Central Issues of Philosophy

General Issues of Philosophy

Central Issues of Philosophy

Edited by

John Shand

WILEY-BLACKWELL

A John Wiley & Sons, Ltd., Publication

This edition first published 2009

Blackwell Publishing was acquired by John Wiley & Sons in February 2007. Blackwell's publishing program has been merged with Wiley's global Scientific, Technical, and Medical business to form Wiley-Blackwell.

Registered Office
John Wiley & Sons Ltd, The Atrium, Southern Gate, Chichester, West Sussex, PO19 8SQ, United Kingdom

Editorial Offices
350 Main Street, Malden, MA 02148-5020, USA

9600 Garsington Road, Oxford, OX4 2DQ, UK

The Atrium, Southern Gate, Chichester, West Sussex, PO19 8SQ, UK

For details of our global editorial offices, for customer services, and for information about how to apply for permission to reuse the copyright material in this book please see our website at www.wiley.com/wiley-blackwell.

Library of Congress Cataloging-in-Publication Data

Central issues of philosophy / edited by John Shand.
    p. cm.
  Includes bibliographical references and index.
  ISBN 978-1-4051-6270-8 (hardcover : alk. paper) – ISBN 978-1-4051-6271-5 (pbk. : alk. paper)
1. Philosophy.   I. Shand, John, 1956–

  B72.C46 2009
  100–dc22

                                                                                    2008046998

A catalogue record for this book is available from the British Library.

Set in 10/12 pt Goudy by SNP Best-set Typesetter Ltd., Hong Kong
Printed and bound in Singapore by Fabulous Printers Pte Ltd

1   2009

For Norman
A good brother

Contents

Preface

I should like to thank all those who contributed to this book. Their hard work and care has, I think, produced something truly useful to students who are encountering philosophy for perhaps the first time. Even for those more advanced, the book will be illuminating.

John Shand, 2009

Contributors

Barry Dainton is Professor of Philosophy at the University of Liverpool, and works mainly in metaphysics and the philosophy of mind. He was educated at the City University London and Oxford. He is the author of *Stream of Consciousness* (2000; second edition 2006), *Time and Space* (2001), and *The Phenomenal Self* (2008).

Matti Eklund received his Ph.D. from MIT in 2000, and is now Associate Professor of Philosophy at Cornell University. Research interests include metaphysics, philosophy of language, and philosophy of logic.

Luca Ferrero (Harvard Ph.D.) Assistant Professor of Philosophy at UW–Milwaukee. He has been a Humanities Fellow and Visiting Assistant Professor at Stanford University. He works on the philosophy of agency, personal identity, and practical reasoning. Recent (forthcoming) papers include "Conditional Intentions," *Nous* and "What Good Is a Diachronic Will?," *Philosophical Studies*.

Keith Frankish is Senior Lecturer in Philosophy at The Open University. He is the author of *Mind and Supermind* (2004) and *Consciousness* (2005), as well as numerous articles and book chapters. He has a particular interest in dual-process theories of reasoning, and is co-editor with Jonathan Evans of *In Two Minds: Dual Processes and Beyond* (2009).

Michael Huemer received his Ph.D. from Rutgers University in 1998 and is presently Associate Professor of Philosophy at the University of Colorado. He is the author of *Skepticism and the Veil of Perception* (2001), *Ethical Intuitionism* (2005), and various academic articles in epistemology, ethics, and other areas.

Maria Kasmirli is a research student in philosophy at the University of Sheffield. She has held positions at Keele University and the University of Wolverhampton, and has taught philosophy for The Open University. She has a broad range of interests in the philosophies of mind and language, with a particular focus on the nature of conversational implicature.

Jeffrey Ketland is Senior Lecturer in Philosophy at the University of Edinburgh. His undergraduate degree is from Cambridge and his Ph.D. from the LSE. His main areas of interest are logic, semantics, and philosophy of mathematics. Publications include "Deflationism and Tarski's Paradise" (1999; *Mind* 108) and "Empirical Adequacy and Ramsification" (2004; *BJPS* 55).

Peter Lamarque is Professor of Philosophy at the University of York. He is the author of *Fictional Points of View* (1996), *The Philosophy of Literature* (2008), and co-author, with Stein Haugom Olsen, of *Truth, Fiction and Literature: A Philosophical Perspective* (1994). He was editor of the *British Journal of Aesthetics* from 1995 to 2008 and edited *Philosophy and Fiction* (1983), *Concise Encyclopedia of Philosophy of Language* (1997), and (with Stein Haugom Olsen) *Aesthetics and the Philosophy of Art: The Analytic Tradition: An Anthology* (2003).

Marc Lange is Professor of Philosophy at the University of North Carolina at Chapel Hill. He works in philosophy of science and related regions of metaphysics and epistemology. His books include *Laws and Lawmakers* (forthcoming), *An Introduction to the Philosophy of Physics* (2002), *Natural Laws in Scientific Practice* (2000), and *Philosophy of Science: An Anthology* (2007), as well as many journal articles.

Mark LeBar is Associate Professor of Philosophy at Ohio University in Athens, OH. His primary research project is a defense of eudaimonism (of the sort common to ancient Greek ethics) as a contemporary view, with contributions to make in normative ethics and metaethical theory.

Robin Le Poidevin is Professor of Metaphysics at the University of Leeds, where he has taught since 1989. He took his first degree, in Philosophy and Psychology, at Oxford, and a doctorate at Cambridge. He is the author of *The Images of Time* (2007), *Travels in Four Dimensions* (2003), and *Arguing for Atheism* (1996).

Daniel Nolan is Professor of Philosophy at the University of Nottingham. He is the author of two books, *Topics in the Philosophy of Possible Worlds* (2002) and *David Lewis* (2005). He works in a range of areas of philosophy, but primarily metaphysics.

Paul O'Grady is a lecturer in philosophy and fellow of Trinity College Dublin. He has published papers in epistemology and philosophy of religion and is the author of *Relativism* (2002).

Duncan Pritchard is Professor of Philosophy at the University of Edinburgh. His main research interest is epistemology, and he has published widely in this area, including a monograph, *Epistemic Luck* (2005), and a textbook, *What Is This Thing Called Knowledge?* (2006).

Greg Restall is a philosopher at the University of Melbourne. His interests include logic and the history of twentieth-century philosophy, and he is the author of *An Introduction to Substructural Logics* (2000), the textbook *Logic* (2006), and with J. C. Beall, *Logical Pluralism* (2006).

R. M. Sainsbury is Professor of Philosophy at the University of Texas at Austin and a Fellow of the British Academy. Before moving to Texas in 2002, he was Susan Stebbing Professor of Philosophy at King's College London. He was editor of *Mind* for the last decade of the twentieth century, and is the author of books on topics in philosophy of language and logic: *Russell* (1979), *Paradoxes* (third edition 2008), *Logical Forms* (second edition 2000), *Departing From Frege* (2002), and *Reference Without Referents* (2005). He is currently working on a book on the semantics and ontology of fiction.

John Shand studied philosophy at the University of Manchester and King's College, Cambridge. He is an Associate Lecturer in Philosophy at The Open University. He is author of *Arguing Well* (2000), *Philosophy and Philosophers: An Introduction of Western Philosophy* (second edition, 2002), editor of *Fundamentals of Philosophy* (2003), and *Central Works of Philosophy* 5 vols. (2005–6).

Paul Snowdon has been Grote Professor of Mind and Logic at University College London since 2001. Before that he was a Fellow of Exeter College Oxford. He has written about the philosophy of mind, primarily perception, and metaphysics, primarily the problem of personal identity, but also about the history of twentieth-century philosophy.

Helen Steward did her graduate work at the University of Oxford before becoming a Fellow of Balliol College, Oxford, in 1993. She moved to the University of Leeds in 2007. Her first book, *The Ontology of Mind*, was published in 1997. She is currently working on topics in the philosophy of action, specifically as they relate to the free will debate, and her next book, *A Metaphysics for Freedom* will be out in 2009.

Daniel Stoljar is Professor of Philosophy in the Research School of Social Sciences, Australian National University. He was an undergraduate at the University of Sydney and received his Ph.D. from the Massachusetts Institute of Technology. He author of *Ignorance and Imagination: The Epistemic Origin of the Problem of Consciousness*, and of many articles on the philosophy of mind and related issues. He is also the co-editor of *There's Something About Mary: Essays on Phenomenal Consciousness and Jackson's Knowledge Argument*.

Philip Stratton-Lake is Professor of Philosophy at the University of Reading. He is the author of *Kant, Duty and Moral Worth* (2000), and editor *The Right and the Good*, by W. D. Ross (2002), *Ethical Intuitionism: Re-evaluations* (2002), and *On What We Owe to Each Other* (2004).

Matt Zwolinski is an Assistant Professor of Philosophy at the University of San Diego, and an Affiliated Scholar at their Institute for Law and Philosophy. He has published on the morality of sweatshops and price gouging, libertarianism, and the role of the separateness of persons in liberal theory. He is currently working on a longer project on exploitation.

Introduction: An Essay on Philosophy and the Four Philosophical Virtues

John Shand

This book aims to be as perfect and comprehensive an introduction to the central issues of philosophy as is possible.

Of course there is more that can be said about each issue than is said here, but taking all the chapters together, the heart of philosophy is openly exposed and presented in a manner that can be readily understood by the curious. What partly distinguishes the approach of this book from some other introductory works is that in each chapter the author does not just head straight off into discussing the issue, assuming the reader will understand why and in what way distinctively philosophical questions may be raised. The ground is prepared by explaining why and in what way the issue gives rise to distinctively *philosophical* concerns. Why, after we have thought about the issues in all the usual everyday and scientific ways, might we suppose that there is something more to be said? Why is there something left over, some unfinished business?

For example, why after looking at the anatomy of the eye and its route to the brain, and noting cases where people suffer from illusions and see things that are not really there, do we suppose there are additional matters we might raise about the issue of perception? Well, the clue here is the word "looking" in the previous sentence. Suppose we were to wonder how we could be sure which, if any, of the ways things look is how they really are. In that case, it would be no use gathering more evidence based on how things look – that would be circular – for whether how things look tells us accurately how things are is just what is in question. It would be like trying to check the truth of a newspaper headline by buying another copy of the same paper.

Consider, then, the example of the state. States have the right, if they are legitimate, to use force to limit what we might do. We could look all over the world and note the varying extent and ways states limit what people do. But no amount of gathering such factual information would answer the question of what *ought* to be the extent and sort of limits the state should impose. What is the legitimate reach of the state? What ought it to be doing and not doing? This is not something that may be answered by assembling only facts; rather it is something that has to be decided by assessing arguments that go beyond the facts, arguments that are philosophical in character.

Take then the issue of language and meaning. We might want to find out what "la mer" means in English. To do this we can look in a suitable bilingual dictionary once we have recognized the expression as French. We discover it means "the sea." But how do words and other linguistic expressions, written or spoken, those funny squiggles and noises, get meaning at all? One might think the problem is solved by a dictionary, even where one is considering a single language. Look up a word like "sea" and you get a definition of what it means. But the definition just uses more words; if there were just words to give words meaning, going on and on, then no words would ever have meaning; there must be something outside the circle of words that gives words meaning. Look at it another way: you land on another planet, and notice a pattern decorating a rock – what makes it a language, if it is one, something that says something, rather than a mere pretty decoration? It's no use simply asking the local aliens to tell you, for you would already need to know (even before you translated what they said) which among their sounds and gestures, assuming they make any, constitute attempts at communication – but that was just the problem in the first place. The worry about how language gets its meaning is an issue for philosophy.

These are just a few examples. I hope they give the flavor of the idea that when many or all of the facts are known or agreed upon about the issues examined here, there are still vital matters that may be raised.

Each chapter in the book gets you going in thinking philosophically about the issue at hand, shows you around the ways it has been considered, leaves you knowing what is going on, what to expect, and which way is up, so that you may then head off and read with understanding the further more difficult classic readings suggested at the end of each chapter. The chapters have each been written by a distinguished expert in the appropriate field, experienced and skilled at conveying ideas in an accessible and engaging manner.

As has been said, this book deals with the central issues that arise in philosophy. Each chapter explains in what way there are distinctively philosophical concerns that might be raised. The term "issues" is used, rather than "problems," because one possible response made by some philosophers has been to deny, on examining such issues, that there are any real *philosophical* problems involving them at all. It is highly characteristic of philosophy to reflect on what it is doing in this way, and not merely carry on doing it, to step back and consider whether what it is doing is in its entirety the right way of going about things. By analogy, imagine you are trying to open a door, and in the attempt to do this you find that the key will not turn in the lock; you struggle on and on, fiddling with the key, oiling the lock, trying different keys, only then to find that when you try the door handle it was not locked in the first place. You just did not think of it; you thought all along, assumed, that the door was locked, when in fact you could just have walked straight through. The "locked door problem" was spurious as a *locked* door problem; there was an issue as to how to open the door, but no problem once it is considered the right way. By contrast, to take another analogy, a plumber might wonder if he is using the right sized spanner, or indeed the right tools, to sort some problem out; but he will rarely be in the position of raising the question of whether, given that water is leaking all over his head from some hidden pipe work, there is a problem and whether tools are needed at all to solve it. Some philosophers think some or all so-called philosophical problems are like the not-really-locked door case: if you can manage to think about it in the right way, you will see that there is not really a *problem* at all, but, rather, only the appearance of a problem, a pseudo-problem; there is instead an *issue* that has been raised that you only need to get clear about to have it go away. Getting clear, however, about the issues so as to bring about the dissolution of the problems they seem to throw up can be very difficult; one still has to present good arguments. If it were easy, one would not in all likelihood have supposed there was a problem where there is none in the first place. Not all philosophers take this approach in any case; indeed, although it is a perfectly respectable position to hold, such philosophers are probably in a minority. Most philosophers, by contrast, think that the issues raised in this book do raise genuine philosophical problems that have to be resolved by being solved, not dissolved by exposing the error of our coming to think there is a problem. Of course, there is a partial way: one might decide that only some of the issues when examined raise genuine philosophical problems, but others do not.[1] One might say that in identifying apparent philosophical problems, raised by the central issues philosophy usually addresses, as not truly philosophical problems, philosophers would be doing themselves out of a job – and one would have a point.[2] It should be emphasized that for most philosophers, all the issues in this book do raise genuine problems that require solutions that are distinctively matters for philosophy, so that they cannot be either eliminated or exported into the sciences.

So, what is philosophy and what is it to take an issue and consider it philosophically? Philosophy is partly a matter of its subject matter and partly a matter of its method in addressing the issues making up its subject matter.

Let us consider some characteristics of philosophy as it is practiced. The starting point may be considered as the assumption that some ways of thinking about things are more defensible or justified, when assessed by the merits of the arguments for and against them, than others. This might seem obviously so. However, one might suggest, as some have, that no view is any more intellectually defensible or justifiable than any other, and that all we have are *different* views, but not ones that at bottom may be said to compete with one another, in the sense of its being more defensible or justifiable by some process of argument to hold one view rather than another. This is a sort of intellectual nihilism, a position where there is no good reason for thinking one thing rather than another because no argument is better than any other in the sense of providing greater or lesser justification. What you think is in all cases utterly arbitrary, but not random as it will doubtless be determined by circumstance; the choice of what to believe, to the degree that choice is involved at all, is purely a matter of taste. How *this* position about the fundamental pointlessness of trying to distinguish the merits of what we think by arguments may be justified, and presented in a way that gives anyone a reason to believe it, without thereby contradicting its main claim, is something of a mystery. A professional philosopher who spends his time advocating a position that says of itself that there can be no possibility of giving any justification for it or any reason to accept it has a thin excuse for drawing his salary. If one accepts such a view, then there is no point in going on to *argue* about the merits of anything as against anything else. Fortunately, most philosophers do not take this intellectually suicidal view, although it is still considered as a possibility within philosophy.

The next step is to free oneself of how one happens to think about fundamental issues just because of where and when one is brought up, and to do so no matter how cherished or indeed uncomfortable it may make one feel. Such ways of thinking may become ingrained habits one has ceased to notice, let alone question. You may be surprised how much you enjoy it; stepping out on your own, albeit with the help of great thinkers from the long history of philosophy who have also done so, may make you nervous, but it can bring a feeling of exhilarating liberation too. One might come to accept the beliefs that surround one as perfectly justifiable, and that holding them is the right thing to do. But to be a philosopher, to think about one's beliefs philosophically, is to make such beliefs one's own and do so by thinking through the arguments for and against them for oneself. Philosophy is about coming to one's views by critically assessing the range of arguments for them in an open minded flexible way. Accepting ideas on the basis of mere examined authority or because of their longevity is not good enough. Partly the motivation might be said to be not to end up believing nonsense, of which there is certainly enough around. In addition, one must think in a determinedly open-minded way, with no holds barred; think, as one might say, to the limits. Partly this is a matter of shaking off habitual ways of thinking. No one should exaggerate the extent to which this task is easy, for to do so is to underestimate the continuous effort that is needed to guard against supposing one is thinking freely and openly when one is not. This is as much a matter of emotional psychology and willed determination as it is of becoming skilled at understanding arguments. Not everyone is suited by temperament to this. Sometimes the habits of thought, exacerbated by social pressures to conform to a common view, are too difficult to be overcome. In this sense philosophy can only flourish in a free society. In order to begin to use arguments properly as the basis of what one believes one has first to be *open* to argument. If you would rather not think about your basic beliefs, or in some sense are unable to do so, if you would rather accept what everyone else believes just because it means going along with the majority, if you would rather rely on self-proclaimed authorities and the mere longevity of a view to come to an outlook on things, then philosophy is perhaps not for you. Not to open one's mind in this way is not necessarily wicked or weak. Whether one ought to take up philosophy comes down to what matters to you. If it matters to you that you have views that you have come to because you have open-mindedly and determinedly looked at the reasons for and against them yourself, if you are in a continuing manner willing to change your mind should good reasons to do so appear, then thinking philosophically is what you are probably already doing. Take heart that you are of course not alone in this thinking; you may build upon the ideas of hundreds of philosophers who have thought about the same basic issues. In a figurative sense, connecting to the philosophical cultural tradition gives one a much bigger brain; being philosophical doesn't mean you have to think about things starting with nothing and without help. If, however, you find this open thinking prospect disturbing, even frightening, a swim into what seems like an endless insecure sea of ideas, you may find that it will make you unhappy. Perhaps your happiness, being untroubled, matters more to you. No one would guarantee that philosophy brings happiness. But before you opt for bovine contentment, there is a warning. Taking one's beliefs on trust from ways of thinking that one merely happens to find around one, ways of thinking that maybe no one has fully thought through and assessed the reasons for in an open-minded way, could well lead one to believe things that are going to let you down, and do so, because in the end they are simply false or poorly examined. Such naive trust would be rather like driving away in car that one knows nothing about – do you really want to drive a car without checking the brakes first? A lot of the time believing poorly justified, superficially thought through, or false things may not matter; but there are times when such ideas are put to the test by circumstances – something runs out in front of the car – and then one can find appalling consequences following.

The subject matter of philosophy is reflected in the chapter titles of this book: Truth, Knowledge, A *Priori* Truths, Perception, Reality and Thought, Existence, Modality, Mind and Consciousness, Self and Personal Identity, Action, Free Will, Language and Meaning, Scientific Inquiry, Causation and Laws of Nature, Ethical Value, Ethical Choice, Artistic Value, Existence of God, State, Liberty. Philosophy aims to get a fundamental and general understanding of the problems raised by the issues as expressed by the concepts that form the titles.

This sounds daunting, but it is not hard to understand. It's mainly a matter of distancing oneself from particular matters connected with the issues to gain an understanding of the issue generally. Take, for example, the issue of truth. It's one thing to ask whether this or that particular claim is true, it is another to ask what, in all the cases where we say something is true, we are to understand by it. It's one thing to ask whether a person's statement "Henry the VIII had six wives" is true, it is another to ask what we are to understand by any claim that a statement is true. Take the example of causation. It is one thing to assert that smoking causes cancer, it is another to consider what we should understand by the claim that anything causes anything else. On first pass, the answers to these implied questions may seem obvious; but in fact if you start to think about them carefully, you find that matters are far from as straightforward as they seem. Thinking these matters through by considering the arguments about what view we should hold is the subject matter of philosophy.

Given that we have a notion of how philosophy is going to treat the issues, the next question that may occur is why does philosophy pick *these* issues. Again, the answer is not too hard to find. There are many issues that we feel we have to deal with and sort out in our lives, both for our own sake and for the sake of others, and this sorting out involves coming to what we may think is a justifiable view on them. But some issues are more fundamental and more important than others, and they are so because of the wide implications of the view we take on them and the way that they are involved in the most fundamental ways we think about the world and ourselves. This is partly reflected in the rather grand abstract concepts in which the issues are expressed, such as "self," "free will," "liberty." Concepts may be considered as the building blocks of articulate organized thought. Without them, it may be claimed, it would not be possible to think about anything, because to think about something is to apply a concept to it. To think about a cat, to think that it is a *cat* that is passing by, is to have in some sense an understanding of the concept "cat" and then apply it to something we are aware of so that it comes before our minds *as* something or other. However, it is one thing not to be able to think about cats without possessing the concept of a cat, it is another simply not to think about cats at all. This seems perfectly possible. We might get about in the world without thinking about cats without any great problems arising; we might simply never encounter a cat. However, the issues philosophy is concerned with are reflected in concepts without which it would hardly be possible to say that we had thoughts about the world, or indeed anything, at all. It would be incredible to claim that we still had thoughts about the world if we did not have an idea of what something being *true*, or *existing*, or *causing* something involved. Such concepts seem indispensable to our thought, our capacity to think. It seems important then that we gain the best understanding we can of these fundamental concepts and that we do so on the basis of the available arguments. So this is what the core of philosophy does: it steps back from the particular application of the most indispensable basic concepts that are needed to understand things, needed for us to think about things, to look at those concepts in their most general form, without which no thought would be possible at all, and aims to make sense of what is going on when those concepts are involved in our thoughts. Philosophy, in short, seeks to understand the concepts that undergird all the other concepts we use, so that we can make sense of what we are doing when we use them. Without doing this, we are just going on blindly applying them, perhaps in ways that are mistaken or confused. Without examining our basic concepts, it may be argued, we would in thinking about things not really know what we were doing. If for human beings the unexamined life is not worth living, as Socrates claimed,[3] it is certainly at least unexamined, and for some merely living a life like that is a betrayal of the noblest aspect of our existence as human beings.

If one takes the view that philosophy is at bottom simply a matter of thinking for yourself about what one's most basic views should be on the basis of arguments, then philosophy is not some esoteric sideshow, a matter of cold pedantic logic-chopping, done when one is able to take time out from the real concerns of life. One should also not lose sight of the philosophical wood among the philosophical trees. Philosophy involves in the end getting hold of a worldview, one shaped by reflective argument; a view of how generally speaking the world hangs together. In this sense philosophy is not by any means just a matter of dryly grinding through arguments while taking especial care that the logic is correct; it also involves a certain kind of sensitivity to the salience of the matters that might be considered, and a capacity of imagination to connect and synthesize these matters in a way that leads one to a coherent outlook. One's philosophical outlook spreads out like ripples on a pool, impinging on and permeating beliefs that directly shape one's view of life, one's view of the world and one's place in it, views that in turn determine one's actions or failures to act, actions which can have good or terrible consequences. If living your life in a way that is as thought through as you can manage matters to you, then philosophy is a necessity and not an optional luxury that may be safely left for one's days off. We are all philosophers insofar as we are willing to open our mind as to what our basic beliefs should be, and are prepared to judge and re-judge them according to the available arguments. You may then be a half-decent philosopher and not even know it. It's just a matter of how much effort you're prepared to put into it and how far and deep you are prepared to go in thinking things through. You may be more of a philosopher than you think; indeed, the fact that you've had the curiosity to pick up this book suggests that you are. The aim of the book is to send you on your way significantly more of a philosopher than when you began reading it, knowing what philosophy involves and how it tackles the issues central to it.

As a kind of summary, here is what might be said to be *The Four Philosophical Virtues*:

1   Think for yourself and allow your views to be guided by critically assessing the range of genuine arguments for and against them, and by learning from what others have said who have thought deeply about the issues.
2   Be prepared to question views even when they seem obvious, are believed by many others, have been believed for a long time, or are beliefs that you hold dear or through habit.
3   Keep a truly open mind by being willing to change your views according to the merits of the arguments and don't be driven into a corner in defending a position dogmatically even when you feel the argument is running against you.
4   Acknowledge that an intelligent and honest person may hold views different or opposed to yours.

Further Reading

I have tried to keep this section simple and straightforward so as not to over-face the reader. Further reading for the particular issues explored in the book is to be found at the end of each chapter. What is suggested here is more general works or classic works that will stimulate philosophical thought. There is a vast number of works one might put forward, so I've had to be extremely ruthless. If I suggested all that I might, then there would be a danger when presented with it of not knowing where to start. I've divided the further reading into three sections: general introductory works, classics of the philosophical literature by famous philosophers that are nevertheless reasonably accessible, and a philosophical reference work that should help you out, whatever philosophy book you're reading. Two of these are online and free.

Among the general introductions, a highly accessible and intelligent book, written in the form of dialogues or debates you might be said to be listening in to, is Stephen Law, *The Philosophy Gym* (2003). It covers all sorts of important topics, and shows how they can be treated philosophically and what the arguments about them might be. An overview of the history of philosophy, done by concentrating on the great thinkers, explaining what they said and how it should be understood, is John Shand, *Philosophy and Philosophers: An Introduction to Western Philosophy*, (2nd edn., 2002). A marvellously inspired, surprisingly wide-ranging little book that lays bare beautifully some of the hardest questions in philosophy is, John Cottingham, *Rationalism* (1984).

Turning to classics of philosophy, I suggest four books to start off with. The idea of recommending one reads these is that that way you get direct experience of the great philosophers, rather than reading or hearing about them second hand. They need not be read in the order presented here. Descartes, *Meditations on First Philosophy*. This appears in many editions and was first published in 1641. It fundamentally shaped modern philosophy. The book is unusual in addressing the reader directly, almost in a homely manner, and engaging him in the author's personal journey of philosophical understanding. No one could fail to be held by the premise of the journey, that of the individual standing back to consider: what do I really know having reflected on the fact that many things I once thought true turned out to be false? The next book is a cornerstone of political philosophy, of thinking about how we should live together in groups, and it is John Stuart Mill, *On Liberty*, first published in 1859. Again, there are other editions. Its influence on political thought throughout the world could hardly be overestimated. A book that has introduced students to philosophical thinking for many years, and has notably never been out of print, is Bertrand Russell, *The Problems of Philosophy* (1912). It may be quirky in places, but it gets you thinking. It would be impossible not to suggest something from the origins of western philosophy in Ancient Greece. If philosophy is a matter of thinking for yourself guided by open argument, then Greece around 600 BC is where humankind started to think philosophically in a substantial and systematic way. The apogee of that thought must surely be Plato, *Republic*, which appears in numerous translated editions; it was written around 375 BC. Many of the central issues of philosophy are explored in this book, many with an astonishing prescience. In its determination to follow arguments where they will and its lack of appeal to supposedly self-verifying authorities, it was humankind's coming of age. Finally, giving a rather different view of things, and involving a different strand of the western philosophical tradition, that of continental existentialism, there is, in my view, the only philosophical novel ever written that might be considered a literary masterpiece, Jean-Paul Sartre, *Nausea*, first published in 1938. In it one finds philosophical ideas and issues embedded in the narrative and characters, rather than as is often the case in supposedly philosophical novels, people making set speeches about philosophy.

A work which give an insight into the life and mind of a great philosopher, at the same time as explaining his ideas, is Ray Monk, *Ludwig Wittgenstein: The Duty of Genius* (1991).

A reference work I recommend, a kind of bedside companion to reading any work of philosophy, that will avoid, one hopes, on occasion, several hours of head scratching on encountering difficult terms and ideas, is Ted Honderich (ed.) *The Oxford Companion to Philosophy* (2nd edn., 2005). It contains many entries that present in a nutshell essential aspects of philosophy, the meaning of philosophical terms, explications of philosophical positions and ideas, and outlines of the ideas of famous philosophers. Longer articles on many core philosophical subjects, of high quality, are found in two free online sources: http://plato.stanford.edu/contents.html and www.iep.utm.edu/.

Notes

1   The most famous representative of the dissolving approach to philosophical problems, at least on one view of what he was about, is Ludwig Wittgenstein in his later works, such as the *Philosophical Investigations*, which first appeared in German in 1953. This approach tends to unpick so-called philosophical problems piecemeal, one-by-one as they come along, in order to show how our philosophical perplexity is based on a confusion of not seeing that things are, when properly understood, all in order and problem free. To use a metaphor of Wittgenstein, one must show the fly the way out of the fly bottle. A more brusque global approach, which sweeps all philosophical problems away in one go by showing how considering them as problems is in some way spurious, is found in the earlier work of Ludwig Wittgenstein, in particular in his *Tractatus-Logico Philosophicus*, which first appeared in German in 1921. The approach of global dismissal is present also among some members of the logical positivist group of philosophers that emerged from the meeting of the "Vienna Circle" in the 1920s. Most brutal in eliminating philosophical problems is A. J. Ayer in his *Language, Truth and Logic*, the second and final edition of which was published in 1946. The selective or partial approach is also found in a philosopher such as Immanuel Kant in his *Critique of Pure Reason*, published in two editions in 1781 and 1787. Kant sought to set the boundaries to human knowledge at the bounds of possible experience. Science was to be made secure against scepticism, but the pursuit of knowledge in respect of metaphysical problems, in the sense of arriving at definitive solutions to them, was ruled out, and shown to involve only irresolvable endless speculation. Such partial approaches are also found in the pragmatist movement around the turn of the last century, as in the work of Immanuel Kant in his *Critique of Pure Reason*, published in two editions in 1781 and 1787. Kant sought to set the boundaries to human knowledge at the bounds of possible experience. Science was to be made secure against skepticism, but the pursuit of knowledge in respect of metaphysical problems, in the sense of arriving at definite solutions to them was ruled out, and shown to involve only irresolvable endless speculation. Such partial approaches are also found in the pragmatist movement around the turn of the twentieth century, as in the work of William James, such as *Pragmatism: A New Name for Some Old Ways of Thinking* (1907), whose general approach is to argue that if "solving" some problem one way rather than another makes no difference to how we go on living in the world, then the problem may be thought of as not genuine. Heir to the pragmatists in modern times is the influential movement of naturalism. Although rather more complex, the essential idea is that philosophical problems when properly understood may be assimilated by science, and become problems to which science will find the solution. The doyen of this position, although there are many later proponents expressing the idea

in a variety of ways, is W. V. O. Quine, his most famous work being *Word and Object* (1960). Selective in the sense of focusing in on one area of philosophy is found in Gilbert Ryle, *The Concept of Mind* (1949). In this, Ryle aims to show that the problems of philosophy of mind are spuriously generated by the grammar of the way we talk about mind, mental states, and mental events, making it seem as though what are talked about is peculiar kinds of objects or things, whereas in fact the mind and its properties are not any kinds of objects or things at all, but, rather, matters of behavior and dispositions to behave.

2　Ludwig Wittgenstein, with an integrity few have matched, retired from philosophy to teach in a remote Austrian junior school after deciding that in his *Tractatus Logico-Philosophicus* he had solved, or one might say eliminated, all the problems of philosophy. But after a few years, he was drawn back into doing work in philosophy, having realized with the help of critics and friends that his annihilation of philosophy was not as conclusive as he thought.

3　Socrates in Plato, *The Apology* 38a., in *The Last Days of Socrates*. The edition below also includes the dialogues by Plato, *Euthyphro*, *Crito* and *Phaedo*.

References

Ayer, A. J. (1975). *Language, Truth and Logic*, London: Penguin.

Cottingham, John (1984). *Rationalism*, London: Paladin.

Descartes, René (1968) [1641]. *Meditations on First Philosophy*, London: Penguin.

Honderich, Ted (ed.) (1995; 2005). *The Oxford Companion to Philosophy*, Oxford: Oxford University Press.

James, William (1907). *Pragmatism: A New Name for Some Old Thinking*, New York: Longmans, Green.

Kant, Immanuel Kant (1976) [1781; 1787]. *Critique of Pure Reason*, tr. Norman Kemp Smith, London: Macmillan.

Law, Stephen (2003). *The Philosophy Gym*, London: Headline.

Mill, John Stuart Mill (1974) [1859]. *On Liberty*, London: Penguin.

Monk, Ray (1991). *Ludwig Wittgenstein: The Duty of Genius*, London: Penguin.

Plato (1969). *The Apology* in *The Last Days of Socrates*, London: Penguin.

Plato (1974). *Republic*, London: Penguin.

Quine, W. V. (1960). *Word and Object*, Cambridge, MA: Harvard University Press.

Russell, Bertrand (1912). *The Problems of Philosophy*, Oxford: Oxford University Press.

Ryle, Gilbert (1949). *The Concept of Mind*, London: Hutchinson.

Sartre, Jean-Paul (1965) [1938]. *Nausea*, London: Penguin.

Shand, John (1993–4; 2002). *Philosophy and Philosophers: An Introduction to Western Philosophy*, 2nd edn., Chesham: Acumen Publishing; 1st edn., London: UCL Press/Penguin.

Wittgenstein, Ludwig (1961) [1921]. *Tractatus-Logico Philosophicus*, tr. D. F. Pears and B. F. McGuinness, London: Routledge.

Wittgenstein, Ludwig (1974) [1953]. *Philosophical Investigations*, tr. G. E. M. Anscombe, Oxford: Blackwell.

1

Truth

Jeffrey Ketland

Introduction: What Is the Philosophical Problem of Truth?

We each hold various beliefs, and assert various statements and propositions, on matters mundane, historical, scientific, and so on. One feature of such beliefs, statements, and propositions is that they may be *true* or *false*.[1] But what exactly does it mean for a statement, belief, etc., to be *true*? Intuitively, the *truth* of a statement consists in its representing the world correctly, or in the world being as the statement says it is. As explained below, this is a formulation of the *correspondence theory* of truth. However, philosophical questions immediately flood in. A preliminary question concerns the *kinds* of things that may be true or false: beliefs, claims, opinions, assertions, etc.[2] Call these *truth bearers*. (A truth bearer can be false, of course.) Despite their apparent diversity, there are plausibly two basic kinds: *linguistic items* (e.g., statements, sentences) and *propositions*.[3]

What are the main philosophical issues here? First, it seems clear that *truth matters to us*. It is important to us whether the information we hear (or accept) is true or false. Much can turn on this. We postpone trying to answer why truth matters until the final section. A second question often causes confusion for the beginning student: how do we *determine* if a statement is true or false? Are there general *procedures* or *criteria* for determining whether a statement is true or false? Does truth consist in being *justified* in the right way? Call this the *Epistemological Question*. This question is *not* what philosophers intend when they discuss the philosophical problem of truth. Rather, they are interested in what it *means* to say, of a belief, statement or proposition, that it is true. That is, how is the concept of truth to be *analyzed*? Call this the *Analytic Question*. This question goes back to Plato and Aristotle, and earlier, and has ramifications throughout modern philosophy, affecting debates about the nature of existence, knowledge, meaning, reference and valid reasoning. In general, the epistemological question is a more difficult one to answer than the analytic question. The bulk of the discussion below focuses on the analytic question: what does "true" mean?

Next, we get a little clearer about what a definition is. A *definition* of a concept, or a word, is usually given by specifying conditions for that concept, or word, to apply to things. For example, we may define "bachelor" as follows:

A person x is a bachelor if, and only if, x is an unmarried adult male human.

We may also call this an *analysis* of the concept of being a bachelor. Analogously, we might look for a definition of truth, of the form:

(D)   A is true if, and only if, . . . A . . .

where A is a truth bearer, and " . . . A . . ." indicates some condition that A satisfies.

Below, we assess a number of proposed definitions of truth, each listed as (D₁), (D₂), (D₃), etc. A point to bear in mind, however, is that one might reject the demand for such a definition, or analysis, of truth. For perhaps truth is simply a primitive, indefinable concept.

Correspondence Theories of Truth

A correspondence theory begins with commonsensical formulations of the following sort: a statement is true just if it *agrees with reality*; or *represents reality as it is*; or *things are as it says they are*; or *says of what is, that it is*; or *designates an existing state of affairs*; or *corresponds to the facts* (or *to a fact*). These are, so to speak, correspondence locutions, and they seem to fall into two main kinds:[4]

(D₁)   A is true iff A says that such-and-such is the case, and such-and-such is the case.
(D₂)   A is true iff A corresponds to a fact.

The first of these, (D₁), is a descendant from Aristotle's formulation, "to say of what is, that it is, is true" (*Metaphysics*). We call it the *classical correspondence definition*. It forms the basis for the semantic conception of truth, developed by Alfred Tarski. The second, (D₂), has a long history too, and we call it the *correspondence-to-fact definition*. For the purposes of this section, we concentrate on (D₂), although the reader should bear in mind that (D₁) is an acceptable, and perhaps preferable, formulation of the correspondence theory.

The correspondence-to-fact definition says that truth involves a *correspondence relation* between truth bearer and a *fact*. Unless we are prepared to treat the notions of *correspondence* and *fact* as basic and primitive, it remains to elucidate them further. What is a fact?[5] Usually, truth bearers and facts are taken to be distinct kinds of entities.[6] Consider the statement "Edinburgh is north of London." Since it is true, the corresponding fact might be something like *Edinburgh's-being-north-of-London*. This is a "complex," whose constituents are Edinburgh, London, and the relation *North-of*. In modern parlance, such complexes are called *states of affairs*. Not every state of affairs is a fact; for some states of affairs *obtain*, some do not.[7] This leads to a definition of "fact" as "state of affairs that obtains." Then, the correspondence-to-fact view becomes:

(D₃)   A is true iff A corresponds to a state of affairs that obtains.

Thus, the statement "Edinburgh is north of London" is true iff the corresponding state of affairs (with its constituents, Edinburgh, London and *North-of*) obtains. Assuming the towns Edinburgh and London to be mind-independent entities, the truth of "Edinburgh is north of London" depends on mind-independent reality. This is an attractive feature of a correspondence view, in that it permits truth to depend upon mind-independent reality.

If facts are obtaining states of affairs, what is *correspondence*? Correspondence might be understood as "conventional correlation" of truth bearer and state of affairs (c.f., the conventional correlation of *green-light signals* and *permission to proceed*, on foot or in one's car). For example, the sentence "this is a cat" is correlated with states of affairs that involve the presence of a cat, in the vicinity of the speaker; a statement made using this sentence, by a particular speaker in a certain context, is true just when one such state of affairs obtains in the vicinity of the speaker. This view takes account of the presence of context-sensitive expressions, such as "this," "here," "I," in speech acts. A difficulty with this view, however, is that it gives no indication how states of affairs get correlated with context-*insensitive* claims, like "neutrinos lack mass" or "the French Revolution occurred in 1789."

Another view treats correspondence as a kind of "picturing" relation. To illustrate:

	Name	*Predicate*	*Name*
Truth bearer:	"Edinburgh	is north of	London"
[correspondence]	⇓	⇓	⇓
State of affairs:	Edinburgh →	*Being-north-of* →	London
	Object	*Relation*	*Object*

In a sense, the sentence and the corresponding state of affairs have the same "logical structure." The names in the sentence refer to the objects in the state of affairs (and the predicate in the sentence refers to the constituent relation). The truth bearer, in some sense, *pictures* its corresponding state of affairs, in analogy with how a map pictures, or represents, some region of territory. Truth bearers are therefore *representations* of reality.

A standard objection to the correspondence-to-fact view is that it leads to skepticism, the doctrine that reality is unknowable (for example, perhaps we are brains-in-vats, but don't realize it). To avoid skepticism, one might urge that in order to *know* a fact, one must be able to *directly cognize* the fact. But *mind-independent facts* seem so different from our mental states that we could never achieve this cognitive feat.

An obvious reply to this is that the correspondence view is a theory of *truth*, not knowledge. It answers the analytic question, not the epistemological question. A second reply is that, in any case, the correspondence theory itself seems to play no role in the argument for the unknowability of *facts*. The objection equally condemns our ability to know any *mind-independent* objects whatsoever: cats, stones, trees, electrons, comets, etc. Finally, note that the doctrine that cats, stones, trees, etc. (and facts about Edinburgh and London) are mind-independent is *not* assumed by the correspondence theory itself. Definitions (D_2) or (D_3) don't imply that the states of affairs are mind-independent. The correspondence theory is thus logically neutral on such questions.

Another objection is simply to that one should repudiate facts altogether. Facts, understood as obtaining states of affairs, are very unlike ordinary physical things: chairs, cups, rocks, fish, etc. One might accept the existence of the towns London and Edinburgh, and perhaps even the abstract relation *North-of*. But is there a further entity, *Edinburgh's-being-north-of-London*? Perhaps, fact-*talk* is merely a convenient manner of speech. Instead of "I am aware of the fact that p," one can say, "I am aware that p." Instead of "it is a fact that p," we say simply "p." The repudiation of facts need not entail that one cannot make sense of truth. For example, the semantic conception of truth, discussed below, was presented as a correspondence theory, but avoids postulating facts, or sentence-to-fact correspondence.

If repudiation of *all* facts goes too far, maybe repudiation of *some* of the weirder ones is wise. For the correspondence-to-fact view requires a specific fact for *every* truth. Consider "London is not north of Edinburgh," which is true. If this corresponds to a fact, it must be *London's-not-being-north-of-Edinburgh*: some sort of *"negative"* fact. Is there such a thing? True statements containing *"not"* are just the start of the trouble, for there are compound statements containing *"or," "and," "if-then," "for all," "there is," "it is necessary that," "believes that,"* and so on. When such a statement is true, is there always a fact? If "Sherlock Holmes does not exist" is true, is there a corresponding fact, the *non-existence-of-Sherlock-Holmes*? A way round this problem is to assume corresponding states of affairs only for the simplest sentences (the *atomic* sentences). Then, truth for the compound sentences (built up from these atomic sentences using *"not," "and,"* etc.) may be defined using a "recursive definition," similar to the kind pioneered by Tarski.[8]

Epistemic Theories of Truth

Around the turn of the twentieth century, several authors criticized the correspondence view and proposed to define truth in terms of some notion of *idealized justification* or *idealized rational acceptability*. Call these views *epistemic* theories of truth. Such views answer the analytic question (what is the meaning of "true"?) via a *prior* answer to the epistemological question. So, we point out first that there are various criteria we use to select which statements to accept and which to reject. These criteria involve observation, reasoning, mathematical proof, and so on. And second, it is proposed that the analytic question be answered by saying that a statement's *truth* consists in its *meeting these criteria*. The first point is not the point of dispute here, as it concerns matters of epistemology, not the definition of truth *per se*. The second is. For why should the fact that a statement meets certain epistemic criteria *imply* its truth? And why should its failing to meet these criteria imply its falsity?

The simplest criterion involves the statement's being *justified* (e.g., being supported by observational evidence). However, introductory epistemology courses explain that one must distinguish between a statement's being *true* and its being *justified* to some degree. Justified statements and beliefs are sometimes false; and there are truths we have no justification for believing. For example, we lack any justification for believing that Plato sneezed on his 30th birthday, and we also lack any justification for believing that he *didn't*. But logic alone tells us that *either* he did sneeze *or* he didn't sneeze. Hence, either the proposition, or its negation, is true. So, there is a truth we have no justification to believe. Hence, there is a gap between truth and justification. So, defining "A is true" as "A is justified" doesn't work. Still, might we hope to define truth in terms of criteria involving *idealized* justification? There is a baffling variety of such proposals, but we focus on three:

(D_4)   A is true iff A is verifiable, in principle.
(D_5)   A is true iff A belongs to the maximally coherent system (of beliefs).
(D_6)   A is true iff A would be accepted, in the ideal limit of rational inquiry, by anyone who investigates.

To use the technical jargon, (D$_4$) expresses *verificationism about truth*; (D$_5$) expresses the *coherence theory of truth*; and (D$_6$) expresses *long-run pragmatism*.

It is perfectly reasonable to accept statements that are justified either by observation or by logico-mathematical reasoning. So, "there is margarine in the fridge" is justified by observation – i.e., *looking* inside the fridge. "The period of a pendulum varies with the square root of its length" is justified by performing certain experiments. "There are infinitely many primes" is justified by a mathematical proof. Such justification procedures are examples of "verification." Definition (D$_4$) says: A is *true* just when it can be "verified" in such a way.

Such a view, however, has severe problems.[9] We *cannot* verify, by direct observation, the statement "the period of a pendulum varies with the square root of its length," for it is a *generalization*, and thus requires indefinitely many experiments. Furthermore, some statements accepted on the basis of observation are *mistaken* (consider the Müller-Lyer illusion). Furthermore, the view implies that *all* truths can, in principle, be verified. But perhaps there are statements, mathematical, scientific or historical, which are true but unverifiable, even in principle. For example, "Plato sneezed on his 30th birthday." Either this or its negation "Plato did *not* sneeze on his 30th birthday" is true, but is either verifiable?

The problem may be that the evaluation criteria are too restrictive. Presumably rational inquiry involves more than just direct, sensory, observation and logical reasoning. Perhaps the statements we ought to accept, as we proceed in inquiry, should form a *holistic, coherent, system*. Thus, though we cannot directly verify the pendulum law, it nonetheless *coheres* with the experiments we have done, and with further background laws of physics. So, perhaps the property of idealized justification we seek is this: *being an element of the maximally coherent system of beliefs* (or *statements*). The coherence definition (D$_5$) says: a belief (or statement) is true just when it belongs to this system. The intended notion of a maximally coherent system is not merely that of a complete consistent system, from logic.[10] Maximal coherence is meant to involve a richer property, wherein all the various beliefs or statements *mutually support one another*.

On a pure coherence theory, to be true is to belong to the maximally coherent system. The standard objection, from Russell, is that it is difficult to see why a maximally cohering system of beliefs is different from a complete, consistent, highly coherent *fictional story*. Complete consistent stories may contain falsehoods and omit truths. No matter how coherent Jane Austen's *Pride and Prejudice* may be, do we count its statements as true? In general, a proposition's belonging to a maximally coherent system need not entail its truth; and, conversely, its being true needn't entail its belonging to a maximally coherent system.

In order to deal with this objection, the most obvious thing is to include observational criteria, thus combining the coherence theory with verificationism. But still there are problems. Even if my *present* system of beliefs, conditioned by experience, is as coherent as possible, future experience may lead to further revisions. And why should *my* system be the same as *your* system? Somehow we must "aggregate" these systems, and consider their evolution into the future, under the guidelines of rational inquiry.

This motivates long-run pragmatism, advanced by C. S. Peirce. The notion of justification is *rational acceptability in the limiting case of inquiry*. The definition says that a proposition is *true* just when it is acceptable in the ideal limit. But do we have any reason to suppose that there *is* such a limit; that there will be convergence, amongst all who investigate? Perhaps our theories will forever be overthrown; perhaps they will forever be partial and incomplete.

Even if inquiry does gradually converge, to "Scientific Consensus," might it still not be the case that we are, in reality, sadly deceived brains-in-vats? We cannot simply *define* reality to be what "Scientific Consensus" says it is at the end of inquiry. If we do this, we have ruled out, by fiat, the possibility of radical error.

Intermezzo: The T-scheme and Material Adequacy

General definitions of truth are controversial. So, consider instead just the single proposition *that all men are mortal*. What does it mean to say of *this* proposition that it is true? Aristotle gives us a hint: a proposition is true exactly if things are as it says they are. So, this proposition is true if and only if all men are mortal. We are led to the following:

1   The proposition *that all men are mortal* is true iff all men are mortal.

For sentential truth bearers, the well-known example, from Tarski, is:

2   The sentence "snow is white" is true iff snow is white.

Sentences (1) and (2) are called *T-sentences*. They are "instances" of the general schematic principles:

The proposition that *p* is true iff *p*;
The sentence "*p*" is true iff *p*.

These are versions of what is known as the *T-scheme*.[11] To construct a T-sentence, we replace "*p*" by any declarative English sentence. There is, of course, no requirement that this sentence be true! That would be circular. So, the following is fine:

3   The proposition *that pigs can fly* is true iff pigs can fly.

Also, there is no (obvious) domain restriction on the sentences we may substitute in order to obtain T-sentences. They may involve any subject matter whatsoever. Thus:

4   The sentence "2 + 2 = 4" is true iff 2 + 2 = 4.
5   The sentence "torture is always wrong" is true iff torture is always wrong.

The T-sentences, (1)–(5), seem trivial or platitudinous. A complaint is that the T-sentences aren't *general* definitions, of the form (D). They don't tell us in general what it is to be true. They just tell us *one-by-one*, what it is for "snow is white" to be true, for "pigs can fly" to be true, and so on.

So, what exactly is the status of T-sentences? Consider "pigs can fly." We surely need empirical evidence to decide whether to accept, or reject, this biological hypothesis. But we do not need empirical evidence to know that this hypothesis is true if, and only if, pigs can fly. Hence, accepting a T-sentence is independent of particular empirical evidence. All we need is to grasp are the relevant propositions involved, and the concept of truth. To use the jargon, T-sentences are *analytic*: we accept them in virtue of understanding the concepts they use.[12] But, a T-sentence is not a *general* definition, of the form (D). Rather, T-sentences are *partial definitions* of truth, each one specific to a particular truth bearer.

Suppose we wish to construct a *general* definition of truth, of the form (D). How should a proposed *general* definition be related to the *partial* definitions? Consider the following absurd definition of truth:

(D*)   A sentence A is true iff A contains 27 letters.

Why is this absurd? The reason is that (D*) *does not imply the corresponding T-sentences*. In other words, one *cannot* show, from (D*), the following,

6   The sentence "snow is white" has 27 letters iff snow is white.
7   The sentence "2 + 2 = 4" has 27 letters iff 2 + 2 = 4.

And so on.

So, a proposed definition of truth counts as "correct" or "adequate" when it *implies* the corresponding T-sentences. Such a definition of truth is called *materially adequate*.[13]

The Semantic Conception of Truth

Is it possible to construct truth definitions which *are* materially adequate? This was Tarski's aim in his 1935 article, "The Concept of Truth in Formalized Languages," presenting the *semantic* conception of truth, which he regarded as a version of the correspondence theory (although whether it is one remains controversial).

On the semantic conception, truth bearers are sentences, understood as strings of letters. For example, "fish swim" is the string "f," "i," "s," "h," "s," "w," "i," "m." The truth or falsity of a string of letters only makes sense *relative to some language*. For example, "fish swim" is true in *English*, but could be false in another language. So, the semantic conception deals not with an absolute concept "A is true," but rather with a *relative* concept, such as "A is true in *English*," "A is true in *Spanish*," etc. In general, "A is true in L," where L is called the *object language*.

The object language might be a formalized language or it might be part of a natural language, such as *Spanish* or *Hindi*. The language *in* which we talk *about* the object language is allowed to be distinct from the object language, and is called a *metalanguage*. In the discussion below the metalanguage is *English*. For example, one may use *English* to talk about truth and falsity in *Spanish*.

Citing the classical correspondence definition, Tarski's version of the T-scheme is:

(T)   The sentence x *is true in L iff p.*

A T-sentence is constructed by replacing "x" with a name of a sentence, and replacing "p" by the translation of the sentence. For example, if the object language is *German*, a possible T-sentence is:

8   The sentence "schnee ist weiss" is true in *German* iff snow is white.

This T-sentence might not be trivial or analytic for *you*. It will, however, be trivial or analytic for a bilingual *English* speaker who also speaks *German*. If the metalanguage contains the object language, we see the effect of what is called "disquotation":

9   The sentence "snow is white" is true in *English* iff snow is white.

The general procedure for constructing a Tarskian truth definition is as follows. First, one specifies an object language L, on the assumption that one may translate from L into the metalanguage; one next constructs, in the metalanguage, a definition of "A is true in L"; and finally, one proves that this definition is materially adequate.

For example, suppose L is a language with just two sentences, X and Y, whose translations are "dogs bark" and "fish swim." There are only two T-sentences, namely,

10   X is true in L iff dogs bark.
11   Y is true in L iff fish swim.

A materially adequate truth definition for L may be given as follows:

12   A is true in L iff [(A is X and dogs bark) or (A is Y and fish swim)].

(The reader might try to show how to infer (10) from (12).)

For object languages of any serious interest, however, one cannot write down such definitions, as there are infinitely many sentences to deal with. For example, suppose that L contains the logical connective "*not*" and one basic sentence, say X, whose translation is "dogs bark." Then L has infinitely many sentences: X, *not-X*, *not-not-X*, *not-not-not-X*, etc. Because of this, one cannot write down a truth definition like (12). Instead, one gives what is called a *recursive definition*, as follows:

13   X is true in L iff dogs bark.
14   *not-A* is true in L iff A is not true in L.

This recursive definition is adequate. The method may be generalized to include other logical connectives, such as "*and*," "*or*" and so on.

When the object language contains names, predicates, connectives, and quantifiers (the phrases "for any" and "there exists"), the situation becomes more complicated. One must first define two auxiliary semantic concepts: *reference* (or *denotation*) and *satisfaction*. Satisfaction, roughly, is the relation of a predicate, such as "loves," to the things it applies to. For example, a pair of objects [*a, b*] *satisfies* the predicate "loves" if, and only if, *a* loves *b*. Reference is the semantic relation that holds between a name and what it stands for. For example, the name "Bertrand Russell" refers (in *English*) to the philosopher Russell himself.

A final point. One might think that *English* contains its *own* truth predicate: i.e., a predicate meaning "is true in *English*." However, this assumption leads to a paradox, the notorious Liar Paradox. Informally, consider the so-called liar sentence "this sentence is not true," which attributes *untruth* to *itself*. Call the liar sentence G. Informal reasoning leads to a contradiction. For, G is equivalent to "G is *not* true." But the T-scheme tells us that G is equivalent to "G is true." So, we conclude "G is true" is equivalent to "G is *not* true." A contradiction! In short, the T-scheme is *inconsistent*. Tarski drew several conclusions from this, as well as using it to prove some powerful mathematical results.[14] In particular, the conclusion that the common-sense concept of truth is inconsistent.

We next turn to some objections to the semantic conception of truth.

A preliminary objection is that the semantic conception deals with truth for sentences, not propositions. But perhaps propositions are basic, and we should define *sentence*-truth in terms of *proposition*-truth. For example, as follows: a sentence is true relative to some language iff the *proposition* that it expresses, relative to that language, is true. This is attractive, but not without problems. The main problem is that it is rather unclear what propositions really are; some philosophers simply reject them, in favor of sentences, whose syntactical structure is much clearer.

A second objection is that Tarski shows how to define "A is true in *L*," a language-relative notion of truth, but not an absolute notion, "A is true." Thus, the single, univocal, notion of truth has fragmented into seemingly unrelated concepts: "true-in-*English*," "true-in-*Spanish*," etc. In reply, note that it just does not make sense to talk of sentences as being merely true or false. For sentences, their truth must be relative to a language.[15]

A third, and rather threatening, objection concerns a lacuna. The semantic conception seems not to *explain* the semantic notions involved: reference, satisfaction and truth. For example, *German* contains the noun "schnee," whose translation in *English* is "snow." A Tarskian truth theory for *German* thus contains the partial definition,

15   The word "schnee" refers in *German* to snow.

This is a semantic fact about *German*. But it doesn't give any indication as to *why* the noun "schnee" refers, in *German*, to snow. The point generalizes to other semantic concepts. One might argue that a Tarskian theory should be extended, adding a separate *theory of reference*, which explains *why* expressions refer to whatever they do, perhaps in terms of how expressions are used, and causal connections between speakers, the expressions they use, and the referents of the expressions.

A forth objection concerns whether Tarskian semantic methods can be *generalized* to real-life natural languages, which exhibit a variety of poorly understood features, including more complicated ways of constructing sentences, context-sensitive expressions, evaluative predicates, and phenomena such as ambiguity and vagueness. One cannot summarize the overall situation easily, but there is a large amount of work in semantic theory, generalizing Tarski's approach to many of these phenomena.[16]

Finally, is the semantic conception a correspondence theory? This is disputed. Tarski himself stated that it was, and others followed him. The semantic conception of truth is based on the classical correspondence definition (D_1), rather than the correspondence-to-fact definition (D_2). So, *if* the classical correspondence definition is a correspondence theory, then surely so is Tarski's. For (D_1) meets the *correspondence intuition*: truth depends on how reality is. The point of difference is that a Tarskian definition of truth doesn't introduce *facts*, and doesn't introduce a *sentence-to-fact correspondence relation*.

Deflationism

The proposition *that snow is white* is true iff snow is white. Thus, to assert the *truth* of this proposition is equivalent to asserting the proposition itself. Similarly, to claim that "snow is white" is true is equivalent to claiming that snow is white; and so on. To assert "A is true" is equivalent to asserting A. These equivalences are encapsulated by one or other version of the T-scheme. The Tarskian semantic conception took (a consistent version of the) T-scheme as an *adequacy condition* on definitions of truth. But given that the T-sentences are platitudes, an attractive suggestion is that the concept of truth is *fully* captured by the T-scheme alone. If correct, perhaps nothing more, or little more, needs to be said. The problem of truth has been *deflated*: we arrive at *deflationism*.[17] If this is right, the view that truth has any sort of "nature," requiring metaphysical analysis, is a philosophical error – a muddle.

Deflationary suggestions were made by Frege, Ramsey, Ayer, and Wittgenstein. An early version noted that since "A is true" is equivalent to A, the predicate "true" might seem *redundant*. However, this is too quick, as there are other contexts where it is not so obvious how to eliminate the predicate "true," a point emphasized by both Tarski and Ramsey.

Still, the T-sentences are analytic platitudes about truth, and deflationism tries to exploit this to the maximum. While there is no exact consensus on what deflationism is, beyond some rather unclear claims that truth is not a property, or that the problem of truth is a "muddle," there are several deflationary theses commonly defended. First, that the notion of truth is, really, a *logical* notion; second, that the sole *reason* for having a truth predicate in a language consists in its *logical utility*, third, that the theory of truth is *neutral* on non-truth-theoretic matters; and forth, that the concept of truth plays no *essential role in explanations*.[18]

To explain the claim that truth is a logical notion, consider the logical expression "*and*." To understand "*and*" is to know how to reason with it. One may infer "A *and* B" from the two assumptions A and B. One may infer A from "A *and* B," one may also infer B. To understand "*and*" is just to understand these logical rules. With truth there is an analogy. From A, one may infer "A is true"; and from "A is true," one may infer A. Thus, there are logical rules for reasoning with the truth predicate, and these seem analogous to the logical rules for reasoning with other logical notions, "*and*," "*not*," "*or*" and so on.

This brings us to the second claim, concerning the logical usefulness of a truth predicate. Suppose that one is so impressed with Harvey's knowledge that one wishes to endorse *everything* Harvey says. If one had a lot of spare time, one could begin asserting the following "infinitely long" statement:

16   If Harvey says that penguins waddle, then penguins waddle; *and* if Harvey says that fish swim, then fish swim; *and* if Harvey says that plastic is edible, then plastic is edible; . . . and so on.

In a sense, (16) is an "infinite conjunction" of statements of the form "If Harvey says that *p*, then *p*." However, note that with the predicate "true," one may simply say:

17   Everything Harvey says is true.

Thus, using the truth predicate and the rules for reasoning with it, one may re-express a certain *infinite* conjunction (16) as a single *finite* statement (17). Similarly, even if we do not know *what* John said, we may still *repudiate* it by saying, "what John said is not true." Even if we do not know specifically what the Dalai Lama said, we may indirectly *endorse* his statements by saying "whatever the Dalai Lama says is true." The T-scheme accounts for this logical utility of the truth predicate. Furthermore, in order for the truth predicate to have this logical utility, nothing more is required beyond the T-scheme: there is no need for talk of facts, correspondence, or notions of justification.

The third claim concerns the neutrality of the T-scheme. Again, there are technical results which confirm this. Accepting the T-scheme makes no difference to one's background views on non-truth-theoretic matters. One may accept the T-scheme (more exactly, a consistent version) irrespective of whether you think "electrons are *mind-independent entities*" or you think "electrons are *logical constructions from sense-data*." The T-scheme is thus metaphysically neutral.

The final deflationary claim is that, while a truth predicate has a certain logical utility, the predicate plays no essential explanatory role whatsoever. Truth is thus "insubstantial," in some sense. A popular argument for accepting an empirically successful scientific theory, is that the best explanation of its empirical success (i.e., its making true predictions), consists in the theory itself being *true*. Does not the truth of the theory explain the truth of the predictions? The deflationist may reply, however, that uses of the notion of truth may be *eliminated* from particular explanations, by using the T-scheme. For example, we observe energy release when uranium-235 is subjected to irradiation by neutrons. The best explanation, one might say, is that Einstein's theoretical law "$E = mc^2$" is *true*. However, the phenomenon is just as easily explained by the ground-level claim that $E = mc^2$. If this is right, there is no need to bring in truth: truth is *dispensable* in scientific explanations.

Let us turn now to some objections to deflationism.

A major objection is that the T-scheme, unless restricted, is *inconsistent*. It leads to the Liar Paradox. It is unclear what deflationism has to say. If consistency is wanted, some T-sentences must be rejected. The problem of explaining *which* ones is non-trivial. The deflationist might, on the other hand, settle for an inconsistent theory of truth. But the cost is high, as it requires unappealing revisions in logic. (The semantic conception, whatever its faults or lacunae, is *not* inconsistent. It was part of Tarski's intention to develop a consistent theory of truth.)

The T-scheme may, in fact, be weakened (in various ways), to restore consistency. The objection now is that it becomes too *weak* to give a *usable* theory of truth. We would like to be able to say, in general, that:

18 For any sentence A: *not-A* is true iff A is not true.
19 For any sentences A and B: *A-and-B* is true iff both A and B are true.

Principles like these are used in our reasoning all the time. However, a deflationary theory of truth based on the T-scheme (or a consistent version) does *not* imply the generalizations (18) and (19). Note that these sorts of generalizations are always built-in to a Tarskian semantic theory of truth.

A third objection to deflationism concerns the *normative* dimension of truth: *true* beliefs are what we *aim* to believe, or what we *ought* to believe. Our cognitive inquiries are guided by a normative rule of the form,

20   Aim to believe a proposition if and only if it is *true*.

It might seem that this normative feature is not accounted for by deflationism. However, perhaps the deflationism can reply to this objection as follows. The *formulation* of this rule as a single statement is really just an example of the logical utility of truth predicate, which has already been explained. The single rule, (20), is equivalent, by the T-scheme, to a *schematic rule*, of the form

21   Aim to believe that *p* if and only if *p*.

So, the truth predicate allows us to reformulate the *schematic* normative rule as a single normative rule. And the schematic normative rule (21) doesn't appear to involve truth at all, at least not explicitly.

Concluding Remarks

This chapter has covered quite a lot of material, and I must apologize that certain logical technicalities have entered as we moved beyond the more basic material on the correspondence and the epistemic theories. However, this is virtually unavoidable, as all important work in philosophy concerning truth since the last 1960s is of a nature similar to the material in Sections 4, 5 and 6 above. However, it is hoped that the interested reader may take the broad survey above as a useful starting point for further study.[19]

Finally we return to the question raised at the start, concerning *why truth matters*. The correspondence theorist may answer this as follows. Truth matters because truth involves *agreement with reality*, and it is *reality* that matters to us. In general, it matters to us whether food norishes us, or loved ones are unharmed, or surroundings are safe, or prospects are good, and so on. Various political and social phenomena also matter to us. To a physicist, the nature of the physical world matters. To a historian, the past events matter. In short, truth matters because reality matters.

Further Reading

Three excellent general resources are the textbook Kirkham (1992) and the anthologies, Blackburn and Simmons (1999) and Lynch (2001). The anthologies are comprehensive and the editorial contributions are very clear. Two shorter expository pieces are Haack (1978: ch. 7) and Glanzberg (2006), at the online *Stanford Encyclopedia of Philosophy*, which also has several valuable truth-related articles. Three further expository books are Engel (2002), Künne (2003) (which contains much interesting historical material), and Blackburn (2006). Each of these has a rather deflationary approach.

Regarding specific accounts of truth, David (1994) defends a correspondence-to-fact view against deflationism, while Horwich (1990; 1999) defends a version of deflationism. The semantic conception is set out in Tarski (1935; 1944). The coherence theory is defended in Walker (1989) while Putnam (1981) defends a form of pragmatism. The identity theory is defended in Dodd (2000).

Beyond these pointers, the literature on truth is simply huge.

Notes

1   Throughout, we concentrate on truth. A sentence is *false* if and only if its negation is true.

2   Sometimes non-linguistic non-propositional entities are called "true" – e.g., a "true friend," a "true Scotsman," etc. We set such uses aside, and concentrate on truth as applied to statements, beliefs, etc.

3   A proposition is the *content* of a statement, or the *content* of a mental state. This allows us to say that sentences with the same meaning express the same proposition, and that what you believe to be the case is exactly the same as what I believe.

4   Henceforth, we use "iff" as an abbreviation for "if, and only if."

5   Some authors, even scientific authors, use the word "fact" to mean roughly "statement accepted on the basis of observation." This is *not* what we mean, for such statements may be *false*, and therefore do *not* correspond to any fact.

6   The term "truth maker" has been suggested for what makes a truth bearer true. We note here that there is a theory of facts which *identifies* facts with *true propositions*. Thus, the correspondence relation between true proposition and fact is the *identity relation*. This view is called *the identity theory*. See Dodd (2000) for a defense of the identity theory.

7   One might think that there are no states of affairs that *don't* obtain. If so, facts are states of affairs, period.

8   There is an objection to the correspondence view (the "Slingshot Argument") which concludes that *every* truth corresponds to the *same* fact: the *Big Fact*. The reader may consult Neale (2001) for details.

9   It is unclear how to *verify* statements about certain topics, such as morality or religion. The verificationist might regard such statements as neither true nor false, or meaningless.

10   *Consistency* means that for no statement A, can one prove both A and *not-A*; while *completeness* means, for any statement A, either one can prove A, or one can prove *not-A*.

11   A *scheme* is a kind of linguistic frame into which various sentences may be substituted. Some authors write "schema."

12   There, however, is a fly in this ointment, which is that some T-sentences are false, because of the "Liar paradox," briefly mentioned below. However, one can restrict the set of T-sentences, and together they may be understood to *implicitly* define truth.

13   As an application, the epistemic definitions (D_4), (D_5), and (D_6) are *not* adequate in this sense.

14   In more detail, the result is known as Tarski's *Indefinability Theorem*: if a consistent language L is "sufficiently rich," the concept of truth in L is not itself definable *in L*. If the metalanguage for L contains a definition of truth in L, the metalanguage is, in some sense, "richer" than the object language.

15   To be more exact, the truth value of a sentence – a string of symbols – is relative to an interpretation of those symbols.

16   Consider a natural language L with context-sensitive expressions, such as "I," "now," and "here." The semantic theory is modified as follows. The notion of *truth* (in L) is replaced by the notion of *truth* (in L), *relative to certain parameters*. These parameters specify the speaker, the time, and the location of a speech act.

17   Two popular forms of deflationism are *disquotationalism* (truth bearers are sentences) and a *minimalism* (truth bearers are propositions). For our purposes, they needn't be sharply distinguished.

18   See Horwich (1999: 262) for a clear summary of what he takes his version of deflationism to involve.
19   We have, alas, not discussed debates about meaning, relativism/rationalism, statements possibly lacking truth values (e.g., moral statements; vague statements), and possible revisions of classical logic. We have not discussed the technical work (some devoted to studying the semantic paradoxes) of increasing relevance, particularly to debates about deflationism, which have dominated the recent philosophical literature

References

Blackburn, S. (2006). *Truth: A Guide for the Perplexed*, London: Penguin.

Blackburn, S. and Simmons, K. (eds.) (1999). *Truth*, Oxford: Oxford University Press.

David, M. (1994). *Correspondence and Disquotation: An Essay on the Nature of Truth*, Oxford: Oxford University Press.

Dodd, J. (2000). *An Identity Theory of Truth*, London: Macmillan.

Engel, P. (2002). *Truth*, Central Problems of Philosophy, ed. J. Shand, Chesham: Acumen Publishing.

Glanzberg, M. (2006). "Truth," *The Stanford Encyclopedia of Philosophy* (online).

Haack, S. (1978). *Philosophy of Logics*, Cambridge: Cambridge University Press.

Horwich, P. (1990; 1998). *Truth*, Oxford: Oxford University Press.

Horwich, P. (1999). "The Minimalist Conception of Truth," in Blackburn and Simmons.

Kirkham, R. L. (1992; 1995). *Theories of Truth*, Cambridge, MA: MIT Press.

Künne, W. (2003). *Conceptions of Truth*, Oxford: Oxford University Press.

Lynch, M. (ed.) (2001). *The Nature of Truth*, Cambridge, MA: MIT Press.

Neale, S. (2001). Facing Facts, Oxford: Clarendon Press.

Putnam, H. (1981). *Reason, Truth and History*, Cambridge: Cambridge University Press.

Russell, B. A. W. (1967) [1912]. *The Problems of Philosophy*, Oxford: Oxford University.

Tarski, A. (1935). "Der Wahrheitsbegriff in den formalisierten Sprachen," *Studia Philosophica*, I, 261–405; tr. "The Concept of Truth in Formalized Languages," in Tarski 1956.

Tarski, A. (1944). "The Semantic Conception of Truth and the Foundations of Semantics," *Philosophy and Phenomenological Research* 4: 341–376; repr. in Blackburn and Simmons and in Lynch.

Tarski, A. (1956). *Logic, Semantics, Metamathematics: Papers by Alfred Tarski from 1922–1938*, ed. J. H. Woodger, Oxford: Clarendon Press.

Walker, R. (1989). *The Coherence Theory of Truth*, London: Routledge; extracts repr. in Lynch.

2

Knowledge

Duncan Pritchard

Two Platitudes about Knowledge

There are many kinds of knowledge. I may know that Paris is the capital of France, or know how to bake a cake, or know where my keys are, or know who was the inventor of the zip fastener, and so on. To keep matters simple, we will focus on a particular kind of knowledge which is of central importance, what is known as *propositional knowledge*. Propositional knowledge, as the name suggests, is knowledge of a proposition. A proposition is, roughly, what is expressed by a sentence which says that something is the case – e.g., that Paris is the capital of France, or that the earth is flat. In focusing on propositional knowledge, then, we are focusing on *knowledge that* such-and-such is the case, rather than, say, on *knowing how* to do such-and-such, or *knowing where* such-and-such is, and so on.

Everyone agrees that knowledge entails true belief, in the sense that if one knows a proposition, *p*, then one believes *p* and *p* is true. (Of course, one might think that one knew a certain proposition which turned out to be false, but in such a case one would thereby discover that one did not really know it after all). Everyone also agrees that there is a lot more to knowledge than merely true belief.

It is easy to formulate cases of true belief that are not also cases of knowledge. For example, imagine a gambler – let's call him "Lucky" – who believes that the horse that will win the next race is Lucky Lass, where this belief is formed simply on the basis that he likes the name. Suppose further that Lucky Lass does indeed win the next race. Would we say that Lucky *knew* that Lucky Lass would win? Surely not, since his belief is simply the result of guesswork and guesswork is by itself no route to knowledge. And yet he does have a true belief in this proposition.

The tricky task for those working in the theory of knowledge (otherwise known as *epistemology*) is to explain what else is required for knowledge over and above true belief.[1]

There are two very natural ways of explaining why Lucky's true belief does not qualify as knowledge. The first is to note that Lucky's belief is only true as a matter of luck. That is, given how he formed his belief, that belief could very easily have been wrong. Compare Lucky's belief in this regard with the belief held by someone who we would regard as having known that Lucky Lass would win. Let us suppose that unbeknownst to Lucky, the race was fixed and the fixer was a local gangster who we'll call "Mr. Big." Since Mr. Big knows that the race is fixed in Lucky Lass's favor, we would naturally regard him as knowing that Lucky Lass will win. Notice, however, that given how Mr. Big has formed his true belief, it is not a matter of luck that his belief is true. That is, his true belief could not have very easily been wrong. There is thus a lot to be said for the idea that a pre-condition on knowledge is that it is not a matter of luck that one's belief in the target proposition is true. Call this intuition about knowledge, the *anti-luck platitude*.

A second way in which one might naturally explain Lucky's lack of knowledge is in terms of the fact that his true belief was not in any way the product of ability, but rather simply due to a lucky guess. In contrast, Mr. Big's true belief *was* formed through ability. After all, he saw for himself that all the other horses in the race were drugged and hence, given what he knows about the performance of drugged horses, he thereby knows that Lucky Lass will win. One way of putting this point is by saying that when one knows it is of some credit to one that one has a true belief. In the case of Lucky, however, it is of no credit to him at all that he formed a true belief, since his belief is only true by luck. There is thus a lot to be said for the idea that a pre-condition on knowledge is that one's true belief in the target proposition is gained via ability. Call this intuition about knowledge, the *ability platitude*.

These two platitudes have been extremely influential on contemporary theorizing about knowledge. Interestingly, one might be tempted to suppose that they are just two ways of putting the same point, such that there is in effect just one "super" platitude in play here. After all, one might naturally suppose that any true belief that was gained via ability would not be true as a matter of luck, and that any non-luckily true belief must have been gained via ability. If this were right, then we would be well on the way to understanding what knowledge is, since we would just need to say more about what satisfying these two platitudes would involve. As we will see, however, matters are not quite so straightforward. Indeed, we will see that these two platitudes in fact impose two independent constraints on knowledge.

Gettier-style Cases

Traditionally, the way of explaining what knowledge is in a manner that is consistent with both the ability and the anti-luck platitudes is to appeal to a *justification* condition, where satisfying this condition involves the agent being able to cite good grounds in favor of what one believes. Such an account of knowledge is known as the "tripartite" account of knowledge, since it defines knowledge as having three parts: justification, truth, and belief.

When it comes to the example just described involving Lucky and Mr. Big this proposal fares pretty well. After all, Lucky is unable to offer any good grounds in favor of what he believes, unlike Mr. Big who can offer excellent grounds in favor of why he thinks that Lucky Lass will win. The proposal does not fare well when it comes to other cases, however. One problem concerns the fact that we often attribute knowledge in cases where the agent concerned is unable to offer any good grounds in favor of what she believes. We will consider one example of this type later on. First, though, we need to look at an even more fundamental problem facing the tripartite account.

Consider the following example. Suppose that our agent – we will call him "Edmund" – comes downstairs one morning and forms his belief about what the time is by looking at the grandfather clock in his hall. The belief he forms, let's say, is that it is 8.20 a.m. Suppose further that this clock has been very reliable in the past and Edmund knows this, and also that Edmund has independent grounds for thinking that the time is roughly 8.20 a.m (e.g., it's light outside, he usually gets up around this time, and so forth). Finally, let us stipulate that Edmund's belief is true, it is 8.20 a.m. Edmund thus has a true belief in this proposition, and he is also in a position to offer excellent grounds in favor of his belief – i.e., his belief is justified. According to the tripartite account, then, he must know that the time is 8.20 a.m. Here comes the twist, however. As it happens, and unbeknownst to Edmund, the clock stopped working twenty-fours hours previously and is stuck at the time 8.20 a.m. Does Edmund know what the time is? Surely not. After all, one cannot find out what the time is by looking at a stopped clock. The moral of the story is thus that whatever knowledge is, it is not justified true belief.[2]

These cases are called "Gettier-style" cases, since they were first formulated as an objection to the tripartite account in a famous article by Edmund Gettier (1963).[3] There is a recipe for creating such cases. First, you take a belief that is formed in a way which would normally result in a false belief (e.g., in this case, a belief that is formed by looking at a stopped clock). Next, you set up the case such that the agent has good citable grounds in favor of her belief (e.g., in this case, Edmund has excellent grounds for believing that the time is indeed 8.20 a.m). Finally, you add the further detail that the belief so formed is, as it happens, true anyway.

Here is a second example which further illustrates this recipe for Gettier-style cases. Imagine a farmer – who we'll call "Roddy" – who is looking into a field and sees what looks to be a sheep. On this basis, Roddy comes to believe that there is a sheep in the field. As it happens, though, what he is looking at is not a sheep at all but merely a big hairy dog that looks like a sheep. Ordinarily, then, if one were to form this belief on this basis one would end up with a false belief. Nonetheless, Roddy has excellent grounds in favor of his belief – the big hairy dog does, after all, look just like a sheep, and he has no reason to doubt what he sees. Moreover, as it happens, Roddy's belief is true since there is a sheep in the field hidden from view behind the big hairy dog. Roddy thus has a justified true belief which does not count as knowledge (since one can't come to know that there is a sheep in the field simply by looking at a big hairy dog).[4]

What is interesting about Gettier-style cases is that they demonstrate that merely having a justification in favor of what you truly believe is insufficient to deal with the constraint on knowledge imposed by the anti-luck platitude. For in all such cases what you have is a justified true belief which doesn't count as knowledge because the belief in question is only luckily true – i.e., it could very easily have been wrong. In the case of Edmund, for example, had he come downstairs a minute earlier or a minute later (or if the clock had stopped a minute earlier or a minute later), then he would have formed a false belief by looking at this clock. The same goes for Roddy. Had there not been a sheep hidden from view behind the big hairy dog, then he would have formed a false belief by looking at the big hairy dog. In both cases, then, the belief formed is only luckily true even though it is justified.

A second point to notice about Gettier-style cases is that they *do* satisfy the constraint on knowledge imposed by the ability platitude. After all, both Edmund and Roddy form their respective beliefs through ability – i.e., these cases are not like the case of Lucky who gains a true belief simply by guesswork. Recall that Edmund has every reason to trust what this clock tells him, and Roddy is indeed looking at something that looks very much like a sheep.

Nevertheless, merely forming one's belief through ability does not appear to suffice for knowledge. Instead one must in addition form one's belief in a way that is non-lucky. The demands imposed by the ability and anti-luck platitudes are thus distinct.

The Lottery Puzzle

There is another type of example which illustrates that the demands imposed by these platitudes are distinct. Imagine a fair lottery with *extremely* long odds (a billion-to-one, say). Now suppose that our agent – we'll call her "Lottie" – is in possession of one of the tickets for this lottery, a ticket which, as it happens, is a losing ticket (though Lottie doesn't have any inkling of this yet). Lottie now reasons to herself that given that the odds against her winning are so high, her ticket must be a losing ticket. On this basis, she forms the (true) belief that she has lost the lottery and so tears up her ticket.

I think we would find Lottie's behavior rather puzzling, and part of the reason for this is that intuitively Lottie cannot come to know that her ticket has lost simply by reflecting on the long odds involved even though her belief is in fact true. Indeed, we would probably say to Lottie that she shouldn't have ripped up her ticket because, for all she knew, she had won the lottery. This example is thus itself a Gettier-style case, in that it is an example of justified true belief which, intuitively, is not knowledge. This is not the only import of this example, though.

What is interesting about this case is that while Lottie is unable to come to know that she has lost the lottery simply by considering the odds involved, she can come to know that she has lost by reading the results in a reliable newspaper. What is mysterious about this, however, is that the probability that the newspaper has printed the wrong result is surely much higher than the probability of her winning. From the point of view of the probability that her belief is correct, then, there is a greater probability that her belief is true if she forms it by reflecting on the odds involved than by forming it by reading the result in a reliable newspaper. And yet Lottie can come to know this proposition by the second method but not by the first.

This is the so-called "Lottery Puzzle."[5] What it demonstrates is the surprising fact that whether or not you know is not a function of the probabilistic strength of your supporting evidence – that is, one might have evidence in favor of one's belief which makes it very probable that one's belief is true and yet *lack* knowledge even though possessing evidence in favor of one's belief which does not make it as probable that it is true *can* suffice for knowledge. The way out of the puzzle is to recognize that whether or not your belief is only luckily true – and hence, in line with the anti-luck platitude, not a case of knowledge – is not directly related to the probabilistic strength of your supporting evidence.

In order to see this, notice that what is wrong with Lottie's true belief that she has lost when it is based on the consideration of the odds involved is that this belief very easily have been wrong. Imagine, for example, that Lottie had been in possession of the winning ticket and formed her belief about whether her ticket had lost in this way. In such a case she would have ended up forming a false belief via this method. Matters are different, however, when it comes to forming one's belief by looking up the result in a reliable newspaper. This is because had Lottie won the lottery then we would expect Lottie to form a true belief via this method. After all, had Lottie won then different results would have been published in the reliable newspaper, results which corresponded to the numbers on her ticket.

So the probabilistic strength of the evidential support you have for your belief does not itself determine whether your true belief is only true by luck, since a very high probabilistic strength of evidential support is consistent with one's belief being only luckily true, while a relatively low probabilistic strength of evidential support might be enough to ensure that your belief is not luckily true. More generally, the lottery case further illustrates the point made above that the demands imposed by the ability and anti-luck platitudes are distinct. After all, whether Lottie forms her true belief by considering the odds involved or by reading the results in a newspaper, it is surely through ability that she forms her belief. Merely forming one's belief through ability is thus not enough to ensure knowledge, because even a belief so formed could still be only luckily true.

Externalism and Internalism about Knowledge

One way of responding to the challenge posed by the Gettier-style cases and the lottery case could be to say that what we need to do is simply define knowledge as non-lucky justified true belief. This would then explain why the agents in these cases lack knowledge, since in each case their justified true beliefs were only luckily true.

One problem facing this proposal, however – which we alluded to above – is that it is far from obvious that we do think that in order to have knowledge you must be justified in what you believe, at least if by "justification" here we mean that the agent concerned is able to cite good grounds in favor of what she believes. In order to see this, consider the following case. Imagine that our agent – we'll call him "Chick" – possesses a highly reliable ability to tell the difference between male and female chicks. Chick believes that he is distinguishing between the chicks by using his sight and touch, but let us stipulate that he's mistaken in this regard and that he is actually doing this via his smell. Suppose further that Chick doesn't have any good reason for thinking that he's reliable in this regard. For example, perhaps the reason why he believes that he's reliable is because someone he trusts told him this, but that this person was in fact trying to deceive him on this score but accidentally told him the truth nonetheless. It should be clear that Chick is unable to offer any good grounds in favor of what he believes. Nevertheless, it is far from obvious that Chick does not know that, for example, the two chicks he has in his hands are of a different gender. After all, he really does have a highly reliable ability to tell the two apart. Moreover, given that he has this ability, it is not a matter of luck that his belief is true – he couldn't have easily been mistaken – and thus he satisfies the constraints laid down by both the ability and anti-luck platitudes even though he lacks justification for his belief.

Intuitions about what to say about such cases differ widely, with some epistemologists arguing that Chick lacks knowledge and others arguing that he has knowledge. If you think that Chick does have knowledge then the conclusion to draw is that one can meet the constraints laid down by the ability and anti-luck platitudes without thereby meeting a justification condition. In particular, it seems that one can satisfy the ability platitude without thereby meeting the justification condition, such that it is only the satisfaction of the former that is essential for knowledge. On this view, then, the conclusion that one should draw is that knowledge should be defined as non-lucky true belief that is the product of ability. In contrast, if you think that Chick *lacks* knowledge then you are committed to holding that there is at least sometimes more to knowledge than a non-lucky true belief that is the product of ability.

Those epistemologists who ascribe knowledge in cases like that of Chick are called *externalists*, while those who deny knowledge to Chick are called *internalists*. Essentially, the debate between externalists and internalists boils-down to whether you think that knowledge requires justification, with internalists making this demand – and so denying knowledge to Chick – and externalists allowing that there are cases in which agents possess knowledge even while lacking justification for what they believe – thereby enabling them to attribute knowledge to Chick.[6]

Externalists hold that knowledge is often relatively easy to come by. Indeed, they often allow that very small children and intellectually sophisticated animals – neither of which are likely to have beliefs that satisfy a justification condition – can have knowledge. In contrast, internalists hold that knowledge is much harder to come by. Notice, though, that this isn't a strike against internalism in itself, since it isn't in any way absurd to suppose that perhaps we do know an awful lot less than we think we know.

The debate between externalism and internalism has seemed to many to be intractable; a straightforward clash of intuition that will not admit of a resolution. Nevertheless, one conciliatory proposal in this regard that has been relatively popular is to argue that externalists and internalists are in effect speaking past one another by focusing on different "grades" of knowledge. That is, one might argue that we need to distinguish between a low-grade type of knowledge – what is sometimes called "brute" or "animal" knowledge – and a high-grade type of knowledge – what is sometimes called "reflective" knowledge. The thought is that while it can suffice for low-grade knowledge to merely have a true belief which satisfies the constraints laid down by the anti-luck and ability platitudes, if one wishes to have high-grade knowledge then it is essential that one also possesses, in addition, a justification for one's belief.[7]

The advantage of viewing the matter in this way is that one can do justice to both externalist and internalist intuitions. On the one hand, one accommodates the externalist intuition that Chick does count as possessing *bona fide* knowledge. On the other hand, one accommodates the internalist intuition that there is something epistemically deficient about the epistemic standing of Chick's belief. We would, after all, prefer to possess high-grade knowledge rather than low-grade knowledge – viz., it would be better to be like Chick but to have a justification for the target belief than to be like Chick and lack a justification. Perhaps, then, the choice between externalism and internalism in epistemology is not as stark as it first appears.

Anti-luck Epistemology

It was noted earlier that cases like Gettier-style cases and the lottery case demonstrate that having a true belief that is formed through ability does not suffice to ensure that one has a non-lucky true belief, and thus does not suffice for knowledge. The moral drawn from this was that the ability and anti-luck platitudes impose distinct demands on knowledge. One might wonder, however, whether having a non-lucky true belief might suffice for knowledge, in the sense that such a belief is of its nature acquired through ability and so satisfies the constraint laid down by the ability platitude. For if this were true, then it would seem that it is the anti-luck platitude which is the dominant epistemological platitude, with the ability platitude essentially just a product of the anti-luck platitude. That is, if this were true then one could simply understand knowledge as non-lucky true belief, what we might call an *anti-luck epistemology*.[8]

Interestingly, however, simply meeting the constraint imposed by the anti-luck platitude will not suffice for knowledge, and it is important to understand why. Consider the following case. Imagine an agent – we'll call him "Temp" – who is in a room and who regularly forms his belief about the temperature of the room by looking at the thermometer in the corner. Suppose further that this is a perfectly reliable way of forming beliefs about the temperature of the room, in the sense that every time he forms a belief in this way his belief is true. Here's the twist. Unbeknownst to Temp, the thermometer is broken and is simply fluctuating randomly within a certain range. That the thermometer is broken doesn't in any way undermine the reliability of the belief so formed, however, for the simple reason that there is someone hidden in the room next to the thermostat who ensures that every time that Temp goes over to the thermometer to find out the temperature, the reading on the thermometer matches up with the temperature in the room.

What is significant about this case is that Temp's true belief about the temperature in the room is clearly not lucky. After all, given the existence of the person hidden in the room, he is destined to form a true belief by forming his belief in this fashion; his true belief could not have easily been mistaken. Clearly, however, Temp does not have knowledge in this case, since one cannot come to know what the temperature of a room is simply by looking at a broken thermometer (any more than one can find out the time by simply looking at a broken clock). Moreover, the right diagnosis of why this is the case seems to be that Temp's true belief is not in any way a product of his abilities. Indeed, if anything, the truth of his belief is entirely the product of someone else's abilities – i.e., that of the person hidden in the room helpfully adjusting the thermostat. It thus follows that we cannot simply regard the constraint laid down by the ability platitude as a consequence of the constraint laid down by the anti-luck platitude. More generally, given the conclusion that we drew earlier that we could not treat the constraint laid down by the anti-luck platitude as flowing from the constraint laid down by the ability platitude, we can conclude that the constraints laid down by these platitudes are independent of one another in *both* directions. We are thus back to the thesis that knowledge is non-lucky true belief that is the product of ability.

As it happens, cases like the Temp case also illustrate why a certain kind of radical externalism about knowledge is unsound. One such view is reliabilism, and it holds that there is nothing more to knowledge than reliably formed true belief (i.e., true belief that is formed in a way that is more likely to lead to the truth than to falsehood).[9] On this view, while having a justification for one's belief might be epistemically advantageous, in that justified beliefs are more likely to be reliably formed beliefs, they are not essential, since what is important is just that the belief is reliably formed. For example, such a view, in keeping with other externalist proposals about knowledge, can allow that Chick has knowledge since his belief is, after all, being formed in a reliable fashion.

Notice, though, that Temp's belief is also formed in a highly reliable fashion, and yet he does not count as having knowledge. The same diagnosis for why Temp lacks knowledge also explains where the reliabilist account goes awry. It is not reliability *per se* that we are interested in when it comes to knowledge, but rather the specific kind of reliability that is directly connected to the agent's cognitive abilities. That's why Chick can count as having knowledge – at least by externalist lights – while Temp cannot: Chick's true belief, but not Temp's, is the product of his reliable cognitive abilities, and not simply a true belief that is reliable.

Virtue Epistemology

Whereas reliabilism is not attractive as an account of knowledge, there is a closely related view which retains much of the spirit of reliabilism but which is not susceptible to some of the same problems. This view is known as *virtue epistemology*. The most basic form of virtue epistemology holds, in essence, that knowledge is non-lucky true belief that is formed via the reliable cognitive abilities of the agent.[10] So construed, the view responds very directly to the two platitudes that we have been discussing here. According to this proposal, reliability in one's belief-forming processes is important, but the mere fact that a process is reliable will not suffice to ensure that an agent has knowledge, even if one adds the further proviso that the agent's belief is not luckily true. Rather, what is required is that the reliability be directly related to the cognitive abilities of the agent. In effect, what this form of virtue epistemology does is make explicit what is already implicit in the ability platitude –viz., that when we think of an agent's abilities as being knowledge-conducive, we are already thinking of them as reliable (that is, an unreliable cognitive ability is not a *bona fide* cognitive ability at all).

We noted earlier that Gettier-style cases and the lottery case demonstrate that merely having a true belief formed through (reliable) ability will not suffice for knowledge since it will not suffice to exclude the possibility that the belief is only true as a matter of luck. Some virtue epistemologists, however, have argued that there is a way of dealing with this problem which ensures that we can treat the constraint imposed by the anti-luck platitude as simply flowing from the constraint imposed by the ability platitude after all.

According to this version of virtue epistemology, knowledge is to be understood, roughly, as true belief that is because of cognitive ability. Notice that all mention of the true belief being non-lucky has been dropped. The thought is that so long as the agent's true belief is properly attributable to her cognitive ability – i.e., *because of* her cognitive ability – then this will suffice by itself to eliminate any knowledge-undermining epistemic luck.[11]

On the face of it, this proposal might seem quite appealing. Take Edmund's belief regarding the time. Although he possesses the relevant reliable cognitive abilities – he knows how to tell the time, for example – it is not because of these abilities that his belief is true, but, rather, down to the good fortune that he happened to look at the clock at the only time in the day in which it was displaying the right time. Or consider Lottie's belief that she has lost the lottery. Again, although this belief is the product of her reliable cognitive abilities – she has worked out the ramifications of the odds of her winning flawlessly, for example – it is not because of these abilities that her belief is true since had she been holding a winning ticket right now she would have continued to believe that she had lost.

It thus seems that we don't need to think of the anti-luck platitude as imposing a separate constraint on knowledge after all, just so long as we understand the relationship between true belief and cognitive ability correctly.

Unfortunately, this more robust form of virtue epistemology which dispenses with a separate anti-luck constraint on knowledge – while certainly offering a very elegant account of knowledge – does not pass muster. The reason for this is that there are cases of knowledge where the agent's true belief is not because of her cognitive ability, and cases in which the agent's true belief is because of her cognitive ability which are not thereby cases of knowledge.

The best way of illustrating the first claim is by considering cases of testimonial knowledge. What is significant about testimonial knowledge is that because of its social dimension it is knowledge that one can acquire by riding "piggy-back" on the cognitive abilities of others. Suppose, for example, that our agent – we will call her "Jenny" – gets off the train in an unfamiliar town and asks the first person she meets for directions. Suppose further that this person has first-hand knowledge of the area and communicates this to Jenny, thereby enabling her to form a true belief about where she needs to go. Intuitively, we would say that Jenny *knows* the way to go. Indeed, if one cannot gain testimonial knowledge in this way then it seems that we know an awful lot less than we think we do. Interestingly, however, it isn't at all right to say that Jenny's true belief is because of *her* cognitive abilities, as opposed, for example, to it being due to her *informant's* cognitive abilities (or at least their combined cognitive abilities). It thus appears to be a case in which an agent has knowledge even while having a true belief that is not because of her cognitive ability.[12]

It is important to be clear about the claim that is being made here. The thesis is not, for example, that Jenny is not exercising her cognitive abilities in a relevant fashion *at all* – i.e., this example is not a counterexample to the ability platitude.[13] After all, in order to maintain the intuition that Jenny has knowledge in this case, we need to suppose that she is indeed exercising a great deal of judgment. For one thing, we would expect her to be discriminating about who she asks for directions – i.e., if the first person she met had turned out to be a small child or someone who was clearly a tourist, then we would have expected her to find another potential informant. For another, we would expect Jenny to exercise discrimination when it comes to evaluating the truth of the testimony provided to her by the informant. If this testimony were clearly false, for example, then we would expect her to recognize this and disregard it accordingly.

Jenny's belief is thus a product of her cognitive abilities. The key point, however, is that the social nature of testimonial knowledge of this sort entails that it is not because of her cognitive abilities that her belief is true, and thus cases like this do count against the kind of virtue epistemology at issue.

The best way of illustrating the second kind of problem for this type of virtue epistemology – i.e., that there are cases in which the agent has a true belief that is because of cognitive ability but which is not thereby a case of knowledge – is via the following sort of scenario. Suppose that our agent – we'll call him "Barney" – gets a good clear view of a barn in good cognitive conditions (e.g., good lighting etc.,) and on this basis forms the belief that there is a barn in front of him. Suppose further that Barney has lots of relevant cognitive abilities which are working to enable him to form this belief and that his belief is also true – he is indeed looking at a barn. Here's the twist. Imagine that, unbeknownst to Barney, he is in "barn facade county," a county where all the barn-shaped objects bar this one are not in fact barns at all but fakes (perhaps, for example, there is some elaborate tax-dodge taking place here). If Barney had been looking at one of these fakes, then he would have formed the false belief that what he is looking at is a barn rather than the true belief that he actually forms. Does Barney know that what he is looking at is a barn? Surely not. His true belief, after all, is just too lucky to count as knowledge since he could very easily have been mistaken in this regard. Notice, however, that the truth of Barney's belief, while due to luck, *does* seem to be because of his cognitive abilities, in that it is these cognitive abilities that have led him to form a true belief.[14]

We can further emphasize this point by noting that the sort of epistemic luck in play in this case is very different from that in play in standard Gettier-style cases. In Gettier-style cases, such as the case involving Roddy described above, it is plausible to suppose that the truth of the agent's belief is not because of his cognitive abilities, and the reason for this is that something intervenes between the agent's belief and her cognitive abilities, albeit in such a way that does not prevent the agent from having a true belief. In the case of Roddy, for example, his cognitive abilities do not hook-up with the target of his belief – the sheep in the field – at all, but instead are led astray by the big hairy dog that is standing in front of the sheep. All Gettier-style luck is of this "intervening" sort.

Notice, however, that the kind of epistemic luck in play in the example involving Barney is not of this intervening sort. After all, Barney really does see a barn in the sense in the sense that his cognitive abilities do indeed put him in touch with the target of his belief, the barn. Instead, the epistemic luck in play here is of an "environmental" variety, in that it simply concerns the fact that this is not an epistemically friendly environment – i.e., it is not an environment in which one's cognitive abilities can easily enable one to have a true belief. However, it is because the epistemic luck in play is not of the intervening sort that it seems entirely right to say that Barney's true belief is because of his cognitive ability, unlike in Gettier-style cases, like that involving Roddy.

It thus follows that one can have a true belief that is because of one's cognitive ability and yet lack knowledge. Again, then, we find that we need to respect both the anti-luck and the ability platitudes.

Concluding Remarks

The less robust version of virtue epistemology was thus right all along: knowledge is non-lucky true belief that is the product of the agent's reliable cognitive abilities. We have thus answered one of the central questions of epistemology – viz., "What is knowledge?" Notice, however, that we have left many more central issues of epistemology unanswered. For example, why does knowledge have this structure? It is, after all, far from obvious why knowledge should have these properties. A related question in this regard concerns why we regard knowledge as such an important philosophical notion, a question that we might expect our analysis of knowledge to throw some light on.[15] And perhaps an even more pressing epistemological issue that has not been engaged with here is the question of whether we have any knowledge.[16]

Nevertheless, while there are many questions that have not been answered in this essay, the hope is that we have learned enough about epistemology to gain a grip on what this key area of philosophy involves and thus provide a foundation for further explorations in this direction.[17]

Further Reading

I have offered further readings that are specific to particular points raised in this essay in the endnotes as we have gone along, so the purpose of this section is to guide you towards some general readings in epistemology that you may find useful. The literature in this regard is vast, so rather than aim for comprehensiveness I will instead simply focus on directing you towards a few key texts within a number of relevant categories. (For a comprehensive survey of further readings in epistemology, see Pritchard 2006: 163–6).

To begin with, there are some freely available articles on the internet that provide a useful introduction to the theory of knowledge. The best of these is almost certainly Steup (2005). If you are a member of an academic institution, then you may also have free access to Klein (2005) as well (if not, then viewing this article will require a subscription). For a general introduction to epistemology which does not presuppose any prior familiarity with the field, see Morton (1997) or Pritchard (2006). For a more advanced textbook on epistemology that offers a non-partisan overview of the central issues, see Audi (1998). Note, however, that there are some first-rate, albeit more idiosyncratic, advanced textbooks available. See, for example, Craig (1990), Williams (2001), and Welbourne (2002). When it comes to reference works, the only dictionary of epistemology that I am aware of is Blaauw and Pritchard (2005). There are, however, a number of encyclopaedias, the best of which is currently Dancy and Sosa (1993). There are also some excellent volumes available which, while not being encyclopaedias as such, serve a similar purpose. See, for example, Greco and Sosa (1999), Moser (2002) and Steup and Sosa (2005). Finally, there are a number of superb anthologies available in epistemology. The most accessible is probably Bernecker (2006), but see also Bernecker and Dretske (2000) and Sosa and Kim (2000).

Notes

1   Some – most notably Williamson (2000) – have argued that this task cannot be completed, and thus that we should regard knowledge as unanalyzable. For my own part, I am far more optimistic on this score, as we will soon see.
2   The example of the stopped clock comes from Russell (1948: 170–1), though he did not himself recognize that it was an example of justified true belief which is not a case of knowledge.
3   The *locus classicus* for discussions of Gettier-style cases is Shope (1983).
4   This example is adapted from one offered by Chisholm (1977: 105).
5   For more on the lottery puzzle, see Hawthorne (2004).
6   For more on the externalism/internalism distinction, see Kornblith (2001).
7   The *locus classicus* for discussions of "animal" and "reflective" knowledge is Sosa (1991).
8   For further discussion of anti-luck epistemology, see Pritchard (2005; 2007).
9   The *locus classicus* for discussions of reliabilism is Goldman (1986).
10   See, for example, Greco (1999; 2000), who describes this type of virtue epistemology as "agent reliabilism."
11   Versions of virtue epistemology of roughly this sort can be found in Sosa (e.g., 1991; 2007), Zagzebski (1996) and later work by Greco (e.g., 2002).

12 This example is adapted from one offered by Lackey (2007), albeit to support a slightly different thesis.
13 This is the moral that Lackey (2007) draws from this example.
14 This example is due to Ginet, but it first appeared in print in Goldman (1976).
15 The *locus classicus* for discussions of the value of knowledge is Kvanvig (2003).
16 According to the radical sceptic, we have very little knowledge, if any. For an overview of the contemporary literature on radical skepticism, see Pritchard (2002).
17 I am grateful to John Shand for some very helpful comments on an earlier draft.

References

Audi, R. (1998). *Epistemology: A Contemporary Introduction to the Theory of Knowledge*, London: Routledge.
Bernecker, S. (ed.). (2006). *Reading Epistemology*, Oxford: Blackwell.
Bernecker, S. and Dretske, F. (eds.) (2000). *Knowledge: Readings in Contemporary Epistemology*, Oxford: Oxford University Press.
Blaauw, M. and Pritchard, D. H. (2005). *Epistemology A–Z*, Edinburgh: University Press.
Chisholm, R. (1977). *Theory of Knowledge*, 2nd edn., Englewood Cliffs, NJ: Prentice Hall.
Craig, E. (1990). *Knowledge and the State of Nature: An Essay in Conceptual Synthesis*, Oxford: Clarendon Press.
Dancy, J. and Sosa, E. (eds.) (1993). *A Companion to Epistemology*, Oxford: Blackwell.
Gettier, E. (1963). "Is Justified True Belief Knowledge?," *Analysis*, 23, 121–3.
Goldman, A. (1976). "Discrimination and Perceptual Knowledge," *Journal of Philosophy*, 73, 771–91.
Goldman, A. (1986). *Epistemology and Cognition*, Cambridge, MA: Harvard University Press.
Greco, J. (1999). "Agent Reliabilism," *Philosophical Perspectives*, 13, 273–96.
Greco, J. (2000). *Putting Skeptics in Their Place: The Nature of Skeptical Arguments and Their Role in Philosophical Inquiry*, Cambridge: Cambridge University Press.
Greco, J. (2002). "Knowledge as Credit for True Belief," in M. DePaul and L. Zagbeski (eds.), *Intellectual Virtue: Perspectives from Ethics and Epistemology*, Oxford: Oxford University Press.
Greco, J. and Sosa, E. (eds.) (1999). *The Blackwell Guide to Epistemology*, Oxford: Blackwell.
Hawthorne, J. (2004). *Knowledge and Lotteries*, Oxford: Oxford University Press.
Klein, P. (2005). "Epistemology" in E. Craig (ed.), *Routledge Encyclopedia of Philosophy*, London: Routledge, www.rep.routledge.com/article/P059.
Kornblith, H. (ed.) (2001). *Epistemology: Internalism and Externalism*, Oxford: Blackwell.
Kvanvig, J. (2003). *The Value of Knowledge and the Pursuit of Understanding*, Cambridge: Cambridge University Press.
Lackey, J. (2007). "Why We Don't Deserve Credit for Everything We Know," *Synthese*, 158, 345–61.
Morton, A. (1997). *A Guide Through the Theory of Knowledge*, Oxford: Blackwell.
Moser, P. K. (ed.). (2002). *The Oxford Handbook of Epistemology*, Oxford: Oxford University Press.
Pritchard, D. H. (2002). "Recent Work on Radical Skepticism," *American Philosophical Quarterly*, 39, 215–57.
Prichard, D. H. (2005). *Epistemic Luck*, Oxford: Oxford University Press.
Prichard, D. H. (2006). *What Is This Thing Called Knowledge?*, London: Routledge.

Prichard, D. H. (2007). "Anti-luck Epistemology," *Synthese*, 158, 277–97.

Russell, B. (1948). *Human Knowledge: Its Scope and Its Limits*, London: George Allen & Unwin.

Shope, R. K. (1983). *The Analysis of Knowing: A Decade of Research*, Princeton, NJ: Princeton University Press.

Sosa, E. (1991). *Knowledge in Perspective: Selected Essays in Epistemology*, Cambridge: Cambridge University Press.

Sosa, E. (2007). *A Virtue Epistemology: Apt Belief and Reflective Knowledge*, Oxford: Oxford University Press.

Sosa, E. and Kim, J. (eds.) (2000). *Epistemology: An Anthology*. Oxford: Blackwell.

Steup, M. (2005). "The Analysis of Knowledge," in E. Zalta (ed.), *Stanford Encyclopaedia of Philosophy*, http://plato.stanford.edu/entries/knowledge-analysis/.

Steup, M. and Sosa, E. (eds.). (2005). *Contemporary Debates in Epistemology*, Oxford: Blackwell.

Welbourne, M. (2001). *Knowledge*, Chesham: Acumen.

Williams, M. (2001). *Problems of Knowledge: A Critical Introduction to Epistemology*, Oxford: Oxford University Press.

Williamson, T. (2000). *Knowledge and Its Limits*, Oxford: Oxford University Press.

Zagzebski, L. (1996). *Virtues of the Mind: An Inquiry into the Nature of Virtue and the Ethical Foundations of Knowledge*, Cambridge: Cambridge University Press.

3

A *Priori* Truths

Greg Restall

Philosophers love *a priori* knowledge: we delight in truths that can be known from the comfort of our armchairs, without the need to venture out in the world for confirmation. This is due not to laziness, but to two different considerations. First, it seems that many philosophical issues aren't settled by our experience of the world – the nature of morality; the way concepts pick out objects; the structure of our experience of the world in which we find ourselves – these issues seem to be decided not on the basis of our experience, but in some manner by things *prior* to (or independently of) that experience. Second, even when we are deeply interested in how our experience lends credence to our claims about the world, the matter remains of the remainder: we learn more about how experience contributes to knowledge when we see what knowledge is available independent of that experience.

In this chapter we will look at the topic of what can be known *a priori*. We will start with some examples of truths which we have thought to be uncontentiously *a priori* known.

Examples

From logic

I can know that if every student has either passed an exam or completed an assignment, then either every student has passed an exam, or some student has completed an assignment. I can know this without concerning myself with the details of which students have passed an exam or have completed an assignment, for I can reason as follows: Let's suppose every student has either passed an exam or completed an assignment. We want to show that either every student has passed an exam or some student has completed an assignment. Suppose I choose a student. By hypothesis, he or she has either passed an exam or completed an assignment. If the assignment is completed, then I can conclude that some student has completed an assignment, which gives us what I wanted to show. If this piece of reasoning fails for *every* student, then we see that *every* student has completed an exam, which also gives us our desired conclusion.

This piece of argumentation suffices to prove what we wished to show. It used no details of students, assignments or exams. The form of the reasoning would work for any claim of the structure: if every F is either G or H, then either every F is G or some F is H. Valid deductive reasoning seems to give us *a priori* knowledge on the basis of logical structure.

From semantics

It seems that I can know that all bachelors are unmarried, without going to the trouble of interviewing bachelors and checking their marital status. I know this because if I find out that someone is married, then this counts decisively against their being a bachelor. I know this because this is how I understand the terms "married" and "bachelor." It seems that the meanings of the expressions I use governs *how* I treat the evidence I may find. I don't wait to learn of the marital status of a number of bachelors to conclude a generalisation on the basis of this evidence. I use this generaliation to govern the evidence I encounter.

From mathematics

Take a case of mathematical reasoning. A salient example in the development of our understanding of the *a priori* and is relationship with logic and the analytic is *the intermediate value theorem*, which states that every continuous function f of real numbers, where the value $f(-1)$ that it takes on the input -1 is smaller than 0, and whose value $f(1)$ that it takes on the input 1 is greater than 0, has *some* input value x between -1 and 1 where the output $f(x)$ is 0. A continuous function which is *below* the origin line at -1 and *above* the origin line at 1, must have *crossed* the line at some point between -1 and 1 (see figure 3.1). In other words, any continuous path (a path without jumps or breaks) starting on one side of a line and ending up on another side of that line must have at least one point at which it *crosses* the line.

This is *obvious*. We can see that it is true in many cases, and furthermore, we may find it very difficult to know what it would be for it to be false in any case at all. For many years, mathematicians claimed that they could *see* that the theorem is true in full generality, without being able to offer anything resembling a proof. The key is the notion of *continuity*. A function is continuous if it has no breaks or jumps – and making this notion precise, in

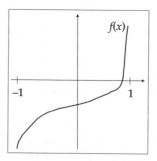

Figure 3.1 A continuous function

the development of the Calculus in the work of Bolzano and Weierstrass (see Coffa 1993: chs. 2 and 3) was required for this piece of *a priori* knowledge to make the transition from something which seems obvious but is hard to justify, to something which could be proved on the basis of an analysis of the concepts involved.

From indexicality

I may have amnesia and not remember where I am. However, wherever I am, if I say "I am here now" this seems to be something which is true, and which I can *know*. You use external evidence to find where I am, but I don't need to take in any evidence to convince myself that I am *here*. Evidence enters the picture when I want to know where "here" is, but as it stands, this is an item of *a priori* knowledge.

This case has interesting features, for while it seems to be a tautology for me to say that I am here now, that is not something that *you* can know *a priori*. You can know that whenever I say "I am here now" that I am speaking truly, but you cannot always know *what* I am saying. To see this consider me speaking to my spouse at the end-of-school-year concert, which I have unexpectedly been able to attend: "Zachary *doesn't know that I'm here now*, he thinks that I'm still at work." I can know *a priori* that I am here, but Zachary, to learn that fact, must see me in the audience.

From ethics

Consider the judgment that making other people happy is, all things considered, a *good* thing to do. Perhaps when you consider this judgment you remember particular acts in which you have made others happy. But upon reflection, it seems that there's no reason to appeal to this or that experience, or this or that *evidence* that happiness is a good thing. Perhaps it is bound up in the very notions of happiness, others, and goodness, and we reasonably could come to that conclusion on the basis of reflection on those notions. Many believe that our fundamental ethical principles are known *prior* to the evidence. Such statements certainly don't look like they can be refuted (or proved) on purely empirical grounds, and the fact that they concern what *should* happen seems to mean that mere description of how the world *is* cannot count decisively against the kind of claim about how it *should* be,

Are these good examples of *a priori* truths? How do they fare when we attend to the connections, if any, between *a priority*, necessity, analyticity, and infallibility? What have philosophers said about the notion of the *a priori*, and does the notion survive close scrutiny? These are the questions we will examine in the rest of this essay.

Definitions

As we have seen in our initial meeting with examples, an *a priori* truth is something that can be known independently of any particular evidence or experience. This rough and ready idea has been the basis of the claim to *a priority* for each of our examples. You do not need to know anything about the world in order to verify that if all Fs are G or H, then either all F are G or some F are H, or that all bachelors are unmarried, and I need to take in no evidence to know that I am here. Or so the reasoning has gone.

This does not mean that the notion of *a priori* knowledge is unproblematic. We have not given a characterization what is necessary for knowledge to be independent of the external evidence, and neither have we had anything to say about what is to count as evidence, and of the evidence we have, what it means for some of it to be *external*.

Similarly, there is confusion on another aspect of the notion of independence. It is one thing to say that knowledge can be acquired without appeal to some antecedent experience. It is another to say that that item of knowledge cannot have its status as knowledge undermined by further experience of the outside world. This is a much stronger requirement. I may be convinced of some reasonably complicated mathematical result (such as the intermediate value theorem) by way of stepping carefully through some proof, with the help of a mathematically sophisticated friend. Although aided by props and outside support, this can count as *a priori* reasoning, for none of the props are essential to the content of what is conveyed, if I come to understand the proof. However, my confidence in my understanding of the proof could be shaky – although I think I have understood it, I may not be confident. In such a circumstance, my belief in the theorem may be undermined if my mathematically sophisticated friend then tells me that actually, that proof contained a subtle mistake and that mathematicians now believe that the theorem is false. My trust of my friend and in her authority as an expert may override my *a priori* knowledge, if I am not confident in that knowledge. This further information – that my expert friend tells me that the so-called theorem is *false* – is anything but *a priori*. This means that my knowledge of the intermediate value theorem, if it could be undermined by the claims of an expert, does not count as *a priori* in a stronger sense that requires unrevisability.

Whether the independence needed for *a priority* requires infallibility and unrevisability on the basis of any empirical evidence is a controversial issue (see, for example Casullo 2006; Kitcher 2000; Field 2000).

There are many other current debates concerning the nature of *a priority*. To take them in turn, we would do well to attend how thinking about the *a priori* has developed from Kant to the present day. While there is no doubt that the *a priori* played an important role in Ancient, medieval and early modern philosophy, the central importance of the notion, and its currently use is indelibly shaped by the work of Immanuel Kant.

The Synthetic A *Priori*

Before Kant's *Critique of Pure Reason*, the three allied notions of necessity, analyticity and *a priority* were not clearly distinguished. In Kant's defence of the synthetic *a priori*, the notions of the *analytic* and the *a priori* come apart. For Kant, an important class of truths can be known *a priori* but not through analysis. They are *synthetic a priori*. In our list of examples of *a priori* truths, the boundary between the analytic and the synthetic occurs in the split between logical and semantic/conceptual truths (which are analytic) and truths of arithmetic and geometry, which for Kant can be shown *a priori* only by the operations of the intuitions of time and space and not by analysis. While a considered discussion of Kant's account of the *a priori* is beyond us, we should venture into this territory just a little, for Kant's approach to the *a priori* set the scene for crucial developments into the twentieth century and beyond.

The distinction between the analytic *a priori* and the synthetic *a priori* is sharply drawn: for Kant, the boundary is found at the limits of what is possible through the *analysis* of concepts. Purely formal logic shows structural relationships between concepts (so Aristotle's syllogisms show formal and analytic conceptual relations between judgments), and the analysis of concepts into constituent parts grounds another kind of deduction between judgments. To say that *Gilles is a bachelor* is in part to say that *Gilles is unmarried*, and so, the conditional judgment *if Gilles is a bachelor, then Gilles is unmarried,* and the corresponding generalization *all bachelors are unmarried,* can be shown to be true, *a priori*, by means of the analysis of concepts.

Nothing, according to Kant, can do the same thing with judgments such as simple arithmetic claims like: 8 + 5 = 13, or geometric claims, such as the claim that the interior angles of triangles add up to 180 degrees; let alone claims such as the *Intermediate Value Theorem*. In each case here, the reasoner must engage in some rational deduction in order to demonstrate the claims (and since the rational deduction is *pure* and not *empirical*, it is *a priori*, well enough), but his kind of reasoning goes beyond what is analytic. In the case of arithmetic reasoning, try as you like, you will not find the concept of 8 in the concept of 13, or *vice versa*. You will pass through 8 on the way to *counting to* 13, and you will hit 13 exactly after taking as many steps counting from 8 that one takes when counting to 5 – this is one way to show that 8 + 5 = 13, *a priori*. But, for Kant, this is not an analytic deliverance of some formal meaning: this is the kind of demonstration possible for one who has the concept of *time* – the concept of one thing coming *after* another, which is crucial to our practice of counting.

The same goes for geometric reasoning, but here, the requirement is not the concept of *time*, but the concept of *space*. We must use our spatial intuition in order to engage in *a priori* spatial reasoning. It is not for nothing that presentations Euclid's *Elements* are filled with diagrams, and geometrical reasoning is filled with instructions to "extend a line from point A through the intersection of lines *l* and *m* until it intersects line *k*" and the like – they are instructions to engage in our spatial reasoning by way of our spatial intuition. (Note here Kant does not mean our *hunches* by the notion of "intuition" but rather, our grasp of concepts and the way we structure them together, pre-conceptually.) The findings of this synthetic *a priori* reasoning are as firm and as necessary as any analytic truth, despite the fact that it may be (in some sense) a contingent matter that we have the intuitions that we do. These intuitions of space and time are, for Kant, *pure*, because we have them antecedently to the acquisition of empirical concepts: we do not learn the pure intuitions of time and of space by example or by experiment: rather, we use these intuitions to structure the empirical intuitions we have *in* time and *in* space.

The "contingency," in some sense, of our having *these* temporal and spatial intuitions instead of others does not lead to the contingency of the judgments involving them: any more than the contingency of your having the concept of a *leg before wicket* and a *dismissal* means that it is not necessary that any batsman out by way of a *leg before wicket* has been *dismissed* by the *bowler*: what is contingent is your having the concept, and your ability to express (or understand) that necessary truth. It would not be any less necessary if we did not have the concepts needed to express it. Though it must be noted that in the case of the socially mediated practice of cricket, if no one has the concept of *lbw* or *dismissal* or *bowler*, then it is plausible no one can play cricket, either. Were we to not possess the spatial and temporal intuitions that we have, then we could not form these numerical or spatial judgments. Despite the internal and contingent nature of the forms of pure intuition, for Kant the link between the necessary and the *a priori* is fixed.

As we will see in the next section, philosophical orthodoxy has not remained Kantian on the matter of the *a priori*. Nonetheless, Kant has able defenders on the identification of necessity with *a priority* and the restriction of analyticity to a strict subset of the *a priori*.[1]

The *A Priori* and the Analytic

It is perhaps not surprising that with Kant's key examples of synthetic *a priori* knowledge coming from mathematics, it was from developments in mathematics that revolutionary new ideas took their root. In the first instance, these ideas came from the nascent discipline of the calculus and the theory of real numbers and functions. We don't have space to recount the intellectual trajectory in any detail, suffice to say that by the eighteenth and nineteenth centuries, since the pioneering work of Newton and Leibniz, the mathematical practice of differentiating and integrating functions was well established and largely well behaved, but – for both the pure mathematician and the philosopher – it was anything but well understood. What is it for a function to be continuous? Can we make the notion of "no jumps or gaps" precise, in a way that is amenable to reasoning? In the work of Bolzano and Weierstrass, Cauchy and Dedekind, through the nineteenth century, advances were made on these fronts. Results such as the intermediate value theorem were provided with *proofs* in the nineteenth century. The necessary ingredient wasn't the ingenuity to fill in a missing step in a calculation or a new technique for solving puzzles, but something much more fundamental, a new *definition*. Bolzano and Weierstrass's definition of what it was for a function to be continuous[2] allows one to *prove* the intermediate value theorem using logic alone. As a matter of logic, any continuous function *in that sense of continuity we have defined*, such that $f(-1) < 0$ and $f(1) > 0$ has some point t between -1 and 1 where it crosses the line – where $f(t) = 0$. The derivation is purely formal, on the basis of definition, without the need for a diagram, picture or any requirement to *see* the conclusion. Advances in mathematics gave the analytic the means to recover lost ground – and to go much further.

It did not go unnoticed that to make sense of the *derivation* of results such as the intermediate value theorem, we needed an expanded notion of logic in order to accommodate reasoning with definitions such as these. The construction "*for every . . . there is a . . . such that whenever . . .*" in the definition of continuity is a complex nesting of what we now understand as *quantifiers*, and it took the development of logic in the nineteenth and twentieth centuries in the work of Peano, Frege, Russell, and Whitehead to give an account of formal deductive consequence in a vocabulary so expressive. With the expansion of the notion of a definition (to include the Bolzano–Weierstrass definition of continuity) and the expansion of the notion of logic (to include what we now recognize as classical first-order logic), the landscape of the territory between the *a priori* and the *analytic* changed shape.

The development of the tools of logic beyond their Aristotelian bounds gave shape to an important question: where exactly are the bounds of logic? What makes an item of vocabulary a logical constant? This became a live issue with the work of Russell and Whitehead, who appealed to an axiom of *infinity* in the type theory of *Principia Mathematica*. They acknowledged that it was not satisfactory to conceive of this as a logical notion in exactly the same way as other logical axioms. But why? What is the ground for calling something a logical notion? Clearly a claim that there are infinitely many things is not empirically verifiable in any straightforward fashion, so in some sense it may be thought to be *a priori* if it is, in fact, true. But could a logical axiom be the kind of thing we could *debate*? Contemporary discussions of the bounds of logical concepts have not settled on a sharp delineation beyond broad agreement that what is known as "classical first-order logic" is a uncontroversially within the scope of logic properly so called (see Etchemendy 1990; Shapiro 1991; Sher 1991).

Now, not only did the new mathematics and logic make possible the thought that the truths of calculus could be true "by definition" without the aid of pure intuition, but advances in geometry and set theory paved the way to do the same thing for space and time, Kant's core notions of geometry and numbers.

Advances in thinking about Euclid's fifth postulate, the *parallel postulate*, led to the construction of formal models of geometric theories in which space behaved radically differently (in the work of Lobachevsky, Reimann, and others, and the question naturally arose as to whether these non-Euclidean geometries did any better than Euclid at characterizing our pre-theoretic concept of space. Advances in theories of sets, classes and types, in the work of Frege, Russell, and Whitehead, and others, meant that such fundamental notions of *number* were having their internal structure plumbed and various analyses of the notions were proposed in order to more clearly articulate the commitments in a theory of number, and to propose various *definitions* of that notion.

At the height of logical positivism, analyses of notions such as *space*, *time* and *number* had been proposed, refined and developed. Carnap's *Aufbau* proposed a logical framework for the definition of concepts, for relating them to sense experience, and for analyzing necessity and *a priority* as due to *analyticity*, which in turn was a purely *conventional* matter. It is up to us which language we use, the adoption of one language over another is an arbitrary or pragmatic matter, and *relative* to that choice of language, a space of necessities and possibilities is defined, which can be analyzed *a priori* using the tools of logic. It is up to us that we define logical, numerical, geometrical concepts in the way that we do, in just the same way that we define other terms of our language. Relative to that definition, some truths are necessary and others are contingent, and this matter is purely linguistic, relative to the choice of language employed. Necessity and possibility; *a priority* and *a posteriority* as internal questions are to be answered relative to a linguistic framework. The *external* question, of whether to employ *this* language or *that* one is a pragmatic affair, to be answered not by asking which language better reflects *truth* (for any question of truth is relative to the choice of a language in which that truth is expressed), but rather, by other concerns such as ease of use, better fit with practical or theoretical virtues or other aims of inquiry. The choice, say, between the employment of a non-Euclidean or Euclidean geometry is not the empirical question of which one is *correct*, in the absence of some prior choice of how we are to identify what counts as a *point* and what counts as a *line*. Once we have made that choice – and choice indeed it is, are points abstract, located in experience, are lines the paths of uninterrupted light beams, or to be identified in some other empirical fashion? – then the properties expressed in that language become a matter of empirical or logical investigation, depending on the language chosen at the outset. On this view, the only necessity is *verbal* necessity – necessity grounded in the analytic, the choice of language. What is *a priori* and *necessary* is true by convention, the conventional choice of a linguistic framework.

In this way, by the end of the first third of the twentieth century, the theoretical landscape had inalterably changed. In the analytic tradition at least, Kant's intuition was largely banished in favor of logic, language and convention.

Gödel and Quine

Such a consensus did not survive. The decline of the logical positivists' identification of necessity and *a priority* with analyticity, and the split between necessary truth-by-convention and contingent truth-on-the-basis-of-reality came in two fronts: one another new mathematical result, and the other, a powerful philosophical metaphor.

The mathematical result is Gödel's justly celebrated incompleteness theorem. Gödel's result dealt a deathblow to the naïve identification of necessary and *a priori* truth (in some language) with what is analytically true (in that language). Gödel showed that in the case of very many mathematical theories – in particular, any theory strong enough to include a small proportion of modern mathematics – there are statements which are true *of* that theory but are not provable *within* that theory, and this can be straightforwardly *proved a priori*. This would not be a problem if it applied to *some* theories, for we could say that even though theory T is incomplete, the theory we are using to reason *about* T is the *real* theory, whose notion of necessity is to be identified with analytic truth relative to *it*. But Gödel's theorem will apply to this theory too, if it is consistent. For any theory (if true), we can construct a stronger theory including truths the first theory missed out. The only mathematically realistic theories to escape Gödel's incompleteness are theories that are *inaccessible* – theories whose axiomatic basis is so complicated as to not be *in principle* enumerated. Such theories are not candidates to be languages in Carnap's sense, for they are not the sort of thing that can be used as frameworks governing our use of mathematical vocabulary. Carnap's program is dealt a deathblow on mathematical grounds.

Not only was Carnap's program dealt a blow by Gödel – these results provide grist for the mill for anyone concerned with the epistemology of mathematics. Which mathematical claims are knowable *a priori*? How are we to account for mathematical truth and our access to that truth? Gödel's results show that this branch of *a priori* truth is a very delicate matter (Franzén 2004; Potter 2000; Smith 2008). One contemporary proposal is to see that numerical vocabulary as introduced by *abstraction* over a relation of equinumerosity. If the Fs are equinumerous with the Gs we say that the number of Fs is the same as the number of Gs (Wright 1983). In this way it could be (in some sense) *a priori*, without reducing to logic, and we do not need to identify the truths of arithmetic with any formal theory, because what we take to be true concerning numbers may well depend on our conceptual apparatus in other matters. (What numbers we are able to countenance depends on what predicates we can construct.) Matters here are, of course, subtle, both philosophically and mathematically (Burgess 2005; Fine 2002).

Gödel's results showed that the *a priori* is not to be identified with the analytic in some language. Quine's arguments against *analyticity* not only led analytic truth into disrepute, but brought down the *a priori* with it. Quine's compelling metaphor of the web of belief, and the attack on the analytic/synthetic distinction apply not only to analyticity but also to the *a priori*.

In a series of papers, including "Truth by Convention" (1936), "Two Dogmas of Empiricism" (1951), culminating in a book *Word and Object* (1960), Quine led a sustained attack on the logical positivism of his mentor, Carnap. In "Truth by Convention" he argued that the Carnap's distinction between conventional and empirical truth is unsustainable, and along with it, there is no place for the distinction between internal and external questions. In "Two Dogmas," Quine argues that the notion of synonymy required in any account of analytic truth is anything but unrevisable or knowable *a priori*, and so cannot play the role required of it in the logical positivist programme. Instead of privileging a class of statements as *a priori* and immune from revision on internal grounds (to be changed only on external grounds on the basis of a pragmatic *choice* for one vocabulary over another), Quine argues that the network of beliefs is so interconnected that a difficulty in one area may be fixed by a revision in another, whether that area is close to the periphery of perception statements, some way in at the level of generalisations and lawlike statements, or deep in the center, at the level of mathematics and logic. All is of a piece, and the entire edifice of commitments stands under judgment from the tribunal of experience *together*. Only as a whole does a theory (an entire epistemic standpoint) serve to be confirmed or disconfirmed by evidence, and any part of it can be revised to better fit that evidence. The epistemology is explicitly *holist*, and *a posteriori*. Putatively *a priori* claims seem independent from experience because they are *general*, applying regardless of the experience we receive from the world and therefore telling us nothing about the world of experience, but nonetheless, perhaps they are revisable in the light of other statements in just the same way as any other claim.

Such a wide-ranging attack on the *a priori* was unprecedented: in Quine's vision of philosophy, none of the notions of *a priority*, analyticity or necessity play a central role. Philosophy is continuous with the empirical sciences: it differs only in generality.

Kripke and Kaplan

The *a priori*, analytic and the necessary were not without friends in the second half of the twentieth century, despite Quine's attack. Among defenders of the of the notion, closer attention was paid to the relationship between the analytic and the necessary, and this shed new light on possibilities for theories of the *a priori*. Two great insights came from Kripke and from Kaplan.

From Kripke (1972) we learned an example of what may be necessary but not *a priori*. The famous examples are all *identity* statements. Take the claim that Hesperus is Phosphorous, where Hesperus is a name for the morning star, and Phosphorous is a name for the evening star. It is plausible that Hesperus *is* Phosphorous, and that this truth is not merely contingent. That planet (said, pointing to Hesperus) is the very same thing as that planet (pointing to Phosphorous). There is no way that they could differ, for there is no "they," it is merely an "it" pointed to twice. So, says Kripke, we should conclude that the claim that Hesperus is Phosphorous is necessary. But can we know that Hesperus is Phosphorous *a priori*? This seems to not be the case: As a matter of contingent fact, we learned our names in a context in which the Morning and Evening Stars were the same planet. Had things been different, the last body seen in the morning and the first seen in the evening, could have well been different celestial bodies. In that case, the sentence "Hesperus is Phosphorous" would not only fail to be *a priori*, it would fail to be true. The only way we can reassure ourselves that we are in *our* circumstance rather than that circumstance is to to engage in astronomical observations and theorizing. We learn that Hesperus is Phosphorous only *a posteriori*.

From Kaplan (1989) we learned the opposite lesson. Not only are some necessities not *a priori*, but some contingent things *can* be known *a priori* in reverse, not all *a priori* knowable truths are necessary. I can know, it seems, that I am here now. This claim is true, and in some sense, analytically true. However, it is contingent. Had things been different, I wouldn't have been *here*, I would have been elsewhere. The logic of indexicals (and demonstratives, such as *this* or *that*) has subtle connections with necessity. The presence of contextual features to be filled in at the circumstances of utterance mean that we can exploit our understanding of these features (or the lack thereof) to generate interesting cases of knowledge, independent of our external evidence.

There are many current issues in these areas: the logic of necessity and names is controversial, and so is the issue of how to extend Kripke's ideas from names to natural kind terms such as *water* and H_2O, as we shall see in the next section. Similarly, when it comes to indexicals and demonstratives, How far are we to go in contextually settled parameters such as that of location, speaker and time of utterance? Does this example mean that we can know statements to be true *a priori*, without knowing what propositions those statements express? What exactly is the item of knowledge claims in these circumstances? What notions of analyticity are in play in these examples? Is the discussion of analyticity merely *ignoring* Quinean objections, or do advances in linguistics and semantics such as those found in Kaplan, Montague and others give us the tools to defuse Quine's objections? (See Russell 2008).

Externalism and Skepticism

Kripke's example has shown us that the behavior of concepts we have may depend on external factors beyond our immediate grasp, and the ability for us to acquire a concept may depend, in a straightforward manner on external factors. If this is the case, then we seem to have the following puzzle. Consider this argument (Boghossian 1997):

1   If I have the concept water, then water exists.
2   I have the concept water.

Therefore,

3   Water exists.

We seem to know the first premise *a priori*, on general semantic grounds. If I have the concept water, this could only have been acquired in an environment in which someone has been in the presence of water. On the other hand, it is true that we *do* have the concept water. (How could we have formulated this argument if we didn't possess the concept?) It seems to inescapably follow that water exists. But if the premises are known *a priori*, then it seems that the conclusion is known *a priori* too, for it is the conclusion of a valid argument. How can this be? Can we truly know that there is water *a priori*?

This is a stripped down version of an argument raised by Putnam's famous *brain in a vat* thought experiment. It seems that we have proved that skepticism is impossible, given the externalist nature of or concepts.

This seems like too much of a success for *a priori* knowledge: some have thought to resist the argument at the conclusion: to say that warrant is not always transmitted from premises to conclusion of an argument, even when those premises are *a priori* known (see, e.g., Wright 1991). Others have sought to clarify the premises: while premise 1. is true, if read in the form it appears to take, it cannot be known *a priori*. What can be known *a priori* is that

1*   If I have the concept water, then whatever plays the water role exists.

That may not be water, were we to be systematically deceived by a demon, or to be running in a computer simulation. From this premise, all we are entitled to derive is the weaker conclusion 3*, that whatever plays the water role exists, and this is much less surprising as an example of *a priori* knowledge.

A *Priori* Truth from Above and from Below

I'll end with a short sketch of two constructive pictures of the nature of a priori truth. The first is the framework in which the above disambiguation can be made out: it is the Two-Dimensionalist account of necessity, analyticity and the *a priori*. Originating in work of Davies and Humberstone (1980) analyzing the distinction between necessity and analyticity in the presence of operators for *actuality*, the two-dimensional framework has been adopted for a wide-ranging perspective on the connection between necessity – conceived of as truth in all possible worlds (where a possible world is how things could have been *had things gone differently*) and *a priori knowability* as true in all epistemic scenarios (where an epistemic scenario is a way that things as they are *could be taken to be*). In this case, there are epistemic scenarios in which Hesperus is not Phosphorous, and epistemic scenarios in which water is not H_2O, but some other material plays the water role. However, water (the substance that plays the watery role) is of necessity H_2O, so water is H_2O in every possible world. Understanding what might play the role of an epistemic scenario is not straightforward (Chalmers 2004), but this broad approach to analyticity, necessity and the *a priori* has motivated a great deal of contemporary philosophy (e.g. Jackson 2000).

This approach to grounding the *a priori* in truth-in-all-epistemic-alternatives is a "top-down" *all at once* account of the *a priori*. It is hostage to giving an account of what is true in an epistemic alternative, and it gives little insight into how that might be found in any concrete case. The main rival to this sort of account of *a priority* is to be found in the *inferentialist* traditions, exemplified currently in the work of Brandom (1994) and Peacocke (2004). In this tradition, we return to the connection between the *a priori* and reasoning: if fundamental inferences involving concepts are to be *a priori*, then perhaps we can use these inferential proprieties to give an account of what it is to possess that concept – indeed, what it is to *be* that concept. To possess the concept of conjunction is, in part, to be disposed to use the inference rules of conjunction elimination (from (*p* and *q*) to infer *p*) and conjunction introduction (from both *p* and *q* to infer their conjunction (*p* and *q*)). To possess a concept such as the color concept *green* is to place it in a network of inferences with other color concepts, as well, perhaps to place it inferentially in a network of *input* and *output* rules governing circumstances where it is permissible to introduce the concept or to exploit it.

Such accounts of the *a priori* have the great advantage of paying attention to the fine detail of each concept under discussion, and to play an important role in grounding the propriety of inferences employing these concepts. However, they have he great *disadvantage* of requiring a great deal of attention to every single case. Furthermore, it is an open question of whether a non-circular reason can be given for why some concepts may be *introduced* by definition or stipulation and others may rejected as incoherent or defective. If concepts are individuated by their inferential roles, then why can we not justify any questionable inference by the adoption of a concept which just happens to take that inference as one of its defining conditions? (Williamson 2003). Perhaps some combination of a top-down two-dimensional approach and bottom-up inferentialist one will provide resources to respond to these concerns.

As we have seen, since Kant the notion of the *a priori* has waxed and waned in its philosophical fortunes: at some times it has been the centerpiece of philosophical concerns, and at others, it has been peripheral. Just as the relationships between metaphysics, semantics and epistemology vary between philosophical positions and fashions, we may also draw the connections between the notions of necessity, analyticity and the *a priori* (or truth in *all* possible worlds, truth *independent* of experience, and truth determined *only* by meaning) in correspondingly different ways. The different ways we treat the *a priori* reflect broader concerns and larger themes in philosophy, and bring to light our views of the aims and methods of philosophical inquiry.

Further Reading

There is much to read on current work on the *a priori*. A useful complement to this article is Carrie Jenkins' survey article (2008). It is especially good on the twists and turns of contemporary efforts to define the notion of the *a priori*, and the debate over whether what is *a priori* is unrevisable.

For another, longer general treatment of the current debate, Albert Casullo's article in Moser's *Oxford Handbook of Epistemology* is very clear, as is his 2006 book. For an excellent collection of core readings, Moser's *A Priori Knowledge* is invaluable.

For an entertaining and illuminating account of the *a priori* in Kant, its attempted capture in the work of the logical positivists, and the eventual disintegration of that program, you must read Alberto Coffa's *The Semantic Tradition from Kant to Carnap*.

The best account of Quine's criticisms of analyticity and (implicitly) *a priority* are still Quine himself: both "Two Dogmas" and *Word and Object* are models of clarity. For Gödel's theorems, Smith's new *Introduction* is second-to-none.

The best overview of the mechanics of the two-dimensional account of the *a priori* is to be found in Chalmers' long paper "Epistemic Two-dimensional Semantics," but a little book that shows how the general approach can be applied to a vast range of philosophical issues is Jacksons *From Metaphysics to Ethics*.

For an introduction to inferentialism, the first port of call must be Brandom's *Articulating Reasons*, but the interested reader must move beyond this short introduction, either to the big book *Making it Explicit*, or to Peacocke's very different *The Realm of Reason*.

Notes

Thanks to John Shand for the invitation to write this chapter, for supererogatory patience in waiting for its arrival, and for very useful comments on the initial draft, to Allen Hazen for very many discussions on the issues contained herein, and to my graduate students at the University of Melbourne, who have put up with many more discussions about *a priori* truth than is healthy.

1   Hanna (2001; 2006) is a clear and lucid contemporary exponent of this view.
2   (f is continuous at x if and only if for every $\delta > 0$ there is an $\varepsilon > 0$ such that whenever $|x' - x| < \delta$, $|f(x) - f(x')| < \varepsilon$).

References

Boghossian, Paul (1997). "What the Externalist Can Know A Priori," *Proceedings of the Aristotelian Society*, 97 (2), 161–75.

Brandom, Robert B. (1994). *Making It Explicit*, Cambridge, MA: Harvard University Press.

Brandom, Robert B. (2000). *Articulating Reasons: An Introduction to Inferentialism*, Cambridge, MA: Harvard University Press.

Burgess, John P. (2005). *Fixing Frege*, Princeton, NJ: Princeton University Press.

Casullo, Albert (2006). *A Priori Justification*, Oxford: Oxford University Press.

Chalmers, David (2004). "Epistemic Two-dimensional Semantics," *Philosophical Studies*, 118 (1), 153–226.

Coffa, J. Alberto (1993). *The Semantic Tradition from Kant to Carnap*, ed. Linda Wessels, Cambridge: Cambridge University Press.

Davies, Martin and Humberstone, Lloyd (1980). "Two Notions of Necessity," *Philosophical Studies*, 38 (1), 1–30.

Etchemendy, John (1990). *The Concept of Logical Consequence*, Cambridge, MA: Harvard University Press.

Field, Hartry (2000). "A Priority as an Evaluative Notion," in Paul Boghossian and Christopher Peacocke (eds.), *New Essays on the A Priori*, Oxford: Oxford University Press, 117–49.

Fine, Kit (2002). *The Limits of Abstraction*, Oxford: Oxford University Press.

Franzén, Torkel (2004). *Inexhaustibility: A Non-exhaustive Treatment*, vol. 16 of *Lecture Notes in Logic*, Wellesley, MA: Association for Symbolic Logic and A. K. Peters Ltd.

Hanna, Robert (2001). *Kant and the Foundations of Analytic Philosophy*, Oxford: Oxford University Press.

Hanna, Robert (2006). *Rationality and Logic*, Cambridge, MA: MIT Press.

Jackson, Frank (2000). *From Metaphysics to Ethics: A Defence of Conceptual Analysis*, Oxford: Oxford University Press.

Jenkins, Carrie (2008). "A Priori Knowledge: Debates and Developments," *Philosophy Compass*, 3 (3), 436–50.

Kaplan, David (1989). "Demonstratives: An Essay on the Semantics, Logic, Metaphysics, and Epistemology of Demonstratives and Other Indexicals," in Joseph Almog, John Perry, and Howard Wettstein (eds.), *Themes from Kaplan*, New York: Oxford University Press, 481–614.

Kitcher, Philip (2000). "A Priori Knowledge Revisited," in Paul Boghossian and Christopher Peacocke (eds.), *New Essays on the A Priori*, Oxford: Oxford University Press, 65–91.

Kripke, Saul A. (1972). *Naming and Necessity*, Cambridge, MA: Harvard University Press.

Moser, Paul K. (ed.) (1987). *A Priori Knowledge*, Oxford Readings in Philosophy, Oxford: Oxford University Press.

Moser, Paul K. (ed.) (2002). *Oxford Handbook of Epistemology*, Oxford: Oxford University Press.

Peacocke, Christopher (2004). *The Realm of Reason*, Oxford: Oxford University Press.

Potter, Michael D. (2000). *Reasons Nearest Kin: Philosophies of Arithmetic from Kant to Carnap*, Oxford: University Press.

Quine, W. V. O. (1936). "Truth by Convention," in *Philosophical Essays for Alfred North Whitehead*, New York: Longmans, Green and Co., New York, 90–124; repr. in *The Ways of Paradox, and Other Essays* (1966).

Quine, W. V. O. (1951). "Two Dogmas of Empiricism," *Philosophical Review*, 60 (1), 20–43.

Quine, W. V. O. (1960) *Word and Object*, Cambridge, MA: MIT Press.

Rey, Georges (1998). "A Naturalistic A Priori," *Philosophical Studies*, 92 (1), 25–43.

Russell, Gillian (2008). *Truth in Virtue of Meaning*, Oxford: Oxford University Press.

Shapiro, Stewart (1991). *Foundations without Foundationalism: A Case for Second-order Logic*, Oxford: Oxford University Press.

Sher, Gila (1991). *The Bounds of Logic*, Cambridge, MA: MIT Press.

Smith, Peter (2008). *An Introduction to Gödel's Theorems*, Cambridge: Cambridge University Press.

Williamson, Timothy (2003). "Blind Reasoning," *Aristotelian Society Supplementary Volume*, 77 (1), 249–93.

Wright, Crispin (1983). *Frege's Concept of Numbers as Objects*, Aberdeen: Aberdeen University Press.

Wright, Crispin (1991). "Scepticism and Dreaming: Imploding the Demon," *Mind*, 100 (1), 87–116.

4

Perception

Daniel Stoljar

Introduction

Perception is one of the distinctive and central ways in which we come to know about physical objects in our surroundings, and about their properties. At the moment, I know that there is a yellow banana on the desk before me. How do I know that? Well, I can see the banana, see its color, and thereby see, and so know, that there is a yellow banana on the desk. Similarly, I know that there is a car just parked outside on the driveway. How do I know that? By hearing the car, hearing it stopping and thereby hearing that there is a car outside.

Perception in the sense at issue is *sensory* perception. I come to know about physical objects in my surroundings by perception when I come to know about them via one of the traditional senses: sight, hearing, touch, taste, and smell. But the concept of perception, at least as used by English speakers, is much wider in its application than this. For one thing, it is perfectly legitimate to say that one *sees* the force of an argument, but one doesn't mean by this that one *visually* sees it. (Perhaps all that is meant is that one knows that the argument has force.) Likewise, one might say that one knows that one's arms are folded by bodily perception (sometimes called "proprioception") or that one knows that one is upright by the sense of balance. But, while both of these involve processes importantly analogous to sensory perception, they do not involve the traditional senses. There are various questions that arise when we ask to what extent phenomena like proprioception, or seeing the force of an argument, are similar to and different from sensory perception. For our purposes here, however, we can afford to set these further cases or alleged cases of perception aside, and concentrate on the sensory, and in fact primarily the visual, case.

Is sensory perception the *only* way in which I come to know about physical objects in our surroundings? Certainly I could have come to know that there is a yellow banana on my desk without actually seeing the banana. Somebody I trust might have told me that there is a banana on my desk. In that case, I would have come to know that there is a banana not by sight but by testimony. On the other hand, there is clearly a sense in which testimony itself relies on perception too. In order that I learn from someone else that there is a banana on the desk, I needn't have seen the banana, but I must at least have heard what was said, and this too is form of perception. However, the nature of testimony, and its relation to perception, is a major philosophical topic in its own right, and one we will set aside here.

What Is the Philosophy of Perception?

Perception – from now one we can take it as understood that we have sensory perception in mind – can be and has been discussed from any number of different intellectual points of view. Neuroscientists and cognitive scientists are concerned with what goes on in someone's brain or mind when they perceive. Medical researchers are interested in various sorts of diseases or degradations of the perceptual systems. Cognitive anthropologists are interested in the ways in which the concept or concepts of perception are articulated differently in different cultures.

In the branch of philosophy known as "philosophy of perception" the concern has been different. One strand of discussion here – a strand that dominated discussion in the 1950s and 1960s – is concerned mainly with the traditional epistemological problem of the external world, the problem of, in what sense, and to what extent, we are justified in making knowledge claims about the external world, i.e. the world of physical objects independent of the mind (Cf. e.g. Ayer 1956). Another strand, one which came to prominence in the 1970s, concerns the logical form of perceptual reports – sentences of the form "S sees o," or "S sees that o is F" (cf. e.g. Jackson 1977). In all of these cases, however, one might discern a central question lurking in the background. That question is: what is perception such that it plays the epistemological role that it does? It is this question has been central to the recent debate about perception and it is this that will be our focus here.

Perhaps the first thing to say about the question "What is perception such that it plays the epistemological role that it does?" is that it is not very easy to interpret. For example, one might think the sciences of perception are best placed to tell us what perception is. Aren't they therefore best placed to tell us what perception is such that it plays its epistemological role? If so, what is left for philosophy to say about the nature of perception?

One answer to this question denies that the sciences *are* the best placed to tell us what perception is. Presumably scientists themselves rely on perception. Scientists test their hypotheses using observational or perceptual data, and conduct experiments designed to yield such information. This suggests that they could not tell us what perception is except by using perception. And this looks suspiciously circular, and in consequence seems to undermine the idea that scientific theories could tell us about perception.

This line of thought is suggestive but difficult to sustain. In the first place, it is not clear why it is objectionable to rely on perception to explain perception. After all, neuroscientists presumably rely on their brains to explain some aspect of the brain. And it is surely impossible to explain logic without relying on logic. We do not regard these facts as undermining either the project of explaining the brain or logic; why could not something similar be true in the case of perception? In the second place, implicit in this line of thought is the idea that philosophy represents a form of inquiry that is quite different from science. But is that really true? For one thing, the use of logic and conceptual analysis are as much a part of science as of philosophy. For another, philosophers seem to both advance and presuppose empirical claims somewhat as scientists do, even if those claims tend to be more abstract than the average claim made by scientists.

The Argument from Hallucination and the Sense-data Theory

Instead of trying to identify a kind of inquiry, the philosophy of perception, which is somehow distinct from any science of perception, a better way to understand our question "what is perception such that it plays our epistemological role it does" is to consider what is perhaps the most famous line of reasoning in philosophy of perception, the so-called "argument from hallucination." This argument begins from a consideration of two possibilities, so what we need first is to have those possibilities squarely before us.

The first, which we may call "case 1," is the case I described earlier, in which I know that there is a yellow banana on the desk in front of me by seeing it. To fill out this case, we might add that, in the envisioned circumstances, I am in good light, I am well fed and rested, I have not taken any drugs, and in general my cognitive faculties are functioning as well can be expected. Such a case, in other words, is in every way a normal case of perception in which I come to know something by sight.

The second possibility – we will call it "case 2" – is very much *not* a normal case of perception. In this case, there is no banana, I don't see a banana, and I don't know that there is a banana – if there isn't one, you can't know that that there is. Rather, in case 2, I *seem* to see a banana, and *seem* to know that there is one. To fill out this case, you might imagine that, far from sitting in front of my desk, I am in fact lying in a hospital bed in a fever and because of this I hallucinate that I am in front of my desk seeing a banana. The intuitive idea is that, while case 1 and case 2 are quite different – one involves a desk, the other a bed – nevertheless they seem to me to be the same. They are, in an intuitive sense, indistinguishable from my point of view.

I have described case 2 as a case of "hallucination," and it is because of this that the argument from hallucination is so called. However, it is important to distinguish the case of hallucination from a different case which philosophers usually call the case of "illusion." What marks case 2 as a case of hallucination is that here there is no banana at all, and so (of course) no banana that is yellow. But suppose, to vary the example, there *is* a banana and I do see it, but that I somehow misperceive its color. Perhaps, for example, I have been fitted with lenses that make yellow bananas look to have the color of grass. In that case, I would not be suffering from a hallucination but from an illusion. An argument from illusion can be constructed that is similar in structure to the argument from hallucination I am going to concentrate on. As an aid to comprehension, it might be helpful in what follows to keep in mind the distinction between hallucination and illusion, and to ask yourself whether the same points go through in the two cases.

Now the mere existence of case 1 and case 2 is not controversial, or at least ought not to be. But the argument from hallucination ("AH"), which as I said is a piece of reasoning that begins from reflection on these cases, is controversial or anyway leads to a highly controversial conclusion. What is that argument?

The first premise of AH is that, *in case 2, I perceive something*. The rationale behind this premise can be brought out in various ways. Some might think it just obvious that, even though I am hallucinating in case 2, nevertheless I perceive something. Others might argue that, since it is clear that there is something that I perceive in case 1, and since case 2 is in an important sense indiscernible from case 2, there is something that I perceive in case 2.

The second premise of AH is that, *if I perceive something in case 2, I perceive something mental in case 2*. The rationale behind this premise can likewise be brought out in various ways. For example, it might be pointed out that there is no good physical candidate for the thing that I perceive in case 2, and, given that mental and physical are often taken as opposites, that this makes it very plausible that it is a mental thing that I perceive in this case. Others might take it as obvious in case 2 that I perceive a mental thing.

The third premise of AH is that, *if I perceive something mental in case 2, I perceive something mental in case 1*. The rationale behind this premise is that case 1 and case 2 are indistinguishable from my point of view. If they are indistinguishable from my point of view, then there is no reason for me to say that case 2 is in any different from case 1. But then if something happens in case 2 – for example, that I perceive something mental – it likewise happens in case 2.

The conclusion of the argument is that in case 1 I perceive something mental. Moreover, since case 1 is exemplary – that is, it is simply a stand in for any case of perception – this conclusion generalizes to perception as such. In other words, the conclusion of the argument provides one answer to our question, "What is perception such that it plays the epistemological role that it does?" According to this answer, perception is a process whereby what I directly see is something mental, and moreover this is true both in cases of veridical perception and in cases of hallucination.

The answer to our question that we have just arrived at – that perception, even in hallucinatory cases, is a process whereby I directly see something mental – is a version of what is called in the philosophical literature the "sense data theory." The proponent of the sense data theory is not suggesting that one never perceives physical objects, like bananas. Rather, perceiving a banana is according to this theory a complicated process. I perceive a banana *by* seeing something mental, e.g. a mental banana. To put it differently, according to the sense data theory, I never see physical objects *directly*. Instead I see something else, and only in virtue of that do I see physical objects. One might think that in a sense this is obviously true; isn't it true that I see the surface of the banana and only because of that see the banana? However, while there is a sense in which this is true, it doesn't affect the sense-data theory. For the surface of a physical object is itself a physical object of a kind. Hence, even if I perceive a physical object by perceiving its surface, I perceive the surface of a physical object by perceiving something mental, or so anyway says the sense data theory.

Adverbialism and Meinongianism

How plausible is the sense data theory and the argument for it? It is fair to say that, while of course there are exceptions (e.g. Robinson 1994), the consensus view among recent philosophers of perception is that the sense data theory is false. There are various reasons for the consensus. Some argue that the theory is false to the way perception appears to us in introspection. Some argue that it leads to skepticism. Some argue that it is inconsistent with materialism. And some argue that it is incoherent given that mental items are not the sorts of thing that one can see.

There are a lot of philosophical considerations lying behind each of these points. We will not be able to go into them in detail. Instead, let us agree provisionally with the majority that the sense data theory is false. It immediately follows that the argument *for* the sense data theory – viz., the argument from hallucination – is unsound, and so it must contain a mistake somewhere; but where exactly? At this point the consensus breaks down. While there is consensus *that* the argument from hallucination is mistaken, there is no consensus on *how* exactly it goes wrong.

One traditional proposal about how the argument goes wrong is called "adverbialism." If we take the surface grammar of claims like "I perceive a banana" as our guide we would think that, when such claims are true, a relation obtains between me, on the one hand, and the banana that I see, on the other. For the adverbialist, however, surface grammar is in this case misleading. Sentences like this should be interpreted, not as expressing a relation between me and something *else*, but, rather, as saying something about me considered in abstraction from my surroundings. Adverbialists put this point by saying that the sentence "I perceive a banana" should not be interpreted as having a structure like "I own a banana" – which really does express a relation between a banana and me – but rather as having a structure something like "I perceive banana-ish-ly." More generally, the adverbialist holds that any true perceptual report is made true, not by a relational fact but by a non-relational fact. Perception is simply a "modification of the subject" as it was sometimes put; that is, it does not involve a relation between perceivers and their environment but rather involves something about perceivers considered in abstraction from their environment. When it is true that I perceive a banana, on this view, it is not the case that a relation obtains between me and something else, all that happens is that I have a certain sort of property.

But how does the adverbialist respond to AH? Well, the adverbialist will not deny that in case 2, I perceive something. Given the adverbialist account of what the sentence "I perceive a banana" means, that sentence will be true in case 2 because in that case I do indeed have the property of perceiving banana-ish-ly. So there is no problem with premise 1 of the argument, when the relevant claim is interpreted as the adverbialist insists. Nor does the adverbialist object to premise 3, the claim that *if* I see something mental in case 2 I see something mental in case 1. That premise is conditional in form, and there is nothing in adverbialism to contradict it. What the adverbialist *does* object to, however, is the antecedent of the conditional; equivalently, what the adverbialist objects to in AH is premise 2. Premise 2 says that in case 2, I see something mental. But to see something mental in the relevant sense means to stand in a relation to a particular object, and the adverbialist thinks that in no case of perception do you stand in a relation to anything, mental or not. All that is true is that you perceive in a certain way. In consequence, it is not the case that in case 2, I perceive *something*; all that is true is that I perceive in a certain way.

Adverbialism was a very popular proposal at one time, but most contemporary philosophers reject it. One problem derives from what is often called the transparency or diaphanousness of perception. According to this idea, which is originally due to G. E. Moore (1922), when I reflect on my perceiving the banana, I find myself focusing on a particular object, viz., the banana. This suggests rather strongly that there is a relational structure to perception, contrary to adverbialism. If Moore's observation is correct, it is hard to avoid the conclusion that in perceiving something I do indeed stand in a relation to a banana. Hence if it is really true in case 2 that I perceive something, then it will be true that I stand in a relation to something.

Another problem for the adverbialist has come to be called the "many properties problem" (Cf. Jackson 1977). Suppose that on a particular occasion I see a red round thing and a blue square thing. The adverbialist might analyze this situation by saying that I sense red-ly and round-ly and blue-ly and square-ly. But suppose now that on a different occasion I see a blue round thing and a red square thing. How is the adverbialist to analyze that? One the face of it, the only thing they have available to say is, again, that I sense red-ly and round-ly and blue-ly and square-ly. But that does not distinguish the two experiences I just described: seeing a red round thing and a square blue thing is different from seeing a blue round thing and a red square thing. So the problem for adverbialism is that it fails to draw distinctions between experiences that are different.

Adverbialism is one traditional proposal about where the argument from hallucination goes wrong. A very different proposal begins from the idea that what is going on in AH is related to one of the traditional puzzles of philosophy, the puzzle of negative existentials. To illustrate the puzzle, suppose I say, referring to the Loch Ness Monster, "Nessie does not exist." Claims of this sort – negative existentials, as they are called – are surprisingly difficult to interpret. In general, if a statement of the form "*a* is not *F*" is true then a particular exist-ing thing, *a*, would lack the property of being *F*; for example, if "Socrates is not bald" is true, then a particular thing, Socrates, would lack the property of baldness. If we apply this to the case at hand, the statement "Nessie does not exist" is true just in case a particular existing thing, Nessie, lacks the property of existence. But this in turn implies that Nessie exists! So the negative existential statement apparently has the paradoxical property that if it is true it is false. But if so, how can I truly say – as surely I can – that Nessie does not exist?

One solution to this problem relies on an idea often attributed to the nineteenth-century German philosopher, Alexis Meinong. (Whether the idea is in fact Meinong's need not concern us here.) According to this idea, it is possible to draw a distinction between two modes or ways of being, which are often called "subsistence" and "existence." Loch Ness (the lake) exists, but the Loch Ness Monster, Nessie, does not. Nevertheless both subsist, and moreover, for the sentence "Nessie does not exist" to be meaningful, all that is required is that Nessie subsists (i.e. it is not required that she exists). This idea raises a number of ques-tions; but for us what is important is its connection to AH. What is this connection? Well, the first premise of the argument is that, in case 2, I perceive something. But, the proponent of the Meinong-inspired View says, this is ambiguous between subsistence and existence. Is what is being claimed that I see something that *exists* or merely that I see something that *subsists*? To the extent that the distinction is available to us, it is tempting to say that in case 2 the banana does not exist but only subsists. But then it would not follow that in premise 2, the thing that exists is mental. For the reason for saying that it is mental is only that there is nothing physical that exists which could be the thing that I perceive.

This Meinong-inspired response is different from the sense data theory. Instead of saying that, in case 2, I am related to a mental banana, this view says that in case 2, I am related to a subsisting, but not an existing, banana. But it has proved to be just as unpopular (if not more so). The main problem is that while it is possible to distinguish the *words* "subsists" and "exists," nobody has a clear idea about what difference in fact these words are supposed to mark. What is it to say that Nessie, or a banana, subsists but not exist? Unless there is a clear answer to this question, we only have an illusory answer here to AH.

Representationalism

The adverbialist and the Meinongian together were the traditional non-sense-data responses to AH in the twentieth century. But neither of them is very attractive on their own terms.

Perhaps because of this, in more recent times, two further proposals have been developed. In the next few sections we will discuss the first of these proposals, representationalism, in some detail.

Representationalism can itself be understood in various ways. However, on one natural way of understanding it, the representationalist begins with the observation that, that while we may *see* a banana in case 1 but not in case 2, presumably we may *believe* that there is a banana on the desk in both cases. In case 1, for example, I *know* that there is a banana in front of me. Since knowledge entails belief – if you know that p, then you believe that p – it follows that in such a case I believe that there is a banana as well. Now, in case 2, I don't know that there is a banana in front of me (because there isn't). So this cannot be the reason that I believe that there is a banana. Nevertheless, it is plausible in this case that I believe that there is a banana anyway. After all, in case 2, it seems to me that there is a banana, and I have no particular reason to distrust my senses. So that is why I believe that there is banana. Of course I am wrong and my belief is false. But for my belief to be false I must have it. So both case 1 and case 2 are reasonably described as involving belief.

Having noted this point about belief, the representationalist goes on to suggest that we should think about perception somewhat in the way that it is natural to think about belief. Now, in philosophy of mind and language, belief is what is called a *propositional attitude*. If I believe that there is a banana on the desk, I am related in a certain kind of way to a proposition, viz., the proposition that there is a banana on the desk. I might bear this relation to, and so believe, a different proposition, as when I believe that there is no banana on the desk, or that a watermelon is on the desk, or that the Democrats will win. And I might have a different attitude to the same proposition, as when I *hope* (out of hunger, say) that there is a banana on the desk. For the representationalist, perception is, or at least involves, a propositional attitude too, just as believing and hoping do. We might put this by saying that, just as one might believe or hope that there is a banana on the desk, so too one might *perceptually represent* that there is a banana on the desk.

So the representationalist wants to say that there is a propositional attitude, which we might call "perceptual representation," that is rather like belief. How like belief is it? Well, in one sense it is very like belief. For example, just as belief is a propositional attitude that can be true or false, so perceptual representation is attitude that can be veridical or non-veridical. In case 1, I veridically represent that there is a banana on the desk, whereas in case 2 I non-veridically represent the same thing. Indeed, some early defenders of representationalism thought that perception is so much like belief that it is identical to belief (or at least to belief of a certain kind); a related view is that perceptual appearance is identical with a disposition or inclination to believe (cf. Armstrong 1968).

In more recent developments of representationalism, this identification of perception either with belief itself or with an inclination to believe has mainly been rejected (Cf. Evans 1982). There are a number of reasons for this. First, I can perceptually represent it to be the case that *p* even if I have no inclination to believe that *p*, and in fact do not do so. For example, suppose I hallucinate a banana on my desk not because I am in a coma in a hospital bed but because I have knowingly taken a drug that induces such hallucinations. Since in such a case I know about the drug I will have no inclination to believe that there is a banana on my desk; nevertheless it will appear to me to be so, and in that sense I will perceptually represent that it is so. Second, I may be inclined to believe that *p*, and do so, even if I do not perceptually represent that *p*. For example, suppose I am blind and someone I trust tells me that there is a banana on my desk. Third, take a case in which I do indeed have the inclination or disposition to believe that *p*. Whenever one has a disposition like this, it is natural to go on to ask what grounds or explains the disposition. At least in some cases, however, an appropriate answer will surely be, "I perceptually represent that there is a banana on the desk, and that is why I am inclined to believe it." If so the representation and disposition are distinct since the presence of the first explains the presence of the second.

Conceptual and Non-conceptual Content

In addition to these arguments against the identification of perception and belief, it is sometimes suggested that the two differ in psychologically and epistemologically more far reaching ways too. It natural to say that when I believe that there is a banana I must possess or have the concept of a banana, where "having the concept of a banana" means, roughly, knowing what it is to be a banana or understanding what it is to be banana. It can't be true that I believe that there is a banana on the desk unless I have the concept of a banana (and of a desk for that matter).

On the other hand, when I perceptually represent that there is a banana, I do *not* require the concept of a banana – or so, at any rate, it seems plausible to think. For example, suppose I am new to the country of bananas and have never come across them before. When I see one on a desk, it seems correct to say both that I perceive a banana and that I have no idea what a banana is. In such a case, I will lack the concept of a banana and yet according to the representationalist I will perceptually represent that there is a banana. So a further way in which perception and belief might be distinguished is that if you believe something then you must have the relevant concepts whereas if you perceive something then you don't.

The distinction between perception and belief that we have just made focuses on what is required of you in order that you believe something or perceive something. To believe something it is required that the believer has certain concepts, whereas to perceive something it is not. However, a lot of philosophers put this point differently. They don't say that in order to believe something you must have certain concepts. They rather say that when you believe something the content of your belief is conceptual. Correlatively, they don't say that in order to perceive something you don't need to have certain concepts; they rather say that when you perceive something, the content of your perception is non-conceptual. In other words, this way of drawing the distinction between perception and belief says that there is a specific sort of content that a perception has, non-conceptual content, and that this distinguishes it from belief, which has its own special sort of content, conceptual content. And different philosophers have gone on to develop theories of it can be for the content of your belief to be conceptual, and what it can be for the content of your perception to be non-conceptual.

This way of drawing the distinction between belief and perception is controversial (Cf. Stalnaker 1998). Suppose I believe something, say that there is a yellow banana on the desk. As we noted before, the usual assumption in philosophy of mind is that if I believe something then I stand in a relation to a certain proposition, in this case the proposition that there is a yellow banana on the desk. Now according to the representationalist, I believe that there is a yellow banana on the desk because it perceptually appears to me that there is a yellow banana on the desk. But this makes it look as if the thing that I bear the relation to in believing, i.e. the proposition that there is a banana on the desk, is the very same thing as the thing that I bear a relation to standing in a relation in perceptually representing. But then it is impossible to say that the first is conceptual while the second is not. As a matter of logic, you can't say that A is identical to B and that A has a property which B lacks; similarly you can't say that the content of belief just is the content of perception, and yet the first is conceptual while the second is not.

However exactly the distinction between conceptual and non-conceptual content is made out, it is important to note that not everyone agrees that perception is non-conceptual or indeed that belief is conceptual for that matter. Some philosophers (e.g. Stalnaker 1998) think that one might truly be said to believe something even in cases in which one lacks the relevant concept; for example, we sometimes say that a dog believes that his owner has thrown the ball, but it not clear that we would want to say that a dog has the concept of ownership. And other philosophers have argued that, given the epistemological role of perception, in particular its role in providing us with justified belief and knowledge about the world, perception must be conceptual (cf. McDowell 1994). Their intuitive thought is that only something sufficiently like belief could justify a belief, if that is right then perception and belief can't be distinct in this sense.

Perception as Representational versus Perception as Relational

We have been looking at the representationalist idea that perception is analogous to, even if not quite identical to, belief. But, to return now to our main line of discussion, what does representationalism have to do with the argument from hallucination? We have seen how adverbialism and the Meinong-inspired view try to answer this argument, but it may be obscure how (if at all) the representationalist does so.

To bring this out, notice that in presenting the AH we routinely talked of perceiving *something*, such as a banana. But when we talk about perceiving something we don't have in mind the idea that we perceive propositions. Even if we *believe* propositions, we don't *perceive* them, at any rate not by sensory perception (cf. Thau 2001). Rather, what we perceive by the senses are physical objects, like bananas, and perhaps properties of these objects, like their movement or color. In other words, there is a distinction to be drawn between two different ideas we might have in mind when we talk about perception. The first idea is the one introduced by the representationalist: perception as a propositional attitude, e.g. the notion of perceptual representation. The second idea is the one that is or seems to be in operation in AH: perception as relation between a person and a physical object (Cf. Schellenberg forthcoming). In the light of this distinction, it might seem that, far from having any response to AH, the representationalist has missed the point entirely. That argument is about perception considered as a relation, but the representationalist is talking about something else, viz., perception considered as a representation.

One option for the representationalist at this point is to deny the distinction between perceptual representation and perception relations. But this seems implausible, and in any case does nothing to resolve the difficulty. The better option is to agree that there are these two notions here but to offer an account of the relation between them. There might be various ways to do this but a relatively straightforward way is to suggest what perception in the relational sense entails perception in the representational sense but not vice versa. So on this view, for example, it is necessarily the case that if I see (i.e. perceive in the relational sense) a banana on my desk, I perceptually represent that there is a banana on the desk; on the other hand, I may perceptually represent that there is a banana on the desk without actually seeing the banana on the desk. To put it differently, for the representationalist, the relation between perceptual representation and seeing is rather like the relation between knowledge and belief. If I know that there is a yellow banana on the desk, this entails that I believe that there is a yellow banana, but not vice versa; similarly if I see a yellow banana on the desk this entails that I perceptually represent that there is a yellow banana on the desk, but not vice versa.

There are number of questions that arise for this suggestion. For one thing, in the case of knowledge and belief, many philosophers think not only that knowledge *entails* belief but that knowledge can be *analyzed* in terms of belief plus various other conditions; is the representationalist saying that that is also true in the case of perception, i.e. that seeing is to be analyzed as perceptual representation plus some further conditions? Moreover, it is true *in the first place* that if I perceive something then I perceptually represent that such and such is the case? These are questions that have been pressed with some force in recent times by an approach in the philosophy of perception called "disjunctivism." We will turn to disjunctivism at the end of this chapter. For the moment, let us concentrate on how the representationalist who adopts this account of the representation/relation distinction might answer the AH.

As we have seen, the first premise of the argument says that in case 2, I perceive something. For the representationalist, however, this is false. It is true of course that in case 1 I perceive something, and it is true that in both cases I perceptually represent that there is a banana. But is not true that in case 2 I perceive something. In case 2 I perceptually represent that there is banana not because I see the banana but because of hallucinating that there is a banana while in hospital.

It might be objected that all a proponent of the argument from hallucination has in mind when he or she says in case 2 that I perceive something is that in that case I am in a state of perceptual representation. This seems unlikely given the point mentioned before: that we perceive objects and not propositions. But in any case, even if this is what was meant, the representationalist can now respond that premise 2 of the argument is false. Premise 2 says that if I perceive something in case 2, then I perceive something mental in case 2. If "I perceive something" is interpreted to mean "I perceptually represent that such and such is the case," then this premise is false. For, from the fact that I bear a relation to a proposition, it does not follow that the proposition is mental. Indeed, it clearly isn't true that the proposition is mental. Propositions are abstract objects and so are neither mental nor physical on any ordinary understanding of those notions.

Our guiding question was: what is perception such that it plays its epistemological role? The answer of the representationalist is that perception is a relation between a person and an object or property that entails that a person perceptually represents that a certain proposition is true. This answer is different from any we have looked at so far. First, it is different from the sense-datum theory. The sense datum theory says that I perceive a physical object by seeing something mental. The representationalist disagrees. It is true that, for the representationalist, when I perceive something, I bear a relation to a proposition. But I do not see or perceive that proposition. Second, it is different from the adverbialist. The adverbialist says that when one perceives a banana one does not thereby stand in any relation to a banana. The representationalist disagrees. Perceiving a banana does involve standing in a certain kind relation to a banana, even if perceptual representation does not. Third, it is different from the Meinongian. The Meinongian says that when one hallucinates a banana one stands in relation to a subsistent rather than an existent banana. The representationalist disagrees. It is true that propositions can be true or false, and as a result of this perceptual representation can be veridical or not; but nowhere need the representationalist appeal to an exists/subsists distinction.

The Phenomenal Character of Perception

The representationalist provides an attractive answer to AH. Nevertheless, there are a number of controversial aspects of the position. One source of controversy we have already mentioned, and will return to – the distinction between representational and relational aspects of perception. But another source concerns an important theme in the whole discussion of perception, a theme I have so far been ignoring. This is the phenomenal or sensory character of perception.

In a normal case in which I perceive something, such as the yellow banana, it not only is the case that I come to know something it is also true that I enjoy a certain conscious episode. Many philosophers use the phrase "what it is like" to capture this aspect of perception. The idea is that when I see a banana or seem to see one, there is something it is like for me to do this. In this way, perception seems to contrast strongly with belief. When I believe something, say that snow is white, there seems to be no particular reason to suppose that there is thereby something it is like for me to believe this. For example, if I am out cold in a coma it might well be true to say that I believe that snow is white, but it is not true to say that I am enjoying any sort of conscious episode.

Not only does perception seem to be the sort of state that has phenomenal character, the phenomenal character of perception plays a role in the two cases we have been concentrating on. Case 1 seems to be a case in which I have a certain sort of experience. And in a sense case 2 seems to involve the very same experience. The type of experience I have in case 1 just is the type of experience I have in case 2. What it is like for me to perceive a banana just is what it is like for me to hallucinate the banana. The phenomenal character of the two episodes is the same.

So there is something it is like to perceive a banana, and moreover what it is like to perceive a banana in case 1 is just what it is like to seem to perceive a banana in case 2. But so what? What question does this raise for the representationalist? Well, according to them, in both cases I perceptually represent that such and such is the case. In both cases, we might say I am in state with a certain *representational character*. But as we have seen, what it is like for me to perceive in case 1 is just what is like for me to perceive in case 2. In both cases, in other words, I am in a state with a certain *phenomenal character*. Now the question is: what is the relation between phenomenal character and representational character?

One answer to this question is often attributed to the eighteenth-century philosopher Thomas Reid. (Again, whether it is in fact Reid's view need not detain us.) On this view the two elements, phenomenal and representational character, are simply two distinct properties of perception. It is true that they go together, but this correlation is simply a matter of contingent fact rather than flowing from the nature of either representational or phenomenal character. At least without further modification however, this Reid-inspired view is implausible. It predicts, for example, that a particular perceptual episode might have the representational character of seeing a banana, and yet has the phenomenal character of climbing Mt. Everest.

A different answer is that the phenomenal character of my seeing a banana and its representational character are identical, i.e., numerically one and the same. This proposal obviously avoids problem of the Reid-inspired view, but it nevertheless faces other difficulties. The problem this time is that states or episodes with the same phenomenal character seem in principle anyway to be associated with distinct representational characters. And if that is the case then it is impossible that the phenomenal character of an experience is strictly identical with its representational character.

Why is it the case that the phenomenal character of an experience can be associated with distinct representational characters? Well, on the representationalist view, when I see a yellow banana, it follows that it perceptually appears to me that some proposition is true. But which proposition exactly? Up to now we have been tacitly assuming that the proposition is (what philosophers call) a *general* proposition, i.e. that there is a yellow banana. In other words, we have been assuming that seeing *a* yellow banana entails representing that there is a yellow banana. But it seems perfectly possible that I see, not simply *a* banana, but *this* banana, i.e., this very one. In that case it is natural to suppose that the proposition that I perceptually represent to be the case is (what philosophers call), a *singular* proposition, proposition about a quite specific banana, e.g. that this banana is yellow. However, once it is granted that I may perceptually represent singular propositions of this sort, it is short step to the idea that different representational characters may be associated with distinct phenomenal characters. For imagine that we have two numerically distinct but duplicate bananas. It seems reasonable to say that what it is like to see *this* banana is what it is like seeing *that* banana, i.e. since the bananas are duplicates. Hence these two episodes of seeing have the same phenomenal character. Nevertheless, they will have different representational characters, since in the first case I perceptually represent the singular proposition that this banana is yellow, while in the second case I perceptually represent the distinct singular proposition that that banana is yellow.

The fact that representational character may come apart from phenomenal character means that the relation between them cannot be one of identity. But we have seen that the relation cannot be mere contingent correlation either. At this point it is very natural to say that the relation is one of *supervenience*. The invocation of supervenience here is analogous to its use in other areas of philosophy. For example it is common for moral philosophers to say that, for any two actions, if they are alike in respect of the natural characteristics, then they are alike in respect of their moral characteristics. Likewise the representationalist can say that, for any two experiences, if they are alike in respect of representational character, they are alike with respect to their phenomenal character. This idea permits us to explain why case 1 and case 2 are phenomenally identical. They involve the same state of perceptual representation, i.e. a perceptual appearance with the same content. So, given supervenience, they involve the same phenomenal character.

The Inverted Spectrum

The idea that the phenomenal character of a perceptual state supervenes on its representational character seems on the face of it more plausible that the other proposals about how these two features are related. Indeed, this supervenience claim is often thought of as constituting representationalism itself (cf. Byrne 2001).

However, while the supervenience claim is plausible and central, it has nevertheless generated a surprising number of puzzles. Some of these puzzles involve cases in which the supervenience thesis is apparently false, i.e., cases in which two experiences have the same content but differ in phenomenal character. A fairly straightforward example, but by no means the only example, is provided by the inverted spectrum hypothesis. Suppose it perceptually appears to Boris that there is a yellow banana on the table. One could imagine someone who was inverted with respect to Boris – call her "Doris" – so that she too is having a perceptual experience as of there being a yellow banana, and yet Doris has the experience that Boris would have just if he were to see a blue banana. We can imagine that Doris and Boris are disposed to speak and act in precisely the same ways; both will insist that they are seeing a yellow banana, that they are not seeing a blue banana, and so on.

Now, in such a case it seems reasonable to say that the phenomenal character of Boris and Doris's experience are different; what it is like for Boris is not what it is like for Doris. On the other hand, it has seemed plausible at least to some people to say that the representational character of these experiences is the same. To motivate this idea, one might think that the representational character of the experience is a function of the properties in the world that cause or control the experience. But it seems clear that the property of being yellow (perhaps we might think of this as the property of reflecting light at a certain wavelength) just is that property. If so, then Boris and Doris have exactly the same representational character.

How might a representationalist respond to this objection? One option that has been explored in some detail is due to Sydney Shoemaker (1996; 2002). Shoemaker proposes that the representational character of the experience is more complicated than we have been suggesting so far. Boris and Doris might represent being yellow, but they also represent a different property, which Shoemaker calls an appearance property. Shoemaker goes on to say that there are various possibilities for what this further property could be. One possibility (which Shoemaker himself does not endorse) the appearance property might be what philosophers sometimes call primitive colors. These are properties that physical objects seem to have but don't. Such a view would say that both Boris and Doris have non-veridical experiences in the case at hand – a position that Shoemaker calls "figurative projectivism."

In order to avoid the suggestion that perceptual appearances of color are routinely non-veridical, Shoemaker himself suggests that the property could be something else, e.g., the property of causing a particular experience in me, or of being disposed to cause a particular experience in me. Other authors have suggested different possibilities. (Cf. Egan 2006). In general, the question of how a representationalist is to deal with the inverted spectrum is one of the most active areas of the philosophy of perception.

Veridical Perception and Veridical Hallucination

The sort of problem for representationalism that is generated by the inverted spectrum has its source in the idea that phenomenal character might come apart from representational character. A different problem has to do with the notion of veridical perception. John Searle (1983) for example, argued that if I am in state of perceptual representation, this state is veridical only if the state bears a relation to the object seen. So, for example, my perceptual representation that there is a yellow banana is veridical only if the banana that I see is causing the appearance in question. Searle drew the consequence that content of the experience not only includes a self-referential element, it also includes a reference to a causal relation.

Searle's suggestion about the content of experience, like Shoemaker's, has generated a number of questions. One problem is that it seems to portray perceivers as being overly sophisticated. Presumably very young children and animals can have experiences of yellow bananas. But do they really have experiences about their experience? And do they have experiences about bananas causing this experience? To suppose so seems objectionable. However, it is not quite clear why a proponent of this sort of causal view might not appeal the conceptual/non-conceptual distinction here. If to perceive a banana does not require having the concept of a banana, why does perceiving that the banana is causing this very experience require either the concept of causation or of this experience?

A very different objection to Searle's proposal is that it excludes the possibility of veridical hallucination. To see this possibility, let us imagine a case that is in some ways like case 2 – in such a case I seem to see a banana, I seem to know that there is a banana and so on. But now let us fill out the case in the following way. The reason that I seem to see a banana is that I have been given some sort of drug by a mad scientist. But, strange as it seems, I am in fact in front of my desk and there is a yellow banana on it. On the one hand, this case seems like a case of hallucination. On the other hand, it seems as if the hallucination is in this case veridical. The problem for the view that the concept of perception includes a causal element is that it rules out this possibility.

One might try to respond to this by accepting that verdicial hallucinations are implausible. But this seems unsatisfactory. For one thing, veridical hallucination seems perfectly possible. In addition, the possibility of veridical hallucination is important in the history of philosophy of perception in a different way. It has been common since Grice (1961) to argue that, in order to distinguish veridical hallucination from cases of genuine seeing, there must be a causal relation between the thing seen and the state of seeing itself. Grice's question was: how to distinguish veridical hallucination from perception proper? His answer was that in genuine cases of perception there is a causal relation between the thing seen and the state of seeing. A representationalist might take account of Grice's point by saying that in a case of genuine seeing, the object seen causes a perceptual appearance as of there being an object. But if veridical hallucination is impossible we lose this argument for the causal theory of perception.

Instead of denying that veridical hallucination is a possibility, there is a different way for the representationalist to respond to Searle. Searle's idea is that, in order for a perceptual state to be veridical, the object seen must cause the state to come into being. But there are two different things that might be at issue when we focus on a perceptual state's being veridical. On the one hand, we might be asking whether the *proposition* that characterizes the state is *true or not*; on the other hand, one might be asking whether the *state* itself *correct or not*. More particularly, suppose that perceptual representation is a state that in a certain sense aims at being a state of veridical perception, rather like belief is a state that aims at being a state of knowledge, according to some philosophers (e.g. Williamson 2000). And suppose moreover that a state is a state of veridical perception only if the thing seen always causes the state in question. In that case, the state of perceptual representation is correct only if it is caused or brought about in a certain kind of way; to put it more briefly, it is correct only if it is case of seeing. However, it does not follow from this that the proposition that characterizes the state has the content Searle says it does, i.e., is true only if the state is caused or brought about in a certain kind of way. To suppose otherwise is to confuse these two ways in which a state can be veridical.

Disjunctivism

The central question of perception that we have been focusing was this: What is perception such that it plays the epistemological role that it does? I motivated that question by considering the argument from hallucination. As we saw, there is considerable agreement that the argument from hallucination is wrong, but much less agreement about where. So far I have considered four responses to this argument, and so four responses to our central question: the sense-datum view, the adverbial view, the Meinong-inspired view, and representational view. In this last section I want to consider briefly a fifth response, that of the disjunctivist.

All of the proposals we have so far in considered agree that there is something very important in common between case 1 and case 2. The adverbialist says that in both cases I perceive banana-ishly. The sense-data theory says that in both cases I directly see a mental banana. The Meinongian says that in both cases I see a banana that subsists. And the representationalist says that in both cases I perceptually represent that there is a banana.

The key point about disjunctivism is that it denies this. For the disjunctivist the two cases share nothing important psychologically in common. It is true that in both cases I *either* see a banana *or* seem to see a banana. But, for the disjunctivist, this commonality is fake. It is like the commonality between a raven and a writing desk. True, both a raven and a writing desk have in common, viz., the property being either a raven or a writing desk; but this does not indicate that the things that fall under this property have anything deeply in common. Similarly, says the disjunctivist, we might say that both cases share the property of being *either* a case of seeing *or* a case of seeming to see; but this does not indicate that the things that fall under this property have anything deeply in common.

How does this view of perception respond to AH? Well, according to the first premise of that argument, in case 2 I perceive something. For the disjunctivist, this premise is false, at least if by "perceive" we mean "see." It is simply false that I perceive a banana in case 2. Nor is it true that I perceive something. Nor is it true that I am in a state that is psychologically like perceiving. All that is true is that in case 2 I hallucinate or seem to see a banana. For the disjunctivist, in other words, the two cases – the perceptual case and the hallucinatory case – involve psychologically different states. The argument from hallucination trades in part on the idea that we are inclined to describe both cases in the same way; but this is precisely what the disjunctivists wants to resist.

The main problem with disjunctivism is that it is difficult to shake the feeling that there *is* something in common here. So we would need a significant argument for the hypothesis that there is not. Is there such an argument? Well one line of thought here is to suggest that disjuncivism is the only way in which one could resist AH. On this view, one is either a distjunctivist or a sense-datum theorist. Given that choice, one might well go for disjunctivism. Indeed, one might go further and say that if one's choices are disjunctivism, on the one hand, and one of either sense-datum theory adverbialism or meingongianism on the other, then the choice is clear. But of course with the development of representationalism the logical situation looks very different.

There is however a more searching line of thought for the disjunctivist to develop here. This is to criticize the representationalist's key notion of perceptual representation. As we have seen, the representationalist not only thinks that I do perceptually represent, but in addition they think perceiving a banana in the ordinary sense entails perceptually representing that there is a banana. Now, for the most part we have adopted this notion uncritically and formulated representationalism in terms of it. However, it is open to the disjunctivist to deny that there is any such thing, and in consequence, deny that seeing a banana entails perceptually representing that there is such a banana. If the notion of perceptual representation, and use of that notion by representationalists, can be shown to be not of reasonable clarity, then representationalism is not the answer to the argument from hallucination that it appears to be.

At this point the philosophy of perception meets up with much larger questions about philosophical methodology, about what can be accepted as clear and why. The disjunctivist thinks that the representationalist is in the grip of a kind of philosophical fantasy, supposing there is thing called perceptual representation when in fact there is not. The representationalist thinks that the disjunctivist is suffering from a willful failure of imagination, denying that there is a thing called perceptual representational when in fact there is. The difficulty in adjudicating this debate is that it is hard to see the standards of clarity from which one can criticize the notion of perceptual representation, and why we should accept those standards. So perhaps our conclusion should be this: if representationalism is a genuinely available option in the philosophy of perception, it is hard to see the rationale for disjunctivism; but if it is not, as it might not be, disjunctivism is more plausible.

Further Reading

These are the works where it is suggested you go next after reading this chapter. A. Byrne and H. Logue (2009), *Disjunctivism: Contemporary Readings*. Tim Crane 2007, "Intentionalism," in Ansgar Beckermann and Brian McLaughlin (eds.), *Oxford Handbook to the Philosophy of Mind*. Susanna Siegel, "The Contents of Perception," *The Stanford Encyclopedia of Philosophy*, Edward N. Zalta (ed.), forthcoming URL = http://plato.stanford.edu/archives/fall2008/entries/perception-contents/.

Note

Bibliographical note: the literature on the philosophy of perception is huge. Rather than aiming for comprehensiveness, I have tried here to keep bibliographical references to a minimum. The items in the Further Reading section are my recommendations about where to go next.

References

Armstrong, David (1968). *A Materialist Theory of the Mind*, London: Routledge and Kegan Paul.
Ayer, A. J. (1956). *The Problem of Knowledge*, London: Pelican.

Byrne, A. (2001). "Intentionalism Defended," *Philosophical Review*, 110, 199–240.

Byrne, A and Logue, H. (forthcoming). *Disjunctivism: Contemporary Readings*, Cambridge, MA: MIT Press.

Crane, Tim (2007). "Intentionalism," in Ansgar Beckermann and Brian McLaughlin (eds.), *Oxford Handbook to the Philosophy of Mind*, Oxford: Oxford University Press.

Egan, A. (2006). "Appearance Properties," *Nous*, 40 (3), 495–521.

Evans, G. (1982). *The Varieties of Reference*, Oxford: Oxford University Press.

Grice, H. P. (1961). "The Causal Theory of Perception," *Aristotelian Society*, supple. vol. 35, 121–53.

Hinton, J. M. (1967). "Visual Experiences," *Mind*, 76, 217–27.

Jackson, F. (1977). *Perception*, Cambridge: Cambridge University Press.

Martin, M. (1997). "The Reality of Appearances," in M. Sainsbury (ed.), *Thought and Ontology*, Milan: FrancoAngeli, 81–106; repr. in Byrne and Logue (forthcoming).

McDowell, J. (1994). *Mind and World*, Cambridge, MA: Harvard University Press.

Moore, G. E (1922). *Philosophical Papers*, London: Routledge.

Robinson, H. (1994; 2001). *Perception*, London: Routledge; paperback (2001).

Schellenberg. S. (forthcoming). "The Particularity and Phenomenology of Perceptual Experience."

Searle, J. (1983). *Intentionality*, Cambridge: Cambridge University Press.

Shoemaker, S. (1996). *The First Person Perspective and Other Essays*, Cambridge: Cambridge University Press.

Shoemaker, S. (2002). "Introspection and Phenomenal Character," in D. Chalmers (ed.), *Philosophy of Mind: Classical and Contemporary Readings*, Oxford: Oxford University Press, 457–72.

Siegel, Susanna (2008). "The Contents of Perception," in Edward N. Zalta (ed.), *The Stanford Encyclopedia of Philosophy*, fall 2008 edn., forthcoming URL: http://plato.stanford.edu/archives/fall2008/entries/perception-contents/.

Stalnaker, R. (1998). "What Might Nonconceptual Content Be?," in Enrique Villanueva (ed.), *Concepts*, Atascadero, CA: Ridgeview Publishing, 339–52.

Thau, M. (2001). *Consciousness and Cognition*, Oxford: Oxford University Press.

Tye, M. (1995). *Ten Problems of Consciousness*, Cambridge, MA: MIT Press.

Tye, M. (2000). *Color, Content and Consciousness*, Cambridge, MA: MIT Press.

Williamson, T. (2000). *Knowledge and Its Limits*, Oxford: Oxford University Press.

5

Reality and Thought

Matti Eklund

Introduction

One of the most famous allegories in the history of philosophy is Plato's cave allegory, from the *Republic*. The allegory concerns prisoners in a cave. Being chained, the prisoners can only see a wall of the cave; and all they can see of the world are what they see on this wall: the shadows of the objects outside.

The allegory can be used to raise many philosophical issues.[1] Here is one: how do we know that we are not in the same situation as the prisoners in the cave, in that we only ever see reality distorted? Maybe there is something about our senses or, more generally, our minds that makes it the case that we always have a distorted view on reality. For example, maybe our senses – our windows on the outside world – systematically deceive us. We are all familiar with the fact that sometimes things can look different from what they really are like; their shapes, sizes, and colors can be different from what they appear to be. What if this is so on a much grander scale than we ordinarily suspect? What if the senses *always* deceive us?

Used in the way indicated, the cave allegory serves to raise the problem of *skepticism*. More specifically, it serves to raise the problem of *global* skepticism: do we know anything at all? There is also what is sometimes called *local* skepticism. Someone who has become convinced that global skepticism is false – that is, convinced that there are some things we do know – can still worry about our knowledge concerning a particular subject matter. For example, she can worry about whether we can ever know what other people think, or whether we can ever know anything about the past, or whether we can ever know anything about what is morally good, etc.

There are many different responses to global skepticism. One response, obviously, is simply to embrace it and try to learn to live with it. Only few philosophers have taken that line.[2] Typically, philosophers discussing the matter have taken it upon themselves to respond to skepticism. There are many types of responses. The responses I will focus on here are those that problematize the nature of thought, the nature of reality, or the relationship between thought and reality. According to the responses I will consider, skepticism is false. But since, *given certain underlying assumptions about thought and reality* – assumptions that otherwise seem natural – skepticism is true, it follows that these assumptions must be rejected. On this type of view, skepticism is false, but false for an instructive reason. The argument why skepticism is false shows something interesting about thought and reality.

One assumption that, arguably, underlies the challenge of global skepticism is that reality is what it is independently of our minds: that reality is *mind-independent*. This is an assumption about reality we all tend to take for granted in our daily lives. We assume that the vast majority of things around us are what they are independently of what is going on the minds of thinking beings. Some of the objects around us and their features are, to be sure, *causally* dependent on thinkers and their minds. We can first think about how to build the new house, and then build it in the way we planned. Then the house and its features are causally dependent on thinkers and their minds. Our plan for the house is a contributing cause to what the house is like. But there is another sense in which even the house we built is mind-independent. The truth about the house is objective. Or at any rate, that is what we tend naturally to assume. A label for this natural assumption is *realism*. For much of the discussion I will discuss opposition to the natural assumption. Opposing views tend to go under the names of *idealism* or *antirealism*.[3]

If, contrary to what we naturally think, reality somehow is what it is because we take reality to be that way, then skepticism should not seem to be as much of a threat. Compare here the story of the three baseball umpires. One says "there are balls and there are strikes and I call them as they are." The other says "there are balls and there are strikes and I call them as I see them." The third says, "there are balls and there are strikes *but they are nothing until I call them.*" The third umpire's point is that what makes something a strike is that he decides to call it a strike. If the umpire calls it a strike, that's sufficient for it to be one – even if replays show the pitch to be outside the plate. One can think that *all* of reality is, in the relevant respect, like what balls and strikes are like on the third umpire's view. How we view reality helps determine what reality is like, in the same sense that the umpire's calls determine which pitches are balls and which are strikes.[4] Then, one can hold, the threat of skepticism is defused. The idea is that the threat only arises if reality is held to be mind-independent and so potentially hidden from us.

Putting the argument briefly: (1) Skepticism is false. (2) But if reality were mind-independent, skepticism would be true. (3) So, reality is mind-dependent. I have not said, and will not say, anything in favor of either premise (1) or premise (2) of the argument. My aim is not primarily to *defend* the argument. I am only laying it out to illustrate one way that one can argue that reality is mind-dependent.

Mind-dependence Claims

An argument like the one just laid out would, if successful, show that reality is somehow mind-dependent. But merely saying that reality is mind-dependent isn't saying anything very specific. What exactly might a claim to the effect that reality is mind-dependent amount to?

Let us consider some ways of making such a claim more precise. Here is a first attempt, what I will call *extreme antirealism* (EA):

(EA)   For any fact about the world, this fact obtains *because we think it obtains*.

Thesis (EA) represents an immediate way to understand the talk of reality as mind-dependent. It is easy to see why skepticism should seem less serious if reality were mind-dependent in the sense of (EA). For certainly – the thought goes – we can know what we think about reality, even though a mind-independent reality might be, so to speak, hidden from us.

But one problem is that (EA) is implausibly radical. It seems to imply that when we change our minds about some matter, the corresponding fact changes too. Do we want to say that the earth used to be flat when people believed it was but it changed its shape when people came to think the earth was round instead? What about when only some people were convinced of the roundness of the earth, what was the shape of the earth at that point? Incidentally, what about the word "we" in (EA) – who are "we"? What about cases not of whole communities of people changing their minds over time but where people believe different things? Take an example. Some believe God exists; some believe God doesn't exist. What does (EA) say about a case like this?

One way to go for someone who seeks to defend (EA) is to say that different realities exist for different people. If you believe God exists, then God exists "for you"; if I believe God doesn't exist, then God doesn't exist "for me." It is however hard to make adequate sense of claims such as "If you believe God exists, God exists for you." One can understand "God exists for so-and-so" to mean precisely that so-and-so believes that God exists. So understood, these claims are true. But they cannot possibly help support radical philosophical claims about reality. For what they say is in effect rather uninteresting. If "God exists for you" just means that you believe that God exists, then the exciting-sounding claim "If you believe God exists, God exists for you" just means that if you believe God exists, you believe God exists. The trouble is to make sense of these claims so that they come out true yet not completely trivial: they must be able to rescue (EA) from the objection, but they cannot do that if all they amount to is that we believe different things

There is another problem with (EA) as stated – using the "we" – which is worth mentioning. If reality is mind-dependent in the sense of (EA), skepticism is defused only if I can know what "we" think. But this is so only if I can know what others think. But is it so clear that I can know this? Knowledge of the thoughts of others seems just as problematic as knowledge of an independent reality. This suggests that the "we" in (EA) should be replaced by an "I." Thus reformulated, (EA) comes to seem still more radical.

In fact, most philosophers who believe reality to be somehow mind-dependent do not opt for (EA). A more popular view would be something along the lines of what I will call *moderate antirealism* (MA),

(MA)   A fact obtains because at the end of inquiry we would believe that it does.

A few words are in order about what "end of inquiry" means here. The locution tends in these discussions to have a somewhat special meaning. It does not mean simply: the point at which we have decided to give up our investigations. Rather, what it means is: the (hypothetical) point at which we have exhausted all our means of finding out the answers – when we have used all our sound knowledge-gathering strategies, and milked them as much as we possibly can. We have, at the hypothetical end of inquiry, employed our knowledge-gathering strategies to the fullest, and we have done as much as can possibly be done when it comes to drawing conclusions from the data assembled.

Good questions can be raised about exactly what (MA) comes to: in particular, concerning exactly what the knowledge-gathering strategies mentioned might be. Since we can and do develop new ways to find out about the truth about the world, the knowledge-gathering strategies cannot be meant to be exactly our current ones. We are talking about some sort of idealization of our current strategies. But it is unclear exactly how we should think of the idealization. In slogan form, the knowledge-gathering strategies are supposed to be *in principle available* to us. But much work is needed to clarify what the in principle availability is supposed to amount to.

Importantly, (MA) does not, given how we understand "end of inquiry", imply that what facts there are somehow fluctuates with what we believe. The idea is, rather, that we have our methods of inquiry, and what is true is exactly what we would hold to be true at the end of inquiry, after we have done all we can possibly do to figure out whether it is true.

(MA) can be nicely illustrated and motivated as follows.[5] Take the threat of skepticism as presented in the French philosopher René Descartes' (1596–1650) *Meditations on First Philosophy*. Descartes considers the possibility that there is an evil genius constantly deceiving him, and worries that there is no way that he can know whether there is such a genius, and whether he is constantly being deceived. The point is that if he cannot know that there isn't such a genius, he cannot know anything at all: for no matter what he takes himself to know, he may just have been deceived into believing it by the genius.

Here is a response to Descartes. Consider first a case where I am dealing not with the powerful genius that Descartes actually envisages but with a less powerful genius, whose deceptions I can see through. Then there are some things I can do – there are some tests I can perform – such that the outcome of these tests could show that I have been deceived. Although the possible existence of such a genius may be sufficient for some skeptical worries to arise – I have not performed all possible tests I can perform so as of now I cannot rule out that I am being deceived – these worries can be seen as not so serious, precisely because in principle we can overcome it. But now suppose I am dealing not with such a lesser genius, but with a genius such that *whatever* I do to see whether, say, the genius's supposed flowers are real flowers, I am unable to figure out whether I am deceived. The fake flowers are such good fakes that they cannot be distinguished from the real thing. This more powerful genius is more like what the genius envisaged by Descartes seems to be like. But then one might ask: what is the difference between the fake and the real thing? Wherein are the flowers really fake? The joke seems to be on the genius. In his zeal to create fake flowers which cannot be distinguished from the real thing, the genius has created real flowers for you.

Suppose we find plausible what has just been suggested. Then we have some motivation for (MA). For what this little story is supposed to make plausible is that "fake flowers" which cannot be distinguished from real flowers even at the end of inquiry are real flowers. To be an F (a flower, say) is nothing more than to be believed to be an F at the end of inquiry, where "end of inquiry" is to be understood as earlier.

(MA) is less radical than, and to my mind more believable than, (EA). But it shares some of (EA)'s problems. By appealing to the end of inquiry, we get around having to say that *whenever* people have different beliefs there are different facts of the matter. For people with different beliefs can still agree with each other at the end of inquiry. But we are not able to rule out the possibility that because of people's different starting points and different methods of inquiry, they might have different beliefs even at the end of inquiry. There is still a problem regarding the "we."

Projectivism

(EA) and (MA) are both radical claims. They both deny that there is mind-independent truth. However, there is a more fundamental assumption which these claims do not put in question: that thought *aims to represent reality*. All that defenders of (EA) and (MA) insist is that reality is mind-dependent in the way outlined, and that this makes it easier for thought accurately to represent reality. The underlying assumption can be rejected. Consider thought about what is beautiful, or funny, or tasty, and maybe also about what is morally good. Specifically, consider thoughts like *the ocean is beautiful*, or *the Marx brothers are funny*, or *blueberries are tasty*. These thoughts seem superficially like the thoughts *the ocean is deep*, *the Marx brothers are five*, or *blueberries can be found in Iceland*. But one may think that the superficial similarities conceal important differences in nature and function. The former thoughts may be more like expressions of preference than like expressions of belief: they are, in different ways, like thoughts of the form *Hooray for__*. These latter thoughts don't aim in any way to represent reality. They are not, for example, true and false. If I say, sincerely, "Hooray for Iceland," the statement that I root for Iceland will be true. But "Hooray for Iceland" will not itself be true. On the view we are considering, "blueberries are tasty" will in these respects be like "Hooray for Iceland." If I say, sincerely, "blueberries are tasty," then the statement that I value the taste of blueberries will be true. But on the view we are considering, "blueberries are tasty" will not itself be true.

The sort of view described is known as a *projectivist* view. The idea behind the label is that according to the view we "project" attitudes onto the world. We are really only giving voice to attitudes, but on the face of it, it is as if we are trying to describe the world: it is in that sense we project our attitudes onto the world. A general projectivist view deals with skepticism in a very radical way. Since the question of truth or falsity does not arise for the relevant thoughts, the question of whether have knowledge of their truth does not arise either.

Projectivism has always seemed considerably more plausible in the case of specific subject matters – matters like those I have brought up as examples – than as a general philosophy of thought. Maybe not all forms of thought which seem to aim to represent reality in fact do so. But the idea that we, or our thoughts, never even aim to represent reality has tended to seem preposterous; much more so than the claim that reality is in fact mind-dependent. Certainly some thoughts – most thoughts we would express in natural language by the ordinary use of declarative sentences – do seem to represent reality.

Direct Realism

In many respects, Plato's cave allegory is an especially useful way to raise the problem of skepticism. For example, focus on some features of the allegory helps explain one response to skepticism which also has implications for the relation between thought and reality.

What the prisoners see in the cave are only images – representations – of the objects in the world outside. They are not in a position to know whether the images faithfully represent the outside objects; and indeed the images are distorted.

Consider the parallel: we only know how the world appears to us, but – so the skeptical challenge goes – we cannot know whether our appearances accurately represent the world outside.

One can question an assumption that can almost go unnoticed: the assumption that what we are immediately acquainted with are "appearances" – representations of objects – rather than the objects themselves. An opposing view – often called the *direct realist* view – emphasizes that we see *objects*, not *representations of objects*, so our situation is *not*, in the relevant respect, like that of the prisoners in the cave. What underlies the seeming threat that skepticism poses is a *representational* theory of thought. The direct realist holds we do not have to infer from some representations what reality is like, but that we must rely on such inferences if a representational theory is right.

My own view on this suggested way out of the skeptical threat is that direct realism, whatever in the end its fate, just cannot serve to underwrite this rather facile response to skepticism. For suppose we perceive objects "directly", as the direct realist holds. Still, the direct realist, like anyone else, will have to contend with the fact that sometimes we take ourselves to see an object when there is no object there, and sometimes we see objects as having features quite different from the features they actually have, and the direct realist will have to have some account of this. We do not always visually perceive exactly the objects that are in our visual field exactly as these objects are in and of themselves. The direct realist will have to make room for this in her theory. But once she allows for this, why can she not allow that this can happen on a much more grand scale, and undetectably? The skeptical challenge can be raised again.

Certain other responses to skepticism – I am here thinking primarily of views like Martin Heidegger's existential phenomenology – also take off from the idea that skepticism seems problematic because of underlying assumptions about the mind. For example, it is sometimes said that the problem of skepticism in modern philosophy depends on assumptions about the mind being somehow *detached* from, or *separate* from, the world: without such an assumption, it is believed, the mind–world gap would not seem so unbridgeable. Proponents of this alternative view emphasize that we are part of the world we inhabit, and claim that the problem of skepticism arises because we mistakenly see an opposition between the thinking subject, detached from the world, and the external world.

I am again doubtful, and for the same reason that I am doubtful of the usefulness of direct realism. Regardless of whether we think of the mind as somehow detached or separate – whatever exactly this means, I do think that the whole issue is rather obscure – there remains the fact that we are sometimes wrong, and one might then come to worry about whether we may be mistaken on a considerably more grand scale. No general assumptions about the mind need be involved.

The skeptical thought I keep referring to here is of the form "We are sometimes wrong. So for all we know, we are always wrong." The form of argument "Sometimes, P. So for all we know, always P" is not valid. It can be that there are certain types of facts about the world such that I know I sometimes have knowledge of them, even though I do not always have knowledge of facts of that sort.[6] Hence, if the skeptical thought was put forward as a compelling argument for skepticism, it would fail. But it would be wrong to see the skeptical thought mentioned as purporting to be a compelling argument for skepticism. It should rather be seen as posing a challenge: what justifies the assumption that we are not always in that predicament? And this challenge, whether serious or not, seems as significant whether we hold on to the representational view of the mind or we replace this view with a direct realist view, or a view of the mind as, so to speak, not detached from the world.

Berkeley's idealism

The Irish philosopher George Berkeley (1685–1753) famously argued for the mind-dependence of the external world and addressed potent objections to the view. Berkeley is famous for the dictum "to be is to perceive or to be perceived" (*esse est percipi vel percipere*): in order to exist, an object must be present in some mind or itself be a mind. This position immediately suggests an objection: does this mean ordinary objects don't exist when we don't perceive them? Berkeley himself brought up this objection and replied by saying that even when none of us earthly creatures perceives an object, that object is still always perceived by God. Hence the object still exists, as it is present in God's mind.

There is nothing in Berkeley's position, as so far laid out, that promises to be of help in a response to skepticism. For on the view as laid out, to know what there is, we must know what is in all minds, including God's mind, and how are we supposed to know what is in God's mind? In this way, Berkeley is in a worse position to respond to skeptical threats than the proponent of theses (EA) or (MA) above would be.

According to another traditional idealist position, the *phenomenalist* view (which Berkeley elsewhere goes for), to say that such-and-such exists is just to say something about appearances: to say that there is a table in front of me is to say nothing more than that my senses do or will present me with table-like appearances of a certain kind. The question of whether there may not *really* be a table there despite what my senses tell me is then misbegotten. Nothing more need be true in order for there to be a table before me than that appearances will be such-and-such. Of course, on this type of view appearances can still mislead. But the only sense that can be made out of talk of appearances being misleading is that they conflict with other actual or possible appearances. The suggestion that the totality of possible appearances can be misleading is ruled out.

An argument Berkeley gives for his idealism is the following: In order for a judgment accurately to represent reality, it must, he thinks, *resemble* reality. But mind and matter are two different types of thing, and mind cannot resemble matter. The only way there can be real resemblance is if reality, like thought, is mental; if reality too is mind and not matter. Proper discussion of this argument of Berkeley's would involve problematizing the sense in which accurate thinking about reality would have to resemble reality: whether the resemblance necessary really is such that mind cannot resemble matter.

Another argument Berkeley employs to argue for his idealism is sometimes called Berkeley's "master argument." The point of this argument is that one cannot even conceive of an unconceived object – for if one tries to do so, one thereby conceives of the object! The supposition that there are unconceived objects is then in a certain way self-defeating. But someone who believes in a mind-independent reality ought certainly to think it possible that some objects are never conceived of. Realism is then committed to a thesis which is self-defeating.

Berkeley's point can be illustrated and motivated by comparing cases other than those of conceiving of objects. Certainly one cannot see an unseen object, or hear an unheard object. For if one sees the object, the object is seen; and if one hears an object, the object is heard.

(One can certainly see a *hitherto* unseen object and hear a *hitherto* unheard object, but that is different.) By analogy, Berkeley reasons, one cannot conceive of an unconceived object.

A well-known and popular response to Berkeley is to distinguish between on the one hand features of the representation, or to be precise the vehicle of the representation, and on the other hand features of the content of the representation. When I think of a pink elephant, my thought is not itself pink. What is represented (the elephant) has a feature not shared by the vehicle of the representation (the thought). Sometimes the vehicle of the representation can have features not shared by the content. My representation can itself be mental without my thinking of the object I represent to myself as something mental. Compare: I can represent to myself an object as big as the sun – for example by thinking of the sun – even though my representation itself obviously is not as big as the sun. Talk of "conceiving of an unconceived object" can, given the distinction, come to two different things. On the one hand, it can mean conceiving of an object which is in fact unconceived. On the other hand, it can mean conceiving of an object *as* unconceived. Conceiving of unconceived objects in the first sense may be self-defeating, but all the believer in mind-independence needs is that we can conceive of unconceived objects in the second sense distinguished.

Secondary Qualities

A different argument for idealism proceeds by way of consideration of the case of color, or generally what are known as *secondary qualities* – colors, smells, sounds, tastes, etc. There could be creatures whose color perception is quite different: their color perception could be inverted as compared to ours. (In fact, the hypothesis I am about to consider goes under the name the *inverted spectrum* hypothesis.) Consider some such hypothetical creatures. Take something that we would judge to be clearly red; say, a ripe tomato. These other creatures might be such that the tomato does not look red to them, but rather looks, say, green. They might, we can further suppose, get by as well as we do in the world: there would not seem to be anything in their interaction with the world to indicate that anything has gone wrong in how they represent it. Further (so the argument goes) any claim to the effect that it is us rather than these hypothetical creatures (or, for that matter, them rather than us) who know the relevant facts is arbitrary: for we and they are surely in the same situation. One possibility is that then somehow both we and they know what the world is like in the relevant respect. Another possibility is that neither we nor they do.

To say that neither we nor they know the facts about color is to adopt a form of local skepticism: skepticism about color facts. Turn then to the former option. It might seem like a non-starter. We and those other creatures perceive the tomato differently. Hence, it is natural to think, either we or they must get things wrong; hence either we or they fail to know the truth. But maybe there is a way to say that both we and they know the facts. It is by, so to speak, distinguishing between essential and non-essential features of our representations of the world.

Compare ordinary maps. Elevation might be represented one way in one map and another way in another map – in one a color scheme may be used and in another lines may be used – but that does not mean that either map gets things wrong. Similarly there may be a type of feature of objects that gets represented one way by one type of creature and another way by another type of creature, but that the representations are different doesn't mean that either is inaccurate, any more in this case than in the map case. Taking this route with respect to color and other secondary qualities means saying that these are features of *the world as we represent it* rather than features of *the world in itself*.

A complication with respect to the inverted spectrum hypothesis concerns how we could ever know that some creatures perceive color differently in this way. Suppose some creatures would call the things we regard as red "green" and vice versa. That is hardly good evidence for taking them to perceive the world differently: it could just be that they use the words "red" and "green" differently from how we use them. More generally, one can suspect that there is no way it could ever be verified that there are creatures like this. But such complications are irrelevant to present concerns. For the situation can obtain even though it cannot be verified that it obtains.

Now, saying that, in some way or other, secondary qualities are not features of the world in itself is relatively standard. What is worrisome, however, is if the considerations having to do with secondary qualities generalize. And it has been argued that the considerations do generalize. Berkeley famously argued that a straightforward generalization from the arguments concerning secondary qualities shows that what goes for secondary qualities also goes for primary qualities. The idea is that just as objects can appear to have different colors from different points of view, objects have different shapes and sizes from different points of view: but if so, then if the so-called secondary qualities are not objective, the so-called primary qualities are not objective either.

All these points are in principle consistent with realism: they do not imply that there is no mind-independent reality. Nor do they imply that we cannot have knowledge of this mind-independent reality. But the more features of our representations are said to be *mere* features of our representations, the more elusive the world-in-itself should seem. Hence, although the points are in principle compatible with the realist view, they serve to put pressure on it. And we might feel forced either to embrace skepticism after all, or to reject realism.

The worry is that on the view considered many features of our representations do not correspond to the independent reality, so even if – in some sense – our thoughts accurately represent the world, the world in itself remains elusive.

A historically important view which would serve as a response to the worry stressed is the view of the German philosopher Immanuel Kant (1724–1804), transcendental idealism, which distinguishes between the world-of-our-experience and the world-as-it-is-itself. On this view, we cannot have substantive knowledge of the world-in-itself, but we can have knowledge of the world-of-our-experience. Moreover, this knowledge is all we should have expected or asked for in the first place: it satisfies the demands properly imposed on objective knowledge. Some later theorists in the Kantian tradition regarded the posited world-in-itself as a wheel turning idly in the philosophical theory and proposed to do away with it. The world-of-our experience is all there is.

Language, Thought, and Reality

Let me in this last section turn briefly to the relation of language to thought and reality. Since the early part of the twentieth century, much philosophy has been devoted to language, and part of the reason is arguably the supposed connections of language with thought and reality.

First, language and thought. Consider a particular thought – say, the thought that Bill is tall. When I express this thought in language I use a sentence, "Bill is tall", with a subject term, "Bill", and a predicate term "is tall." The thought is not identical with the sentence that expresses it. One way to see this is that one and the same thought can be expressed by different sentences in different languages. But does the thought still have a form similar to sentences expressing it? That is to say, is the thought a complex built up of simpler constituents, corresponding to how the sentence is built up of simpler constituents? Or might thoughts be more like *images* or *maps* than like *sentences*, as far as their structure goes? Any discussion of how to properly resolve this issue would require a more involved discussion than can be attempted here. Let me just note that a working assumption behind much philosophical thinking about these matters is that the structure of language parallels the structure of thought; so we can learn how thoughts are built up by considering how sentences are built up.

Second, on the relation between language and reality. A traditional view is that entities can be divided into *particulars* (or "individuals"), which can be referred to only by subject terms, and *universals*, which also predicate terms can refer to. Socrates is a particular; wisdom is a universal. We think there are such things as Socrates, Venus, the Milky Way, Kilimanjaro, etc. We also think there is wisdom, redness, rectangularity, beauty, etc. The former can be referred to only by proper names. The latter can be referred to by both predicates ("is wise", "is red", "is rectangular", "is beautiful", . . .) and the corresponding proper names ("wisdom", "redness", "rectangularity," "beauty", . . .) The former are located in only one place. The latter are located, if they can be said to have location at all, in many places: redness is located wherever there is something red, rectangularity is located wherever there is something rectangular, etc.

A certain worry one might have regarding the particular-universal distinction just described has to do with the fact that the types of entity postulated correspond to the linguistic categories in the languages we use. It can reasonably be suspected that this is why we believe in entities of just these types: and why should we think that the world's categories should match up with our linguistic categories this neatly? For instance, could there not in principle be other languages, without sentences of subject-predicate form, such that these languages capture the structure of reality equally well or even better than our actual languages do?

One response to such skeptical worries is to say about reality's structure something analogous to what is often said about secondary qualities. Just as – if we believe what was earlier urged – different creatures can perceive color differently yet each represent the world fully accurately (compare the analogy brought up earlier: different maps can represent elevation differently yet each represent elevation fully accurately), different languages with different structure can represent the world fully accurately. This is a way of denying that the world in itself has any particular metaphysical structure, specifically, that the world in itself either is, or is not, built up from such fundamental constituents as particulars and universals.

Conclusion

In the discussion here, I have for the most part sought to illustrate the question of the relation between thought and reality through considering the threat of skepticism. Some theorists – certain idealists and antirealists – would defuse the skeptical threat by holding the relation between thought and reality is, in one particular way, more intimate than we initially believed: by saying that reality is mind-dependent. I also mentioned how certain other theorists hold that the relation between thought and reality is, as it were, more intimate than we initially might have believed: these theorists would insist that the skeptical threat arises because of a mistaken view of the mind, leading us to think of mind and reality as more deeply separate than they are. It must be stressed that it may well be that both these lines of thought regarding the response to the skeptic can be mistaken: maybe the proper response to skepticism turns on other questions regarding knowledge; maybe the proper response is not nearly so theoretically involved as the responses concerned here. I have focused on presenting these responses to skepticism only because that strikes me as a useful entry point into the issue of thought and reality.

Further Reading

As indicated in one of the footnotes, the discussion of the cave allegory is not meant to be faithful to Plato's purposes in presenting it. Plato's own presentation is in the *Republic* (2004: book 7). For a good discussion of how Plato meant the cave allegory, see Julia Annas (1997).

Leo Groarke (2008) is a useful over view of ancient skepticism, for example the views of Pyrrho and of Sextus Empiricus.

Useful discussions of modern debates over realism/antirealism can be found in Alexander Miller's (2005) *Stanford Encyclopedia* entry on Realism, and in chapter 5 of Simon Blackburn's (1984). Two of today's main critics of realism are Michael Dummett and Hilary Putnam. Putnam's best work on this topic is perhaps his (1981), which also discusses skepticism. Dummett is famously difficult. Perhaps the best introduction to his views is in the essays collected in his (1978). His (1991) is a book-length defense of his views. In his (1992), Crispin Wright suggests a novel understanding of how realism and antirealism should be understood. Arguably, Wright's book constitutes the most important recent development.

Descartes' classic discussion of skepticism is in the *Meditations on First Philosophy*. The response to Descartes' argument that I discuss is from O. K. Bouwsma (1949).

A projectivist view on moral discourse is defended in Simon Blackburn (1984) and in some of the essays in Blackburn (1993)

Berkeley's *main works are Treatise Concerning the Principles of Human Knowledge (1710)* and *Three Dialogues between Hylas and Philonous (1913)*. A good introduction to Berkeley's views is in Winkler (1989).

Kant is difficult. It is hard even to state his view in general terms without running into conflict with how some interpret him. The reader should be aware of this when reading my brief summary of Kant's transcendental idealism. Two good recent overviews of Kant's philosophy are Allen Wood's (2005) and Paul Guyer's (2006). Kant's most important work on the topic is his *Critique of Pure Reason* (1781; 2nd edn., 1787). His *Prolegomena to Any Future Metaphysics* (1783) is somewhat more accessible.

A classic appeal to direct realism as a response to the skeptical threat is in the work of the Scottish philosopher Thomas Reid (1710–1796). Some important works here are an *Inquiry into the Human Mind on the Principles of Common Sense* (1764) and *Essays on the*

Intellectual Powers of Man (1785). A contemporary work which argues for direct realism in this way is Michael Huemer (2001).

Heidegger's classic defense of existential phenomenology is in his *Sein und Zeit* (*Being and Time*). Charles Guignon (1983) and (2001) provide good introductions to Heidegger's thought.

My discussion of primary qualities and secondary qualities follows the discussion in Blackburn (1999), which generally is a good introduction to many central philosophical problems.

Notes

Thanks to Peter Goldstein and Rachelle Rubinow for their helpful feedback.

1 As the formulation in the main text suggests, I am not using the allegory for its *original* purpose. While the allegory arguably does serve to illustrate skepticism regarding the senses, it is not meant to indicate any more general skepticism. Moreover, there are details in the allegory I skip over, as they are not germane to the present topic. For further readings on Plato's own use of the cave allegory, see the Further Reading section.

2 Though some have. Among the most famous such philosophers are ancient skeptics such as Pyrrho and Sextus Empiricus. For more information on these thinkers, see the Further Reading section.

3 One difference in the use of the labels is that the label idealism is more often applied to traditional views; the label antirealism is more often applied to contemporary views. At the level of content, the idealist more than the antirealist tends to maintain the view that reality is somehow intrinsically mental.

4 I hope and trust that the point of the example comes across even for readers not very familiar with baseball.

5 In the following paragraphs, I am in effect reproducing some of the discussion in O. K. Bouwsma's article "Descartes' Evil Genius."

6 Blackburn (1999: 22), gives the following nice example: "Some banknotes are forgeries. So for all we know, they all are forgeries." Here it is especially easy to see that the argument is not valid. For the very existence of forged banknotes is arguably dependent upon the existence of real banknotes to forge. If so, then we can conclude from the premise that some banknotes are forgeries that some banknotes are not forgeries – the denial of the conclusion of the argument.

References

Annas, J. (1997) "Understanding and the Good: Sun, Line, and Cave," in R. Kraut (ed.), *Plato's Republic*, Lanham, MD: Rowman & Littlefield, 143–68.

Berkeley, G. (1710). *Of the Principles of Human Knowledge*.

Berkeley, G. (1913). *Three Dialogues Between Hylas and Philonous*.

Blackburn, S. (1984). *Spreading the Word*, Oxford: Oxford University Press.

Blackburn, S. (1993). *Essays in Quasi-realism*, Oxford: Oxford University Press.

Blackburn, S. (1999). *Think: A Compelling Introduction to Philosophy*, Oxford: Oxford University Press.

Bouwsma, O. K. (1949). "Descartes' Evil Genius," *Philosophical Review*, 58, 141–51.

Descartes, R. (1996) *Meditations on First Philosophy*, tr. John Cottingham, Cambridge: Cambridge University Press.

Dummett, M. (1978). *Truth and Other Enigmas*, Cambridge, MA: Harvard University Press.

Dummett, M. (1991). *The Logical Basis of Metaphysics*, Cambridge, MA: Harvard University.

Groarke, L. (2008). "Ancient Skepticism," in E. Zalta (ed.), *Stanford Encyclopedia of Philosophy*, Stanford, CA: Stanford Uiniversity Press.

Guignon, C. (1983). *Heidegger and the Problem of Knowledge*, Indianapolis: Hackett.

Guignon, C. (2001). "Heidegger," in D. Pereboom and C. Guignon (eds.), *Existentialism: Basic Writings*, 2nd edn., Indianapolis, IN: Hackett, 183–210.

Guyer, P. (2006) *Kant*, London: Routledge.

Heidegger, M. (1927/96). *Being and Time*, tr. J. Stambaugh, Albany, NY: State University of New York Press.

Huemer, M. (2001) *Skepticism and the Veil of Perception*, Lanham, MD: Rowman & Littlefield.

Kant, Immanuel (1781; 1787). *Critique of Pure Reason*.

Kant, Immanuel (1783). *Prolegomena to Any Future Metaphysics*.

Miller. A. (2005). "Realism," in E. Zalta (ed.), *Stanford Encyclopedia of Philosophy*, Stanfrod, CA: Stanford University Press.

Peirce, C. (1901), "Truth and Falsity and Error" (in part), in J. M. Baldwin (ed.), *Dictionary of Philosophy and Psychology*, vol. 2.

Plato (2004) [ca. 380 BC]. *The Republic*, tr. C. D. C. Reeve, Indianapolis, IN: Hackett.

Putnam, H. (1981). *Reason, Truth and History*, Cambridge: Cambridge University Press.

Reid, T. (1764). *An Inquiry into the Human Mind on the Principles of Common Sense*.

Reid, T. (1785). *Essays on the Intellectual Powers of Man*.

Winkler, K. (1989). *Berkeley: An Interpretation*, Oxford: Clarendon Press.

Wood, A. (2005). *Kant*, Oxford: Blackwell.

Wright, C. (1992). *Truth and Objectivity*, Cambridge, MA: Harvard University Press.

6

Existence

Robin Le Poidevin

The Riddles of Existence

Suppose, one day, someone who is in the right place at the right time and with all the right equipment is able to establish, beyond all reasonable doubt, that beneath the placid surface of Loch Ness there lurks a huge, ancient, reptilian and possibly dangerous beast with a long neck. How might such a discovery be announced in the newspapers? Very probably one of the headlines would be "Loch Ness Monster Exists!," or perhaps, more familiarly, "Nessie exists!" And just about everybody would know what was meant by that: that somewhere beneath the placid waters, etc., etc. Or suppose that a team of physicists pondering the mysteries of space, time and the universe hit upon a solution to some long-standing difficulties in cosmology and publish in a popular science journal an article entitled "Parallel Worlds Exist." Again, this announcement would be widely understood – at least by those who had grasped the concept of parallel worlds. Or suppose that a mathematician, having worked for decades on a mathematical theorem long thought impossible to prove (call it "Gumley's Theorem"), stumbles at last upon a proof. "Of course, the proof existed all along," he might explain to an excited public, "It's just that no one had discovered it!" Yet again, this remark would not create widespread puzzlement.[1]

It seems that we know what is meant by "*x* exists," whether the "*x*" in question is the Loch Ness monster, a parallel world, or a proof of a mathematical theorem. Yet if we really *do* know what we are talking about, this is really rather puzzling. For we are dealing here with three very different kinds of thing, and if we were asked to say just what it is that they have in common, in virtue of which we can say that they all exist, we would probably be stuck for an answer. So here we have the first riddle of existence: What does it mean to say that something exists?

The second riddle is related to this, and emerges when we consider the variety of items above: do we employ the same sense of "exists" when we say "a proof of Gumley's Theorem exists" as when we say "the Loch Ness Monster exists," or "a parallel world exists," or even "God exists"?

The third riddle of existence involves its mirror image: non-existence. We can, it seems, say quite intelligibly such things as "Mondas was the tenth planet of the Solar System," or "the White Witch has made it forever winter in Narnia." Yet neither Mondas nor the Witch exist, so those two statements are not about anything at all! How, then, can they be meaningful? On the other hand, if we cannot speak meaningfully about what does not exist, then a statement like "The Skipton *sumo* Club does not exist" cannot be both meaningful and true. So the third riddle of existence is how we can speak meaningfully, or think coherently, about non-existent objects.

The fourth riddle concerns those items that exist in some sense, but in a less full-blooded way than do you or I: shadows, holes, and mirror images – things we might call "half-existent" objects. We are certainly talking about *something* when we talk about these, and we can say things that are true or false of them ("that shadow is growing longer," "that hole has been filled in," "the mirror image of my face makes the mole appear on the right"), but are they *things*, exactly?

The fifth riddle concerns the boundaries of existence. When does a person come into existence? At the moment of conception? At some point during the development of the embryo? When it starts to be capable of feeling? Contemplating such questions, we might be inclined to think, not just that we do not know exactly when the person comes into existence, but that there is *no objective fact of the matter*, that it is actually indeterminate, when it does so. There are some times when it definitely does not, and other times when it definitely does, but there are times in between when it is neither definitely true nor definitely false that it does. The boundary between existence and non-existence, it seems, can be vague, but how precisely do we express this idea?

The sixth and final riddle of existence is one of the most perplexing of all philosophical problems, but also one that provokes very different reactions. For some, it is the most profound problem we can ask; for others, not worthy of serious attention. It is this: Why does anything exist at all? Why is there not just *nothing*?

In what follows, we shall explore, or at least make a start at exploring, each of these riddles.

Does Ontology Rest on a Mistake?

The word "ontology" is used in two ways. A person's, or theory's, ontology is just the catalogue of things they, or it, suppose to exist. The ontology of idealism, for instance, is restricted to mental items; the ontology of materialism to matter.[2] But when we talk just of ontology, rather than *x*'s ontology, we mean the philosophical study of existence. Ontology as a study asks what kinds of things exist, and nowadays metaphysicians take this to be a substantial and meaningful question. But in the twentieth century there was an influential tradition of suspicion about this question, and in some quarters that suspicion lingers on. So, before going much further into our examination of the nature of existence, we should satisfy ourselves that there is indeed something to examine.

Consider cases where we ask ourselves questions about what exists which are clearly not intended as philosophical: Are there any books on building your own house in the library? Is there a mouse in the kitchen? Is there any beer left in the fridge? It is quite clear how we should set about answering such questions: go and see. Other existential questions – questions about what exists – are similarly parochial, as we might put it, but concern a rather different domain: Are there any prime numbers between 618 and 734? Is there an obtuse angle in this parallelogram? Are there any numbers that cannot be expressed in terms of two integers (such as 22 over 3)? Here, we do not "go and see" in quite the same way as we did in response to the first set of questions. Finally, consider the kinds of question scientists might pose from time to time: Is there any chlorine in this gas sample? Are there any alpha-particles in this cloud chamber? Is there a genetic link between eye color and height? Here, going and seeing might involve some quite sophisticated tests and theoretical background.

So when we ask parochial existential questions like these, we often have in mind a particular way of discovering the answers, and the method of finding out will be very different in different cases. Now the fact that we use very different methods for discovering the existence of books, mice, beer, numbers, angles, gases, alpha-particles, and genetic links suggests that we are dealing with very different kinds of existential fact. What it is for a mouse to exist is a very matter from what it is for a number to exist, or for a genetic link to exist. The fact that the questions start off in the same way "('Are there … ?' or 'Is there … ?')" does not necessarily imply that, at bottom, these are all concerned with the same kind of fact.

Of course, the existential questions philosophers ask tend to be much more general: Are there physical objects? Are there numbers? Are there unobservable entities? And the assumptions here are, first, that these questions do have something in common – they are all concerned with the nature of reality – and second, that answers to the everyday, parochial questions will not help us answer these more general, philosophical, questions about existence. The odd thing, however, is that it ought to follow, from the "parochial" truth that there is a mouse in the kitchen, that there are physical objects (since a mouse is a paradigm physical object), and from the truth there are prime numbers between 618 and 734 that there are numbers. And if this kind of inference is acceptable (as surely it is) then it seems that, by doing a little rodent-related detective work, or mathematics, we can answer philosophical questions.

Ontologists will naturally protest. Their question about what exists is at a deeper level, they say, than questions about mice or prime numbers: deeper, note, not just more general. But perhaps they are mistaken. In asking what really exists, or what ultimately exists, they assume that "exists" has a single meaning, applicable to different kinds of thing. But when we set about answering the parochial questions, the criteria we used were so different, that there are grounds for thinking that "exists" means different things, depending on whether we are talking of physical objects like mice, or abstract things like numbers, or something in between, as when we talk of theoretical entities like genetic links. For a *physical object* to exist (it might be proposed) is for it to occupy space. For a *number* to exist is for it to be includable in mathematical calculations. The answers to the parochial questions may not always be easy to find, but they do not require us to engage in philosophy, and once we have answered them, then we do not need to do any further work to answer the philosophical questions. So ontology is really redundant.[3]

To meet this kind of challenge, ontologists need to show that there is a generally applicable notion of existence, suitable for different domains, and whether or not a candidate for existence satisfies that notion is not settled by any amount of detective work, or mathematical proof, or scientific investigation. So let us move on to the question "what is it to exist?"

The Analysis of Existence

What we would like, ideally, is an informative account of what it is to exist. A natural approach to this task is to ask how we typically become aware of the existence of something, and in most cases, that is because it directly or indirectly impinges on us in some way (the bed-side table, when we stumble into it in the dark; the first star to appear in the evening; a distant relative we have just discovered). So our first account of existence is this:

An object exists if and only if it has effects.

It might be objected right away that non-existent objects have effects: six-year-old Sophie is frightened of the Grinch, for instance. But here we should say that it is Sophie's *idea* of the Grinch that has this effect. But even with this initial objection out of the way, it is clear that the first account will not do at all. "An object exists if and only if it has effects." Effects on what? Why, on other things, presumably. But first, it seems odd to make the existence of any object logically dependent on the existence of other objects. What if there were only one object in the world? It could not affect anything else, since there would be nothing else for it to affect. Yet it does, surely, still exist. Second, since only existent objects can be impinged on, the account is really short for "An object exists if and only if it has effects on other things *that exist*," and this defines existence in terms of existence, which is hopelessly circular.

In reply to the lonely object objection, we could say that something only needed to be *capable* of affecting things in order to count as existent:

An object exists if and only if *it is possible* for it to have effects on other things.[4]

So a lonely object still counts as existent. But this still does not get over the circularity objection, since, even if the objects it could affect do not actually exist, they must be possibly existent. And there are other worries, too. First, there is something distinctly odd about defining an actual quality (existing) in terms of what is possible, rather than in terms of what is actual. What is it about the actual nature of this object, we want to ask, by virtue of which it could affect things? Second (and this worry also applies to the first analysis), if we are looking for as comprehensive account of existence as possible, one that would allow, or at least not automatically rule out, non-physical objects such as numbers, then this will not be it. For numbers are abstract objects, not existing in space and time at all: if they do exist, they do so timelessly and non-spatially.[5] So the "only if" of the analysis seems too restrictive. Third (and again this applies to the first analysis), the property of being able to have effects cannot be *constitutes* existence, since this seems to be a matter of what an object *does*, or *could do*, rather than what it is for that object simply to exist. The causal account provides, at best, a *criterion* of existence, a test that only existing things can pass, but not an *analysis*, something that captures the core of existence.

Let us, then, take a look at a quite different approach:

An object exists if and only if it has properties.

This does not automatically rule out abstract objects such as numbers, since "properties" here could include mathematical properties, and not merely physical ones. It also focuses on something that an object cannot possibly lack, even if it is the only thing in existence. It also tells us what kind of thing existence is. Existence, as we might put it, is the most general kind of property there is: it is the property of *having properties*. It is sometimes suggested, however, that existence is not a property, though the point is sometimes put in terms of language: "exists" is not a predicate.[6] The reason often given is that, once we have described something – in terms, e.g., of its being red and round and made of wood – we do not add anything to its description by saying that it exists. This does not help to define it any more precisely. What we are saying, rather, is that the properties that we have just mentioned are all exemplified (indeed co-exemplified – that is, exemplified by the same thing). How might we defend the analysis against this objection? Far from being inconsistent with the fact that "Jeff exists" does not add anything to the description of Jeff as five foot ten, left-handed, and wearing Chanel No. 5, the analysis actually explains this. For if the analysis is correct, "Jeff exists" is actually entailed by "Jeff weighs 11 stone" (or some other description), and what is entailed by a description adds nothing to that description. For instance, since "the apple is colored" follows from "the apple is green," the first statement adds nothing to the second. We would not on that account, however, insist that being colored was not a genuine property.

A worry, however, remains, and that is that the analysis allows in too much. Consider the non-existent being Superman. There are plenty of properties we can correctly ascribe to Superman: that he is very tall, enormously strong, is able to fly, etc. So Superman has properties. Yet Superman does not exist! So the third analysis above must be wrong. This would be too hasty, however. Superman does not *really* have these properties: he is merely represented as having them. But then, does it not follow that he has the property of *being represented as* being very tall, etc.? To rule this out, we would have to modify the analysis as follows:

> An object exists if and only if it has properties independently of any representation of it as having those properties.

Non-existent objects continue to be a problem, however. They are, in fact, the third riddle of existence we need to discuss.

Non-existent Objects

Perhaps ascribing properties to fictional objects and other non-existent things does not, absurdly, commit us to their existence. But if not, then it is not at all obvious how we can speak meaningfully about such objects, for our talk would be about nothing at all! How can there be contentful thought or talk about *nothing*? There may be no one satisfactory solution for all cases, but one strategy that recommends itself is that any sentence of the form "A is such-and-such," where there is no A in existence, can be paraphrased in terms of things that do exist, or in terms of properties. To take a rather obvious example, when we say "The average householder in St Mary Mead owns 1.5 cars," we do not mean to assert something about a particular person who owns 1.5 cars, but rather assert something more complicated, namely that dividing the number of cars owned by householders in St Mary Mead by the number of householders results in 1.5. Only existing things are thus picked out.

Can we generalize this strategy? Suppose that, one day, Anne says "The discoverer of the proof of Gumley's Theorem is a genius." It turns out that Gumley's Theorem has not yet been proved (and let us suppose, to avoid complications, that it never will be), so Anne has not actually referred to an existing person. To make sense of what she has said, we might propose the following paraphrase: "There is someone who discovered Gumley's Theorem and who is a genius." We have now removed any phrase that looks as if its function is to refer to a specific person. Terms like "Jeff" or "the current secretary of the parish council" are used to pick a particular person. But "someone" (as in, for instance "there is someone in this room") is not used in this way. So what Anne says, or rather its real content, is entirely intelligible, although, admittedly, her statement is a false one.[7]

But now look what this strategy does to statements like "Othello, the Moor of Venice, suspects his wife Desdemona of infidelity," "Bugs Bunny likes carrots and is much given to saying 'What's up, doc?'," "Nicholas Nickleby is appalled by the brutality of Dotheboys Hall," "Mr Spock is highly logical," and so on. These are statements about fictional characters, and we would ordinarily treat them as true. But if we paraphrase them in the way that we paraphrased Anne's statements, we obtain: "*There is* a person called 'Othello', who is Moor of Venice, and who suspects his wife Desdemona of infidelity," "There is a rabbit who likes carrots and who is given to saying 'What's up, doc?'," etc. But these statements, implying as they do that the characters in question really exist, are false. So it seems we should distinguish between a statement like Anne's, which is clearly based on a mistaken belief in an individual's existence, and a statement that is knowingly made about a fictional character. This second kind of statement could be regarded, not as an assertion, but as a pretended assertion made within a game of make-believe. So, while watching a performance of *Othello*, we might pretend that what is happening on stage is not merely a representation of a jealous husband, but a real case of one, and so pretend to refer to him.

Suppose, however, that we wish to make a statement like "Othello does not exist." On the one hand, in order to make sense of the name "Othello," we have to imagine ourselves participating (at least minimally) in the fiction, to the extent of pretending that the name "Othello" actually names someone. But when we assert the non-existence of Othello, we have to step outside the fiction, and drop all pretense, for of course within the fiction, Othello *does* exist. Unfortunately, once we step outside the fiction, "Othello" ceases to function as a name, and we once again face the problem of making intelligible statements about non-existents. We could then fall back on the first strategy, which involved paraphrasing, and suppose that "Othello does not exist" is shorthand for some such statement as "There is no person who is called 'Othello', who is Moor of Venice, who suspects his wife of infidelity, etc." The trouble with this is that it is a general statement, not about a specific individual at all, yet "Othello does not exist" seems to be about a specific individual, not merely a general assertion to the effect that there is no one answering a certain description.

Perhaps we can relate "Othello does not exist" to the kind of statement we encounter in literary criticism, such as "Othello is one of Shakespeare's more convincing tragic characters," or "Othello represents a recurring theme in Shakespeare, that of the possessive nature of love." In this kind of statement, the fictional status of the character is not in question – these are not statements that are made within the fiction, or that require any pretence – but the reference does seem to be to a specific individual. One approach to these critical statements is to treat them as about an actual object, but an abstract one, rather than a concrete, flesh and blood one. The expression "Othello," in the context of literary criticism, functions more like the expression "the number two," or "justice," than "Queen Victoria," or "the Albert Hall." If we can extend this treatment to "Othello does not exist," then we could represent the meaning of this statement to be that the abstract object named here is not a concrete object (concrete objects providing the paradigm of existent things).

"Half-existent" Objects

There is a group of objects that satisfy the "having properties" analysis of existence, but which we would be reluctant to grant full existence to. Perhaps a suitable, though paradoxical, name for these objects would be "half-existent" objects. Holes, shadows and reflections fall into this category. Consider a hole, for instance. It certainly has properties: it has certain dimensions, things can fall into it or through it, and it has a particular location in relation to other objects. But what *is* it, exactly? Is it a region of space? No, because even if we think that space exists as an object in its own right, independently of the things that it contains, any hole that we are likely to come across would be moving through space (as a result of the rotation of the earth, for instance). As it moves, it remains the same hole, but different parts of space would fill it. Also, regions of space would have smaller regions as parts, but we never say that a hole has holes in it! And if we do not think of space as an object in its own right, but just as a network of spatial relations between things, then there is no object to identify the hole with. Either way, then, the hole is not the same as a part of space.

A clue to how we should view holes is provided by the thought that, if we were to remove the objects surrounding the hole (the rest of the blanket, or a patch of ground), the hole would disappear. That suggests that the hole, though existent, has a dependent existence: it depends on the existence of other things. But does it depend on the existence of particular things? Suppose a wall is built from stones, with a hole in the middle, an entrance into a castle, perhaps. But as the stones around the entrance begin to crumble, they are replaced. Eventually, none of the original stones remains, but the shape and location of the entrance is unchanged. We might imagine after a while that the stones are replaced by bricks. Provided the size and shape of the aperture remains exactly the same, is this not still the same entrance? If so, and similar observations apply to other holes, then it seems that holes do not depend on particular objects, but rather on objects that are arranged a certain way.

Shadows seem to present a similar kind of case. Suppose we cast a shadow on a wall by means of a piece of paper. We then put another piece of paper, exactly the same shape and size, on top of the first. We then remove the first piece of paper. The shadow is now being cast by the second piece of paper, but is it the same shadow? If so, then, like holes, although shadows depend for their existence on other objects, they do not depend on particular objects. There is, however, this difference between shadows and holes. There is a logical, rather than causal connection between a hole and the objects that bound it. The *cause* of the hole would be the activities of the builders, or diggers, and so on. In contrast, the shadow seems both logically *and* causally dependent on the object that casts it. It is logically dependent, because a shadow is necessarily a shadow of something: we don't ever come across a shadow on its own. And it is causally dependent, for in order for the shadow to be cast, the object has to block the light that would otherwise illuminate the area where the shadow is. But how can a connection be both logical and causal? Doesn't one exclude the other? Perhaps a way of resolving this apparent conflict is to say that the shadow is logically (rather than causally) dependent on a causal interaction between an object and light.

What of reflections in the mirror? Here we have another interaction of objects with light, for without the light, there is no mirror image. Unlike holes and shadows, however, the mirror image is dependent on a particular object. We cannot replace that object and get exactly the same image. But mirror images are not just the objects they are images of, for they have different, and indeed incompatible properties. We do not change in size as we move towards and away from a mirror, but our mirror images do change in size. If you wave your right hand, your image's *left* hand waves back. Moreover, whereas the mirror image disappears if you move right away from the mirror, or the light goes off, you remain in existence. On the other hand, if you are looking at your mirror image, are you not also looking at yourself? And how can this be if you and your image are not the same?

It is a favorite question among those who encounter philosophy for the first time (which is not to suggest that it loses all interest when you have been studying philosophy for years) whether a tree, for example, continues to exist when no one is looking at it. Let us give the commonsense answer that *of course* the tree continues to exist: its existence is not at all dependent on its being perceived. Is the same true of mirror images? If you are inclined to say "no" to this question, then the result is another difference between such images, on the one hand, and holes and shadows on the other, and that is that mirror images are dependent, not just on other objects, but on our minds. Perhaps our minds are the true location of such images. If so, then we may wonder whether they really fit our analysis of existence.

There seem, then, to be objects that are not at all fictional, but are logically dependent on others for their existence. They are, however, a miscellaneous bunch, and no one analysis will capture them all.

The Boundaries of Existence

If the kind of objects we have just been discussing form a kind of twilight zone between existence and non-existence, the temporal boundaries of existence form another. When does a person die? When the heart stops beating? When the brain ceases to function? When consciousness is permanently lost? Suppose we say: when the brain ceases to function. What marks that, exactly? When the last neuron ceases firing? Or some time before? Whatever point we take as marking the instant of death, we find that it is not an instant at all, but a process that has different stages, and we have to take another decision as to which stage is the crucial one. In other words, the boundary between life and death is an indeterminate one. Does that mean, then, that the difference between existence and not existing at all is not an all or nothing matter?

This is one instance of a kind of phenomenon we are very familiar with, a gray area where we are not sure what to say. Another instance of this phenomenon concerns words like "tall." Some people are clearly tall, and others are not, but since "tall" is not defined in terms of any specific height, there are cases in between the clear-cut ones where it does not seem appropriate to say either that someone is tall, or that they are not tall. Or consider the term "red." An old-fashioned British telephone kiosk is clearly red, but there is a continuous scale of color where red merges into purple on one side of the spectrum, and into orange on the other. At one point does a color cease to be an orangey kind of red and become plain orange? There are cases where it is just indeterminate.

So, given that there are gray (or orangey-red) areas where we are not sure whether a particular word (like "living," or "tall," or "red") should apply, how do we explain this? There are three stances we could take. The first is to say that there really is indeterminacy in the world here: the boundaries between different properties are vague. There are cases where there is just no fact of the matter as to whether a person is tall or not, or still in existence or not. But does it make sense to suppose that there *world itself* is vague, rather than our concepts that are so? Suppose we allow that the indeterminacy is in the world. Then a rather strange consequence arises. Let us say that at 4 o'clock Jeff is very definitely still alive (though not exactly in the pink). At half-past four, he is very definitely dead. Somewhere in between there are times where there is no fact of the matter as to whether Jeff is alive or not. That is one level of indeterminacy. But is there then a definite cut-off point between the times at which Jeff is alive, and the times at which there is no fact of the matter as to whether he is? Presumably not, since we are assuming the boundaries of existence (i.e. definite existence) to be vague. So there is now another level of indeterminacy, where there is no fact of the matter as to whether it is the case that (1) Jeff is alive or (2) there is no fact of the matter as to whether he is alive. But surely this just amounts to there being no fact of the matter as to whether Jeff is alive. In which case, there *ought* to be a definite cut-off point between Jeff's being alive, and there being no fact of the matter, etc. But if we have to allow that there is such a sharp boundary, then why not concede that there is a sharp boundary between being alive and being dead?

The second stance is to say that there is a definite point at which a certain term applies, but we cannot always tell exactly when it is. This has something to recommend it in the case of existence. There was a definite point at which Jeff died, but we could not tell which it was. In contrast, treating "tall" in this way would be most implausible. Just consider it: there is a definite height (it might be five foot and ten inches) where anyone of that height or more is tall, and anyone less than that height is not. But no one knows what that height is! One wants to ask: who settles which is the appropriate height? It seems more reasonable to suppose that we know all there is to know about "tall," but not all there is to know about "living." But there is still something odd about the suggestion that Jeff dies at a very definite (though unlocatable) point. We expect Jeff's demise to be intimately connected with the various process of deterioration going on in his body and brain. But those processes are entirely continuous: there are no sudden and dramatic changes in state. (I am assuming that Jeff died peacefully in his sleep, rather than having his head cut off by a guillotine.) It does not seem at all plausible that one of the many continuous and tiny changes, no larger or apparently more significant than the changes that preceded it, was nevertheless the point that marked the moment when Jeff shuffled off his mortal coil. Why this particular point? What was so special about it? Or was Jeff's death quite independent of the changes taking place in his body? That cannot be right.

Doubts about the first two approaches may well incline us towards the third, and that is to say that any indeterminacy is due to our language. Some concepts are just not sufficiently precisely defined for us to be able to identify exactly how they fit onto the world. Or rather, they fit it, but rather loosely. Now this seems exactly the right thing to say about adjectives like "tall." Though a term of height, "tall" is not defined in terms of specific heights, so it is no surprise that it provides no guidance when we are considering people between, say, five eight and five foot eleven. Now perhaps what goes for "tall" also go for "living"? There are various states of organisms that clearly indicate life, and others that clearly indicate the absence of life. But the meaning of "living" is not tied very specifically to certain states rather than others: it is defined at a rather higher level of generality. A similar vagueness attaches to the word "person." We might ask ourselves, when contemplating Jeff, whether we are dealing with a living person or not. But "person" is not so precisely defined that it enables us always to say whether we are being presented with a living person or not.

This third approach to indeterminacy may seem the most reasonable, but when we reflect on the fact that it presumes that the world itself, and all that exists therein, is entirely determinate, we realize its implication: that reality, in itself, is not divided into the living and the non-living, or into persons and non-persons, but these distinctions are, to some extent, merely conventional. And that is a consequence we may not be happy with.

Why Does Anything Exist?

And so to our final riddle: why does anything exist? Why isn't there just *nothingness*? Now, one rather quick answer to this is that there are some objects that just have to exist, namely abstract objects like numbers. For what makes mathematics true if not the numbers and their relations? And is mathematics not necessarily true? How could merely contingent objects make necessary truths necessarily true? It is, of course, rather controversial whether numbers and their ilk do satisfy the analysis of existence we suggested earlier, namely a thing's having properties independently of any representation of that thing as having those properties. It might be thought that numbers have no existence outside of mathematical thought. But let us leave that dispute aside and narrow our question: given that there are contingent objects, objects that might not have existed, why are there in fact any contingent objects at all?

This challenging question deserves a book to itself (or perhaps several). Here we can only look briefly at two attempts to answer it.

The first approach compares the question to the wail of the disappointed lottery entrant: "*why* didn't I win?" Actually, very few people entering a lottery can have asked this question, simply because no one who reflects on the chances involved can seriously expect to win a lottery. The answer to the question "why didn't I win?" is that the chances of winning were only one in a million (or whatever). Now, if we think of the (presumably infinite) ways the universe might have been, only one of them consists of there being no contingent objects. There is only one way for there to be no contingent objects: there are no variations on this particular theme. But if there is an infinite number of ways altogether, all but one of them involving some contingent object or other, then the probability of there being no contingent objects is infinitely small. And an infinitely small chance is the next thing to no chance at all.

This very simple and attractive solution does, however, rest on two assumptions that might be questioned. The first is that any given way the universe could have been is intrinsically no more, and no less, probable, than any other way. Only then can we take the probability of any given way to be determined by the total number of possible universes. The second is that we can make sense of chance in this context. We talk of the chances of a coin's landing heads, but this is against the background conditions: that the coin is not biased, that the throwing is a normal throwing, and so on. The conditions in which one tosses a coin determine, we say, the chances of its landing heads. But what determines which, of a number of ways the universe might be, is the one that is to be actualized? The hand of God?

A second, a rather less compromising, approach to the question "why isn't there nothing?" is to say that the idea of there being nothing at all is not, ultimately, a coherent one. There are various ways in which we might try to establish this, but here is one that tells us something interesting about the world. When we say something true about an object, our assertion is made true by some feature of the object. "This book is green" is made true by the book's actually being green. But what if I had said "this book is not blue." Since that is true, is it then made true by what you might call a *negative* feature of the book, its "non-blueness"? Non-blueness seems a strange kind of property. Or take absences. I say, entering a room, "Jeff is not here." Is that made true by an actual absence in the room, Jeff's non-existence? Again, this sounds strange. A more natural way of looking at these cases is to suppose that negative assertions, like "the book is not blue" and "Jeff is not here" are made true by positive features. It is the book's greenness that makes it true to say "the book is not blue," for (paradigmatic) greenness excludes (paradigmatic) blueness; it is Jeff's being elsewhere that make it true to say "Jeff is not here," being elsewhere excludes being here. So, although we can make true negative statements, there are no negative features in the world, only positive features. What about "there are no unicorns"? Since this means that there are no unicorns anywhere, we can't say, as we did with Jeff, that there are unicorns somewhere else. Here, it is the existence of everything in the world that makes it true that there are unicorns, because everything that exists has features that exclude being a unicorn. So, for any negative statements to be true, something has actually to exist. But that means that the proposition "there is nothing" could not possibly be true, for there cannot be negative truths without existing things, and just one existing thing would make it false that there is nothing.

One attractive feature of this solution is that we face the problem of negative truths anyway, and it would nice if, in solving that problem, we also provided an answer to why there is something rather than nothing. But is that approach to negative truths satisfactory? Consider again "there are no unicorns." The mere existence of everything else cannot be enough to make this statement true, since the existence of everything else is actually compatible with there being unicorns. (Your nature might exclude your being a unicorn, but it doesn't exclude unicorns elsewhere.) So we have to add another fact, that these are all the objects that exist. But isn't this just a negative fact, the fact that there are *no* other objects?

Further Reading

A detailed discussion of a number of the issues raised here is C. J. F. Williams' *What Is Existence?* (1981). Despite his chosen title, he proposes that the question should be immediately replaced by the question "what does 'exist' mean"?

The classic paper that sets out to undermine ontology is Rudolf Carnap's "Empiricism, Semantics, and Ontology," which originally appeared in the *Revue Internationale de Philosophie* (1950). It is reprinted with some amendments in Paul Benacerraf and Hilary Putnam (eds.) *Philosophy of Mathematics* (1983: 241–57). Carnap argues that there are only two legitimate kinds of question about existence: the internal questions, concerning the applicability of certain kinds of concept within a conceptual scheme (or "framework"), and "external" questions, concerning the usefulness or otherwise of adopting that conceptual scheme. Traditional ontological questions fit into neither category and so are illegitimate.

The idea behind the slogan " 'exists' is not a predicate" is expressed by Kant, in the *Critique of Pure Reason*, in a passage which tries to demolish the ontological argument for the existence of God (*Transcendental Dialectic*, book II, ch. III, section 4). Related to this is Frege's view, put forward in the essay "Concept and Object," that existence is a property of concepts. Thus "unicorns exist" means "the concept unicorn is realized." See also the debate between William Kneale and G. E. Moore, "Is Existence a Predicate?" (1936: 154–88).

Plato's dialogues, in which the idea of the forms is articulated and defended, are readable and, in most cases, readily available. See, for instance, *The Last Days of Socrates* (2003), which contains both the *Apology* and the *Phaedo*; and *The Republic* (2007). Forms were intended to explain, among other things, what things had in common, and the standard name for these shared, general, properties, is universals (expressed by terms like "redness," "roundess," etc. For a discussion of the indispensability of universals, see Bertrand Russell, *The Problems of Philosophy* (1959: ch. 9): "The World of Universals." An argument for the existence of abstract objects is developed in Bob Hale, *Abstract Objects* (1987), and the question of the status of numbers explored in John Bigelow, *The Reality of Numbers* (1988).

The problem of the meaningfulness of statements about non-existent objects was tackled by Bertrand Russell in "On Denoting" (1905). Here he proposes that "The present King of France is bald" be taken to mean "There is an object such that that object is presently King of France, and is bald." Russell's suggestion was supported and extended by W. V. O. Quine in "On What There Is" (1948: 21–38); reprinted with amendments in Quine, *From A Logical Point of View* (1961: 1–19). It is in this paper that Quine expresses his famous slogan, "to be is to be the value of a variable." The contributions of Kant, Frege, Russell, and Quine to the understanding of existence are all discussed by Williams (1981) Peter van Inwagen's "Creatures of Fiction" (1977: 299–308), explores the idea that statements about fictional objects such as "Othello suspects Desdemona" and critical statements about those objects, such as "Othello is a well-developed character," might be susceptible to the same treatment, in terms of abstract objects.

For discussions of what we have called "half-existent objects," see David and Stephanie Lewis, "Holes" (1970: 206–12), reprinted in David Lewis's *Philosophical Papers* (1983: 3–9), and Roberto Casati's *Shadows* (2002).

Approaches to problems of vagueness are discussed in Mark Sainbury, *Paradoxes* (1988: ch. 2). These include the ideas of objective indeterminacy, degrees of truth, and "supervaluation," in which statements containing vague predicates are replaced by more complex statements containing only non-vague ones. A classic paper arguing for the incoherence of the notion of indeterminacy in the world is Gareth Evans, "Can There Be Vague Objects?" (1978).

The probabilistic answer to the question "Why is there anything?," in a rather more sophisticated form than the very telegrammatic version presented here, is put forward and defended by Peter van Inwagen, in "Why Is There Anything At All?" (1996: 95–110). See also E. J. Lowe's reply, which immediately follows it. A book-length treatment of the problem is Bede Rundle, *Why Is There Something Rather Than Nothing?* (2004). Rundle argues, but for different reasons than those presented in this article, that the idea that there could be nothing, although apparently intelligible, actually makes no sense.

Notes

1   The case is not entirely fictional. A mathematical proposition called Fermat's Last Theorem, after Pierre Fermat (1601–1665), the seventeenth-century lawyer and mathematician who first pro-

pounded it, eluded proof until 1993, when Andrew Wiles, a Cambridge academic, offered a 250-page solution that was widely accepted as successful. In an interview, Wiles pointed out that the fact that no one had succeeded in finding a solution didn't mean that there wasn't one. The story of the theorem is told in Simon Singh, *Fermat's Last Theorem* (2002).

2 Idealism says that everything that exists is mental, and the usual way of interpreting this is to say that objects are just collections of ideas. Materialism, in contrast, says that everything is made of matter. Idealism was defended in a series of ingenious arguments by George Berkeley (1685–1753). See particularly the *Principles of Human Knowledge* (1710) and *Three Dialogues between Hylas and Philonous* (1713). Materialism was defended by Thomas Hobbes (1588–1679) in *De Corpore* (1655).

3 The argument just given is a simplified version of the one put forward the prominent logical positivist Rudolf Carnap (1891–1970), in "Empiricism, Semantics and Ontology" (1950).

4 Compare the remark made by the Eleatic stranger in Plato's dialogue the *Sophist*: "My notion would be, that anything which possesses any sort of power to affect another, or to be affected by another even for a moment, however trifling the case and however slight and momentary the effect, has real existence; and I hold that the definition of being is power" (247).

5 The idea that there are abstract things, beyond the world of sense, is a dominant theme in Plato's dialogues: he calls them the "forms," and they include beauty, equality and justice. See particularly the *Apology*, the *Phaedo* and the *Republic*. For Plato, there is no conflict with the causal criterion of existence, since these forms are sources of knowledge. The suggestion that abstract objects are causally inert is characteristic of a position in contemporary metaphysics called, perhaps somewhat misleadingly, "platonism."

6 The suggestion that "exists" is not a predicate, or is not a "real" predicate is made by Immanuel Kant (1724–1804), in the *Critique of Pure Reason* (1781).

7 This treatment of statements apparently about non-existents was proposed by Bertrand Russell (1872–1970), on "On Denoting" (1905).

References

Benacerraf, Paul and Putnam, Hilary (eds.) (1983). *Philosophy of Mathematics*, Cambridge: Cambridge University Press.

Berkeley, George (1710). *Principles of Human Knowledge*.

Berkeley, George (1713). *Three Dialogues between Hylas and Philonus*.

Bigelow, John (1988). *The Reality of Numbers*, Oxford: Clarendon Press.

Carnap, Rudolf (1950). "Empiricism, Semantics and Ontology," *Revue Internationale de Philosophie*, 4; repr. in Benacerraf and Putnam (1983).

Casati, Roberto (2002). *Shadows*, New York: Vintage.

Evans, Gareth (1978). "Can There Be Vague Objects?" *Analysis*, 38.

Hale, Bob (1987). *Abstract Objects*, Oxford: Blackwell.

Hobbes, Thomas (1655). *De Corpore*.

Kant, Immanuel (1781). *Critique of Pure Reason*.

Kneale, William and Moore, G. E. (1936). "Is Existence a Predicate?" *Proceedings of the Aristotelian Society*, supple. vol., 15, 154–88.

Lewis, David (1983). *Philosophical Papers*, vol. 1, Oxford: Oxford University Press, 3–9.

Lewis, David and Stephanie (1970). "Holes," *Australasian Journal of Philosophy*, 48, 206–12.

Plato (2003). *The Last Days of Socrates*, ed. Harold Tarrant and Hugh Tredinnick, London: Penguin.

Plato (2007). *The Republic*, ed. H. D. P. Lee et al., London: Penguin.

Quine, W. V. O. (1948). "On What There Is," *Review of Metaphysics*, 2, 21–38.

Quine, W. V. O. (1961). *From a Logical Point of View*, Cambridge, MA: Harvard University Press.

Rundle, Bede (2004). *Why Is There Something Rather Than Nothing?*, Oxford: Clarendon Press.

Russell, Bertrand (1905). "On Denoting," *Mind*.

Russell, Bertrand (1959). *The Problems of Philosophy*, Oxford: Oxford University Press.

Sainsbury, Mark (1988). *Paradoxes*, Cambridge: Cambridge University Press.

Singh, Simon (2002). *Fermat's Last Theorem*, London: Fourth Estate.

Van Inwagen, Peter (1977). "Creatures of Fiction," *American Philosophical Quarterly*, 14, 299–308.

Van Inwagen, Peter (1996). "Why Is There Anything at All?" vol. 1, *Aristotelian Society*, supple. vol., 70, 95–110.

Williams, C. J. F. (1981). *What Is Existence?*, Oxford, Clarendon Press.

7

Modality

Daniel Nolan

As well as what does happen, we are often concerned about what could have happened. When we are almost run over by a careless driver, we justifiably feel angry: even though no one was hurt, someone easily could have been. When we make decisions, we choose between alternative actions that we think are possible. Politicians and artists are often more inspired by what could be than what is.

If possibility is important, so too is necessity. Some things, like the truths of pure mathematics, are often thought to be necessary: they are unchangeable, and it is hard to even imagine what it would be like for three plus four to equal anything except seven. Some of the things science discovers seem to have a necessity about them, like the fact that nothing continuously accelerates to faster than the speed of light, or that sodium chloride always dissolves in pure water at normal temperatures and pressures. These principles seem to have a different status to truths that seem like mere accidents: there was no necessity in Queen Elizabeth's first child being a boy, for example, or in a stock market crash happening on the day that it did, rather than one day earlier or one day later.

Judgments about what can happen and what must happen, what is possible and what is impossible, and so on are common in discussions of almost any topic. But outside philosophy, there is not much general investigation into what we are trying to capture when we talk and think this way. Some topics connected with possibility and necessity are of particularly interest in metaphysics. These include questions about laws of nature, dispositions, causation, and essence.

One thing that is not immediately obvious is why any of this should be called "modality." The explanation is historical: in medieval logic, possibility and necessity were considered *modes* of propositions, and so the study of possibility and necessity is now known as the study of modality. That study obviously includes related matters, such as the study of impossibility, contingency, and what is expressed by words like "must," "should," "would," and others. The topic of modality does not have exact boundaries, nor would insisting on precise boundaries be very useful.

We seem to be able to inter-define a number of modal expressions. For example, starting with "could," we can say that something is *necessary* if it could not be otherwise (necessarily, $2 + 2 = 4$); something is *impossible* if it could not happen (it is impossible for $2 + 2 = 6$), and something is *contingent* if it could be, but also could be otherwise (it is contingent whether I have two arms and two legs). Something is *possible* if it could be (it is possible for me to go into outer space), but sometimes we use the word "possible" to suggest that while something could happen, it has not or does not: in such cases the relevant thing is only *merely possible*.

Deontic, Epistemic, Alethic

There seem to be several quite different uses of words like "can," "must," "might," "has to," and other expressions that are associated with possibility and necessity. Sometimes these words are apparently used to describe how the world is objectively: "Nothing can accelerate through the speed of light," "Everyone must die in the end.," "It is impossible for it to rain and not rain at the same place at the same time."

These uses of modal expressions are sometimes known as the "alethic modalities." Varieties of alethic necessity discussed include "logical necessity," "metaphysical necessity," "nomological necessity," "temporal necessity," and others. There are no entirely uncontroversial definitions for many of these. The core cases of logical necessity are the theorems of logic: for instance, it is logically necessary that it is not both raining and not raining. Some extend "logical necessity" to include analytic truths: they would usually hold that it is logically necessary that every bachelor is unmarried. It is also common to think that mathematical truths are logically necessary. And some would want to extend "logical necessity" to every claim they think is necessary in the strongest sense.

"Metaphysical necessity" is even more contested. Some do not want to draw a distinction between metaphysical necessity and logical necessity. Another view is that metaphysical necessity is a special grade of necessity that many fundamental principles of metaphysics have: the sense in which it is necessary that a table can have squareness, but squareness cannot have a table, for example. The examples of logical necessity mentioned in the previous paragraph are usually treated as metaphysically necessary as well. Metaphysical necessities may include some truths that are only discovered to be necessary through empirical investigation: since Kripke 1980 and Putnam 1973, many philosophers have thought it is metaphysically necessary that water is H_2O, even though there does not seem to be any *a priori* guarantee that the nature of water would turn out that way.

"Nomological necessity" is the grade of necessity given to things guaranteed by the laws of nature. Typical examples include the necessity that copper is a conductor of electricity, or that objects cannot accelerate through the speed of light. Of course, what is nomologically necessary depends on what the laws of nature are, so new discoveries in science might well cause us to revise our opinions about what is necessary in this sense. Everything metaphysically necessary and logically necessary is normally treated as being nomologically necessary as well: even if the laws of physics are silent about whether 7 is prime, still 7 is not composite in any nomological possibility. Nomological necessity is sometimes called "physical necessity," though sometimes "physical necessity" is reserved for the status of things that cannot be different without different laws of *physics*, in particular. Philosophers disagree about whether the laws of nature are *metaphysically* necessary: if they are, then nomological necessity may just be the same thing as metaphysical necessity, or maybe a special species of it. On the other hand, some other philosophers deny that there are really any laws of nature at all (or that they are only idealisations that do not often apply to real phenomena): if those philosophers are right, then very little will be nomologically necessary except, perhaps, for things that are logically or metaphysically necessary for other reasons. (For an example see Cartwright 1983.)

There are more restricted alethic modalities still. Arguably the sense in which the past is fixed gives us "temporal necessity": things that could have turned out otherwise, but now it is too late for them to be any way except the way they are. There seems to be a type of modality associated with ability or feasibility: there is a good sense in which I cannot run a three-minute mile, or speak fluent Hungarian, even though neither of those things is nomologically impossible. A lot of our talk about what is "impossible" or what "can happen" seems to invoke standards much less generous with possibility than the nomological standard: though perhaps some of these uses involve elements of non-alethic modalities too.

There are other uses of modal vocabulary besides the alethic ones above. There are epistemic uses, where what has to be or can be seems to depend on the state of knowledge or evidence. Consider a tracker who has just discovered that the remains of a fire are still warm, and says "They must have camped here last night." Presumably he is not saying that "they" were forced to camp there last night, or otherwise found it unavoidable: instead, he seems to be saying something to do with what follows from his evidence. Or consider someone who has been searching their bedroom for hours and then says "My glasses cannot be in the bedroom." The "cannot" there seems to be signalling a connection between her evidence, or what she knows, and the location of her glasses, rather than saying something about the alethic possibility of her glasses existing in her bedroom.

Other uses of modal vocabulary seem to relate to what is allowed and what is forbidden, by moral codes or other systems of norms like legal systems or codes of etiquette. Often it seems to be that something is possible if it is permitted, and necessary if it is required: "All tickets must be shown," "A gentleman cannot refuse a challenge," "The perpetrator has to be brought to justice," and so on. One interesting thing about these cases, usually labeled "deontic" modalities, is that deontic necessity does not imply truth. If something is logically necessary, or physically necessary, or epistemically necessary (at least in the sense of following from what is known), then it must also be true. But just because law, or morality, or honor, requires something, it does not follow it is true. Even when the law says that people cannot take things that do not belong to them, still some people do.

One interesting question is what these different uses of modal vocabulary have to do with each other. One plausible suggestion is that there is no genuine ambiguity here, rather words like "can" and "possible" and "must" and "has to" are context sensitive. Compare: "that," used as a demonstrative, can be used to pick out many different sorts of things – but this need not mean that "that" is ambiguous. Instead, the core meaning of "that" seems to be associated with a function from acts of demonstration, or intentions to pick things out, to reference to objects. So "that" means the same in "That is a tiger.," "That is what I've been trying to tell you!," and "I want that for Christmas.," even though it refers to different things when each of these sentences is used. What is common is its being associated with a function from a demonstrative feature of context to an object.

Of course, even if we allow that modal expressions are context-dependent, this leaves us with the question of what it is about context that they are sensitive to. Perhaps it depends on what constraints a speaker has in mind, or are in play in a discourse. Perhaps modal operators signal whether something follows from some background assumptions, given by context: to say it must be that p would be to signal that p is a logical consequence of things taken for granted (this is the view explored in Quine 1966). Or perhaps the influence of context is best understood as restrictions on classes of possible worlds (see below). There are of course other options for explaining the role of context here, and it is safe to say this question remains disputed.

Possible Worlds

Philosophers have paid a lot of attention to "possible worlds" since the 1960s, even though using possible worlds in philosophy goes back at least as far as Leibniz. A possible world corresponds to a complete specification of an alternative way for the world to turn out: complete in the sense that for every proposition p, either p or its negation will follow from the specification. One complete possibility corresponds to how things in fact are: it is normally labeled the "actual world."

Possible worlds have been invoked in a range of areas in philosophy. One important early use was in understanding modal logic. Systems of logic had been worked out that added logical symbols for "necessarily . . ." and "possibly . . ." to propositional logic and predicate calculus. The initial development of modal logic was through proposing systems of axioms, but there were difficulties in understanding the relationships between the different systems, and determining the meta-logical properties of such systems, such as whether the different systems were complete. (A logical system is complete when every sentence that is true in every model of the logic is provable in that logic.)

A breakthrough in the understanding of these logics came when it was realized that they are modeled well by a system that have a number of "worlds" at which propositions can take different truth values, together with an accessibility relation to tell you which worlds are possible from which others. For a proposition to be necessary at one world (call it w_1) is for it to be true at all the worlds *accessible* from w_1. For a proposition to be possible at w_1 is for it to be true at at least one world accessible from w_1. Different modal logics can then be modeled by putting different accessibility relations on worlds. For example, it seems very reasonable to insist that if a proposition is necessary at a world it is true at that world, and if it is true at that world then it is possible at that world, too. This amounts to insisting that the accessibility relation is *reflexive*: that every world is accessible from itself. More controversially, some people think that a proposition can be possibly possible without being possible. This makes most sense when dealing with restricted modalities: perhaps something is not feasible, but there is something feasible we can do to *make* it feasible: then we might want to say it is possibly possible, but not currently possible. This can be represented with an accessibility relation that is not *transitive*. If p is true at world 1, which is accessible from world 2, and world 2 is accessible from world 3, then p is possibly possible at world 3. If world 1 is not accessible from world 3, and no other p-world is accessible from world 3, however, "possibly p" will be false at world 3.

A family of modal logics now called "normal" modal logics can all be represented by varying conditions on an accessibility relation, and many more modal logics can be represented by similar techniques. Insofar as this is only modelling, we do not have to take the "possible worlds" seriously: they are just indexes in a model that stand in a function from sentences to truth-values. But the fact that these models were so illuminating is suggestive, as noted by David Lewis (Lewis 1986: 17–20). "Necessarily . . ." seems to function like "In all possible worlds . . . ," and "Possibly . . ." like "In some possible world . . ." Maybe talk about what is necessary and what is possible is just talk about what is going on in all possibilities, or in some possibility? Some philosophers have thought that this gives us a way to understand, or to analyze, modal discourse – we can see modal talk as a way of generalizing about possible worlds.

Of course, if we do this, we need to find a place for the modal talk we engage in that does not seem to involve *every* possible world, such as the restricted modalities discussed above. (The sense in which it is not possible for me to become a billionaire by the end of the year, for example.) One way to understand them is that they correspond to some restricted subset of all possible worlds: the worlds that obey the same laws of nature (for nomological necessity), or the same current financial situation (for the claim about becoming a billionaire), and so on. Another, similar, approach is the one modeled above on which there is an "accessibility relation" between worlds, so that a world is possible relative to another if it is accessible from it. This more naturally allows us to interpret cases corresponding to failures of transitivity, where something is necessary but not necessarily necessary, or possibly possible but not possible (see above). If these moves improve our understanding of the relationships between different uses of modal vocabulary, they provide another example where philosophizing about possible worlds has been useful.

References to possible worlds can be found all over the philosophical literature. They are used to provide models for claims about chance and probability. They are used to distinguish important varieties of supervenience claims. They have a very important role in theories of the meanings of sentences in natural language: they are the foundation of Montague grammar, for example, an important tradition in contemporary linguistics. They are employed to illuminate the logic of "if . . . then . . ." sentences. They are usefully employed to model mental content, especially what beliefs and desires are "about" (Stalnaker 1984). Many contemporary philosophers would concede that, some way or other, we need to make sense of talk about possible worlds. But exactly what are we talking about?

What Are Possible Worlds?

Once a number of philosophers started to find it useful to talk about possible worlds, the metaphysical question of what possible worlds *are* was not far behind. Notoriously, David Lewis (see especially Lewis 1986) defended the view that possible worlds were alternative concrete universes, the same sort of thing as our own cosmos. Other philosophers argued that possible worlds should be seen as abstract objects of some sort: perhaps as collections of sentences or propositions (Carnap 1956; Adams 1974), perhaps as maximal properties, or ways, that an entire cosmos could be (Forrest 1986), perhaps as uninstantiated maximal states of affairs: a total state of the universe, albeit one that the universe in fact does not have (van Inwagen 1986) or perhaps as a special sort of abstract object in their own right (which I think is Robert Stalnaker's view, though it is hard to tell: see the discussions in Stalnaker 2003).

One way to try to work out the metaphysics of possible worlds is to start from a job-description. Possible worlds should have either sentences or propositions true at them: a possible world where some swans are blue must be able to endorse "Some swans are blue." This true-at relation is called by some, following David Lewis, "representation" (Lewis 1986: 137). But do not be misled by using the term "representation" here. Lewis, for example, thought that a possible world represents claims like "some swans are blue" by containing blue swans as parts of it, not by any sort of reference or meaning.

Different theories of possible worlds handle this true-at or representation differently. Lewis, who believed possible worlds were universes like this one, has one obvious story. Those who think possible worlds are sentences or propositions think that "representation" in this technical sense is *representation* in the more usual sense: a possible world with "some swans are blue" true at it is a proposition that says that some swans are blue, or implies it. Theories that held that possible worlds were states of affairs say that "some swans are blue" is true at a world (state of affairs) *w* provided *w* met the following condition: were *w* to obtain, some swans would be blue. Those who think possible worlds are not analyzable in other terms might think the true-at relation is not analyzable as well, or they might offer an account of the connection. Even though Robert Stalnaker tends to treat possible worlds as not further analyzable (Stalnaker 2003, especially chs. 1 and 2), he does give an analysis of the "true-at" relation: he claims possible worlds are sets of propositions, and for a proposition to be true at a world is for that world to be a member of the proposition (i.e. the set). Because all of these candidate worlds, in their own way, would be able to perform the role that possible worlds are supposed to play, they are all so far viable options.

Whether one of these candidates is better than the others depends in part on what other things possible worlds are supposed to do. For example, some people want a theory of possible worlds to provide an *analysis* of modality, and so require that we be able to specify which things are the possible worlds without relying on other modal notions. (Lewis 1986: 150–7, 167–70, 176, criticizes rival theories for not being able to do this.) To give another example, a theory of possible worlds should provide *enough* possible worlds for all the possibilities there are, and Lewis 1986 pp 157–163 charges that some of his rivals cannot do that, especially when it comes to possibilities of individuals and properties that do not exist but could. Nolan 2004 offers another sort of argument that many theories of possible worlds do not allow for enough possibilities. Of course there are many other things you could argue possible worlds should do that rule out one or more of the usual options.

There may be other ways to narrow down the list of candidates to be possible worlds besides the demands of the role possible worlds are to play. Perhaps arguments can be given that some of these candidates just do not exist: many people would want to say this about Lewis's concrete alternative universes, and there are some who might worry about various different sorts of abstract objects offered as candidates to be possible worlds. Or perhaps, if several groups of objects met all the criteria to be possible worlds, we might think the expression "possible world" was indeterminate between them, or alternatively sometimes picked out one group and sometimes another.

What should we do if no proposed ontology plays all the roles we want for possible worlds? We could decide that possible worlds are not quite as we thought they were. Or we could decide that talking about possible worlds was a mistake. Or we could treat talk about possible worlds as engaging in a "useful fiction." Rosen (1990) is a well-known presentation of a "modal fictionalist" theory.

What Are Possibilities?

The question of what possibilities are is less discussed. Presumably, a possibility does not need to be *complete* like a possible world: when I discuss a possibility of a US president of recent Arab descent, that possibility need not represent anything one way or another about e.g. the exact facts about what every American has for breakfast. You could think that possible worlds were just a special sort of possibility: the complete ones. A common approach to these incomplete possibilities is to identify them with *sets* of possible worlds: where what is true according to a possibility is what all the possible worlds in the set agree upon. Even if we do not identify possibilities with sets of possible worlds, those sets provide a good way of modelling many aspects of possibilities.

Treating incomplete possibilities as sets of possible worlds does have some intuitive drawbacks. One is that possible worlds all agree on necessary truths: so if we model possibilities as sets of possible worlds in the way described, then every possibility will endorse every necessary truth. The idea of possibilities as incomplete, though, may make this unappealing: why should the possibility of a US president of Arab descent incorporate the whole of mathematics, for example? Those who want to treat possibilities as not incorporating all logical truths, let alone all necessary truths, often call these possibilities *situations*. See Barwise and Perry (1983).

If we do not construct possibilities out of possible worlds, we are left with the metaphysical question about the nature of possibilities, or situations themselves. But the options for possibilities are quite similar to the options for possible worlds: and any theory of the nature of possible worlds can usually be modified slightly to yield a theory of the nature of possibilities or situations. For example, the theory of possible worlds as maximal consistent sets of sentences (sets that, for each sentence S, either contain S or the negation of S) has as a close cousin the theory that possibilities are consistent sets of sentences that need not be maximal. Possible worlds can often be construed as just a particular sort of possibility – the possibilities that are maximally specific.

Modality *De Re*

The possibilities for a given object or person are often called the possibilities *de re* ("of the object") for that object or person. This is contrasted with *de dicto* ("of the expression") possibility and necessity, which concerns the possibility or necessity of the proposition involved (at least when the expressions were developed). Questions about modality *de re* are particularly thorny ones, and have attracted a lot of interest from metaphysicians.

Our judgments about what can, and what cannot, happen to an object seem to depend on what kind of object it is. The number 2 can be eternal and lack any physical properties: but can my table? A lump of gold perhaps can survive being flattened out, but a cat cannot: change the relationships between a cat's parts sufficiently, and the cat has been destroyed. There is a lot of controversy about what sorts of changes are possible for people: completely destroying my mind and body presumably kills me, but what if everything except my brain is destroyed and the brain is kept functioning on life-support? What about if my psychology is copied into another human body, or a computer program? Is it possible that I could survive that process, or would we just be left with someone (or something) else psychologically similar?

Many philosophers believe that this is because some kinds of things have *essences* associated with them, and that they have some properties essentially and others only accidentally. Sometimes what it is to have a property essentially is defined modally: for b to have a property G essentially is for it to be the case that necessarily, if b exists, b has G. So if my cup is essentially a physical thing, then each possible world either lacks my cup or alternatively represents that my cup exists and is physical. Properties had accidentally are all the other properties a thing has: presumably my cup containing tea is accidental to it. Some philosophers (following Fine 1994) think that we can understand the essential/accidental distinction in non-modal terms, but by and large they would agree that if a property is essential, it meets the modal condition just mentioned, though this may not be sufficient for a property to be essential.

One problem that arises here for a theory of modality *de re* is that it seems like one and the same object can belong to more than one kind: thought about one way, one answer seems correct, but thought about another, a different answer seems right. Prior to worrying about philosophical issues, you might be inclined to think that a certain lump of gold is *identical* to a certain statue. (The statue is just the lump shaped in a certain way with certain intentions.) But the lump of gold can survive being flattened, while flattening the statue would destroy it. Another modal difference is presumably that the lump of gold could have existed without ever having been made into a statue – but it is much less clear the statue could have existed without being a statue.

There are several responses available here. One is to try to find a privileged kind for each thing to be (Burke 1994): perhaps, despite appearances, only one of the kinds of the statue/lump is relevant. Or a multiple occupancy view could be endorsed, according to which the statue and the lump are distinct, but they happen to occupy the same space and be made up of the same parts (see for example Wiggins 1980). Versions of multiple occupancy views seem to be the most popular. Or perhaps a strongly anti-essentialist stance could be adopted that claims that a lot of our intuitions about essential properties are mistaken, and in fact all sorts of things are possible for all sorts of objects.

A final option is to accept what is sometimes called *inconstancy de re* (Lewis 1986: 248–63). On this view, which *de re* predications are true depends not just on which object is at stake, but other things about how it is thought of or referred to. The most famous approach along these lines is *counterpart theory*, as developed by David Lewis and others (Lewis 1968; Hazen 1979; Forbes 1989). In counterpart theory, I am represented in possible worlds other than the actual one by *counterparts* – things related to me by a *counterpart relation*. But which counterpart relation should be used in evaluating a claim of *de re* necessity can depend on context. Ask about what can happen to a statue, *using a statue counterpart relation*, and you might be told that it could have its limbs somewhat rearranged, but could not be flattened. (That is, it has counterparts with different limb arrangements, but no flattened counterparts.) But ask about the same thing *using a lump counterpart relation*, then it has counterparts that are flattened.

Counterpart theory is not the only way to implement inconstancy *de re*. Another approach is to accept straightforward contingent identity. Suppose there are no worlds where a statue, S, survives being squashed, but there are plenty of worlds where a lump L survives being squashed. If S = L in this world, then that object (the thing which is identical to S and also identical to L) can possibly survive squashing (because it is L), but necessarily does not survive squashing (because it is S). Care has to be taken to set up contingent identity theories so as to avoid contradictions: and indeed my statement of the modal features of the thing which is S and also L will already look contradictory to some. Another way for a theory to endorse inconstancy *de re* is if modal predicates are *Abelardian* (Noonan 1991). If modal attributions mean something different depending on the kind of thing they are applied to, then we can have apparently contradictory *de re* modal predications both being true. If we say that S cannot survive flattening, but L can survive flattening, this looks inconsistent if S = L. But if all we mean is that it has a lump-kind-of-possibility of surviving flattening but no statue-kind-of-possibility of surviving flattening, then this is not inconsistent.

There are other kinds of puzzles for modality *de re*. As well as the cross-kind puzzles discussed above, there are same-kind puzzles. People can survive the complete destruction of one hemisphere of their brain, with the right medical care. They also can survive the loss of a lot of their body. Someone who had the left side of their body (including their brain), might conceivably survive if they received enough medical assistance and the right kinds of prosthetics or transplants were available. (Maybe not with today's medical technology, but we can easily imagine a life support system that could keep someone alive and functioning even with such horrific 50 percent injuries.)

Now consider a possible world where someone (say, me) is bisected vertically and each half is attached to sophisticated life-support. "Lefty" regains consciousness in one room, while "Righty" regains consciousness in another. Just as head-trauma victims today can be rehabilitated even with the loss of a lot of brain tissue, let us suppose Lefty and Righty both are rehabilitated. They both remember my earlier life, they both have my personality, they both care about the people I cared about, and so on. Where have I gone in this example? Have I disappeared? Well, that does not seem right: if I could survive losing my right half, then I could have survived in no worse shape than Lefty is right now. Am I Lefty? That seems plausible until we remember that we could just as well identify me with Righty. Am I both Lefty, and also Righty? Well, Lefty is distinct from Righty, so if I am identical with Lefty I had better be distinct from Righty, it seems. Am I Lefty and Righty put together? Maybe, but then in that world I would be a very odd thing, with two sets of memories and experiences, and no unified sense of self. (See Parfit 1971 for a classic discussion.)

This example mixes issues of modal properties with issues about identity over time (since we would also be puzzled about what to say if such a fission case happened in the actual world). But we can construct purely modal cases too. (See Chisholm 1967 and Chandler 1976 for examples). The interesting thing about these same-kind cases is that a lot of the options in the cross-time cases look less appealing. A multiple occupancy view, where there are two people where I am right now (the one that would be Lefty and the one that would be Righty), seems more odd than the multiple occupancy view about statues and clay. Dominant-kind views like Burke (1994) do not help us. *De re* inconstancy might do better: perhaps both Lefty and Righty are my counterparts, or perhaps I am identical to each of them even though they are distinct from each other in the operation world.

Cases like Lefty/Righty also raise issues about whether there can be differences in *de re* possibility without differences in the qualitative description of possible worlds. Is there a possible world, just like the one described, where I am identical only to Lefty after the operation, for example? Imagine, for example, the situation where you wake up from an accident and find yourself only with the left side of your original body, and then you are told that such a bisection has been carried out and someone very like you, nicknamed "Righty," is in the next room with the right side of your pre-accident body. Is that a possible situation?

There are other ways of asking questions about possible worlds that are the same qualitatively but differ in what objects exist in them. Could there be a world just like this, except that one of the actual electrons is replaced by a merely possible electron that does the same thing as the replaced electron does? Consider a world with two qualitatively identical iron spheres and nothing else. Can there be a world with just the first sphere? If so, would it be any different from the world with just the second sphere?

Views where possible worlds can differ in the identity of the objects in them without there being any other differences are called *haecceitistic* views, and views that say there is no difference in identities of objects without some difference in qualitative arrangements are called *anti-haecceitistic*. (The terminology goes back to the medieval philosopher Duns Scotus.) The debate between these two camps points up a deep divide in how to think about the relation between possibilities for objects and possibilities for arrangements of qualitative features.

How Do We Discover Modal Truths?

A final topic to discuss is the question of how we discover what is necessary and what is possible. When we are dealing with restricted necessities and possibilities, an important part of the story will be a story about how we discover facts about the constraints in play. When I want to know what is financially possible for me, for example, I should look at my bank balance and credit card statements, talk to the bank about what loans they are prepared to make, and so on. A different sort of question arises when we consider unrestricted alethic modality: how can we find out what is possible at all, or what is necessary in the strongest sense?

Some of the answers will be piecemeal. When I want to know whether a formula is a logical necessity, for example, one thing I can try to do is *prove* it from axioms. Likewise for mathematical formula, of course – the first step in telling whether a mathematical formula is necessary is often looking for a proof or disproof of it. But these epistemic stories are only partial. What about the axioms in logic or mathematics, for example? Or other necessary truths, like the truth that all bachelors are unmarried, or that nothing is both a sphere and a cube at the same time?

The logical positivists thought that all of these necessary truths were analytic: knowing the meanings of expressions put you in a position to tell that they were true. According to this line of thinking, the axioms of logic and mathematics were all analytic, and establishing whether a truth was necessary was something that could be done *a priori*.

It may well be that some necessary truths are analytic, such as well-worn examples like "all bachelors are unmarried." But Kripke (1980) and Putnam (1973) have argued that not all of them are, and that a significant range of necessary truths are *a posteriori*. Kripke, for example, argued that when objects were identical, they were necessarily identical. Furthermore, he argued that proper names were *rigid designators*, always picking out the same object in each possible world. But then it would follow that true identity statements using only proper names would be necessary: "Bob Dylan is Robert Zimmerman," for example. But many such identity statements are only discoverable *a posteriori*: if the Sheriff of Nottingham wants to know whether Robin of Locksley is identical to Robin Hood, he has to investigate, and cannot tell *a priori*.

Kripke and Putnam wanted to extend this idea to so-called natural kind terms as well. "Water" and "H_2O," according to them, refer to the same natural kind, and do so rigidly. So an identity statement like "Water is H_2O" would then be necessary. But of course it required considerable chemical investigation to reveal that water is H_2O: that claim is definitely not *a priori*.

The epistemology of modality continues to excite a lot of controversy. Some philosophers continue to maintain that conceivability has an important role in determining whether something is possible, though with caveats to handle Kripkean cases. (See Gendler and Hawthorne 2002 for many examples.) Other philosophers think that many necessary truths reflect truths about the essences of things, truths that can often only be discovered through investigation of the world. One common approach to justifying theories of modality and possible worlds is to point to their usefulness in an overall theory. David Lewis offers a justification of this sort for his theory of possible worlds (Lewis 1986: 3–5). This style of argument has parallels with the use of so-called "indispensability arguments" for the existence of mathematical objects, and "inference to the best explanation" for theoretical posits more generally. (See Colyvan 2001 for a general discussion of indispensability arguments in mathematics, and Lipton 2004 for a general discussion of inference to the best explanation.)

The epistemology of modality is not done in a vacuum: it has close connections to more general questions about the epistemology of metaphysics, the epistemology of mathematics and logic, and even the epistemology of science insofar as science is supposed to deliver *a posteriori* necessary truths.

Further Reading

As well as works referred to above, there are a number of good recent introductions to the philosophy of modality. These include Girle (2003) and Melia (2005). Divers (2002) is perhaps the best systematic survey of issues in the metaphysics of possible worlds.

An important part of philosophy of modality in the twentieth century was concerned with understanding and applying modal logics. Two classic and very informative introductions to modal logic are Chellas (1980) and Hughes and Cresswell (1968, if you can find it, is a better introduction, I think, otherwise 1996). Three excellent, and recent, presentations of modal logic are Beall and van Fraassen (2003), Girle (2000), and Priest (2001).

Loux (1979) is a collection of classic papers on modality and possible worlds. One of the best collections to start with when investigating statue/lump cases like the ones discussed above is Rea (1996).

Finally, no list of recommended further reading would not be complete without mention of two of the great classics of later-twentieth century philosophy, both of which have modality as a central theme: Saul Kripke's *Naming and Necessity* (1980) and David Lewis's *On the Plurality of Worlds* (1986).

References

Adams, R. M. (1974). "Theories of Actuality," *Nous*, 8, 211–31; repr. in Loux (1979).

Barwise, J. and Perry, J. (1983). *Situations and Attitudes*, Cambridge, MA: MIT Press.

Beall, J. C. and van Fraassen, B. C. (2002). *Possibilities and Paradox: An Introduction to Modal and Many-valued Logic*, Oxford: Oxford University Press.

Burke, M. (1994). "Preserving the Principle of One Object to a Place: A Novel Account of the Relations among Objects, Sorts, Sortals, and Persistence Conditions," *Philosophy and Phenomenological Research*, 54 (3), 591–624.

Carnap, R. (1956). *Meaning and Necessity*, enlarged edn., Chicago: University of Chicago Press.

Cartwright, N. (1983). *How the Laws of Physics Lie*, Oxford: Oxford University Press.

Chandler, H. (1976). "Plantinga and the Contingently Possible," *Analysis*, 36: 106–9.

Chellas, B. F. (1980). *Modal Logic: An Introduction*, Cambridge: Cambridge University Press.

Chisholm, R. (1967). "Identity Through Possible Worlds: Some Questions," *Nous*, 1, 1–8; repr. in Loux (1979).

Colyvan, M. (2001). *The Indispensability of Mathematics*, Oxford: Oxford University Press.

Divers, J. (2002). *Possible Worlds*, London: Routledge.

Fine, K. (1994). "Essence and Modality," *Philosophical Perspectives*, 8, 1–16

Forbes, G. (1989). *Languages of Possibility*, Oxford: Basil Blackwell.

Forrest, P. (1986). "Ways Worlds Could Be," *Australasian Journal of Philosophy*, 64, 15–24

Gendler, T. S. and Hawthorne, J. (eds.) (2002). *Conceivability and Possibility*, Oxford: Oxford University Press.

Girle, R. (2000). *Modal Logic and Philosophy*, Chesham: Acumen Publishing.

Girle, R. (2003). *Possible Worlds*, London: Routledge.

Hazen, A. (1979). "Counterpart-theoretic Semantics for Modal Logic," *Journal of Philosophy*, 76, 319–38.

Hughes, G. E. and Cresswell, M. J. (1968; 1996). *An Introduction to Modal Logic*, London: Methuen.

Humberstone, I.L. 1981. "From Worlds to Possibilities." *Journal of Philosophical Logic*, 10, 313–39.

Kripke, S. (1980). *Naming and Necessity*, Oxford: Basil Blackwell.

Lewis, D. (1968). "Counterpart Theory and Quantified Modal Logic," *Journal of Philosophy*, 65, 113–26.

Lewis, D. (1986). *On the Plurality of Worlds*, Oxford: Blackwell.

Lipton, P. (2004). *Inference to the Best Explanation*, 2nd edn., London: Routledge.

Loux, M. J. (ed.) (1979). *The Possible and the Actual: Readings in the Metaphysics of Modality*, Ithaca, NY: Cornell University Press.

Melia, J. (2005). *Modality*, Chesham: Acumen Publishing.

Nolan, D. (2004). "Classes, Worlds and Hypergunk," *Monist*, 87 (3), 3–21

Noonan, H. (1991). "Indeterminate Identity, Contingent Identity and Abelardian Predicates," *Philosophical Quarterly*, 41 (163), 183–93.

Parfit, D. (1971). "Personal Identity," *Philosophical Review*, 80 (1), 3–27

Priest, G. (2001). *An Introduction to Non-classical Logic*, Cambridge: Cambridge University Press.

Putnam, H. (1973). "Meaning and Reference," *Journal of Philosophy*, 70 (19), 699–711.

Quine, W. V. O. (1966). "Necessary Truth," in Quine, *The Ways of Paradox*, Cambridge, MA: Harvard University Press, 68–76.

Rea, M. C. (1996). *Material Constitution: A Reader*, Lanham, MD: Rowman and Littlefield.

Rosen, G. (1990). "Modal Fictionalism," *Mind*, 99 (395), 327–54.

Stalnaker, R. C. (1984). *Inquiry*, Cambridge, MA: MIT Press.

Stalnaker, R. C. (2003). *Ways a World Might Be*, Oxford: Clarendon.

Van Inwagen, P. (1986). "Two Concepts of Possible Worlds," *Midwest Studies in Philosophy*, 11, 185–213

Wiggins, D. (1980). *Sameness and Substance*, Cambridge, MA: Harvard University Press.

8

Mind and Consciousness

Keith Frankish and Maria Kasmirli

The Mind–Body Problem: Old and New

Minds are strange things. In a sense our minds are us. We might lose our limbs and have our internal organs replaced, but provided our minds remained intact we would still be us. Yet minds are hard to pin down. They do not seem to be part of our bodies, in the way that our organs are. A surgeon could examine your brain, but could they see your *mind* – your thoughts, beliefs, desires, hopes, intentions, perceptions, sensations, and feelings? And although our minds are clearly linked to our bodies, we can imagine swapping bodies with someone else, or even having no body at all.

In the past, considerations such as these led many philosophers to hold that our minds are not physical things but immaterial substances – souls – which are completely distinct from our bodies and could survive their death. This view is known as *substance dualism*, since it is the view that we are made of two separate substances, mind and matter. (It is also known as *Cartesian dualism*, after the seventeenth-century philosopher René Descartes, who set out some famous arguments for the view.) Substance dualism may do justice to our intuitions about the mind, but it also creates a new problem: If minds and bodies are completely distinct, then how can they interact with each other? How can an event in an immaterial soul, such as a decision to move one's arm, cause changes in a physical body? And how can changes in a physical body, such as the stimulation of its pain receptors, cause sensations in an immaterial soul? This is the traditional *mind–body problem*.

Nowadays very few philosophers are substance dualists. We now know a lot more about the dependency of the mind on the brain. We know how changes in the chemicals in the brain can affect our minds, and how brain injury and disease can damage it. And scientists are building up extremely detailed accounts of how the brain processes sensory inputs, stores and accesses information, and controls movement, all couched in physical terms and making no reference to the soul. Moreover – despite the claims of psychics – there is no good evidence for the existence of disembodied minds. And finally, the influence of religion, which once supported belief in an immaterial soul, has waned considerably, at least in western civilization. In one sense, then, most modern philosophers are *physicalists*: they reject substance dualism and hold that human beings are composed simply of matter –

or more precisely, of the basic entities posited by modern physics (atoms and their constituents).

Does this mean that the mind–body problem is settled? In its old form, yes. If there is no immaterial soul, then there is no puzzle about how it interacts with the physical world. But a new version of the mind–body problem has emerged, which is currently the focus of vigorous debate. To understand the problem, a little background is needed.

If substance dualism is false, then mental states – thoughts, feelings, experiences, and so on – are states of the body. But what *kind* of states? An answer popular around the middle of the twentieth century was that they are *behavioral dispositions*. A disposition is a tendency to do something in certain circumstances; for example, a glass has a disposition to shatter if dropped. A *behavioral* disposition is a tendency to engage in behavior of some sort. Now different mental states are associated with different behavioral dispositions. For example, a person with a bad mood is disposed to scowl, be impatient, snap at people, and so on. And on the view we are considering, when we talk about a person's mental states we are referring simply to these behavioral dispositions. Thus, on this view, a bad mood is not a *thing* inside a person that causes them to scowl, be impatient, snap at people, and so on; rather, it simply *is* a disposition to do those things. Advocates of this view propose similar analyses of all other mental states – beliefs, desires, hopes, fears, experiences, and so on. So, for example, to believe that it is going to rain soon is to be disposed to behave in ways appropriate to oncoming rain – closing the windows, bringing in the washing, and so on – the details varying depending on circumstances. Thus the mind is not a mysterious inner thing, known only to its possessor, but a pattern of dispositions open for all to observe. This view is known as *philosophical behaviorism*. If it is correct, then substance dualists were making what Gilbert Ryle called a *category mistake* (Ryle 1949). They thought that minds, like bodies, belonged to the category of things (albeit immaterial ones), when in fact they belong to the category of activities and dispositions. Their mistake was a bit like that of a person who thinks that a *university* is a special building, in addition to all the other structures on a campus.

Philosophical behaviorism still has advocates, but there are serious objections to the doctrine and its popularity has decreased sharply since the 1960s. One problem is that it is implausible to extend the analysis to experiences, including perceptions and bodily sensations such as pains. A pain, it seems, is not just a disposition to display pain-related behavior (wincing, crying out, rubbing the affected part, and so on), but an internal state that *causes* one to do these things. This is reflected in the commonsense view that our mental states are private things, of which we have an inner awareness, via introspection.

In response to this and other problems with behaviorism, many philosophers turned to a different view, according to which mental states are states of the brain, identified by their distinctive causes and effects – their *causal roles*. Thus, pains are those neural states that are caused by stimulation of pain receptors and that tend to cause behavior characteristic of pain; perceptions are those states that are caused by stimulation of the sense organs and that tend to cause corresponding beliefs; and beliefs are those long-term states that are caused by perceptions or inferences and that tend to cause appropriate behavior. The view is known as the *identity theory of mind*. The theory comes in different forms, depending on how we conceive of the relevant causal roles and whether we identify mental states with the neurological states that play these causal roles in humans, or, more broadly, with *any* states that play these roles, whatever their precise make-up. The latter view is known as *functionalism*, and it is widely felt to be more plausible, since we want to allow that other species – and even aliens – can have mental states like ours, despite having different neurologies. The identity theory is often coupled with the view that the mind is similar to a computer, and in one form or another it is the dominant view in contemporary philosophy of mind.

Like substance dualism, identity theory does justice to the idea that mental states are the internal causes of behavior, but like behaviorism it does not treat the mind as a non-physical entity, and it holds out the promise of a scientific explanation for mental phenomena. However, it still faces problems. For mental states seem to have some mysterious *properties*, which are hard to explain in scientific terms. Two in particular stand out: *representational content* and *phenomenal feel*.

To say that mental states have representational content is to say that they are *about* things – they represent, or stand for, things beyond themselves, including objects and places that are distant in space and time, and even ones that are non-existent. (Another term often used for this feature is "intentionality," which means *directedness*. Mental states are *directed to* things in the world.) But how do brain states acquire this property? How can neurons and synapses be *about* something? Of course, in a sense representational content is not mysterious at all. The words in a book represent things, but we do not think of them as deeply mysterious. However, it is plausible to think that words derive their content from us. Words only mean things because we have conventions that they do – conventions which ultimately depend on our thoughts. They have *derived* intentionality. But thoughts themselves cannot derive their content from other thoughts. They, it seems, have *intrinsic* intentionality. And this does seem mysterious.

The second property is *phenomenal feel*. Think about some everyday experiences – the sight of a clear summer sky, the pain of a bruised shin, the smell of coffee, the feeling of stroking a cat's fur. Focus on what each of these experiences is *like* – what it feels like subjectively, from the inside. Each has its own character, which is instantly recognizable but very difficult to describe. Philosophers use a variety of terms for this aspect of experience, including, "phenomenal feel," "phenomenology," "qualitative feel," "subjective character," "raw feel," "what-it-is-likeness," and "qualia" (a Latin plural meaning "qualities"; the singular is "quale"). Having experiences with phenomenal feel is central to what we call *consciousness*, and the word "consciousness" is often used to refer to the possession of such experiences. Like content, consciousness seems mysterious. If the identity theory is right, then experiences are just brain states – electrochemical changes in brain cells – and how could such things have an inner feel to them? As one writer puts it, how could soggy gray brain matter give rise to the "technicolour phenomenology" of consciousness? (McGinn 1989: 349). The Australian philosopher David Chalmers has dubbed this the "hard problem" of consciousness (Chalmers 1995).

Content and consciousness are the focus of the new mind–body problem. Subjectively, we know that we have mental states with content and feel, but looking at ourselves from the third-person perspective, as physical beings, it is hard to see how this can be. The problem is to explain how a physical body comes to possess these strange properties. It is widely assumed that doing this would involve providing *reductive explanations* of them. A reductive explanation is one that explains a property in terms of more fundamental, lower-level properties. For example, reproduction can be reductively explained in terms of more basic physiological, cellular, and genetic processes, which can themselves be explained in chemical and physical terms. Many philosophers hold that all properties above the level of basic physics (the science of the fundamental particles and forces) can be reductively explained. This view is a version of what is called *naturalism*, and it seems to be borne out by the huge success science has had in finding reductive explanations. Solving the new mind–body problem would involve providing similar explanations of content and feel, showing how their existence can be explained in terms of more basic and less mysterious properties.

Another way of posing the new mind–body problem is to ask whether content and feel are *physical* properties. By "physical properties" we mean properties that exist simply in virtue of the features described by basic physics – the underlying distribution of subatomic particles and forces. Many philosophers and scientists hold that basic physics (or a fully developed version of it) is a theory of *everything* – that everything can be described and explained in the language of basic physics. Of course, we do not usually describe things in this way; we use everyday non-scientific concepts and concepts from higher-level sciences such as biology. But the idea is that the properties we are referring to are not really distinct from the basic physical ones. They are not extra features of the world, in addition to the basic physical ones, but just those same features under different guises. This is sometimes expressed metaphorically by saying that once God fixed the basic physical facts, he fixed all the facts; there was no more work for him to do (Kripke 1980). For example, I have a digestive system, but this is not an extra property of mine, over and above the basic physical ones. Rather, it *consists in* my having certain basic physical properties – having certain basic physical components arranged in a certain way and performing certain functions. In a widely used phrase, the basic physical properties *realize* the higher-level biological one. It is important to stress that the claim is not that each high-level property can be identified with the *same* set of basic physical properties in every instance. Most higher-level properties can be realized in more than one way; for example, the digestive system involves different physical structures in different animals. The claim is simply that each *instance* of a given high-level property is realized in some set of basic physical properties, differing perhaps from case to case. If we use the term "physical properties" in a broad sense for both basic physical properties and higher-level properties that are realized in basic physical ones, then the view we are considering amounts to the claim that all properties are physical properties.

The claim that all properties are physical ones marries up with the claim that everything is reductively explicable in basic physical terms. Reductive explanations work because, when fully spelled out, we can see that there is *nothing more* to the property being explained than the properties cited in the explanation. The upshot is an elegant and economical picture of the world in which all the complex phenomena around us can ultimately be described and explained in terms of a small number of basic particles and forces. And we can now rephrase the new mind–body problem as that of whether content and feel are exceptions to this elegant picture – whether they are non-physical properties, which are distinct from the underlying basic physical ones and not explicable in terms of them. The view that they are is known as *property dualism*, and it contrasts with *property physicalism*, or just *physicalism* for short.

The problems of content and consciousness have attracted a huge amount of attention from philosophers in recent decades. Of the two, the former is widely felt to be more tractable, and numerous reductive explanations of representational content have been proposed. (One, for example, turns on the notion of *tracking*. The idea is that a cluster of brain cells represents some environmental feature because, under ideal conditions, it is activated only when the feature is present, and thus tracks its presence.) Since there is no space here to consider both topics, we shall therefore focus on consciousness, which is widely felt to pose the major challenge to physicalism.

Property Dualism

One of the best-known arguments for a property dualist view of consciousness runs as follows. If property physicalism is true, then the physical facts are all the facts there are (a physical fact is a fact about physical properties). Thus, if one knew all the physical facts about a creature, one would know all the facts there are to know about it. Yet – the argument goes – this is not so, since the physical facts would not tell one what the creature's experiences were *like*. We might know everything about the neurology of bats, but we would not know what it is like to be a bat, sensing the world by echolocation rather than sight (Nagel 1974). Hence, these facts are not physical ones, and physicalism is false.

The classic statement of this argument is by Frank Jackson, who dubs it the *knowledge argument* (Jackson 1982). Jackson offers the example of Mary, who has been confined since birth to a black-and-white room and has never seen colors. Mary has, however, made a detailed study of the neuroscience of color vision and knows all the physical facts about it, down the very last detail. Yet – Jackson argues – she does not know *everything* about color vision: she does not know what it is *like* to see colors, and would therefore learn something new about color vision if she were to leave her room and experience colors for herself. Hence facts about the phenomenal feel of color experiences are not physical ones.

A large and complex literature has grown up around this argument. There are two broad lines of reply. The first questions the premise that Mary does not know what it is like to see colors. After all, we are still a very long way from knowing *all* the physical facts about color vision. How can we be sure what a person in Mary's situation would and would not know? (In the past many people thought that organic processes such as healing and reproduction could never be understood in purely physical terms.) The second line of reply concedes that Mary would learn something on leaving her room, but denies that she would learn new *facts*. There are various ways of developing this response. One suggestion is that she would merely acquire new *practical* knowledge – abilities to remember, imagine, and recognize color experiences. Another suggestion is that she would simply learn new ways of conceptualizing facts she already knew. When she has color experiences for herself she will acquire new concepts – concepts of the feel of these experiences – which she can apply in introspection. So, for example, she will be able to think that the experience of seeing a banana is "yellowish," where "yellowish" is the concept of the feel of an experience of seeing yellow. Yet it is compatible with this that the properties these concepts refer to are physical ones, and that Mary already knew all the facts about them, under different guises. So, for example, she already knew that banana experiences have the property she now calls *yellowishness*, although she conceptualized this fact differently, using physical concepts. Of course, defenders of the knowledge argument have replies to these responses, and debate about the argument continues.

A second important argument for property dualism is the *zombie argument* (also known as the *conceivability argument*). In outline, it goes like this. We can clearly imagine *zombies* – creatures which are exact replicas of us in all their physical aspects, and which behave exactly like us, but whose experiences have no phenomenal feel to them ("the lights are off inside," as it were). But if phenomenal feels were physical properties, then we should not be able to do this. If we considered the underlying basic physical properties in detail we would see that they were in fact sufficient to confer consciousness, and we would not be able to imagine those properties being present without consciousness. As an analogy, consider a camera. A camera has the property of being able to record visual images. This property is a physical one, which exists in virtue of the shape of the lenses, the chemical composition of the film, and so on, and if we knew enough about those properties we would see that they were sufficient to confer the power to record images. Hence we could not imagine a "zombie camera," which was physically identical to a normal one, but could not record images. If consciousness were physical, the same should go for it.

Again, there are two broad lines of reply, parallel to those for the knowledge argument. The first denies that zombies are clearly imaginable, appealing to similar considerations as before (if we knew all the physical facts about experience, then perhaps we would not find it imaginable that they should hold without consciousness). The second questions whether the imaginability of zombies entails the falsity of physicalism, on the grounds that imagination can mislead us. For example, we can imagine Clark Kent being in the room and Superman not, even though Clark Kent and Superman are one and the same person. Again, defenders of the argument have responses to these criticisms, and a complex and often highly technical literature has built up.

We turn now to some problems for property dualism. First, can the doctrine be reconciled with the naturalistic outlook of science? As we mentioned, science seems on course to develop an elegant picture of the world, in which all phenomena can ultimately be explained in terms of a few fundamental particles and forces. If property dualism is true, must we reject this view and accept that consciousness is not scientifically explicable? (Some people disparagingly refer to property dualists as "mysterians.") In reply, property dualists can argue that their view does not require us to reject our current fundamental science, but merely to *expand* it, recognising new fundamental features and laws. We might treat phenomenal feels themselves as fundamental features of reality, or (as David Chalmers suggests) we might hold that phenomenal feels exist in virtue of more basic "proto-phenomenal" properties, to which they are related in the same way that higher-level physical properties are related to basic physical ones. The new fundamental laws will specify how these phenomenal or proto-phenomenal properties are correlated with basic physical properties. Consciousness will then be explicable in terms of this expanded basic science.

There are precedents for expanding our conception of the fundamental laws and properties in this way; it happened with electromagnetism in the nineteenth century. However, some writers find the dualist's picture inelegant and counterintuitive. They argue that the laws correlating phenomenal or proto-phenomenal properties with basic physical ones would be awkward appendages to the network of basic physical laws – "nomological danglers" as they are sometimes called. ("Nomological" means *relating to laws*.) Moreover, the proposed correlation laws would be unusual ones, linking extremely complex basic physical properties with simple phenomenal feels. Such laws are like no other fundamental laws, and in the words of one writer, they have a queer "smell" to them (Smart 1959: 143).

A second problem for property dualism concerns the *causal role* of consciousness. It seems obvious that the phenomenal feel of a person's experiences can affect their behavior. For example, the excruciating pain of a toothache might cause me to visit the dentist. But on a property dualist view it is not clear that this is correct. For there is strong evidence that all events at the basic physical level – all changes in atoms, molecules, and so on – can be completely explained at that level, in terms of basic physical properties and laws. This is expressed by saying that the basic physical realm is *causally closed*. And if so, then the movements of our bodies can also be explained in basic physical terms, since our bodies are just collections of basic physical particles. Now it does not immediately follow that phenomenal feels have no causal influence. If they are physical properties, then they will possess the same causal powers as the underlying basic physical properties in which they are realized. If, however, they are *not* physical properties, but extra properties over and above the underlying basic physical ones, then it seems they can have no influence within a physical world that is causally closed. If our actions can be completely explained in terms of physical properties alone, then consciousness has no role to play, if it is not physical. (In response, it is sometimes suggested that even if our actions have sufficient physical causes, they might have additional mental causes as well – that they might be *overdetermined*. But even if this were so, we would still never need to appeal to consciousness to *explain* our actions, since they would have occurred anyway, thanks to the physical causes alone.)

This is clearly a serious problem for property dualists. There are three main options open to them. One is simply to accept that phenomenal properties are inert. On this view, consciousness is merely a by-product of brain activity, like the exhaust from an engine, which has no effect on behavior. Such properties are said to be *epiphenomenal*, and the view that phenomenal feels are of this kind is known as *epiphenomenalism*. A second option is to challenge the claim that the basic physical realm is causally closed. Perhaps new causal powers arise in the brains of conscious creatures, which go beyond those of their basic physical components and exert a "downward" influence on the physical world. This view is a form of *emergentism* – the idea that completely new properties and causal powers emerge as matter is organized in increasingly complex ways. The third option involves proposing that phenomenal properties, or rudimentary versions of them, are found at the fundamental level of physical reality, in the basic physical particles themselves – that subatomic particles have a tiny spark of consciousness. This is a version of *panpsychism* – the view that everything has mental properties. It is compatible with basic physics and causal closure, but it also gives consciousness a causal role, since it treats phenomenal, or proto-phenomenal, properties as essential features of the entities mentioned in the causal explanations given by basic physics.

These positions are not easy to defend, however. There is no empirical support for denying causal closure. (Although scientists are far from fully understanding how the brain works, they do understand how brain cells work, what makes them fire, and how their firing affects neighboring cells. And, so far, there is absolutely no evidence of any non-physical interventions in these processes.) And epiphenomenalism and panpsychism are very counterintuitive views. For many philosophers the difficulties here constitute a decisive objection to property dualism.

Physicalist Approaches

We turn now to some physicalist approaches to consciousness. Some writers argue that, although consciousness is physical, we shall never explain it in physical terms. They hold that there is an *explanatory gap* between the physical facts and the facts of consciousness, which we shall never close – perhaps because of the limitations of our minds. Most physicalists, however, hold that a reductive explanation of consciousness is possible. The most popular theories are broadly *representational* in character. That is to say, they attempt to explain the phenomenal feel of experience in terms of the existence of mental states with certain types of representational content. If representational content can itself be reductively explained, then this would give us a reductive explanation of phenomenal consciousness. Of course, providing a reductive explanation of representational content is a big problem in its own right, but, as we mentioned, there are a number of theories of content on the market, and many physicalists feel that reducing the problem of consciousness to one of representation would constitute significant progress.

Representational theories of consciousness divide into two broad kinds. According to those of the first kind, for an experience to have a phenomenal feel is simply for it to have a certain sort of representational content. The theories differ as to the details, but most agree that the relevant sort of content is *non-conceptual*, in that it has a fineness of grain that far outstrips our ability to conceptualize it. (Think, for example, of how many shades of color you can distinguish.) Thus, on this view, to have a conscious experience of a blue circle is simply to have a mental state that represents the presence of a blue circle in a fine-grained, non-conceptual way. (This is not to say that one must actually be perceiving a blue circle; experiences can misrepresent, as in cases of hallucination.) In other words, how an experience *feels* is simply a matter of what it *represents* – the information it carries about the world. Theories of this kind are known as *first-order representational theories*, or FOR theories for short.

A key argument for the FOR view is that when we focus on what our experiences are *like*, we are not aware of any intrinsic features of the experiences themselves, but only of the features of the things in the world they represent. When we focus on what it is like to see a brilliant blue sky, all we are aware of is the blueness of the sky, not any intrinsic features of the experience itself. Our experiences are, as it were, *transparent* (Harman 1990).

Opponents object that many experiences have no representational content at all; they are pure phenomenal feel. Examples often cited are bodily sensations, such as pains, itches, and – to take a slightly risqué example – orgasms. Does a headache represent something? Does an orgasm carry information? FOR theorists respond that these experiences *do* represent something, namely states of our bodies – damage in the case of pains, other kinds of changes in the cases of itches and orgasms. (One FOR theorist describes orgasms as "sensory representations of certain physical changes in the genital region" (Tye 1995: 118).) FOR theorists also allow that these representations typically evoke further reactions in us, such as feelings of distress or pleasure, but they insist that these are distinct from the experience itself and not part of its phenomenal feel. Evidence for this view comes from patients who have had brain surgery to alleviate certain kinds of chronic pain. These patients typically report that they still feel the pain but no longer *mind* it. The experience has the same phenomenal feel but evokes no negative reaction. (The existence of masochism offers further support; experiences which others find disagreeable elicit positive reactions in masochists.)

In response, opponents argue that even if all experiences do have representational content, this does not *exhaust* their subjective character: we are also aware of intrinsic properties of our experiences, in addition to properties of the things they represent. That is to say, experiences are not completely transparent, as FOR theorists claim. There are various arguments here, most involving hypothetical cases where two experiences feel differently while representing the same thing. One much-discussed idea is that two people's visual experiences might be *inverted* with respect to each other, so that, for example, yellow things produce in one the experience that blue things produce in the other, and vice versa. Such inverted experiences, it is argued, would still have the same representational content, since they would indicate the presence of the same color in the environment. (Experiences produced by bananas would all represent yellowness, even if they did not all have the same phenomenal feel.) If this is right, then it would show that phenomenal feel is not simply a matter of representational content. Again FOR theorists have replies, and there is a large literature here, which is intertwined with debates about the nature of representational content itself. This debate over the transparency of experience is a key one in the literature on consciousness.

We turn now to the second group of representational theories, which introduce a further element. In order for an experience to have a phenomenal feel, they claim, it must *itself* be represented within the mind. That is, it must be accompanied by a further thought *about* it or an experience *of* it, or, at least, must be *available* to processes that can generate a thought about it. Without this accompaniment, the experience will be non-conscious, lacking any phenomenal feel. (Think, for example, of what it is like to move your legs when you walk. There is a feeling to this, which you notice if you pay attention to it, but which is normally not conscious.) Thus, on this view, having a conscious experience of a blue circle involves *two* representational states – one representing the presence of a blue circle and another representing the presence of this experience of a blue circle. The latter is said to be a *higher-order representation* – a representation of a representation – and theories of this kind are known as *higher-order representational theories*, or HOR theories for short.

Several versions of HOR theory have been proposed. The main point of disagreement between them concerns the nature of the higher-order representations involved. According to some theories, these are perceptual in character: we have an internal scanning mechanism, which generates perceptions of our own experiences. Theories of this kind are known as *higher-order perception*, or HOP, theories. According to other theories, the higher-order representations are thoughts; an experience becomes conscious when we have a thought about it. (This thought need not itself be a conscious one; one can have a conscious experience without consciously thinking about it. The higher-order thought involved will be conscious only if it is accompanied by a further thought about *it*.) Theories of this kind are known as *higher-order thought*, or HOT, theories.

One problem for HOR theories is that if every aspect of our experience has to be re-represented in order for it to be conscious, then there will be a massive and wasteful reduplication of mental representation, which seems implausible. Some HOT theorists respond that we need not actually form a higher-order thought about an experience in order for it to be conscious, and that it is enough simply to be *disposed* to form one. It is unclear, however, whether a mere disposition could confer an *actual* phenomenal feel. A second problem concerns infants and non-human animals. We assume that infants and many animals have conscious experiences similar to ours. But according to HOT theory, consciousness involves having thoughts about one's own mental states, and this requires possession of psychological concepts, such as that of *experience*. HOP theory also seems to require this, at least if higher-order perceptions feed into higher-order thinking (Carruthers 2000). And it is unlikely that infants and animals meet this condition. There is evidence that children do not develop mental-state concepts until around the age of three, and, with the possible exception of some primates, animals do not appear to possess them either. But if so, then infants and most animals will not possess the resources required for higher-order mental representations, and will, consequently, lack conscious experiences. HOR theorists differ as to whether they should accept this conclusion.

We turn finally to the much-discussed "multiple drafts" (or "fame-in-the-brain") model of consciousness developed by Daniel Dennett. Dennett claims that most theories of con-sciousness, including physicalist ones, implicitly assume that there is a "headquarters" in the brain where information from the different senses is assembled and presented for conscious awareness – a bit like a show on an interior stage. (Dennett dubs this venue the *Cartesian Theater*, since he regards it as a hangover from substance dualism.) Dennett concedes that this view is tempting, but argues that it is both ill-conceived (who is supposed to be watching the inner show?) and contradicted by empirical evidence (neuroanatomy reveals no structure to which all sensory information is routed). Dennett's own view is that there is no single canonical version of experience, but, rather, multiple versions in existence at any one time, like different drafts of an academic essay, each subject to continual editing and revision. Experiences become conscious, not by being displayed on an inner stage, but by achieving a sufficient level of influence within the brain, and in particular, by becoming available to be reported in speech. (Dennett speaks of consciousness as the neural equivalent of *fame* or *political clout*.)

This view has affinities with HOR approaches, in that it identifies conscious experiences with ones that have certain effects on other mental states. However, Dennett's approach has a more radical edge, since he denies the existence of phenomenal feels in the traditional sense. "When you discard Cartesian dualism," he writes, "you really must discard the show that would have gone on in the Cartesian Theater" (Dennett 1991: 134). When we talk about what an experience is like, Dennett argues, we are not referring to some introspectable property of it, but simply to the reactions it evokes in us – its effects on speech, memory, perceptual expectations, emotional state, and other behavioral dispositions. Dennett uses various hypothetical scenarios to motivate this view. One involves two coffee tasters, Chase and Sanborn, whose job is to ensure the consistency of taste of a certain brand of coffee (Dennett 1988). They both agree that, although the coffee itself has not changed, they no longer enjoy their job. They have different explanations for this, however. According to Chase, the coffee produces the same taste experience as always, but he no longer *likes* that experience. According to Sanborn, something has gone wrong with his taste perception mechanisms, and the coffee no longer produces the same taste experience in him. Now, if there were a Cartesian Theater, then these explanations would be clear-cut alternatives, the former corresponding to a change after presentation of the taste in the Theater, the latter to one before it. However, Dennett suggests that the situation is not so simple. We might be able to decide between the explanations in extreme cases; for example, if Chase cannot correctly re-identify other drinks on blind tests, then we shall doubt his explanation. But, Dennett argues, there will always be gray areas where it is impossible even in principle to decide whether the change involves a difference in taste or in the person's reactions to it. We just cannot separate out the taste from our reactions to it in the way that Chase and Sanborn assume. The taste of the coffee is *constituted* by the reactions the coffee triggers in us, and if these have changed, then the taste has changed.

On Dennett's view, then, when we talk about what our experiences are like, we are not referring to some mysterious mental ingredient, presented to us in a private inner realm;

rather, we are referring simply to the activities of our sensory systems and their complex effects on memory, emotion, and behavior. Thus it is not possible for the subjective character of our experiences to vary without some physical change, and zombies and color inversion are not conceivable after all, despite our intuitions. This view, which denies that experiences are introspectable inner objects, has affinities with the behaviorist perspective described earlier. Opponents accuse Dennett of denying that consciousness exists, but he would say that he is merely rejecting a deeply misguided conception of it.

Conclusion: A Matter of Perspective?

Where one ends up on the mind–body problem is to some extent determined by where one starts. If one starts with a first-person perspective, focusing on what it is like, subjectively, to have a mind, then mental phenomena can seem deeply puzzling and resistant to explanation in physical terms. If one starts from a third-person perspective, on the other hand, viewing human beings as complex natural phenomena, then one will probably adopt a physicalist approach, and may be tempted to agree with Dennett in denying the existence of introspectable phenomenal feels. Many philosophers hope to reconcile these perspectives by developing a theory which explains the introspective data in physical terms. FOR and HOR theories can be seen as examples of this. But it may be that the two perspectives cannot be harmonized, and that we shall simply have to make a choice between them. Either way, the debates are fascinating ones, and the questions raised go to the heart of our conception of ourselves and our place in the universe.

Further Reading

We shall start with some recommendations for general works. There are numerous good introductions to philosophy of mind on the market. We suggest beginning with Ravenscroft (2005) or Heil (2004). Smith and Jones (1986) is also excellent. Crane (2003) is a good introduction to the computer model of mind and the problem of mental representation. Frankish (2005) expands on the themes of this chapter and includes edited readings from key texts. The opening chapters of Chalmers (1996), Dennett (1991), and Tye (1995) also provide useful introductions to consciousness, though each reflects its author's own theoretical perspective. A good reference work on philosophy of mind is Guttenplan (1994), which contains substantial entries on key topics and a lengthy introduction. Numerous anthologies of readings in philosophy of mind are available; we recommend Chalmers (2002a) or Lycan and Prinz (2008). Block et al. (1997) is a valuable collection of articles on consciousness, covering most of the topics discussed in this chapter. There is also useful material available on the internet. In particular, we recommend the online *Stanford Encyclopedia of Philosophy*, which is at http://plato.stanford.edu/. (Searching the encyclopedia for "consciousness" throws up a number of excellent articles by leading researchers.) We should also mention David Chalmers's website, currently located at http://consc.net/chalmers/, which contains a wealth of material related to the mind and consciousness.

We turn now to readings on specific topics. Descartes' arguments for substance dualism can be found in his *Mediations*, nos. II and VI, first published in Latin in 1641. The standard modern English edition is Descartes (1986). Kenny (1968) offers a good introduction to Descartes. For classic statements of philosophical behaviorism and identity theory respectively, see Ryle (1949) and Armstrong (1968). The most influential contemporary advocate of property dualism is David Chalmers. See his (1995) for a quick introduction and his (1996) for the full story, including a presentation of the zombie argument. (The latter work is difficult in places, but Chalmers helpfully highlights the more technical sections, so that first-time readers can skip them.) The knowledge argument is set out in Jackson (1982); see also Nagel (1974). Van Gulick (1997) provides a useful summary of responses to the argument, and Ludlow et al. (2004) collects important papers from the debate. Chapters 2 and 3 of Papineau (2002) contain clearly written physicalist responses to the arguments for property dualism, and the appendix to the book offers an excellent account of the reasons for thinking that the physical realm is casually closed. For a property dualist approach to the science of consciousness, see Chalmers (2004), and for property dualist positions on the causal role of consciousness, see ch. 4 of Chalmers (1996) and Chalmers (2002b). Emergentism is defended in Broad (1925), and panpsychism in Strawson et al. (2006), which also contains replies by various authors.

Arguments for the view that we shall never explain consciousness, even if it is physical, are set out in Levine (1993) and McGinn (1999). For some versions of FOR theory, see Dretske (1995) and Tye (1995), and for criticism of the FOR approach see chapter 6 of Carruthers (2000). Versions of HOR theory are defended in Carruthers (2000), Lycan (1996), and Rosenthal (2002) and (2005). Gennaro (2004) is a collection of essays on HOR theory by both defenders and critics. If you want to explore Dennett's view in more detail, the best place to start is with his lively and engaging (1991). For critical responses, see the symposium in *Philosophy and Phenomenological Research* (1993), 53, 889–931). Dennett revises and develops his views in his (2005).

Finally, if you are interested in setting philosophical discussion of consciousness within a scientific context, we recommend Blackmore (2003), which is a lively interdisciplinary textbook on the neurology, psychology, and philosophy of consciousness.

Note

This chapter draws in part on material from the first author's book *Consciousness* (Open University, 2005), which is part of the course material for the Open University course AA308 *Thought and Experience: Themes in the Philosophy of Mind*. The authors thank The Open University for permission to use this material.

References

Armstrong, D. M. (1968). *A Materialist Theory of Mind*, London: Routledge.
Blackmore, S. (2003). *Consciousness: An Introduction*, London: Hodder & Stoughton.
Block, N., Flanagan, O., and Güzeldere, G. (eds.) (1997). *The Nature of Consciousness: Philosophical Debates*, Cambridge, MA: MIT Press.
Broad, C. D. (1925). *The Mind and Its Place in Nature*, London: Kegan Paul & Co.
Carruthers, P. (2000). *Phenomenal Consciousness: A Naturalistic Theory*, Cambridge: Cambridge University Press.

Chalmers, D. J. (1995). "Facing Up to the Problem of Consciousness," *Journal of Consciousness Studies*, 2, 200–19.

Chalmers, D. J. (1996). *The Conscious Mind: In Search of a Fundamental Theory*, New York: Oxford University Press.

Chalmers, D. J. (ed.) (2002a). *Philosophy of Mind: Classic and Contemporary Readings*, Oxford: Oxford University Press.

Chalmers, D. J. (2002b). "Consciousness and Its Place in Nature," in D. J. Chalmers (ed.), *Philosophy of Mind: Classical and Contemporary Readings*, New York: Oxford University Press, 247–72.

Chalmers, D. J. (2004). "How Can We Construct a Science of Consciousness?" in M. S. Gazzaniga (ed.), *The Cognitive Neurosciences*, 3rd edn., Cambridge, MA: MIT Press, 1111–19.

Crane, T. (2003). *The Mechanical Mind*, 2nd edn., London: Routledge.

Dennett, D. C. (1988). "Quining Qualia," in A. J. Marcel and E. Bisiach (eds.), *Consciousness in Contemporary Science*, Oxford: Oxford University Press, 42–77.

Dennett, D. C. (1991). *Consciousness Explained*. Boston: Little Brown and Co.

Dennett, D. C. (2005). *Sweet Dreams: Philosophical Obstacles to a Science of Consciousness*, Cambridge, MA: MIT Press.

Descartes, R. (1986). *Meditations on First Philosophy: With Selections from the Objections and Replies*, tr. J. Cottingham, Cambridge: Cambridge University Press.

Dretske, F. (1995). *Naturalizing the Mind*, Cambridge, MA: MIT Press.

Frankish, K. (2005). *Consciousness*, Milton Keynes: Open University.

Gennaro, R. J. (2004). *Higher-order Theories of Consciousness: An Anthology*, Amsterdam: John Benjamins.

Guttenplan, S. (ed.) (1994). *A Companion to the Philosophy of Mind*, Oxford: Blackwell.

Harman, G. (1990). "The Intrinsic Quality of Experience," in J. Tomberlin (ed.), *Philosophical Perspectives*, vol. 4, Northridge, CA: Ridgeview, 31–52.

Heil, J. (2004). *Philosophy of Mind: A Contemporary Introduction*, London: Routledge.

Jackson, F. (1982). "Epiphenomenal Qualia," *Philosophical Quarterly*, 32, 127–36.

Kenny, A. (1968). *Descartes: A Study of his Philosophy*, New York: Random House.

Kripke, S. (1980). *Naming and Necessity*, Oxford: Blackwell.

Levine, J. (1993). "On Leaving Out What It's Like," in M. Davies and G. Humphreys, W. (eds.), *Consciousness: Psychological and Philosophical Essays*, Oxford: Blackwell, 121–36.

Ludlow, P., Nagasawa, Y., and Stoljar, D. (eds.) (2004). *There's Something About Mary: Essays on Phenomenal Consciousness and Frank Jackson's Knowledge Argument*, Cambridge, MA: MIT Press.

Lycan, W. G. (1996). *Consciousness and Experience*, Cambridge, MA: MIT Press.

Lycan, W. G. and Prinz, J. (eds.) (2008). *Mind and Cognition: An Anthology*, 3rd edn., Oxford: Blackwell.

McGinn, C. (1989). "Can We Solve the Mind–Body Problem?" *Mind*, 98, 349–66.

McGinn, C. (1999). *The Mysterious Flame: Conscious Minds in a Material World*, New York: Basic Books.

Nagel, T. (1974). "What Is It Like to Be a Bat?" *Philosophical Review*, 83, 435–50.

Papineau, D. (2002). *Thinking about Consciousness*, Oxford: Oxford University Press.

Ravenscroft, I. (2005). *Philosophy of Mind: A Beginner's Guide*, Oxford: Oxford University Press.

Rosenthal, D. M. (2002). "Explaining Consciousness," in D. J. Chalmers (ed.), *Philosophy of Mind: Classical and Contemporary Readings*, New York: Oxford University Press, 406–21.

Rosenthal, D. M. (2005). *Consciousness and Mind*, Oxford: Oxford University Press.

Ryle, G. (1949). *The Concept of Mind*, London: Hutchinson.
Smart, J. J. C. (1959). "Sensations and Brain Processes," *Philosophical Review*, 68, 141–56.
Smith, P. and Jones, O. R. (1986). *The Philosophy of Mind: An Introduction*, Cambridge: Cambridge University Press.
Strawson, G. et al. (2006). *Consciousness and its Place in Nature: Does Physicalism Entail Panpsychism?*, Exeter: Imprint Academic.
Tye, M. (1995). *Ten Problems of Consciousness: A Representational Theory of the Phenomenal Mind*, Cambridge, MA: MIT Press.
Van Gulick, R. (1997). "Understanding the Phenomenal Mind: Are We All Just Armadillos? Part I: Phenomenal Knowledge and Explanatory Gaps," in N. Block, O. Flanagan, and G. Güzeldere (eds.), *The Nature of Consciousness: Philosophical Debates*, Cambridge, MA: MIT Press, 559–66.

9

The Self and Personal Identity

Paul Snowdon

Selves and Persons

Philosophers are described, and describe themselves, as offering theories of *the self* and of *personal identity*. It can be asked: what are such theories about? We need to pick out the objects that such questions concern so that we can at least try to test the theories. We can begin by dividing what is in the world in to three broad categories.[1] The broadest category is that of what we might call *purely* physical things, Examples are the tree at the end of your garden, the air, the earth – and so on. We might say that this category is the category of things with physical properties and which, considered in themselves, have no psychological properties at all.[2] Within this category there is massive variation in size, from the very small, individual subatomic particles, to the very large, an object like the sun. In this group, as I mean it, will fall inanimate objects and also plants, and simpler organisms. The second, much smaller category, comprises objects which of course have physical properties, such as shape, size and weight, but which also have what we would recognize as psychological features, such as perceptual capacities, plus broad, and also environmentally directed, goals and a capacity to act, but which lack the advanced psychological capacities that we, typical humans, possess. Examples falling in this category are dogs, cats, and other middle sized and large animals. Finally, there is the even smaller category of creatures like *us*. We have (or seem to have) physical properties, and we share the basic psychological capacities possessed by ordinary animals, but we also, at least characteristically, posses an array of considerably more advanced psychological capacities – including the ability to think, imagine, reason, remember, develop theories and solve intellectual problems. We can think about individual objects in our environment, and determine what kind of objects they are. In particular we can think, in a variety of ways, about *ourselves*, and we recognize ourselves as creatures with that very capacity, the capacity, as we might say, for self-knowledge. It is helpful to have an abbreviated way of expressing this vague and vaguely specified battery of advanced psychological capacities. I shall simply call these advanced powers – self-consciousness. We can now say that when philosophers discuss the topic of the self and of personal identity they are theorizing about aspects of *self-conscious entities*.[3]

Although it might be premature, given the imprecision of the conditions that the term "self-conscious" picks out, there is a temptation to select a noun to stand for things which are self-conscious. Some philosophers use the term "self" and so would formulate questions as about the nature of *a self* or of *selves*. Others employ the term "person." I shall at this stage use both nouns interchangeably.

There are three aspects of these nouns worth noting immediately. The first is that as initially introduced they apply, not to some special or perhaps strange type of object which is part of us (as, perhaps, sometimes it is assumed the word "self" does) but rather to *us*, as one might say, as whole complex things. You are a self, just as you are a person.[4] (This contrasts with the term "mind"; you are *not* a mind, rather you *have* a mind. Mind-talk is thus talk about some restricted aspects of you.) Second, since you are a self and a person, we can say that the thing that you pick out when you use the word "I" *is* the self or person that you are. Hence the question – what is a self or person? – can be formulated by you in these words: what sort of thing am I? what nature do I have? Third, the way I have introduced or explained these nouns it is not being assumed at all that, as one might put it, these nouns express or pick out what we fundamentally or basically are. Consider this analogy. The noun phrase "students of philosophy" applies to you and to me; that complex noun expresses some condition that we fall under, which is to say that we all *are* students of philosophy. But even though you are a student of philosophy if someone were to ask – what sort of thing are you fundamentally? – I would not say – "a student of philosophy" – but would rather say – perhaps – a human being. This is surely linked to the fact that you could cease to be a student of philosophy, while undoubtedly remaining in existence. It can, therefore, hardly amount to what you *fundamentally* are. So, although it is agreed that we are selves and persons as those terms have been interpreted, that does not mean that we should say that what we fundamentally are is a self or a person. Maybe we are fundamentally a different sort of thing which given the way we have developed amount to selves or persons. The introduction and application to us of these nouns does not settle the question as to what we are, or what nature we fundamentally have.

This leads to a question: when philosophers raise issues about selves or about what they call personal identity, are they raising questions about *us*, about ourselves, the things which happen to be selves and persons, or are they raising questions about us only in so far as we qualify as selves and persons, or perhaps, as one might say, about the class of selves and persons? This is an important question, but it would stall proceedings too much if I discuss it here. Rather, I shall dogmatically affirm what I think the correct answer is, which is that they are raising questions about *us*, about the nature we fundamentally have. The reason for saying that is that philosophers express their answers in claims about themselves, and also argue about the truth of claims about selves (and persons) by considering whether the claims apply to themselves.

Some Questions

If we are interested in determining the nature of a type of object, in this case the type of object that *we* are, what kind of questions need asking? I want to focus on two very basic questions. First, for any sort of thing, one question relevant to settling its nature would be to ask: what do such objects *consist of*? What are the elements that *make up* the object? The form in which this question is usually pursued in connexion with selves starts from the assumption that each of us has a body, a body that is intimately related to him or her. Granting that assumption the fundamental question is: are there parts to me other than my body? I call that question – *the self–body problem*. But a second fundamental question to ask when attempting to characterize the nature of an entity is what is required or essentially involved in a thing of its sort *existing over time*. This type of problem is what the problem of *personal identity* deals with: what is required for things of the type we are to persist? An aspect of the division is that the second question relates to existence *over time*, (sometimes called a diachronic question) whereas the first relates to what parts or constituents the object has *at any time* (sometimes called a synchronic question). It would not, of course, be correct to draw a sharp line between these two questions. There must be some connection between what a self consists in, what it is made of, and what is required for it to remain in existence over time. However, it helps to divide the debate into two main questions.

Philosophers have also asked a third question about selves: can anything informative and interesting be said about the conditions for being a person or self? For example, *must* a person or self be a *physical* thing? Are there limits to what types of *experience* something must have if it is a person or self? There are interesting and debated questions here, but I shall restrict myself to the first two.[5]

The Self–Body Problem

Let us take a particular case; call the person or self (one of us) P, and call the body of P B. We can ask: how is P related to B? The fundamental question is: are there any parts of P which are not parts of B? There are a number of possible ways to think about the relation between the parts of B and the parts of P, but I want to present the debate, initially at least, as between two views. The first says that no parts of B are parts of P. The second says that there are no parts of P other than parts of B, and, moreover, each part of B is a part of P. The first view in effect identifies P, the self or person, with something distinct from P's body. The second view holds that B is all there is to P. (There are, of course, other possible views, but I shall ignore them in this introduction.)

According to the first view, which has seemed right to many philosophers and has received assent in various religious traditions, P and B are distinct things. Nothing that is part of my body is part of me. The most famous version of such a view is that espoused by Descartes. His view is called Cartesian Dualism, in recognition of its postulation of a *duality* of basic entities; there are bodies (physical objects) and also things of the sort that a person or self is. Descartes' view is that that the self is a non-physical object (or substance), which being non-physical is not spatially located. In religious language, such items are called "souls."

Are there any reasons for thinking that this dualist view is correct? Now, it is clear that an argument can support dualism only if it at least supports the weaker claim that P and B are *not* identical. So I want to ask the following question: does Descartes give us any reason for thinking that P and B are not identical?

Philosophy is full of arguments purporting to show that an object x and an object y are not the self-same thing. Such arguments work by trying to locate some property P which it can be agreed that x has but that y does not. If such a property can be found then it seems that x and y cannot be the self same thing, since there is some difference between them. The philosopher Leibniz formulated the general principle that we are relying on here; if x and y are the single self-same thing (are identical) then there cannot be any difference between them. This is sometimes called Leibniz's Law. I assume that it is correct. Did Descartes locate any genuine property differences between P and B?

One argument that it is sometimes said that Descartes employed springs from the fact that at a certain stage in his inquiry he is sure that he exists but is not sure that his body exists. (He has not yet found a convincing reason to think that he has a body). In that context he might be read as arguing as follows:

1   It is certain that I (P) exist.
2   It is not certain that my body (B) exists.

Therefore,

3   It is not the case that I (P) am identical to my body (B).

The assumption in this argument is that the words "it is certain that . . . exists" expresses a property of me but something that is not a property of my body (B). There is, therefore, a difference between them.

It is more or less universally agreed that, if Descartes does advance such an argument, the argument is not valid. Consider the following well known parallel case. Looking at an Australian bank being robbed by the man in the iron mask I can think:

4   It is certain that the man in the iron mask is that man.

But since I did not know who he was I could also think:

5   It is not certain that Ned Kelly is that man.

Given those claims could I legitimately conclude that the man in the iron mask is not Ned Kelly? It is obvious that I could not conclude that, since, in fact, he was Ned Kelly. Why did that conclusion not follow? The simplest answer is that "its being certain that . . . is that man" does not represent a property that the object Ned Kelly lacks but the man in the iron mask possesses; rather, it is that I accept the claim that the man in the iron mask is here, but I do not accept the claim that Ned Kelly is here; my difference with regard to these claims is not a difference between New Kelly and the man in the iron mask. In celebration of this obvious mistake such inferences are described as committing the Masked Man Fallacy. Returning to Descartes' supposed argument, we can see that the difference between (1) and (2) above does not represent a difference between me and my body. It is, rather, a difference between my attitude to a claim explicitly about myself and the same claim explicitly about my body.

Descartes has a second argument (presented in the 6th Meditation). The conclusion that P is not identical to B is supposed to follow from two alleged contrasts between P and B. The two contrasts are:

1   P is essentially a thinking thing, whereas,
2   B is not essentially a thinking thing.

Further,

3   B is an essentially extended thing, whereas,
4   P is not an essentially extended thing.

What do these claims, which employ the notion of "essential" features, mean? The definition of "x is essentially F" is – necessarily, if x exists then x is F. An essential property of an individual is one that that individual had to have (assuming that it existed at all). It seems that this notion is one which is entirely commonsensical. For example, it is hard to suppose that my tie might under any circumstances have been a prime number. (How could it have been?) If that is impossible, then my tie is *essentially not a prime number*. On the other hand, my tie might have belonged to someone else; so it is *not essentially mine*, although it does happen to be mine. Although the term "essential property" is technical there seems nothing arcane about the idea of essential properties. Leaving aside, for the moment, whether the premises are true, should we count the argument as valid and not fallacious? Opinions might differ here, but on the face of it whether an object is essentially F or not is a matter of the way that object is, and does not depend on how the object is described. If so, then if an object x is essentially F and object y is not essentially F, then x and y are not one and the same.

The question, then, is whether Descartes has good reason to contrast the essential properties of P and B. Interestingly, the claims about B seem plausible. In order for B to exist it has to occupy space, and it seems that B is not essentially a thinking thing. Some might say that B is not the sort of thing to think at all; however, if we allow that B might think it hardly seems that in order to exist it must think. So, Descartes is right in these two claims about B. In contrast the two claims about himself (about P) are questionable. Why does Descartes think that thinking is an essential property of himself? It seems obvious that there are periods when Descartes does not think, say when he is knocked out or deeply asleep. But it certainly also seems plausible to think that Descartes could have been born so damaged that he did not think at all. So claim (1) above is one we can reject. Claim (4) denies that Descartes has the essential property of being extended. How did Descartes know this, prior to determining his relation to his body? Descartes' reasoning seems to have been that he could clearly think about himself and there is nothing that suggests to him that he must have a body. But as his contemporary Arnauld pointed out, this is hardly convincing. He gives the example of right-angled triangles which prior to Pythagoras had been easily thought of by many without them realizing that Pythagoras' theorem applies to them. Such triangles are necessarily Pythagorean, but no one had recognized this or suspected it before. How does Descartes know that we are not essentially embodied, even though nothing suggests to him that we are? The problem with Descartes' main argument is that the claims about himself, and hence subjects in general, are not properly supported.

Descartes has a third argument worth considering. He presents the argument in his book *The Discourse on Method*, part 5. We can represent the argument as resting on the following premises:

1   I can do F,
2   No thing which has no parts beyond bodily parts can do F, therefore,
3   I am not identical with my body.

The logic of this argument seems impeccable; the question is, again, whether all the premises are true. The values for F for which Descartes thinks the two premises are true are engaging in and understanding conversation and solving problems in general. It is clear that we can understand conversation and solve problems, though we cannot give any very precise statement of what we are capable of in these respects. I am certainly not able to solve every problem, nor to understand every conversation. But it is much more significant to ask why Descartes thought that (2) is true. How, we might say, does Descartes know what bodies are capable of? In so far as Descartes reveals his thinking it seems that he was guided by a sense of what the latest technology indicated matter was capable of. This technology included clocks and moving models of animals. Scrutinizing such objects might indicate that matter is not capable of much, but the obvious question should have been – why suppose that such physical objects are the ones to reveal what matter is capable of? A rather more plausible line of thought than Descartes' would be that we are capable of solving problems etc., and we seem to be coextensive with our bodies, so some bits of matter have very advanced capabilities. This line of thought is in effect a proof of the existence of that extraordinary matter called the central nervous system.

It has been assumed that selves or persons have bodies, but the question has been whether there is any reason to posit any parts to selves other than their bodies. There will be such reasons only if there are reasons to think that the self is not identical to the body of that self. I have just argued that Descartes gives us no reason to think each of us is not identical to his or her body. Are there, though, reasons on the other side to think that we cannot be identical to something distinct from our bodies? The reasons that have been offered by philosophers can be divided into two classes. One sort alleges that there is something incoherent about the theory. The second sort allows that the dualist theory makes sense, but claim that it exhibits other bad features.

I want initially to sketch two alleged problems of the first sort with the dualist approach. The first is the problem of causal interaction. On any plausible view, according to which selves both control their bodies (and act with them) but are also affected by bodily occurrences (for example, they feel pain as a result of bodily injury), there is causal interaction between B and P. Since, however, P has, according to dualism, no physical parts (and so no physical nature) it seems hard to understand how there can be this interaction. Now, it is clear that this argument homes in on an implication of dualism that is in need of investigation, but it is far less clear that there are any principles about causation which rule out in advance the very possibility of such interaction. It is not enough to point out that it is unlike all other known cases of causal interaction, for novel cases might be possible.

The second objection, which I shall call the Individuation Objection, rests on two premises. The first is that if we are to understand the dualist approach then we need to understand talk of non-physical selves as objects or entities, which requires attaching sense to the idea that they can continue to exist over time, and so attaching sense to the distinction between a single enduring self and two selves which exist in succession. It also involves attaching sense to the possibility of there being two distinct selves which are qualitatively the same. The second premise claims that given the non-physical nature of such postulated selves no such understanding is available. Why, though, is that claim correct? Two points are made. The first is that we have no conception of how to tell what is the case with non-physical selves. Is there, for example, a single enduring self or two in rapid succession? We cannot tell. Second, it is pointed out that our understanding of such possibilities with, for example, chairs or suitcases, depends essentially on the idea of space occupation. Thus, there is sense in the idea of two qualitatively identical suitcases because they can occupy different spaces. This spatial understanding is not available with non-physical selves. However, neither of these points is a secure basis for alleging an incoherence. The impossibility of knowing which possibility has occurred does not mean that we cannot attach sense to the distinction. It also does not show any unintelligibility that the grounds for understanding a contrast in one case are not available in another. Maybe other grounds are available, or, maybe, the conjecture is simply primitively intelligible.

These objections were supposed to be ones that are, in a sense, regarded as *a priori*. Another style of objection alleges no *a priori* failings in dualism but points out that by postulating that each of us consists of something other than our bodies, while still holding that we have bodies, is ontologically more complex than holding that we consist of our bodies, and being ontologically more complex it should only be accepted if there are decisive reasons to bring in such entities. So far we have found no such decisive reasons. This style of objection appeals to what is sometimes called Ockham's razor, which says that we should postulate a more complex structure of entities in our theories only if there are explanatory benefits from so doing. This style of argument has been justly popular recently.

Another type of argument worth sketching here which can be treated as trying to show that no part of B is a part of P, derives from Hume. He is credited with proposing the so-called bundle theory of the self, according to which the self consists of the sequence (or bundle) of experiences that that subject enjoys. Since events of experiencing are not parts of the body, if this claim is correct the subject shares no parts with his or her body. Why, though, does Hume think the bundle proposal is correct? In a very famous passage Hume says;

"For my part, when I enter most intimately into what I call *myself*, I always stumble on some particular perception or other . . . I can never catch myself at any time without a perception, and can never observe anything but that perception. When my perceptions are removed for any time, as by sound sleep: so long am I insensible of myself, and may truly be said not to exist."[6]

Despite its fame and influence, this passage is not very convincing. First, it would be a serious mistake to infer that the subject consists of whatever is required for the subject to be aware of him or herself. Let us agree that a subject cannot be aware of themselves unless the subject is having experiences. It hardly follows that the subject *is* the experiences. That is like arguing: I can only see these atoms if there is a microscope, so these atoms are microscopes. Second, Hume misdescribes what he finds in experience. When he, for example, looks in a mirror he sees himself, the very thing he is. Why should we accept the he only observe his experiences, rather than himself? Third, Hume asserts, as if we should agree, that if he has no perceptions then he may truly be said not to exist. This hardly seems true at all; our conception of ourselves is of things which continue in states of total unconsciousness. The invitation to believe the bundle theory is not attractive.

We have so far, then, found no reason to think that there are any parts of P other than parts of B. Is it correct to infer that, probably, P and B are one and the same thing, are, that is, identical? The answer, I believe, is "no." To see how this inference might be mistaken we need to consider a puzzling case which has been of central focus in recent metaphysics. Consider a statue of Einstein that I made a few days ago. Let us call that statue SE (short for statue of Einstein). To make the statue I took a piece of clay (call it C) and shaped it.

At the moment we have SE and C. What is the relation between those objects? We do not initially have a sense that they are not identical, but as we think about them we seem to view them differently. Thus, we can say that SE was created at t, whereas C was created much earlier. We also accept that I can destroy SE without destroying C. As we think about them we seem to credit SE and C with different life histories. But this does create problem for thinking of them as the self-same item. There seem to be differences. If we do conclude that C is not identical to SE we would not think that there is more to SE than C.[7] As we might say; SE just consists of C. A popular way to express this relation is to say that C constitutes SR.[8] For all the arguments so far considered, then, it may be that B constitutes P, without being identical to P.

This issue is completely unsettled but cannot be taken any further here. It is necessary to introduce the debate about selves (or persons) over time.

Personal Identity

Things of our sort are not, characteristically, short lived. We persist over time (often at least three score years and ten) and so have histories. The question is: can we say in an informative way what is both essential and sufficient for our persistence? The way to think of this problem is that it involves three aspects in its formulation. The first element is the idea of possible ways that the world might develop. Suppose that P is standing in a field. One thing that might happen is that a bomb lands next to P and P's body disintegrates. Another possibility is that the bomb lands but does not explode, and P remains standing. These are just some of the possible ways the world can develop. But the second idea is that some ways constitute P's remaining in existence, whereas others constitute P's going out of existence. As envisaged, the first development presumably amounts to the ceasing to exist of P, whereas the second possibility amounts to the remaining in existence of P. The third element is the goal of specifying in an informative way which possibilities carry a creature like P with them and those which do not. For this to be informative the idea is to specify the possibilities in a way which does not pick them out in terms of the verdict. We can, obviously, say that the possibilities in which P survives are the ones which constitute P's remaining in existence. Can we say, though, in an informative way which they are?[9]

The aim is to specify what is essential for the survival of people or selves. How can we work that out? The problem is that in the real cases we encounter in which a person recognisably survives over time there may well be elements which are not *strictly* needed for the person to survive. Further, there may be ways for persons to survive which are quite unlike anything that actually occurs. The usual response is to assume that we have an understanding of what is essential to survival which we can access by being asked to consider and give verdicts on imaginary cases in which various elements which are standardly present are excluded and which may be quite unlike ordinary cases. Imagining such cases and making judgments about them is called engaging in *thought experiments*. Now, it may be that our ability to think about ourselves and keep track of ourselves over time does not reflect a degree or level of understanding that enables us to advance reliable verdicts about such imaginary cases. If it does not, we need another route into the essence of personal survival. I shall, however, develop the problem in the standard way to begin with.

Faced with this problem three main directions of solution have traditionally been proposed and explored.[10] The first of these options is known as the bodily theory. The simple idea is that any self or person has a body, which of course develops over time. We have, surely, an agreed understanding of what it is for a body to remain in existence over time. The theory proposes that a person P will remain in existence as long as that object which is P's body remains in existence. The idea is that the person or self is tied of necessity to that body, and, further, that no more is needed for the person to survive than for that body to survive.

Such a theory seems plausible because, in brief, in the world as we know it, the principle seems to generate only true and acceptable implications. For example, the adult in front of you is the child you saw nearly twenty years ago if and only if the body in front of you is the same body as that you saw nearly twenty years ago. The proposal assumes, surely correctly, that we agree that a single body can grow and develop over time, so that its being the same body does not require that it now looks as it did. We have an agreed understanding of bodily continuity that the theory presupposes. Further, there is something plausible to the thought that the survival of the person does not require more. Thus, a person's character can change radically, so can their attitudes and mental powers.

In discussions of personal identity this approach has not been popular. Why should that be so? Putting it generally there are two types of reasons. John Locke's discussion of personal identity in the seventeenth century brilliantly pioneered such arguments, and as we shall see, he developed a different theory in the light of them. The first type of reason is that when applying the method of thought experiments, there seem to be imaginary but in principle possible cases where the best verdict is that the person and the body come apart. We can divide such examples into two main cases. One sort is where supposedly we start with a person and linked body but things so develop that the body remains but the person does not. We can call these *(B and not P)* cases. The other sort is where supposedly things develop so that the person or self remains but the body does not. Call those *(P and not B)* cases. The claim is, then, that thought experiments reveal the possibility of a double dissociation between the person and the body. Now, there are many suggested examples of both sorts, but I can sketch only a very few.

Here are two candidate *(B and not P)* cases. (1) A person P suffers a terrible car accident in which P's brain is so badly damaged that there is no chance of the return of consciousness, and *a fortiori* no chance of the return of any more advanced mental functioning. P's body is obviously still there. What has happened to P? The verdict that seems reasonable to many philosophers is that since mental functioning is lost, so is the person.[11] (2) We are familiar with what can be called the typical scenario of multiple personality disorder. Very roughly, at t there is a person P linked to a body B. Shortly afterwards, the person linked to B denies that he or she is P, has a completely contrasting character, a distinct set of memories and opinions, etc. Then later it is as if P has returned. What is the correct description of such cases? According to some the correct verdict is that despite the continuous presence of B there is a sequence of distinct persons. Assuming that according to this account the previously present but currently absent person is not there, we have a *(B and not P)* case.[12]

What of *(P and not B)* cases? Here one has to suffice, but in a crucial and much debated case, that of a brain transplant. Imagine there is a person P, with a body B1, at t. Shortly afterwards the brain of P is removed from B and re-housed and reconnected in another human-style body, B2. The normal assumption is that our psychological states, for example, beliefs, and memories, are based in the brain. They will, therefore, be moved across with the brain. The question is: what happens to P? To many it seems obvious that the correct verdict is that P goes with the brain. Thus, when the person in B2 wakes up he or she will be convinced that they are P, retain P's memories and beliefs etc. Surely, they say, it will in fact be P.

The chief difficulty for the bodily theory has been that there seem to be such possible dissociations between persons and their bodies. However, Locke was impressed by a second line of thought. He proposed that the notion of a person should be defined as follows; a thinking intelligent being, that has reason and reflection, and can consider itself as itself, the same thinking thing in different times and places.[13] This definition of "person" has struck many as along the right tracks. Locke, though, inferred from it that for a person to remain in existence after a time t it must lay down memories of what was happening to it at t which a future subject could retrieve. He suggested, in his words, that "as far as this consciousness can be extended backwards to any past action or thought, so far reaches the identity of that person." Locke thereby made the notion of memory the central notion in the analysis of personal existence over time. He also thought that the verdicts that we tend to make about the thought experiments can be fitted onto such an analysis too.

The Lockean approach to the analysis of personal survival is marked by two general features. First, it regards persistence of a person as consisting in the presence of psychological relations across time (in Locke's case the all important relation was memory). Second, it opposes the idea that a person is tied to any material or substantial object (such as an evolving body). It is clear that there can be theories fulfilling these two general requirements which are different from Locke's theory. Such approaches, which we might call neo-Lockean theories, have been developed.[14] They arise out of two general problems in the Lockean model. The first is its exclusive focus on memory and its requirement of a very strong memory link. Why not formulate a weaker memory requirement? Why concentrate solely on memory? Neo-Lockeans have proposed a weaker memory link and also brought other across time psychological links, such acting on a prior intention, into the analysis. Second, there is the worry that the very psychological notions that are being used in the analysis of personal existence presuppose the notion of a persisting person, and so can hardly analyze it.[15] Thus, one might suggest that a creature can remember things only if it has a faculty that, in some sense, records its past. But this requires (or, at least, makes one suspect that it requires) that the very notion of memory rests on the prior idea of a persisting item with a past, and can hardly be used to explain it.[16] The ingenious response suggested by neo-Lockeans was to attempt to define certain artificial psychological concepts which resemble our normal ones but which are explicitly defined in such a way that they do not rest on any requirement that it is the same person involved. The defined terms tended to be expressed using the expression "quasi" – thus they employed the term "quasi-memory."[17]

With this analytic and conceptual liberalisation neo-Lockeanism has seemed attractive to many. But a third traditional alternative appealed to some. The neo-Lockeans denied any links between persons and bodies or even parts of bodies. Why did they think that? The answer is they accepted there could be (*P and not B*) cases. However, the strongest and most influential case was that of brain transplants, and it is clear that acknowledging that possibility does not commit one to denying all links between subjects and all parts of their bodies, since in such imagined cases the brain goes with the person. Further, there is something very radical about the proposal to break all ties between the subject or person and their bodies. The further proposal emerged that a person survives so long as there are suitable and linked psychological states which are grounded in the self same and natural grounding object, which is, of course, the brain. According to this a person is tied to that object which grounds the necessary psychological links.[18]

It cannot be said that there is a decisive objection to this suggestion. Neo-Lockeans object that there are plausible (*P and not B*) cases which reveal that the brain is not essential to survival. It can also be wondered why there is any necessity to the mode of grounding of psychological states that happens to be the mode we in fact have – say, preservation in single enduring entity – being the essential mode for selves or persons in general.

The standard debate about personal identity primarily consisted of exchanges between people occupying one of these three positions.[19] The notions employed in the competing analyses are, basically, those of bodies (and body parts) and psychological states. A case has recently been developed for thinking that this analytical toolbox is excessively restricted. The case starts from noticing that where you are, and hence where your body is, there also seems to be an animal – in your and my cases, an animal of the human variety. What weight, if any, should we give to that object when thinking about ourselves and what is required for us to remain in existence? Three points stand out once we bring the (human) animal into the question. The first we can reach by asking what relation must a neo-Lockean or a brain theorist regard as holding between the subject or person and the human animal? It seems that according to their theories the person and the human animal are not identical. Consider briefly the neo-Lockean view. It accepts that the person can cease to exist even though the body remains, so long as mental functioning ceases. However, if the body remains and there is still life, then, presumably, the animal is still there. This means that the animal cannot be the person or self. According to the brain view, the person goes with the brain, or at least that part of the brain that sustains psychological connections and functions. It is though implausible to suppose that the removal of a brain cannot leave the animal behind, especially since it may be possible to leave enough neural stuff behind to sustain life. So a difference between the animal and the self emerges on the brain conception. Both views, then, entail a person/animal contrast. Second, if we compare the properties that we ascribe to ourselves and those we ascribe to the human animal there is a massive similarity. The animal is conceived, born, enters into human society, lives a life, and dies. And, we would, surely, say the same things happen to us, persons or selves. Indeed, in the course of actual life it would be hard to puts one's finger on any differences between the person and the human animal, on the basis of which we might regard them as different things. Third, there is certainly something that needs explaining if the person/animal contrast is drawn. Let us suppose that you and the human animal where you are different things with different requirements for remaining in existence. Now, you are obviously mentally endowed, but we can ask whether the animal where you are is also mentally endowed. On the face of it the answer is that it is mentally endowed. After all we think of animals in general as having psychological states – perception, emotion, desire, sensation etc. Surely the advanced human animal does not lack such states. Rather, is seems to have those and more; human animals can reason and think and speak. If so, then a view that says that the animal is one thing and the person or self is another seems committed to the presence in the same space at the same time of two things that can think, reason and speak. Although such a consequence does not amount to a contradiction, it does not represent something that we believed when we started thinking about the problem. Moreover, the standard assumption in formulating the problem was that selves are marked out by their advanced psychological capacities. It now turns out that that cannot be right, since there are two things (at least) where you are which possess such properties – you and the animal. A new explanation needs to be provided of what a person or self is. This is sometimes called the Two Lives problem. How can there be two psychological lives where you are?

The introduction of the notion of the animal into the debate, with the recognition of the apparently paradoxical consequence of adopting the person/animal contrast, and the further recognition of the obvious similarities between the person and the animal, has led to the formulation of a fourth approach to the problem, which has been labeled animalism.[20] This proposes that we, the persons and selves we are interested in, are the same things as certain human animals, and so have the conditions for remaining in existence of such animals. Now, it is a matter of controversy what those conditions are, especially at the end of lives. Does an animal cease to exist when it dies or does it remain in existence but dead? Over this different views can be taken. What seems uncontroversial, though, is that neither the presence of psychological states nor the existence of psychological links across time are essential for an animal to survive. If an animal remains in one piece and alive it is there, even if it has lost its psychological capacities. It follows that if one adopts animalism one should say that same about ourselves. Our rich and advanced psychological lives enable us to live as we do and think about ourselves, but we can exist without such a mental life.[21]

Against this animalist position the main objections will be of the same type as those that were brought against the body view which were sketched earlier, and indeed the very same candidate examples are used. Thus, it is claimed that although animalism looks correct, we can bring against it the existence of imaginary but possible cases in which the person or self can come apart from the human animal. Again, there are the two main sorts of alleged dissociations – (A and not P) cases, where a development leaves the animal but removes the person, and (P and not A) cases, where the person remains but the animal does not. Earlier I did not sketch a possible response to this type of argument when it was brought against the body theory. What though can be said? It is clear that if there is to be a line of reply to the view of the imaginary cases that the objection relies on it has to be against what is claimed about the person or the self. In the imagined cases there is very little doubt that we are tracing the animal correctly. The crucial question is: are we tracing the person or the self correctly? There are two very difficult sides, at least, to this aspect of the problem. First, when we are tempted to judge of an imaginary case that either it involves the removal of the person or the continuation of the person, are we sure that what we are initially tempted to say represents what we really, on consideration, think? Second, why are we confident that we are in a position to judge what is happening to the person or self in all these quite exceptional cases? Consider, for example, at this point the first supposed (B and not P) case, which would also work, if it works at all, as an (A and not P) case. Someone is in an accident and loses their capacity to have mental states. Do we think that the person has actually ceased to exist, or do we really think that this represents a terrible accident that has befallen the person, say, your grandfather, who is there but tragically and irrecoverably injured? Once one faces the case in a realistic frame of mind it is hard to feel that we are quite sure the person has literally gone. The most difficult and influential case is that of brain transplants. What happens there to the person or self?[22] There are a range of options to consider here, but one suggestion is that just as someone can lose an organ and donate it to someone else, so they can lose that organ which sustains mentation in them and donate it to someone else. Could not that be the correct way to think about this case?

The main thing when considering this very difficult problem is to not allow oneself to form the conviction that one knows the general direction of a correct solution simply on the basis of a fairly cursory sampling of standard thought experiments. It is possible that the solution to the problem of the self and of personal identity is to recognize that we are advanced mentally endowed self-conscious animals who have convinced ourselves that we have a different nature to the animal. But if that is a defensible solution we are a long way from knowing that it is.

Further Reading

Now, read next on the self, D. Armstrong (1968), *A Materialist Theory of Mind* chs. 1–3, and on personal identity, read H. Noonan (2002), *Personal Identity*.

The self

An excellent introduction to debates about the self is D. Armstrong (1968), *A Materialist Theory of Mind*, chs. 1 to 4. Another clear and helpful introduction to dualism is P. Smith and O. Jones (1986), *The Philosophy of Mind*. The Cartesian dualist view is expounded by Descartes (1641) in *Meditations on First Philosophy* (commonly called *The Meditations*), especially the second and the sixth Meditation, and in *The Discourse on Method*, part 5. Arnauld's devastating criticism of Descartes' main argument is in the fourth set of Objections; Descartes replied. All these can be conveniently found in *Descartes Selected Philosophical Writings* (1988). Influential criticisms of Descartes' view are presented in G. Ryle (1946), *The Concept of Mind* (1946), especially ch. 1, and in P. F. Strawson (1959), *Individuals*, ch. 3, and in his paper "Self, Mind and Body," contained in his (2008) collection, *Freedom and Resentment and Other Essays*, 186–95. The problem of causal interaction is discussed in J. Foster (1985), A. J. Ayer, 254–63, and in H. Y. Wong (2006), "Cartesian Psychophysics" in van Inwagen and Zimmerman (eds.), *Persons Human and Divine*. The objection to dualism that it is ontologically profligate is presented in J. Smart's classic (1959) paper, "Sensations and Brain Processes" in the *Philosophical Review*. The distinction between identity and constitution is clearly introduced in J. Lowe (2002), *A Survey of Metaphysics*, ch. 4, and developed in a profound way in D. Wiggins (2001), *Sameness and Substance Renewed*. The view that the person is the body is defended by B. Williams (1973), "Are Persons Bodies," in *Problems of the Self*. The Humean bundle theory is presented in Hume (1739), *Treatise*, book 1, part 4, section 6. A very interesting diagnosis, with links to Hume, of the difficulty of thinking about ourselves is given by T. Nagel (1987), *The View from Nowhere*, ch. 4. A difficult but interesting discussion of a variety of arguments about the self is Q. Cassam (1997), *Self and World*.

Personal identity

There is an excellent discussion of the general problem by J. Mackie (1976) in *Problems from Locke*, ch. 5. Two other longer but excellent introductions are H. Noonan (2003), *Personal Identity* and B. Garrett (1998), *Personal Identity and Self-consciousness*. The body view is defended by B. Williams (1973), "Personal Identity and Individuation" in *Problems of the Self*. Locke's views are presented in his *Essay*, book 2, ch. 27. Helpful and critical accounts of Locke's theory are contained in Mackie (1976) and Noonan (2003). Two neo-Lockean approaches are D. Parfit (1984), *Reason and Persons* and S. Shoemaker (1984), *Personal Identity*. The circularity problem with the Lockean view is first expressed by Butler in "Of Personal Identity," reprinted in J. Perry (1975), *Personal Identity*. The so-called brain view can be found in Mackie (1976), and in M. Johnston (1987), "Human Beings," in the *Journal of Philosophy*. An especially interesting version is proposed by T. Nagel (1986) in *The View from Nowhere*, ch. 3. The animalist approach is developed in P. F. Snowdon (2004), "Persons, Animals and Ourselves" in Crane and Farkas (eds.), M. Ayers (1990), *Locke*, vol. 2, part 3, especially ch. 25, and E. Olson (1997), *The Human Animal*.

Notes

1   Anyone uncorrupted by philosophy encountering the three categories I shall sketch will surely feel happy (or at least fairly happy) with them. An implication of some philosophical theories to be considered here would be that the list is either overly restricted or confused. The list does though provide a useful way into the discussion, whatever the ultimate outcome.

2   When defining a category of thing in terms of its properties in such a general way care needs to be taken. Thus consider the book you are reading. I think that we would consider a book a physical thing, and hence something that belongs to the first highly general category. But in being a book it has what one might call semantic properties – it says things, or contains features which say things. Saying things is not itself on any ordinary understanding a purely physical property. This indicates that it counts as having solely physical properties only so far as it is considered in itself. The semantic features belong to it in virtue of its relation to people who wrote it and the languages they possess.

3   Two caveats need entering at this point. We may think that we know that only we humans are self-conscious, but we should be cautious about excluding all other creatures. The careful study of other animals is in its infancy. Second, we should not assume the third category can be sharply distinguished from the second. Creatures who are not fully self-conscious may get very close to it!

4   There is a contrast between the term "person" and the term "self." It is not really a matter for dispute that each of us is a person. The term "person" just applies to us. So we can test any claim about persons by asking whether the claim applies to each of us. In contrast, the term "self" is sometimes used in a technical way, which means that it is not automatic that each of us is a self. An example of someone who defines it in such a way is Galen Strawson: "I will restrict myself to the human case and take it that if anything is to count as a self then it must be a subject of experience and must be non-identical with a human being considered as a whole." Such a definition is of course perfectly legitimate, though I am not adopting any such usage myself. Those who speak in some such way face two questions – why suppose that there are selves in your sense? – and – why be interested in that notion?

5   For a thorough discussion of some of these issues see Cassam (1997).

6   Hume, *Treatise*, book 1, part 4, section 6.

7   An elegant candidate for the same relation is one provided by Kripke. He asks us to consider a tree from which all the branches have been shaved, leaving only, we can assume, the trunk. What is the relation between the trunk an the tree? At the envisaged time there are no parts of the tree

that are not also parts of the trunk, but does that mean that the tree is the trunk? Hardly, because there seem to be differences between the trunk and the tree. For example, once the shaving stops the tree will consist in part of leaves, whereas the trunk will never consist of the leaves. This difference seems to mean that we must think of the trunk as constituting the tree a period, but not being identical with the tree.

8   This general metaphysical debate can be traced by reading Wiggins (2001), etc.

9   These informative principles about our persistence conditions are sometimes called – criteria of personal identity.

10   Since I found no reasons to postulate parts to us other than bodily parts my classification of the main approaches ignores theories of self-persistence which assume that such parts exist (for example, dualist theories). It also needs stressing that the three categories of theory that I employ are very broad and that within each one there are variants that are quite different.

11   This simple case resembles a more complex one invented by shoemaker, which he calls a brain zap. See Shoemaker (1984).

12   Locke anticipated such a case in book 2, ch. 27, section 23, of his *Essay*. Wilkes (1988: ch. 1) develops an argument in some detail in favor of the pluralist verdict.

13   See Locke, *Essay*, book 2, ch. 27, section 9. The next quotation also comes from this section. Locke's argument in section 9 deserves very close scrutiny.

14   The two best developed versions are those of Parfit (1984) and Shoemaker (1984). Whatever the final verdict on such theories they are clearly brilliant and profound examples of constructive philosophy.

15   The classical exposition of this worry is by Butler (1975).

16   It is, of course, not clear that there is any circularity here.

17   For the definitions see Parfit (1984: 219–23). The general idea of such definitions can be illustrated by the case of memory, in connection with which it was first developed and has been most discussed. The assumption is that if a single subject recalls his or her earlier history there will be some form of, probably causal linkage between the recalling and the original recalled event. Let us call this linkage L. it is normally conceived of as the laying down of a neural trace and its re-activation. There is no reason why this L linkage should not, in some strange cases, get transferred from one subjet to another, for example, by some mini-neural transfer. Quasi-memory is then conceived of as present so long as a later subject is L-related to an actual earlier occurrence. This relation does not require that it is the same subject. This enables an apparently non-circular psychological definition. Of course, not everyone concedes that this type of definition is satisfactory. See Wiggins (2001: ch.7).

18   Proponents of this type of view are J. Mackie (1976: ch. 5) and Johnston (1987). It is important to realize that this proposal does not claim that the person or self is (identical with) the brain. That suggestion is deeply inconsistent with how we think of ourselves. For example, I think of myself as having a weight, and an appearance, and indeed an extension in space, quite different from any such features that my brain has. The theory says that the person can survive only if the mental features are sustained by or grounded in a particular object. The person can then be thought of as being the total thing which is organized around that object, but which can extend beyond it.

19   I am here simplifying in the way I have so far done by ignoring in my account of the debate positions which require ontologies beyond bodies (and mental states).

20   It has also lead to a downgrading of the bodily theory. It is not so much that animalism is in opposition to the bodily theory, as that there is no evident attraction to stepping straight to the bodily candidate except via the animal one.

21   For presentations of the animalist view see Snowdon (2004), Ayers (1990), and Olson (1997).
22   For attempts by animalists to answer this very difficult question see Snowdon (1991) and Olson (1997: ch. 3).

References

Armstrong. D. (1968). A *Materialist theory of Mind*, London: Routledge and Kegan Paul.
Ayers Locke, M. (1991). London: Routledge.
Cassam, Q. (1997). *Self and World*, Oxford: Oxford University Press.
Descartes, R. (1988). *Descartes: Selected Philosophical Writings*, Cambridge: Cambridge University Press.
Foster, J. (1985). *A. J. Ayer*, London: Routledge and Kegan Paul.
Garrett, B. (1998). *Personal Identity and Self Consciousness*, London: Routledge and Kegan Paul.
Lowe, J. (2002). *A Survey of Metaphysics*, Oxford: Oxford University Press.
Mackie, J. (1976). *Problems From Locke*, Oxford: Oxford University Press.
Nagel, T. (1987). *The View Form Nowhere*, Oxford: Oxford University Press.
Noonan, H. (2003). *Personal Identity*, London: Routledge.
Olson, E. (1997). *The Human Animal*, Oxford: Oxford University Press.
Parfit, D. (1984). *Reasons and Persons*, Oxford: Oxford University Press.
Ryle, G. (1949). *The Concept of Mind*, London: Hutchinson.
Shoemaker, S. (with Swinburne, R.) (1984). *Personal Identity*, Oxford: Blackwell.
Smith, P. and Jones, O. (1986). *The Philosophy of Mind*. Cambridge: Cambridge University Press.
Snowdon, P. (1991). "Personal Identity and Brain Transplants," in D. Cockburn (ed.), *Human Beings*, Cambridge: Cambridge University Press, 109–126.
Snowdon, P. (2004). "Persons, Animals and Ourselves," in T. Crane and K. Farkas (eds.), *Metaphysics*, Oxford: Oxford University Press, 578–96.
Strawson, P. F. (1959). *Individuals*. London: Methuen.
Strawson, P. F. (2008). *Freedom and Resentment and Other Essays*, Abingdon: Routledge.
Van Inwagen, P. and Zimmerman, D. (2006). *Persons Human and Divine*, Oxford: Oxford University Press.
Wiggins, D. (2001). *Sameness and Substance Renewed*, Cambridge: Cambridge University Press.
Williams, B. (1973). *Problems of the Self*, Cambridge: Cambridge University Press.

10

Action

Luca Ferrero

Actions, Agents, and Agency

We are agents. Not only are we capable of acting, but considerable portions of our lives are taken up by our doings, by exercises of our agency. Our actions and doings are essential to much of what we cherish most in our lives, and – arguably – our death can be equated with the permanent loss of our agency. Under these respects, we differ from inanimate objects, artifacts, chemical substances, and natural phenomena such as – for instance – planets, tables, acids, and lightning-storms. When we speak of the "actions" of these things, we simply refer to the operations of some of their characteristic causal powers. But when speak of our own actions and doings, we refer to phenomena that, at least in their paradigmatic form, have all of the following: they are directed at some aim or purpose, they are the subject matter of practical deliberation, the objects of our intentions, the chief manifestations of our freedom, the primary targets of accountability and moral evaluation, and the characteristic objects of demands for rational intelligibility and justification.

What is the nature of our agency and its characteristic manifestations? One might begin addressing this question by considering what difference there is between what *we do* and what merely *happens to us*, between what we perform and what we suffer or undergo. It is uncontroversial that an action is directed at a goal, brings about some transformation in the world, and originates in its agent, at least in the sense that there is a subject who exercises some privileged, direct, and immediate control – although possibly not an exclusive or an ultimate one – over the action's inception and execution. Despite the familiar and uncontroversial character of these observations, it is far from trivial to formulate a satisfactory philosophical account of action and agency.

To begin with, the distinctive features of an action might not be externally observable. For instance, when I raise my arm, I make a movement that might be indistinguishable from the one produced, say, by a spasm, i.e., by the mere rising of my arm. Possibilities of this kind suggest that there is more to action than bodily movements alone. Action is, at least in part, a matter of the operation and existence of mental events and states, such as decisions, intentions, desires, and beliefs. Several questions arise at this point. Which psychological features are required for agency? Which mental states and events are required for action?

How are these mental components related to each other and to the bodily movement? Is the relation causal, justificatory, or both? If the latter, how are justification and causation related? And what is an action, exactly? The movement produced by the proper mental components, the operation of the mental elements alone, or some combination of the movement and the mental elements? Finally, how do the answers to these questions account for the role of the *agent* and the special importance that we attribute to actions both as expressions of our "true selves" and as proper objects of accountability and responsibility?

A further complication is that agency comes in various kinds and degrees. The philosophy of action is primarily interested in *full-blooded intentional agency*. That is, the agency paradigmatically instantiated by situations where the agent is aware of what she is doing and of why she is doing it, she acts as a result of an explicit deliberation, and she sees her conduct as "up to" her rather than as the product of "alien forces." These cases are distinctive of the agency of adult human beings. The nature of full-blooded intentional agency can be fully understood, however, only by appreciating how it differs not just from utterly passive happenings but also from lesser kinds of agency – in the spectrum that goes from the complex intelligent purposive behaviors of higher animals to the simpler teleological processes of lower organisms (such as plant phototropism – e.g., the sunflower's tracking of sunlight – or bacterial chemotaxis – e.g., the movement of a bacterium in response to changes in the gradient of glucose in its surroundings).

Moreover, many things that we describe as our "doings," even as our intentional doings, might fall short of the paradigm of full-blooded intentional agency. For instance, normally we can be said intentionally to fall asleep only in the sense that we intentionally create conditions – say, taking a sleeping pill – that induce us to passively *fall* asleep. The voluntary control of our physiological processes is normally only of this indirect sort. Hence, in their normal operation they are not actions of ours, even if they are the "doing" of our own body (e.g., we can intentionally increase our heartbeat only *by* engaging in some strenuous physical activity or by taking a stimulant). Consider then cases such as sneezing, coughing, and breathing. Although we might have a certain amount of control in inhibiting or *delaying* their occurrences, normally we do not voluntarily initiate them and often we are ultimately unable to resist them. When so, our sneezing, coughing, or breathing are not things that we do in the same intentional way in which we might inhibit or delay their occurrences.

Other cases in which we do not seem to have full intentional control are the behaviors produced by unconscious motivation, compulsion, addiction, and hypnosis. Although we acknowledge that these behaviors originate *within* us, we are reluctant to qualify them as fully intentional since they appear to stem from parts of us from which we are "alienated," i.e., from parts that we do not acknowledge as belonging to our "true" or "deep self."

Finally, an intentional action is not necessarily a deliberate one. It need not be preceded by an explicit and fully articulate deliberation. However, it is the sort of conduct that is the standard subject matter of deliberation. In addition, an intentional action might be executed "automatically," at least in the sense that it might take place outside of the agent's focus of attention. There is, nonetheless, a point past which automatic execution and lack of awareness of one's conduct disqualify a purposive behavior from counting as fully intentional, making it more akin to a manifestation of the lesser kind of agency characteristic of non-human animals.

In keeping with the standard focus of the philosophical investigation of agency, this chapter is primarily concerned with the paradigmatic instances of full-blooded intentional agency; with actions such as – to use a standard example – the deliberate flipping of a switch in order to illuminate a room. The focus on scenarios of this kind should not be interpreted, however, as implying that intentional agency necessarily involves bodily movements, brings about positive changes, and is exercised by single agents in isolation. But limitations of space prevent me from discussing the issues raised by mental acts, omissions, and collective agency, respectively. A final introductory remark: the ultimate aim of the philosophical investigation of action is to understand the nature of *agency*, of the capacity that makes us agents and that usually, although not necessarily, is manifested in our actions. Hence, although it is customary to refer to this investigation as "philosophy of action" (and sometimes as "action-theory"), "philosophy of agency" would be a better and more comprehensive label for it.

The Explanation of Action

A distinctive feature of actions, as opposed to mere happenings, is that we explain their occurrences by appealing to reasons rather than mere efficient causes. Elizabeth Anscombe argues that intentional actions are those to which "a particular sense of the question 'Why?' is given application," the sense in which "the answer, if positive, gives a reason for acting." An action is the kind of happening that can be made intelligible, rationalized, assessed, and justified by appealing to reasons for it.[1]

These reasons need not be explicitly entertained and articulated by the agent. Nor does an agent necessarily act on good reasons. The important point is rather that a conduct is intentional only when it is in principle subjected to a demand for justification in terms of the agent's reasons for it (a request that in the limiting case might be discharged by claiming that one acted "for no reason").

According to Anscombe, reasons are not efficient causes. Donald Davidson rejects Anscombe's anti-causalism. He claims that an action is both caused and rationalized by the joint operation of a belief and a desire. For instance, my desire to illuminate the room and my belief that I have the ability and opportunity to illuminate it by flipping the switch, when properly combined, both cause and rationalize my flipping the switch. These mental states play a dual role. Their efficient causal powers explain the occurrence of the action, their contents rationalize it. Davidson's central argument is that, unless reasons are causes, we cannot account for the distinction between the many reasons the agent might have *to* do something (all the possible justifications she might have for that action) and the reason *for* which she *actually* performed it.[2]

Thanks to Davidson, a causal account of the nature of action and its explanation in terms of belief/desire pairs (possibly augmented with intentions as distinct mental states) became the new orthodoxy, the "standard story about action." This story has not gone unchallenged. As even its defenders noted, so-called deviant causal chains raise serious difficulties. For instance, a climber desires to rid himself of the weight and danger of holding another man on a rope, and believes that by loosening his hold on the rope he could rid himself of the weight and danger. This belief and desire might so unnerve him as to cause him to loosen his hold, but he does not do so intentionally. The belief and the desire do not cause the action "in the right way." The problem, which many consider still unresolved, if not unsolvable, is whether an account of "the right way" can be offered in purely causal terms as the standard story demands.[3]

George Wilson offers a more radical criticism of the causal nature of action-explanation. According to him, the explanation of action is a species of *non-causal* teleological explanation. Talk of "the intention with which" a person acted indicates that the act is directed by the agent at a certain objective. It makes explicit the goal-directed nature of action but it does not specify one of its causal antecedents. Wilson argues that these teleological explanations cannot be analyzed as causal explanations in which the reasons play the role of guiding efficient causes. The dispute over the nature of action-explanation is still open.[4]

The Standard Story

Throughout the empiricist tradition up to the early twentieth century, the philosophy of agency was dominated by *volitionism*, the view that actions are made intentional and voluntary when caused by distinctive conscious mental occurrences called "volitions" or "acts of will." Gilbert Ryle moved a devastating criticism to classical volitionism by showing that it faces an inescapable dilemma: if volitions are *intentional* acts, they can be made so only by other volitions, which gives rise to an infinite regress; if volitions are mere happenings, instead, it is unclear how the combination of two mere happenings (the volition and the bodily movement caused by the volition) might amount to an intentional action.[5]

The standard story of action, although it appeals to mental states as causal antecedents of action, does not run into Ryle's dilemma. The belief/desire pair is not the same as an "act of will." Moreover, the standard story offers an informative account of the rationalization of action. The problem with the standard story is rather that it seems to fail to include the agent. For it seems to cast the agent as the mere passive arena for the interaction of the mental states that cause the action.

This criticism comes in two forms. Some accept the basic outline of the causal story but argue that we need a more complex picture of the psychology of agents, one that goes beyond simple belief/desire pairs. These views are moved by considerations in so called "moral psychology," they want to account for the agent's characteristic *identification* with the springs of her full-blooded intentional conduct, as opposed to the alienation she experiences when her conduct does not stem from her true or core self as in the cases of unconscious motivation or compulsion. Other philosophers worry that the standard story leaves the agent out because it misunderstands the nature of the causal relation between agents and actions. They argue that agents are sources of a distinctive kind of causal contribution. This causality does not fit with the strictures imposed by the "naturalistic" reduction of agency attempted by the standard story, a reduction that is usually accepted by those who pursue the first line of criticism. Let's consider these criticisms in turn.

Agency, Identification, and Reflection

As indicated at the outset, there seems to be an important difference between merely purposive behaviors (such as those produced by unconscious motivation, compulsion, addiction, and hypnosis) and full-blooded intentional actions. Only the latter ones seem to manifest or stem from the agent's "true self." Harry Frankfurt accounts for this difference in terms of the notions of "guidance" and "identification." First, goal-directed behaviors are *guided* throughout their temporal unfolding. They are not the simple products of some triggering causal antecedent. They are, rather, sustained by the agent's ability and readiness to secure the achievement of one's goal by making compensatory adjustments to her conduct when interfered with, and to stay idle when no adjustment is called for. Some behaviors are guided by local mechanisms within the agent's body, like the dilating of the pupil in response to the fading of light. Other behaviors are truly guided by the agent since the agent as a *whole* is responsible for the compensatory adjustments.

Guidance by the whole agent is all that is required for the intentional behavior of non-reflective beings, like animals and children, which are inescapably immersed in their purposive conduct. Reflective beings like us, however, might still be *alienated* from the behaviors stem from this global guidance, since they might not identify with their own motives. A drug-addict, for instance, can be guided by her desire for the drug and yet reach for it "unwillingly" or "in spite of herself" since she does not *identify* with that motive. Identification is required for the behavior of a reflective agent to be fully intentional.

Frankfurt accounts of identification in terms of hierarchical attitudes of a reflective agent. A reflective agent (as opposed to a non-reflective "wanton," to use his terminology) has second-order desires about the first-order desires that are to be effective in determining her conduct. An agent identifies with a first-order motive that moves her to act when this is the motive that she desires, at the higher-level, to be effective in moving her to act. The unwilling addict, for instance, is alienated from her conduct because she is moved to reach for the drug by a first-order desire for the drug that goes against her unconflicted second-order desire *not* to be moved by her desire for the drug. Were it not for her addiction – for the irresistibility of the first-order desire, the agent would be expected to prevent that desire from determining her conduct and, if successful, to identify with her refusal to take the drug.[6]

There is a problem, however, with Frankfurt's view. A hierarchy of motives does not appear to account for identification. The fact that a motive is of a higher order does not guarantee that that motive speaks for the agent. A reflective agent might have motives of an even higher order than the second one, motives that in principle could go against the lower-order ones (e.g., the addict might have a third-order desire against the effectiveness of her second-order desire not to be moved by her first-order desire for the drug). The problem is that there seems to be no principled way to determine at which level in this potentially infinite hierarchy of motives we should stop to locate the agent.[7] Frankfurt's response is centered on the idea of "satisfaction": an agent identifies with a first-order motive when she has a second-order motive for the effectiveness of the first order and she is *satisfied* with the second-order motive in the sense that she has no active interest in changing it. Notice that the satisfaction is a property of the agent's whole psychic structure. The satisfaction described the *absence* of a pressure for change, not a distinct attitude. If the latter, there would still be a threat of regress, since one could continue raise the question of whether the agent identifies (and it is thus satisfied) at a higher order with her lower-order satisfaction.[8]

David Velleman and Michael Bratman agree with Frankfurt that the standard story of action is wanting and that reflection and hierarchy are fundamental to agential guidance, but they maintain that the notion of "satisfaction" is inadequate to stop the regress. A depressed, bored, or lazy agent might have no interest in changing her higher-order motives. She would be satisfied in Frankfurt's sense, but this does not appear a case of genuine identification with one's motives since conditions such as depression, boredom, and laziness always carry the potential for reflective dissociation. According to Velleman, the trouble with Frankfurt is his appeal to second-order motives that do not necessarily arise out of an appreciation of the role of first-order motives as *reasons* for action. Velleman argues that being reflective as a rational agent is a matter of being disposed to do what is justified, to do what makes sense to oneself. More precisely, a matter of a "higher-order motive of rationality" to be moved by a lower-order motive in its capacity as a reason: to acquiesce in being moved by the intrinsic force of a first-order motive only if being so moved is intelligible to the agent (where this intelligibility is a kind of self-knowledge, as explained later). The motive of rationality operates by *reinforcing* pre-existing first-order motives. In full-blooded intentional agency, the agent does not simply flip the switch as a result of the desire to illuminate the room and the belief that flipping it is an effective means (as she would if she were to act impulsively or out of subconscious motives). Rather, her motive is strengthened by the fact that this conduct makes sense to her by comparison to courses of action that, although supported by her first-order motives, are not equally intelligible to her.

There is no regress in Velleman's account because the agent cannot dissociate from the higher-order motive of rationality. This motive drives practical thought and, as such, cannot be made the object of detached critical reflection. The agent is *functionally identical* with the operation of the motive of rationality. She is identical with the capacity for reflection rather than with other specific higher-order desires. Hence, a subject *qua* rational agent cannot ever be alienated from this capacity. She could only disown it by giving up making rational assessments of her motives, i.e., by giving up being a rational agent.[9]

Bratman agrees with Frankfurt and Velleman's criticisms of the limitations of the simple psychological structure of the standard story. He maintains that full-blooded intentional agency results from the integration of the capacity for reflection with the distinctive diachronic dimension of our temporally extended agency. For him, attitudes "speak for the agent" only when their role in the subject's psychology partly constitutes and supports her existence as one and the same agent over time. Bratman subscribes to a Lockean theory of personal identity according to which identity is a matter of psychological continuity. An important contribution to this continuity is provided by "self-governing policies," intention-like attitudes that offer general guidelines about which desires one is to treat as reasons in practical reasoning. When one guides one's thinking and acting in accordance to self-governing policies, one exercises self-governance in one's capacity as an agent because, first, these policies contribute to one's identity over time and thus have authority to speak for oneself and, second, one directs one's thinking and acting in terms of what one takes not as mere motives but as one's reasons for action.

Bratman differs from Velleman in maintaining that identification with a first-order desire is not produced by a *single* higher-order motive or rationality shared by all agents in their capacity as agents. Identification is, rather, due to self-governing policies that can differ from agent to agent. What is common to all agents is only the basic structural role that specific self-governing policies play in securing the temporal identity of each individual agent. Bratman agrees with Frankfurt and Velleman on the importance of reflection and its hierarchical structure (self-governing policies are higher-order attitudes about first-order motives). However, he concedes to the critics of hierarchical views that the attitudes that speak for the agent might not be higher-order ones, although he insists that the nature of self-governance puts pressures toward the existence of a hierarchy.[10]

Reflection plays a prominent role also in Christine Korsgaard's theory of action. She argues that action is necessarily performed by a unified agent; it is an expression of the agent as a whole rather than a product of forces at work in her. Nonetheless, the agent does not exist as a unified author prior to the action. The agent constitutes herself as such author in the very act of choice: action is self-constitution. This is true for agency in general, not just for human agency, although different kinds of agents constitute themselves as different forms of life.

Consider *animal* action. According to Korsgaard, the animal is presented with an "incentive," a motivationally loaded representation of an object. The animal is aware of some features of the object as desirable or aversive in some specific way (e.g., as to be eaten) and she acts on this incentive on the basis of a "principle," which determines what the animal does in the face of that specific incentive (in the example, to eat the object). The principles on which an animal acts are its instincts. They *automatically* tell the animal which responses are appropriate for each particular incentive. The instinctual operation of the incentives is causal but it does not bypass the animal's own guidance. For the instincts are the laws of the animal's causality; they define the animal's will. By operating on them, the animal is not just purposive but also autonomous, at least in the sense that its movements are determined by its own nature.

The self-determination in *human* action is deeper. We are not simply governed by the principles of our own causality. We choose these principles. We are self-conscious and thus aware of the working of incentives within us. We no longer experience incentives as demands but as proposals. Incentives become "inclinations," something we now have to decide whether to satisfy or not. It is only within this space of "reflective distance" that the question arises whether our incentives give us *reasons* to act. Self-consciousness creates the need for principles of reason.

Animal action is purposive since it is guided by a conception of its object. But our self-conscious action requires a conception of its purpose, of what we are doing and why. In this sense, we are agents who adopt intentions. We are conscious of our own causality and it is thus up to us how we exercise it. Our self-consciousness is the source of a psychic complexity unknown to animals. We are conscious of the threats to our psychic unity. For animals, psychic unity is a natural state: the instincts immediately tell them how to deal with incentives. For us, psychic unity is to be achieved. Being a person is being engaged in a particular form of life: the activity to constitute oneself as a *particular* individual given that, as a *reflective* animal, each of us must create, through one's own choices, one's individual self-maintaining form, one's individual "practical identity."[11]

Actions and Agents

Let's now consider the second line of criticism against the standard story of action. This criticism concurs with the first one in denouncing the standard story for leaving the agent out of the picture, but it claims the fault does not lie in overlooking the complexities of reflection but in misunderstanding the nature of the causal relation between agents and their actions. Against the standard story, Roderick Chisholm argues that agents, not their mental states, cause actions. Agents do so by being *additional* primitive elements in the explanatory order.[12] The suggestion that there is a distinctive kind of "agent-causation," however, has been widely criticized because it takes agents as *intruders* among natural events in violation with a widely accepted naturalistic conception of causal explanation.[13]

Jennifer Hornsby offers a different criticism of the causal claims of the standard story. She argues that the purely event-based account of the causal order implicit in the standard story misses the agent's distinctive contribution. The first mistake is to conceive of action as the event of body movement, understood intransitively, rather than as the mov*ing* of the body, understood transitively. If we conceive of action as a body movement, we are induced to explain it by taking the causes of action to be either the mental states of the standard story (thereby missing the agent's role), or the agent itself as in agent-causation (thereby making the agent an intruder in the causal order). According to Hornsby, agents cause bodily movements but these movements are not actions, they are only the effects of actions. An action is, rather, the agent's *causing* of the bodily movements (or, better, her *trying* to move the body, see below) and of the other causal consequences of these movements. In the light-switching scenario, for instance, the action is not the finger movement but the mov*ing* of the finger, i.e., the agent's causing of the finger movement. The agent does not cause the moving of the finger, she causes the finger movement and this caus*ing* is the action. In a similar fashion, the agent is the cause of the other effects of her action, such as the illumination of the room, but her action is not the occurrence of these events, it is her causing them.

Hornsby claims that in explaining an action we are not looking for a causal explanation of the occurrence of a bodily movement or any other effects of the action. We already have an explanation of this occurrence in that we know what caused it, namely, the agent. It is exactly because we already think of this occurrence as the effect of an action that we are interested in understanding *why* the agent caused that effect. In looking to explain the action, we do not want to learn the causal role played by the agent. This is something that we already assume in looking for an explanation of an *action*. We, rather, want to learn things about the agent that make it understandable that she should have brought those effects about, that she should have played the causal role that makes her the author of that action.[14]

The Individuation of Action

When I illuminate a room *by* flipping the switch *by* moving my finger, how many actions do I perform? We might be tempted to say that I am doing at least three separate things. Anscombe and Davidson argue, instead, that I am performing only one action, although one that admits of as many descriptions as its disparate causal effects. For them, there is only one event that counts as my action. This event can be described in terms of any of its effects; for instance, as my moving the finger, my flipping the switch, or my illuminating the room.[15]

If a causal effect of the illumination of the room (and thus of the finger movement) is that a burglar is alerted of my presence, my action can also be described as my alerting the burglar. This is not to say that by flipping the switch I *intentionally* alert the burglar. Only some of the possible descriptions of the action indicate what I do intentionally. At the very least, I am not acting intentionally under any of the descriptions that apply to my action unbeknownst to me. If I have no idea that there is a burglar, I am not intentionally alerting him by flipping the switch, even if the action of unintentionally alerting the burglar is the same action as my intentionally illuminating the room and as my intentionally flipping the switch.[16]

We illuminate the room by flipping the switch. We flip the switch by moving our fingers. However, we do not seem to move our fingers *by* doing anything else. The movement of our finger is a "basic action." An action is basic when the doing is described in such a way that one cannot be said to be acting under that description *by* doing anything else. (This is not to deny that there are causal antecedents of the basic action within the agent, e.g., muscles contractions and neurophysiologic events, but these are descriptions of what one *does*.) Davidson claims that all basic actions are bodily movements. Whatever we do, we do by moving our bodies, and we do not move our bodies by doing anything else.[17]

Contra Davidson, Brian O'Shaughnessy and Jennifer Hornsby argue that a basic action is not a bodily movement but one's *trying* to move one's body. For instance, if someone does not know that her arm is completely paralyzed and she attempts to move her finger, she seems to have done something even if her arm and finger have not moved at all; she has *tried* to move her finger. These philosophers argue that even when we actually succeed in moving our bodies, whatever we do it is something that we achieve *by trying* to do it. The basic description of action is thus always in terms of "trying," even if in ordinary talk, for pragmatic reasons, we reserve the expression "to try" to describe cases where we either fail to move our bodies or we suspect that it is very likely that we might be unable to move them.[18] This view should not be confused with the classical volitionism presented above. The trying *is* the intentional acting. It is not a distinct phenomenon that accounts for the action's intentionality and voluntariness as its causal precursor – whence the immunity from Ryle's criticism of classical volitionism.

Acting Intentionally and Intention

So far I used "acting intentionally" to refer to full-blooded intentional agency. But in ordinary talk we often use "intentionally" more liberally to refer to several distinct, although not necessarily unrelated, aspects of agency. Sometimes we describe a conduct as intentional to indicate that it is goal directed or, more strongly, that it is guided by the agent as a whole rather than a local mechanism. Sometimes we speak of acting intentionally in the narrower sense of acting deliberately, i.e., acting in view of a goal adopted in an explicit and articulate deliberation. In certain contexts, to say that something is done intentionally means that it is not done inadvertently or accidentally. We are also reluctant to claim that something is done intentionally when its outcome, although not deviantly caused, depends to a large extent on chance – e.g., we intentionally roll the dice but we do not intentionally roll a seven with the dice. Doing something intentionally, in this sense, means that one exerts the kind of control and guidance normally expected by proficient agents in the unfolding of that particular activity.[19]

There is an important connection between acting intentionally and the agent's knowledge of what she is doing. Knowledge of what one is doing is necessary for the intentionality of one's action in that one cannot be said to be acting intentionally under a description of the action in terms of unknown and unexpected effects (as in the burglar case previously discussed). But knowledge of the effects is not sufficient to make the action intentional under that description. For instance, if I know that there is a burglar and that my turning on the light is necessarily going to alert him, it might still be that, by intentionally flipping the switch, I do not intentionally alert the burglar; I only *knowingly* do so. Alerting the burglar is an effect of my illuminating the room that I foresee, but I do not intend. Whereas illuminating the room is my goal, alerting the burglar is not. I guide my conduct so as to ensure that it succeeds in illuminating the room. That is, I am expected to make the necessary adjustments to turn on the light. But since I am not aiming at alerting the burglar, I am not making sure that I succeed at it. If it turned out that in illuminating the room I would not be alerting the burglar, I would be under no expectation to find alternate means to alert him.[20]

According to Anscombe, there is another important relation between intentionality and knowledge: in acting intentionally the agent knows what she is doing "without observation." Anscombe's suggestive but somewhat unclear discussion has recently spurred an interesting debate on the relation between self-knowledge and intentional agency. If the knowledge in question is of the intention as the objective of one's action, this knowledge can be claimed to be non-evidential because it is produced by the agent's first-personal responsiveness to the deliberative considerations that support the adoption of the intention. It does not result from a third-personal investigation about one's mental states on the basis of epistemic grounds, including those provided by introspection.[21]

What about the knowledge of one's actual and future intentional *performance*, the kind of knowledge that seems the primary concern of Anscombe's remarks? George Wilson argues that because of its nature as a practical commitment, an intention comes with the expectation of the stability of the case for its adoption. This expectation provides a defeasible ground for the belief that one will continue to carry it out. But the expectation of a stable case is based not on inductive evidence about the immutability of the agent's preferences but on the agent's continuous sense of the intrinsic force and authority of the reasons for action that have been decisive in his adoption of the intention.

Velleman claims that a different lesson is to be learnt from Anscombe: an intention amounts to knowledge only if it appropriately and reliably causes the facts that make the intention true. For him, intention amount to this knowledge and it does so in a non-evidential fashion: an intention is a *cognitive* commitment to the truth of the intention's content; a commitment that provides a reliable connection to the intended action via the operation of the higher-order motive of rationality (as discussed above). The agent's commitment to the truth of doing what she intends to do reliably enlists reinforcement for the motives that favor that action since that is the only action that satisfies the higher-order motive of rationality. It is the only action that makes true the agent's belief that she is going to do what she intends to do. The kind of self-knowledge provided by the intention, therefore, counts as "practical knowledge" in Anscombe's sense, a knowledge that causes what it represents.[22]

What is the relation between acting intentionally and having an intention? Anscombe maintains that acting intentionally just consists in one's conduct being subjected to the demand for explanation in terms of reasons. The term "intention" does not denote a distinct mental state. Defenders of what might be called a "behaviorist" or "outward-looking" conception of agency concur. For them, our talk of intentions indicates distinctive structural features of our performance, including its goal, without committing us to the existence of intentions as distinct causal elements in our psychology. However, one needs not embrace the outward-looking conception to deny the existence of intentions as distinct mental states. For instance, Davidson initially argued that acting intentionally only requires causation by a belief/desire pair. Later he acknowledged the need for intentions as distinct attitudes in order to account for those cases in which one reaches a conclusion about what to do well in advance of the time of action, a conclusion that one might never carry out, as it happens for instance when one is weak-willed. In this later work, Davidson identifies intentions with what he calls "all-out value judgments" about the desirability of an action.[23]

According to Bratman, however, a psychology of belief/desires even if augmented with Davidson's style intentions is too austere to account for the distinctive *planning* structure of our diachronic agency. Bratman argues that prospective intentions are partially specified plans about our future conduct, plans to be filled in as they unfold over time. Intentions *settle* what we are going to do in the future in a way that is usually effective in determining our future conduct. An intention allows the agent to take advantage of more favorable conditions for deliberation in advance of the time of action. It provides a filter for future practical reasoning since one needs only consider options compatible with one's intentions thereby reducing the costs of contingency planning. Last but not least, by settling future conduct, intentions greatly contribute to both intra- and inter-personal coordination of action over time.

For Bratman, intentions are not reducible to a combination of beliefs and desires. They are functionally characterized by a distinctive set of rational pressures. The agent who intends to φ is under several rational requirements: She is to be instrumentally coherent (she is either to take the necessary means to φ-ing or to abandon her intention); her intention is to be consistent with her beliefs (in particular, she is not to believe that her φ-ing is impossible); the intention is to be agglomerated (if the agent intends to φ and she intends to ψ, she is also to intend to [φ and ψ]); finally, the intention is to be stable over time. By comparison, none of these requirements apply to the agent's desires. Moreover, contrary to the claims of what Bratman calls the "simple view," when one does something intentionally one does not necessarily acts with a corresponding intention. At times, we might be pursuing a goal without trying to fit it within a more complex and global coordinated plan of action. When so, one does not have an intention as a genuinely planning attitude but rather a "settled objective" – an objective that is under a pressure for instrumental coherence but not for agglomeration. Our truly distinctive form of agency, however, is the planning agency that calls for the global demands for coordination characteristic of full-fledged intentions, rather than the simpler *local* constraints imposed by "settled objectives" (which, as such, might be the distinctive form of the diachronic agency of the purposive but non-planning agency of non-human animals).[24]

An important and still debated issue about intentions concerns the source of their effectiveness in controlling future conduct. Do they simply cause the intended future conduct or do they, rather, exert rational authority over it? If the latter, what is the nature and source of its authority? Does an intention generate a reason for the intended action *additional* to the considerations that made the action choiceworthy for the agent when the intention was first adopted? If so, Bratman worries that an intention could have an undesirable "bootstrapping effect": when the time of action comes the agent might find herself with a (possibly decisive) reason to act as intended even if she no longer finds the action choiceworthy independently of her intention to perform it.

Finally, for Bratman an intention is not a cognitive but a practical commitment. Adopting the intention is not to discover something about oneself; it is to make a further practical move, although one that might be accompanied by some knowledge about one's future conduct. Hence, Bratman rejects cognitivism about practical reason.[25] The cognitivists claim that the rational demands for consistency and coherence of intentions are grounded in the norms of *theoretical* rationality, in rational demand for consistency and coherence of belief. This is so because an intention to φ is deemed to be either identical to or to entail a belief that one will φ. A cognitivist like Velleman argues that, if one does not believe that one is going to do what one intends to do, there are no grounds for the coordinating role of intentions and for their distinctive rational pressures.[26] Bratman's response in a still ongoing debate is twofold. First, an intention does not necessarily involve a belief about its eventual success. Intention only entails the belief in the possibility of acting as intended. Second, the norms of intention are fundamentally practical. They are grounded not on our nature as cognitive beings but on the requirements for the effectiveness of the distinctive planning character of our diachronic intentional agency.[27]

Further Reading

The best short introduction to the philosophy of action is Wilson (2007). The best book-length introduction is Stout (2005). Three short papers that could serve as introductions to important issues in the philosophy of action are Davidson (1980: ch. 3), Frankfurt (1978), and Kenny (1992: ch. 3). A good collection of essays is Mele (1997).

Notes

1 Anscombe (1963). The beginning of the contemporary philosophical investigation on agency (and of the "philosophy of action" as a distinct area of philosophy) could be dated back to the publication of Anscombe (1963; 1st edn., 1957) and Davidson (1963/1980: ch.1). Although the nature of action and agency has been the object of philosophical interest at least since Socrates, this investigation was usually pursued only as preparatory to discussing issues in other areas of philosophy – such as the metaphysics of free will, the mind–body problem, and the role of voluntariness and intentionality for moral accountability and evaluation. By contrast, the contemporary discussion has largely proceeded on its own terms. Moreover, only rarely has it engaged with the specific accounts of actions advanced in the history of philosophy (the more notable exception is Korsgaard 2009) even if many contemporary theorists have found some inspiration in the views of action advanced by such a diverse group of philosophers as Plato, Aristotle, Aquinas, Hume, Kant, and Wittgenstein. Unfortunately, the philosophy of action in the analytic tradition has for the most part ignored the important works on agency by the early Heidegger, Merleau-Ponty, and Sartre (see especially Sartre 1956), although the views of the former two have recently gained renewed attention in the discussion of "situated and embodied" cognition in the philosophy of cognitive science.
2 Davidson (1963/1980: ch. 1).
3 On action explanation, see Melden (1961: chs. 8–9), Davidson (1980: ch. 1; 1987), von Wright (1971: ch.1), Dretske (1988), Mele (1992).
4 Wilson (1989). See also Schueler (2003). A related debate concerns the issue whether reasons for action should be conceived as (putative) states of affairs rather than mental states. Some argue that the reasons for which the agent flips the switch, say, are things like the "world-involving" fact that, by flipping the switch, she would illuminate the room – not her *belief* that the flipping

would work this way, and the fact that there is something desirable about the room's being illuminated – not her *desire* for it; see Dancy (2000).

5   Ryle (1949: ch. 3). For a defense of classical volitionism, see Prichard (1945).
6   Frankfurt (1988: ch. 2, 4–7, 12).
7   For the criticism of hierarchy and an outline of a non-hierarchical view of identification in terms of the agent's valuing, see Watson (1975).
8   Frankfurt (1999: ch. 8).
9   Velleman (2000: ch. 1, 6).
10 Bratman (2007).
11 Korsgaard (2009).
12 Chisholm (1976).
13 On agent-causation, see Clarke (1993), Alvarez and Hyman (1998), O'Connor (2000).
14 Hornsby (2004).
15 Anscombe (1963); Davidson (1971/1980: ch. 3).
16 On the individuation of action, see also Anscombe (1979), Goldman (1970: chs. 1–2), Ginet (1990: ch. 3).
17 On basic actions, see Danto (1963) and Davidson (1971/1980: ch. 3).
18 On trying, see O'Shaughnessy (1973; 1980) and Hornsby (1980: chs. 1–3).
19 For a representative sample of the various approaches to the study of intention and intentional action, see Anscombe (1963), Austin (1990: chs. 8, 12), Davidson (1978/1980: chs. 5), Hunter (1978), O'Shaughnessy (1980: chs. 17), Searle (1983: chs. 3), Bratman (1987; 1999; 2007), Velleman (1989; 2000), Mele and Moser (1994), Scheer (1994), and Hartogh (2004).
20 On the difference between intended and merely foreseen effects, see Harman (1986: ch. 9) and Bratman (1987: ch. 10). Notice that the difference between doing something intentionally and doing something knowingly but non-intentionally might make a difference in the assessment of the agent's blameworthiness and culpability, as suggested by the so-called doctrine of "double effect."
21 Moran (2001).
22 Velleman (2000).
23 Davidson (1980: ch. 1, 5).
24 Bratman (1987; 1999).
25 Bratman (2009).
26 Velleman (2007).
27 On the relation between intention, prediction, and self-knowledge, see Hampshire (1975: ch. 3), Grice (1971), Velleman (2007), Wilson (2000), Falvey (2000), Moran (2001; 2004). On cognitivism about practical reason, see Harman (1976), Bratman (1999: ch. 13; 2009), Velleman (2000: ch. 1), Wallace (2001), Setiya (2007).

References

Alvarez, M. and Hyman, J. (1998). "Agents and Their Actions," *Philosophy*, 73, 219–45.
Anscombe, G. E. M. (1963). *Intention*, 2nd edn., Ithaca, NY: Cornell University Press.
Anscombe, G. E. M. (1979). "Under a Description," *Nous*, 13, 219–33.
Austin, J. L. (1990). *Philosophical Papers*, Oxford: Clarendon.

Bratman, M. (1987). *Intentions, Plans, and Practical Reason*, Cambridge, MA: Harvard University Press.

Bratman, M. (1999). *Faces of Intention*, Cambridge: Cambridge University Press.

Bratman, M. (2007). *Structures of Agency*, Oxford: Oxford University Press.

Bratman, M. (2008). "Intention, Belief, Practical, Theoretical," in J. Timmerman, J. Skorupski, and S. Robertson (eds.), *Spheres of Reason*, Oxford: Oxford University Press.

Chisholm, R. (1976). "The Agent as Cause," in M. Brand and D. Walton (eds.), *Action Theory*, Dordrecht: Reidel, 199–211.

Clarke, R. (1993). "Toward A Credible Agent-causal Account of Free Will," *Nous*, 27, 191–203.

Dancy, J. (2000). *Practical Reality*, Oxford: Oxford University Press.

Danto, A. C. (1963). "What Can We Do?" *Journal of Philosophy*, 60, 435–45.

Danto, A. C. (1965). "Basic Actions," *American Philosophical Quarterly*, 2, 141–8.

Davidson, D. (1980). *Essays on Actions and Events*, Oxford: Clarendon.

Davidson, D. (1987b). "Problems in the Explanation of Action," in P. Pettit, R. Sylva, and J. Norman (eds.), *Metaphysics and Morality*, Oxford: Blackwell.

Dretske, F. (1988). *Explaining Behavior*, Cambridge, MA: MIT Press.

Falvey, K. (2000). "Knowledge in Intention," *Philosophical Studies*, 99, 21–44.

Frankfurt, H. G. (1988). *The Importance of What We Care About*, Cambridge: Cambridge University Press.

Frankfurt, H. G. (1999). *Necessity, Volition, and Love*, Cambridge: Cambridge University Press.

Ginet, C. (1990). *On Action*, Cambridge: Cambridge University Press.

Goldman, A. (1970). *A Theory of Human Action*, Englewood Cliffs, NJ: Prentice Hall.

Grice, H. P. (1971). "Intentions and Certainty," *Proceedings of the British Academy*, 57, 263–79.

Hampshire, S. (1975). *Freedom of the Individual*, expanded edn., New York: Harper.

Harman, G. (1976). "Practical Reasoning," *Review of Metaphysics*, 79, 431–63.

Harman, G. (1986). "Change in View: Principles of Reasoning," Cambridge, MA: MIT Press.

Hartogh, D. G. (2004). "The Authority of Intention," *Ethics*, 115, 6–34.

Hornsby, J. (1980). *Actions*, London: Routledge.

Hornsby, J. (2004). "Agency and Actions," in H. Steward and J. Hyman (eds.), *Agency and Action*, Cambridge: Cambridge University Press, 1–23.

Hunter, J. F. M. (1978). *Intending*, Halifax: Dalhousie University Press.

Kenny, A. (1992). *The Metaphysics of Mind*, Oxford: Oxford University Press.

Korsgaard, C. (2009). *Self-constitution: Action, Identity and Integrity*, Oxford: Oxford University Press.

Melden, A. I. (1961). *Free Action*, London: Routledge & Kegan Paul.

Mele, A. R. (1992). *The Springs of Action*, New York: Oxford University Press.

Mele, A. R. (ed.) (1997). *The Philosophy of Action*, Oxford: Oxford University Press.

Mele, A. R. and Moser, P. K. (1994). "Intentional Action," *Nous*, 28, 39–68.

Moran, R. (2001). *Authority and Estrangement: An Essay on Self-knowledge*, Princeton, NJ: Princeton University Press.

Moran, R. (2004). "Anscombe on 'Practical Knowledge,' " in H. Steward and J. Hyman (eds.), *Agency and Action*, Cambridge: Cambridge University Press, 43–68.

O'Connor, T. (2000). *Persons and Causes: The Metaphysics of Free Will*, New York: Oxford University Press.

O'Shaughnessy, B. (1973). "Trying as the Mental 'Pineal Gland,' " *Journal of Philosophy*, 70, 365–386.

O'Shaughnessy, B. (1980). *The Will*, Cambridge: Cambridge University Press.

Prichard, H. A. (1945). "Acting, Willing, Desiring," in H. A. Prichard (ed.), *Moral Obligation*, Oxford: Clarendon, 187–98.

Ruben, D. H. (2003). *Action and Its Explanation*, New York: Oxford University Press.

Ryle, G. (1949). *The Concept of Mind*, Chicago: Chicago University Press.

Sartre, J. P. (1956). *Being and Nothingness*, tr. Hazel E. Barnes, New York: Philosophical Library.

Scheer, R. K. (1994). "The Causal Theory of Intentions," *Philosophical Investigations*, 17, 417–34.

Schueler, G. F. (2003). *Reasons and Purposes: Human Rationality and the Teleological Explanation of Action*, Oxford: Oxford University Press.

Searle, J. R. (1983). *Intentionality*, Cambridge: Cambridge University Press.

Setiya, K. (2007). *Reasons without Rationalism*, Princeton, NJ: Princeton University Press.

Stout, R. (2005). *Action*, Montreal: McGill-Queen's University Press.

Velleman, J. D. (1989). *Practical Reflection*, Princeton, NJ: Princeton University Press.

Velleman, J. D. (2000). *The Possibility of Practical Reason*, Oxford: Oxford University Press.

Velleman, J. D. (2007). "What Good Is a Will?" in A. Leist and H. Baumann (eds.), *Action in Context*, Berlin/New York: De Gruyter/Mouton.

Von Wright, G. H. (1963). *Norm and Action*, London: Routledge.

Von Wright, G. H. (1971). *Explanation and Understanding*, Ithaca, NY: Cornell University Press.

Wallace, R. J. (2001). "Normativity, Commitment, and Instrumental Reason," *Philosophers' Imprint*, 1, 1–26.

Watson, G. (1975). "Free Agency," *Journal of Philosophy*, 72, 205–20.

Wilson, G. (1989). *The Intentionality of Human Action*, Palo Alto, CA: Stanford University Press.

Wilson, G. (2000). "Proximal Practical Foresight," *Philosophical Studies*, 99, 3–19.

Wilson, G. (2007). "Action," in E. Zalta (ed.), *Stanford Encyclopedia of Philosophy*, Stanford, CA: Stanford University Press.

11

Free Will

Helen Steward

We usually tend to feel that we have a certain amount of control over our lives. This control is of course not complete. We are hemmed in by circumstances in various ways – and accept, on the whole, that not every path is one which is genuinely open to us. Perhaps I know, for instance, that I am not talented enough ever to become a great composer or a great long jumper, however much effort I put into these things. Perhaps I can also see (though this tends to be easier with other people than it is with oneself) that my upbringing and my environmental circumstances have had a powerful effect on the sort of person I have become, on the choices I have made so far and on the way I am perceived by others – perhaps, for instance, I can see that growing up in poverty on a sink estate in an inner city is relatively unlikely to lead to my becoming a corporate lawyer or a brain surgeon, for a complex mixture of financial, educational and social reasons. But the problem of free will in its most acute form arises from the fear that perhaps there are actually no choices at all – that I am so completely hemmed in by the circumstances in which I find myself that only one future course – the one I in fact end up taking – truly remains available to me. Perhaps, the fear is, the whole course of my life is determined by factors entirely beyond my control and I really have nothing whatever to do with the way in which my future unfolds.

How might this worry arise? One way to make the problem vivid is simply to continue to press the line of thinking I began above. We are used to the nature-nurture debate – to the idea that we are the products of our genetic endowment and our upbringing. But this view already sits rather uncomfortably with the idea that I have free will. After all, I do not choose my genetic endowment. I am simply landed with it. If I just don't have what it takes to be a great long jumper, for example, that's tough – there's nothing I can do about it. But neither do I choose such things as: my parents, my siblings, my school, the social environment I grow up in, the cultural and religious ethos in which I am initially embedded – all these things which we recognize have such a powerful effect on the course of a human life. Of course, I might get to choose some of the elements of this environment later on, once I am a bit older – for example, I can start to choose my friends, my school subjects, my hobbies, and so on. But the worry would be that these later choices would inevitably be the products of a personality formed and shaped entirely by earlier influences – and so are not really down to me in any ultimate sense. I have perhaps become a rather shy nine-year-old, for instance, because of my over-critical parents, and this means that I "choose" to be friends with other shy and quiet people. What looked at first like spontaneous choice, then, it might be argued, is actually just the inevitable working out of predispositions laid down years ago when I began to become the person I am today, under the joint influence of genes and upbringing. And the idea would be that a human life is in the end, no more than this – the complex product of an enormous number of interactions between a genetic program and its environmental embedding. The idea of a free person at the heart of things, autonomously forging her route through the world would have to be regarded, were this true, as a mere comforting fiction in which we perhaps cannot help but take refuge, in order to protect ourselves from the harshness of a rather unappealing reality.

The consequences of this view for a range of our most significant beliefs and important social practices, moreover, would appear to be very severe. If I am not a free person autonomously forging my route through the world, does it really make sense to blame (or praise) me, for any of the things I do? We generally think that it is wrong to blame a person for what they cannot help, but if I, and my actions, are the inevitable products of my genes and the environment in which I find myself placed, then surely it might be wondered whether I can really help being the sort of person I have become, and whether, therefore, I can help doing any of the things I do in consequence of having become that sort of person. But what becomes, in that case, of the notion, crucially important in our relations with others, that we are morally responsible for our actions and can be held to account for them? Does it make sense to feel such emotions as gratitude and resentment towards others if I cannot coherently think of them as responsible for what they have done? And what of the practice of punishment? Doesn't it become unjustifiable to punish someone, if their actions are no more than the inevitable consequences of genetic and environmental factors? Of course, it could still be useful to punish people from a purely utilitarian point of view; it would help to mould and influence their future behavior, perhaps, and also the behavior of others. Its deterrent effect could still be used to justify the practice. But we generally suppose that punishment is *deserved* by those who have done wrong and who are subjected to it as a result. And this might seem to be a thought we could no longer reasonably have, if it were true that all our actions are determined by a complicated mix of genetic and environmental factors. The problem of free will appears to have all sorts of practical implications, as well as theoretical ones, and we therefore cannot afford to hive it off to the academics to sort out amongst themselves. It needs, and deserves, an answer that all of us can live with.

Determinism

A related, but somewhat more abstract way of raising the free will problem, the one which has probably been the most common route into the issue in philosophy, considers the possibility that *determinism* is true. Determinism can be considered, for our purposes, to be the view that every event that ever happens is necessitated by events in the remote past, together with the laws of nature. The enormous success of Newtonian physics made this, at one time, the accepted scientific view of the universe; each movement of, or change in, any entity was thought to be produced by antecedent causal factors, which brought about their effects in conformity with a set of strict, exceptionless laws.[1] But then if determinism is true, the thought goes, it applies also to the movements and changes which we think of as our actions and our choices. Those are also necessitated by events in the remote past, together with the laws of nature. But in that case, one might start to wonder what I really have to do with the events I think of as my actions and my choices. It looks as though it was already settled long ago, before I was born, by the laws and the initial conditions of the universe, that my actions and choices would happen.[2] And this is very hard to square with our view of ourselves as creatures who *make a difference* to the universe – whose interventions make the world go one way when it might have gone another. We tend to think that our actions are things which did not *have* to happen – that we always could have done otherwise than we did. In William James's words "the whole sting and excitement of our voluntary life . . . depends on our sense that things are *really being decided* from one moment to another, and that it is not the dull rattling off of a chain that was forged innumerable ages ago."[3] But if determinism is true, this seems to be an illusion. And rather frighteningly, again, many of our practices of praising, blaming and punishing people begin to look as though they might be thoroughly unjustified. If my actions are just inevitable events in the long rolling out of the consequences of happenings that occurred long before I was born, it doesn't really seem fair to hold me morally responsible for them. The state of the universe and the laws of nature are responsible, not me.

It might be thought that perhaps one could take refuge in the possibility that perhaps determinism is *not* true. Those who believe that determinism and free will are incompatible, but who deny the truth of determinism, and therefore continue to suppose that free will exists, are called *libertarians*. We might think it was good news for the libertarian that most physicists today subscribe to at least some theories which are indeterministic – which allow for laws which are merely probabilistic, and, at the microphysical level, for truly random events, happenings whose occurrence is not necessitated by any prior circumstances. It does not seem as though determinism *is* universally true – so we might have thought we could stop worrying about the free will problem, at least when couched as a problem about its incompatibility with determinism. But the trouble is that even many libertarians agree that the sort of indeterminism which appears to be allowed for by physics doesn't really seem to help all that much with the free will problem. All that this variety of indeterminism seems to introduce into the picture is the possibility that some of my actions and choices, instead of being entirely determined by prior circumstances, are merely probabilistically related to those circumstances, or perhaps alternatively, are not related to prior circumstances at all, being purely random events. But this is no good. We don't just want to have to wait and see whether our actions will happen, or whether we will choose course of action A or course of action B. We don't want the relevant causal connections to be *chancy*. We want to be able to *ensure* that our actions will happen when we decide that they should. We want our wills to impact reliably on the world, to do what we intended to do, and to intend what we wanted to intend. And the introduction of randomness in the universe does not appear to help in the slightest with this. Moreover, even if the universe of fundamental physics *is* indeterministic, it is often said, it doesn't follow that there is any significant indeterminism in the causal relationships which are of relevance to our actions – for example, between neurological antecedents and bodily movements, or between different types of neurological occurrence. Microphysical indeterminism doesn't necessarily entail macrophysical indeterminism. So it is not clear in any case that microphysical indeterminism will do the job we wanted it to do, of disrupting the smoothly inexorable way in which the past gives rise to the future at the levels of resolution in which we are interested.

Not all philosophers are so pessimistic about the possibility that microphysical indeterminism might provide an escape route for the libertarian. It has been argued, for example, that the chaotic amplification of indeterministic processes in the brain might have a role to play in permitting the existence of some important sorts of free action – for example, important moral decisions of the sort that help to form and forge a person's character.[4] But many philosophers have remained skeptical about the idea that the acceptance of microphysical indeterminism could be enough, in and of itself, to solve the free will problem. Perhaps it is a necessary condition of the freedom to which we aspire, but many feel it could not possibly be sufficient; and that we must look elsewhere for the solution.

Compatibilism

In the face of these difficulties with indeterminism, the majority of philosophers have tended to think that the best hope for free will lies in the project of trying to show that despite first appearances, free will is not in fact incompatible with determinism after all – that we can have what we want *even if* determinism is true of the macrophysical universe. This view is called *compatibilism*, and is contrasted with the *incompatibilist* line of thinking I outlined above, according to which determinism cannot be made consistent with the idea of free will. There are a number of different compatibilist strategies. One historically popular move lies in the observation that causes should not be thought of, as they seem to be by the incompatibilist, as events which bring their effects inexorably in their train. The incompatibilist appears to be relying on a conception of laws of nature according to which the laws *make* things happen as they do. But this, it is said, is a mere confusion. Causal laws are just descriptions of regularities that have so far been found to describe our universe successfully. We should not think of them as metaphysical realities, sewn into the fabric of the world, constraining and dictating the shape of things to come. Rather, they are just *post facto* creations of our own, in principle capable of infinite adjustment and alteration so as to conform to what in fact is found to occur in actuality, not pre-existent rails along which the world must run.

But this move is much less popular than once it was, mainly because the regularity theory of causation, on which it relies, is much less popular than once it was. On the whole, the majority of philosophers in recent years have tended to think that the idea that causal laws are mere regularities, and that there is nothing metaphysically real which might explain why the regularities are the way they are, is very unappealing, because it offers no account of what *grounds* the indisputably real patterns in the world. Of course, saying that a law of nature lies behind an indisputably real pattern isn't of itself to offer much of an explanation of that pattern. But, it is suggested, it is nevertheless a far more satisfying stopping place for our thinking than the brute regularity of the pattern itself, even if fully satisfying explanations of why things go the way they do might be forever beyond us. Broadly realist views of causation and law have therefore now largely replaced the regularity theory as orthodoxy, and so this particular compatibilist escape route has not found much favor in recent years.

A much more popular compatibilist suggestion is that it simply does not follow from determinism that no one could ever have done other than they did. We simply need, it is said, to focus more clearly on what we mean when we say that freedom requires the capacity to have done otherwise. We do not mean, surely, that it requires the capacity to perform actions that bear no relations to our choices and intentions – to act in ways which are totally irrational and inexplicable by our own lights. We mean, rather that it requires the capacity to do another thing *should we so choose*. But there is nothing inconsistent with determinism in this suggestion. A determinist can perfectly well accept that I could have done something different *if* I had chosen to do something different. That is a power she has no trouble accommodating at all.

But the difficulty with this move is that it just doesn't seem to be true that the only capacity we are interested in when we are concerned with free will is the capacity to do another thing should we so choose. We are also interested in the capacity to *choose* another thing; which is a capacity we cannot have, it is argued, if determinism is true. If my choice itself is inevitable, it is surely not much comfort to point out that I would have done something else if I had chosen to do something else. I want to know, in addition, that I actually *could* have chosen something else – indeed, the very notion of choice seems to demand the idea of a range of possible options, all of which are genuinely open to me. But this, it is said, I cannot truly have if determinism is true.

Many compatibilists have therefore come to focus on the relation between such things as choices or decisions and what precedes them in the chain of supposed psychological causes. Choices flow, they say, from a complex web of beliefs, desires, moral principles, etc., beliefs, desires, and principles which ought to *rationalize*, that is, make sensible or reasonable, the choice that I make. Now, it is not sensible, they argue, to wish that I might have chosen something other than what is rationalized by my beliefs, desires and moral principles – not, at any rate, not if my beliefs, desires and moral principles have been arrived at in appropriate ways. Surely, I do not *want* the capacity to make completely *mad* choices, choices I can see no reason whatever to make and which do not connect up at all with what I want to achieve and with my beliefs about the best means for achieving it.[5] Deterministic causation of our actions by our beliefs, desires and moral principles is in fact, then, it is argued, just what we should want, provided we can manage to exclude certain sorts of problematic cases in which beliefs, desires and moral principles have been arrived at in ways that seem paradigmatically unfree – e.g. through indoctrination, addiction, personality disorders, phobias, etc. This causation – of choice by the right set of desires, beliefs and principles – just *is*, on this view what choice by the autonomous selves we take ourselves to be really amounts to.[6]

But what *is* the right set of desires, beliefs, and principles? It seems obvious that not any old set will do. For example, I may desperately want some heroin because I am an addict. This incredibly powerful desire certainly "rationalizes" the actions I take to secure it, in that it makes it sensible for me to attempt to secure the means to pay for it (by e.g. engaging in theft, burglary, prostitution) so that I can satisfy my desire. But we do not, generally speaking, regard the heroin addict as a free agent – and this is because, it is argued, there is something wrong with the relationship between him and his own desire. He probably does not *want* to have that desire for heroin himself; he does not *endorse* the desire, or value its object in any way. In his reflective moments, he sees and knows it is a bad thing, something he would prefer to be rid of and with which he does not identify. A range of compatibilist strategies have therefore focused on the possibility that perhaps we might attempt to describe the conditions necessary for free will by describing the relationships that ought to hold amongst the beliefs, desires, principles, etc. of a free agent. Roughly speaking, the idea is that we can *reflect* on the desires, principles, and so on, with which we find ourselves – rank them, for example, in terms of how important they are to our conception of what is truly good, important and meaningful in life, and that only actions caused and rationalized by those which end up endorsed by this type of reflective activity would count as free.[7]

Agent Causation

For the incompatibilist, though, this solution will seem to be no solution at all. If the reflective "activity" itself is a merely deterministic consequence of prior conditions, she will be inclined to think, it is just another set of deterministically guaranteed events, which cannot have been up to the agent; indeed, she may be inclined to put her point by saying that she does not see how there could *be* such a thing as an agent or an action, under the circumstances the determinist describes. She may doubt the very applicability, if determinism is true, of the psychological scheme of explanation that traces choices to such things as beliefs and desires, believing that this scheme already presupposes a conception of an agent who *has* the beliefs and desires and whose impacts on the world cannot merely be reduced to the impacts on the world of those beliefs and desires. The real problem, she may say, is with the very idea that actions are to be thought of as the causal consequences of a mere series of states and events. What we need to recognize is that agency cannot be conceptualized properly in terms of such a causal series. Some causation, that is, the sort that is involved in agency, cannot be captured in terms of mere events causing other events. Some events, they say, must be caused by *agents* if there is to be such a thing as free action – perhaps if there is to be such a thing as action at all – in the world. This special variety of causal relation, thought to be necessary for freedom by at least some incompatibilists, is known as *agent causation*.

The view that there is a special variety of causation operative only when actions occur, though, has seemed unattractive to many. It raises difficult questions for the agent causationist to answer: how, for example, does agent causation relate to the (presumably) common-or-garden variety that relates the various events in our brains and bodies that are known to be involved in the phenomenon of action? Is it operative only when human beings act, or can it also be found in the activity of animals? If we say the former, it has the appearance of being at odds with a naturalistic conception of the place of humanity in the universe. If we say the latter, on the other hand, we must ask how far down the hierarchy of animal life we have to go before agent causation is no longer found – and whether there is a sharp cut-off point. If agent causation is truly a distinctive phenomenon, it might seem as though the cut-off point *should* be sharp. But sharp cut-off points might seem unappealing in the context of a broadly evolutionary conception of animal nature, and of the relations that different species of animal bear to one another.

A less metaphysically committed position, which might be regarded, perhaps, as Kantian in spirit, might agree with the agent causationist that there is something about the way in which we think about and explain purposive action in terms of reasons, which cannot be properly fitted together with the way in which we think about and explain such events as mere bodily movements. But this, the Kantian might say, need not mean that we must look to the world to supply an alternative type of causation to operate in the case of purposive action. Rather, we should recognize that the source of the incompatibility is in the schemes of thought, conceptualisation and explanation that we bring to bear on different kinds of case – the source of the incompatibility is in us, and in our ways of thinking, not in the world. There could be different versions of this kind of view. One kind might stress, as Kant himself did, the difference between *theoretical* and *practical* thought, arguing that when we attempt to explain actions psychologically, by adverting to agents' reasons, our concern is always practical – and in the practical realm, we must regard both ourselves, and those others whose actions we seek to explain in rational ways, as being the source of their own activity, as being free. When, on the other hand, we wish to explain mere bodily movements in terms of their antecedents, we take a more theoretical stance, and we utilize the causal framework we use in general when we want to understand why an event has occurred – that is to say, we look for the events that preceded it, and we assume that there are laws operating in virtue of which the prior events gave rise to the later ones. Another version of this strategy opts for a strict distinction between reasons and causes. Reason-giving explanations, some philosophers insist, are not causal at all – it is a mistake to suppose that when we explain actions by saying something about what the agent thought good or desirable or important about them, we offer a *causal* explanation. We are doing something else entirely. We do not therefore need to suppose that there is such a thing as agent causation to relate agents to the events they bring about – for the explanations which might make it look as though we are committed to the idea that agents cause events are not causal explanations in the first place. Rather, when I say, for example, that I put a bird-bath in my garden because I wanted to attract some birds, I am making my action *intelligible*, explaining what is the *end* or *purpose* it serves; and this type of explanation is simply not in competition with the causal explanation of why my body made the movements it did as I took the bird-bath out into the garden. It has a different kind of point altogether, and therefore can stand alongside the causal explanations of neurophysiology without either usurping them, or being usurped. And if the presuppositions of reason-giving explanations were indeterministic, while those of causal explanations were deterministic, then perhaps we could live with that, tracing the conflict to the operation of differing schemes of explanation, each of which has its own value and integrity.

Against this, though, it has been argued forcefully that reason-giving explanations surely *are* causal explanations of a kind.[8] When I say that I put a bird bath in my garden because I wanted to attract some birds, I do not *merely* rationalize my action; I also say something about the nature of its *causal source* in my desires and beliefs. And if this is right, then it seems hard to avoid the conclusion that the two sorts of explanation *are* in competition. We have one sort of causal explanation tracing my actions (and therefore, presumably, the bodily movements that my actions entail) to me and my reasons, and another sort tracing those bodily movements to such things as neural firings in the motor cortex. And the worry is that if the second explanation is really correct, it can leave no proper room for the first. Neural firings would seem to have their source in prior neural firings, and those in prior ones, and so on, back to times much earlier than the point at which it seems to me I decided to put the bird bath in my garden. So that seems to mean that it was in fact settled that I would decide to do this long before the decision was actually made. But then, how can the decision really have *been* a decision? It seems to be no more than one in a long series of inevitable occurrences, if the determinist's account of the matter is right. It is hard to avoid the conclusion that once reason-giving explanations are regarded as a variety of causal explanation, the elegant Kantian-style solution, according to which we trace the free will problem to the operation of two distinct conceptual schemes, collapses – we are back not only with distinct, but with incompatible conceptual schemes; and if two schemes are truly incompatible, one must go.

Strawson

Perhaps it may be, though, that it is not really open to us to rid ourselves of the scheme in terms of which we do our practical thinking in any case. The importance of the question whether we could possibly live without such concepts as moral responsibility, desert, praise and blame, and the practices and emotions with which those concepts are intertwined, whether any recognisably human form of existence could survive their repudiation, is stressed by P. F. Strawson in his enormously influential article, "Freedom and Resentment."[9] Strawson wishes to agree with the incompatibilist that many varieties of compatibilist "solution" to the free will problem are unsatisfactory. In particular, he is keen to concede to the incompatibilist that it will not do to try to represent the practice of punishment as something that can be essentially grounded solely in such utilitarian matters as crime prevention and deterrence – a strategy sometimes adopted by compatibilists in the attempt to salvage these practices from the wreck which might appear to have been made of them by the supposition that determinism is true. But at the same time, Strawson is clear that the libertarian in the end has nothing but "obscure and panicky metaphysics"[10] to offer us – nothing that could truly help us see our way clear of the difficulties presented by the free will problem. His ambition, therefore, is to give the compatibilist "something more to say" – some facts beyond the purely utilitarian ones, which might supply an adequate basis for the concepts and practices which the incompatibilist fears would be undermined were determinism true, in which to ground our ideas about desert and responsibility, and the associated societal and legal framework of law, punishment and exculpation.

Strawson turns, in order to find these additional facts, to what he calls the "reactive attitudes" – natural human responses to the goodwill – or absence of goodwill – we find demonstrated by other human beings towards ourselves. Such attitudes as gratitude, resentment, hurt feelings, forgiveness, and love belong in this important category – they are attitudes we take towards others which depend, at least in part, upon our beliefs about how what those others do and say reflects their attitudes towards *us*. He contrasts these attitudes with other, more objective and detached attitudes we are sometimes able to take towards others when we regard them as compulsive or deranged in their behavior, and are viewing them as potential objects of social control and policy, rather than as friends, lovers, colleagues, cohabitants, fellow citizens, etc., with whom we might have a more personal, "participant" variety of relationship. The compatibilist, he suggests, can sometimes seem to be insisting that we must entirely replace the personal reactive attitudes with a more objective and detached view, and that this is the rational consequence of the metaphysical truth we recognize when we recognize determinism. But Strawson presses the question whether we can really imagine divesting ourselves of the reactive attitudes. He suggests that the answer to this question is "no" – it is not humanly possible to rid ourselves of the reactive attitudes – an answer which makes it simply useless to ask whether it would be rational to do so, if we only could. These interpersonal emotions and attitudes are part of the indestructible framework within which particular questions of moral responsibility must be raised and answered – the framework itself cannot come up for review. And even if, *per impossibile*, we could conceive of replacing this framework with the dispassionate objective appraisals offered by the proposed alternative perspective, the question whether it would be rational so to replace it could only be answered by reference to the question what the costs and benefits would be to human life as it is lived.

Strawson does not explicitly answer this question – but we are left to infer that life would surely be immeasurably impoverished, were we prevented from ever taking these sorts of attitudes to another human being. And so it could not be "rational" to do what the compatibilist sometimes seems to be suggesting we ought to do, and take the objective stance all of the time to all of our fellow human beings – even supposing it were possible.

Experimental Results

There remain many, though, who believe that a scientific view of human nature really does reveal that the view of ourselves which seems to underpin our participant attitudes is mistaken, whether or not we are actually able to make the necessary adjustments to our thinking. The idea that things are often settled before we come to make the conscious decision that we take to be the cause of our action has been given additional impetus by some experimental evidence obtained in recent years, which has received a great deal of attention in the free will literature.[11] There is experimental evidence to support the view that human voluntary acts are preceded a specific electrical change in the brain (the "readiness potential") which occurs 550 msec. before the act actually occurs. Human subjects, however, become aware of the conscious intention to act only 350–400 msec. after the readiness potential has started. It seems, then, as though the brain begins to prepare for action *before* the person makes the conscious decision to act. The initiation of action, it is concluded, therefore, is actually unconscious. A veto role may remain for the conscious will, which still has time to prevent the motor action once it becomes aware of what is going on; but the initiation itself seems to be an unconscious affair. Some philosophers (and others) have taken this to show that we do not have free will.

The interpretation of these results is, however, enormously controversial. Many philosophers do not think this experimental data bears significantly on the free will problem at all. And any consequences the results might have for free will would of course have to depend on the idea that for an act to be initiated by its agent is for it to be initiated by a conscious volitional event – an idea that has for many years been thought problematic by philosophers of action in *any* case, for the simple reason that most of the intentional activity we undertake does not appear to be preceded by any such conscious volitional events. For example, I just typed the letter "t." I was not aware, immediately prior to typing it, of any conscious volition to do so. But the absence of such an introspectible volition surely has no tendency to imply that it was not me that typed the letter, or that I did not do so freely or intentionally. It is unclear, then, why we should suppose that the fact that the conscious awareness of a decision to press a button succeeds volitional preparation for button pressing in the brain should have any tendency to imply that the act is any less mine or any less free than the many, many acts we appear to perform in the complete absence of an antecedent volitional event.

Free Will and Moral Responsibility

A strategy which attempts to weave its way between compatibilism and incompatibilism proceeds by *conceding* that determinism is incompatible with the ability to do otherwise, but then attempting to divorce this concession from what are often taken to be its most devastating consequences, by arguing that actually the capacity to do otherwise is not a necessary condition for moral responsibility at all. The argument tends to proceed on the basis of a now very famous thought experiment.[12] Let us imagine that there is an agent, Jones, who is considering whether to do a certain thing – say, vote Republican – and another agent, Black, who has a lot of power over Jones. Black can, for example, interfere with Jones's nervous system in various ways in order to ensure that he does certain things. Now, Black very much wants Jones to vote Republican – but he would prefer not to intervene to ensure this unless it turns out to be absolutely necessary. What Black does, therefore, is monitor Jones's thought processes very carefully, perhaps while he is in the voting booth, watching for any signs that Jones may be about to change his mind. If Jones does show any signs of wavering, Black resolves, he, Black, will step in and make a neurological intervention which will result in Jones voting Republican. But in the event, Jones just goes ahead and votes Republican of his own accord. Black does nothing, in the end, except watch and monitor what occurs.

What should we say about this example? Most philosophers think that under the circumstances described, Jones is clearly morally responsible for voting Republican. We could blame (or praise) him for doing so, for instance, and hold him to account for what he has done. And yet it appears very natural to say that Jones could not have done other than vote Republican. For if he had *attempted* to do anything else, Black would have intervened and prevented him; Black was always going to ensure that Jones was unable to leave the voting booth without having put a cross next to the Republican's name. It seems to follow, then, that the possibility of doing otherwise is simply not a necessary condition of moral responsibility at all.

Frankfurt-style examples, as they have become known, have been the basis for the distinctive position known as semi-compatibilism,[13] which argues that though the capacity to do otherwise is inconsistent with determinism, we can afford to be less worried by this fact that we might have thought – since it does not follow that determinism is incompatible with *moral responsibility*. We simply do not require the capacity to do otherwise in order to be morally responsible for the things we do – as Frankfurt-style examples are supposed to show. But incompatibilists have tended to be unimpressed by Frankfurt-style examples. Some insist that Jones, in the situation imagined, still *could* have done other than he did; they point out, for example, that he could certainly have done other than vote Republican *on his own*; or he could have done other than perform the *particular* action he in fact performed (even if he could not have done other than perform an action of the *type* "voting Republican"). Semi-compatibilists have responded that though it may indeed be that various "flickers of freedom" are available to Jones, none is "robust" enough or important enough to ground Jones's moral responsibility. But it remains open to the incompatibilist to respond that the flickers are not supposed to ground Jones's moral responsibility directly; they are supposed, rather, to ground his *agency*. We need, that is, to be able to think of Jones's particular action as something that he need not have performed if it is to count as an action of his in the first place. And while this is something that seems possible in the Frankfurt-style scenario, it does not seem to be possible for it to be true under determinism. If determinism is true, the incompatibilist may insist, each individual action is itself something from which no agent is ever able to refrain – which is as much as to say, she may allege, that it cannot be an action at all.[14]

Conclusion

It seems fair to say that the free will problem remains as far from a solution as it has ever been. It seems likely that its persistence can be traced in part to the modern conception of causation, which (on the whole) eschews talk of such things as causal powers and prefers to suppose causation to be a matter of the production of events by other events. Perhaps action is genuinely not intelligible within the constraints of an event-based picture, and a richer and better understanding of causation is required. But another difficulty, I am inclined to think, is that the customary formulation of the central tension misses an important point. Traditionally, the free will question has been posed in the following way: how is it possible for it to be true of an agent that he could have done otherwise, if determinism is true? But another issue is this: how is it possible for there to be such things as agents and their intentional doings *at all*, if determinism is true? When one imagines the universe as it is alleged to be by the causal determinist, a place in which each event follows inexorably from immediately preceding circumstances according to all-embracing laws of nature, it can seem that that universe permits no space for the phenomenon of action at all. It appears to be a world of mere events in which there seems to be no place of the sort where an agent might interpose herself and make a difference to what then occurs. The compatibilist, doubtless, will want to argue that the idea that an agent needs such a "place" to interpose herself into the series of events is an unnecessary and possibly even incoherent one – that an agent's interpositions must simply form a special subset of the networks of deterministically related events which she envisages as constituting causal reality. But this question needs answering before the traditional one can even be broached.

Further Reading

A very good place to begin exploring further is Gary Watson's edited collection *Free Will* (2003) which contains a number of classic articles, covering a very wide spectrum of views. The article by Strawson which is discussed above is included in this collection. Robert Kane's *Oxford Handbook of Free Will* (2002) is also an excellent introduction – in particular to relatively recent developments in the free will debate. A classical compatibilist view is found in the writings of the eighteenth century philosopher David Hume (see his *Enquiry Concerning Human Understanding* (1975: ch. VIII), "Of Liberty and Necessity." A very readable, more contemporary defence of compatibilism is found in Daniel Dennett's *Elbow Room* (1984). Peter Van Inwagen's *An Essay on Free Will* (1983) offers a careful analysis of different versions of an argument for incompatibilism; though it contains logical notation and may therefore be a bit hard to follow, in places, for total newcomers to philosophy. Robert Kane's book *The Significance of Free Will* (1998) is both an excellent introduction to the issues and an exciting development of a particular libertarian position. Timothy O'Connor's book *Persons and Causes* develops an appealing version of the agent-causationist line. There is an article by Benjamin Libet entitled "Do we Have Free Will?," which explains his own view of what his experimental results do and do not show, in Kane's *Oxford Handbook of Free Will* (see above) and his work is discussed in detail by Daniel M. Wegner in *The Illusion of Conscious Will* (2002). Frankfurt's suggestion that moral responsibility is independent of alternate possibilities is contained in his article "Alternate Possibilities and Moral Responsibility" (1969: 829–39) which is also reprinted in the Watson collection mentioned above. The best place to go for an overview of semi-compatibilism is probably John Fischer's book, *The Metaphysics of Free Will: A Study of Control* (1994); a revised and updated version of the view is presented in John Fischer and Mark Ravizza, *Responsibility and Control: A Theory of Moral Responsibility* (1998).

Notes

1   See e.g. Pierre-Simon Laplace (1995: 2): "We ought then to consider the present state of the universe as the effect of its previous state, and as the cause of that which is to follow. An intelligence that, at a given instant, could comprehend all the forces by which nature is animated and the respective situations of the beings that make it up, if, moreover, it were vast enough to submit these data to analysis, would encompass in the same formula the movements of the greatest bodies of the universe and those of the lightest atoms. For such an intelligence nothing would be uncertain, and the future, like the past, would be open to its eyes."

2   See Peter van Inwagen, *An Essay on Free Will* (1983) for an attempt to lay out an argument of this sort in a precise way.

3   William James, *The Principles of Psychology* (1950: 453).

4   See Robert Kane, *The Significance of Free Will* (1998) for a view of this sort.

5   Though for an opposed view, see, for example, Fyodor Dostoevsky (1992: 19–20): "man may consciously, purposely, desire what is injurious to himself, what is stupid, very stupid – simply in order to have the right to desire for himself even what is very stupid and not to be bound by an obligation to desire only what is sensible . . . this very stupid thing, the caprice of ours, may be in reality . . . more advantageous for us than anything else on earth . . . it preserves for us what is most precious and most important – that is, our personality, our individuality."

6   Different versions of this view of freedom as involving conformity to reason are found in Plato's *Republic* (1961; orig. date of composition ca. 375 BC); Benedictus de Spinoza, *Ethics* (1996, orig. pub. 1677); and Jean-Jacques Rousseau, *The Social Contract* (1968; orig. pub. 1762).

7   See e.g. Harry Frankfurt, "Freedom of the Will and the Concept of a Person" (1971: 5–20); and Gary Watson, "Free Agency" (1975: 205–20), for views of this sort.

8   See in particular Donald Davidson, "Actions, Reasons and Causes" (1980: 3–19).

9   P. F. Strawson, "Freedom and Resentment" (1962: 1–25); repr. in G. Watson (ed.), *Free Will* (2003: 72–93), to which page numbers refer.

10   Strawson (2003: 93).

11   Benjamin Libet, "Unconscious Cerebral Initiative and the Role of Conscious Will in Voluntary Action" (1985: 529–66); "Are the Mental Experiences of Will and Self-Control Significant for the Performance of a Voluntary Act?" (1987: 783–91). For a useful summary of Libet's results and his views about what they do and do not show, see his "Do We Have Free Will?" in Robert Kane (ed.), (2002).

12   This thought experiment was first offered by Harry Frankfurt, "Alternative Possibilities and Moral Responsibility" (1969: 829–39); the example I describe here is a variant on Frankfurt's original case.

13   This position has been developed in detail by John Fischer and Mark Ravizza – see their *Responsibility and Control: a Theory of Moral Responsibility* (1998).

14　For the development of this view, see Helen Steward (2009), "Fairness, Agency and the Flicker of Freedom" *Nous*, 43 (1).

References

Davidson, Donald (1980). "Actions, Reasons and Causes," *Essays on Actions and Events*, Oxford: Oxford University Press, 3–19.
Dennett, Daniel (1984). *Elbow Room*, Cambridge, MA: MIT Press.
Dostoevsky, Fyodor (1992). *Notes from the Underground*, tr. Constance Garnett, New York: Dover.
Fischer, John (1994). *The Metaphysics of Free Will: A Study of Control*, Oxford: Blackwell.
Fischer, John and Ravizza, Mark (1998). *Responsibility and Control: A Theory of Moral Responsibility*, Cambridge: Cambridge University Press.
Frankfurt, Harry (1969). "Alternate Possibilities and Moral Responsibility," *Journal of Philosophy*, 66, 829–39.
Frankfurt, Harry (1971). "Freedom of the Will and the Concept of a Person," *Journal of Philosophy*, 72 (8), 205–20.
Hume, David (1975). *Enquiry Concerning Human Understanding*, ed. David Selby-Bigge, Oxford: Oxford University Press.
James, William (1950). *The Principles of Psychology*, vol. 1, New York: Dover.
Kane, Robert (1998). *The Significance of Free Will*, New York: Oxford University Press.
Kane, Robert (2002). *Oxford Handbook of Free Will*, Oxford: Oxford University Press.
Laplace, Pierre-Simon (1995). *Philosophical Essay on Probabilities*, tr. Andrew Dale, New York: Springer-Verlag.
Libet, Benjamin (1985). "Unconscious Cerebral Initiative and the Role of Conscious Will in Voluntary Action," *Behavioral and Brain Sciences*, 8, 529–66.
Libet, Benjamin (1987). "Are the Mental Experiences of Will and Self-control Significant for the Performance of a Voluntary Act?" *Behavioral and Brain Sciences*, 10, 783–91.
Libet, Benjamin (2002). "Do We Have Free Will?" in Kane.
O'Connor, Timothy (2000). *Persons and Causes*, Oxford: Oxford University Press.
Plato (1961). *The Republic*, in *Plato: The Collected Dialogues*, ed. Edith Hamilton and Huntington Cairns, Princeton, NJ: Princeton University Press.
Rousseau, Jean-Jacques (1968) [1762]. *The Social Contract*, tr. Maurice Cranston, London: Penguin.
Spinoza, Benedictus de (1996) [1677]. *Ethics*, tr. E. M. Curley, intro. Stuart Hampshire, London: Penguin.
Steward, Helen (2009). "Fairness, Agency and the Flicker of Freedom," *Nous*.
Strawson, P. F. (1962; 2003). "Freedom and Resentment," *Proceedings of the British Academy*, 48, 1–25; repr. in Watson.
Van Inwagen, Peter (1983). *An Essay on Free Will*, Oxford: Oxford University Press.
Watson, Gary (ed.) (2003). *Free Will*, 2nd edn., Oxford: Oxford University Press.
Wegner, Daniel M. (2002). *The Illusion of Conscious Will*, Cambridge, MA: MIT Press.

12

Language and Meaning

R. M. Sainsbury

Language and Meaning

> language survives everything – corruption, misuse, ignorance, ineptitude. Linking man
> to man in the dark, it brought man out of the dark. It is the human glory which ante-
> cedes all others. It merits not only our homage but our constant and intelligent study.
> (Burgess 1975)

We use language so effortlessly, so automatically, and so unreflectively that it's easy to forget what an extraordinary phenomenon it is. A few sounds or marks can *mean* something; they can be used to enable us to exchange thoughts of a complexity that has no upper bound; they can be used in some of mankind's greatest aesthetic creations; and of course they can be used in the most humdrum ways as well. How is language possible? What breathes meaning into what are otherwise mere sounds or marks? Do dolphins have a language? Could a crea-ture without language think? Is language use a uniquely human accomplishment? Do lan-guage users deserve special moral consideration?

I'm not going to be able to address (let alone answer) all these questions. Rather, I'll offer a tour of three main themes from recent philosophical approaches to language. The first theme is rather surprising: I consider two versions of the view that there can be no such thing as meaning, at least as we ordinarily conceive it. Willard van Ormon Quine, a phi-losopher at Harvard for fifty years, reached this conclusion by reflecting on the evidence we would need in order to be justified in ascribing meaning. Ludwig Wittgenstein, a very influ-ential Austrian-born philosopher who did much of his philosophical work while living in England (he was particularly associated with the University of Cambridge), challenged our ordinary conception of meaning as involving an indefensible notion of rules which determine in every situation how a word is to be rightly applied: in his striking metaphor, "rails laid to infinity." His challenge has been sympathetically elaborated more recently by Saul Kripke.

The second theme I'll address is the systematic work that has been done in describing meaning in language, work which to some extent presupposes that the kinds of skepticism discussed in the first theme of this chapter are misguided. The work itself involve quite a lot of technicality, but I can give the general flavor of two of approaches without much technical detail. One approach is based on the idea that the meaning of a sentence can be given by the conditions under which it is true, in slogan form: meaning is truth conditions. The other approach is based on the idea that the basic notion of meaning can be defined in terms of speakers' intentions.

The third theme is the relation between the meanings of sentences and what we can reliably use them to communicate. For example, suppose I ask you whether you like music and you reply "I can tell the difference between loud and soft."[1] I would be right to treat you as meaning that you did not like music, although this is not what your words meant, and you did not literally say you did not like music.

We use the word "means" and its cognates for various phenomena with no special connection with language. In "Those spots mean measles," we invoke a notion of meaning centered on the idea of indicating or being a sign of. In "He meant no harm," we invoke a notion of meaning in which it amounts to intending. It may be that both aspects are invoked in linguistic meaning: there's a connection with indicating and being a sign of, and also a connection with the intentions of speakers. However described, most of us believe that we possess a sound and distinctive notion of linguistic meaning. The next section considers challenges to this natural belief.

Skepticism about Meaning

Language is a social art. (Quine 1960: ix)

Quine on rabbits

Imagine you are a linguist in the field, studying a people who speak a radically alien language (there are no bilinguals or similar languages to help you get started). Let's suppose you notice that, mostly, when the aliens utter one of their strange words, "Gavagai," there's a rabbit in their vicinity; and, mostly, if an alien notices a rabbit, she utters "Gavagai." This behavior makes "Rabbit" a sensible tentative translation of "Gavagai." No doubt there will be times when "Gavagai" is uttered when there is no visible rabbit: perhaps the speaker sees old rabbit-tracks, or wishes she had a rabbit. No doubt there will be times when a rabbit is in plain view but no one says anything: perhaps silence is required for rabbit catching, or the aliens see no reason to state the obvious. But it's natural to assume that these more complex data could be factored in, and in the end we would have a solid case for the hypothesis that "Gavagai" means "Rabbit."

This is the natural view that Quine seeks to undermine. One main line of argument is that we have simply assumed that the aliens share a metaphysical picture of the world that resembles ours. But suppose they think of the world as made up momentary things, collected together into bundles. What we think of as a rabbit is thought of by them as a collection of temporal parts of rabbits, a "rabbit-at-an-instant-of-time." The data about "Gavagai" equally support the view that it is true not of rabbits, but of temporal stages of rabbits. Or, of undetached parts of rabbits (for a rabbit is present just when an undetached rabbit part is present); and so on. There are endless distinct possibilities, and the data don't sort out which is correct.

Quine admits that if we already shared some parts of language with the aliens, we could reach a more determinate view. For example, if, when a single rabbit is present, we could ask an alien how many gavagai there are, any plural answer (e.g. "Five" or "Many") would count against the hypothesis that "gavagai" means "rabbit" and in favor of some such hypothesis as that it means "undetached rabbit part." But how are we to justify our supposition that we have really asked how many gavagai there are? Perhaps the alien words for "how many" which we use really mean "how many undetached parts of," in which case a plural answer is, after all, consistent with the view that "gavagai" means rabbit.

Quine calls the difficulty of grounding a determinate meaning for a term in the behavior of its users the "inscrutability of reference." His target is to establish a related thesis, the "indeterminacy of translation." He claims that any sentence of a language can be translated with equal correctness into both of two sentences which, intuitively, have different meanings. Perhaps, so far as any observable data about how the aliens behave are concerned, the one-word sentence "Gavagai" can be translated equally well as "Lo, a rabbit!" or as "Lo, an undetached part of a rabbit!." But the translations don't mean the same as each other, so they can't both mean the same as "Gavagai!." Quine invites us to conclude that the notion of *meaning* which underpins this contradiction is unsound. We must replace it by something closer to observable reality, and less governed by what he calls the "museum myth," according to which a meaning is displayed as some one determinate object among others.

The discussions of Quine's indeterminacy thesis are voluminous and detailed, and I will not attempt to indicate even their most salient features. But here's something we can usefully carry forward: Quine thinks that meaning is a property of behavior, of the use of language. This can be interpreted as an anodyne thesis, if no limitation is placed upon how behavior or use is to be regarded. An anodyne thesis connecting meaning and use is that the meaning of a word is a matter of what it is conventionally used to *mean*. Quine, however, thought that meaning needs to be a property of behavior which can be specified independently of semantic terms, like "meaning" or "reference." That plays a crucial role in his discussion, but it is a challenging and controversial thesis. One moral we might draw from the implausibility of the conclusion he reaches is that he is wrong to admit only such an impoverished conception of behavior as the basis for meaning. Perhaps it's wrong to think of meaning as reducible to "observable behavior" thought of as Quine thinks of it: the motion of matter through space. Perhaps we have to view the world, notably the behavior of others, in terms of meanings if we are to understand what it contains.

Wittgenstein and Kripke on invisible rails

> Whence comes the idea that the beginning of a series is the visible section of rails invisibly laid to infinity? (Wittgenstein 1953)

We all think there's a definite fact concerning what we mean by "+" (the addition function in arithmetic). Ludwig Wittgenstein, however, broaches skeptical reflections designed to undermine our confidence in this opinion. The essence of this skepticism is that it seems there is nothing we can point to which makes it the case that we mean addition by "+," rather than some related function. Our behavior would have been the same, even if we had been applying a function which differs from addition with respect to some relatively large numbers, ones we have never used in a sum.

This Wittgensteinian skepticism is made vivid by Saul Kripke (1982). Kripke invites us to consider an alternative function, quus ("$\oplus$"), which is defined as follows:

x ⊕ y = x + y when x and y are less than 57; otherwise, x ⊕ y = 5.

The skeptical question can then be posed as follows: what facts about you make it the case that you've meant addition by "+" rather than quaddition (the function signified by "⊕")? Let's suppose that you have never done a sum involving numbers larger than 57. So even if you've got all your sums right, you've been behaving just as you would behave if you had been quadding rather than adding. Your behavior doesn't mark you out as an adder rather than a quadder.

The most natural first answer is that I intended to use "+" for addition, not for quaddition. For this to be so, however, I must have been in a mental state with the content *addition* rather than the content *quaddition*, and the original question arises again: what makes my intention have the one content rather than the other?

The second most natural answer is that I exemplify different dispositions depending on whether I am an adder or a quadder. If I'm an adder, I'm disposed (even if the occasion has never in fact arisen) to answer the question "68 + 57?" by "125." If I'm a quadder, I'm disposed to answer the question by "5." Isn't that difference enough?

Kripke says not, on the grounds that what the skeptic required was an answer that would *justify* the claim that "125" is the right answer (which it would not be if the relevant function were quaddition). Concerning the totality of dispositional facts, he writes "How does any of this indicate that – now *or* in the past – '125' was an answer *justified* in terms of instructions I gave myself, rather than a mere jack-in-the-box unjustified and arbitrary response?" (Kripke 1982: 23). At least at this point in the discussion, he thinks the non-skeptic cannot answer the question, and he sums up the predicament thus:

> ultimately, if the sceptic is right, the concepts of meaning and of intending one function rather than another will make no sense. For the sceptic holds that no fact about my past history – nothing that was ever in my mind, or in my external behavior – establishes that I meant plus rather than quus. . . . But if this is correct, there can of course be no fact about which function I meant, and if there can be no fact about which particular function I meant in the *past*, there can be none in the *present* either. (Kripke 1982: 13)

Like Quine's skepticism about meaning, this version (Kripkenstein's as they say) has been widely discussed, and many different responses have been offered. Kripke himself seems to think that relief from skepticism can be found by reflecting on the social character of language, the fact that we are engaged in the practice as a community. Not everyone has understood why many speakers are somehow better able to resist the skeptic than one.

Another line of response is that two questions have been run together under the heading "What's the right answer to '68 + 57'?." There's the question "Which function is being picked out by "+": addition or quaddition? Then there's the question: given which function is at issue, what's the correct answer? One view is that dispositions can give a sufficiently determinate answer to the first question. If the person answering the question is generally disposed to answer "5," and is not disposed to accept corrections, that's in part constitutive of her being a quadder; *mutatis mutandis* if the disposition is to answer "125." Justification for the correctness of the answer is a mathematical matter which arises only when it is determinate which function is intended. That is the second question, and is quite different from the first.

This response can be challenged on the grounds that it fails to do justice to the normativity of meaning. Meaning imposes requirements which someone who grasps it may fail to meet. We might mean addition by "+," but still give the *wrong* answer, say 121, to the question '68 + 57?'. Hence we cannot read off what function is being invoked just from the subject's dispositions to use an expression, and the dispositions can't be even partially constitutive of what the expression means.

We need to re-raise the thought with which we concluded the discussion of Quine's skepticism. The skeptic takes for granted that an account of meaning can be given in other terms (for example, dispositions to use). It's not clear that this reductive approach is justified. No doubt meaning supervenes in some way on use, in that two communities whose use of every expression coincides arguably mean the same by these expressions. But we may not be able to tell exactly how the supervenience works, so we may not be able to answer the question: what facts about use make these facts about meaning as they are? Our ignorance does not mean that there is nothing to know, nor does our ignorance of the details entail that we don't know that the general fact that meaning supervenes on use.

Meaning and Truth Conditions

> To give truth conditions is a way of giving the meaning of a sentence. (Davidson 1967)

Let's suppose that we have somehow managed to resist skepticism about the very notion of meaning. The question arises: how should meaning be described? This question divides into two: (1) What central notions is it appropriate to exploit in describing meaning? (2) What kind of structure should we use?

Let's take a whole sentence, say "Snow is white," and consider what notions it would be legitimate to bring to bear to describe its meaning. In a sense we can't go wrong if we stick with the notion of meaning itself. Perhaps we could say that "Snow is white" means that snow is white. (This might look a bit trivial but it's something a monolingual French speaker doesn't know, so it can't be all that trivial!) We might think that this takes the notion of meaning itself too much for granted. Just as Quine thought we should be able to describe linguistic behavior without using such terms as "meaning," so it's often supposed that we should be able to describe the meanings of sentences without using such terms. Alternative terms may cast light on the notion of meaning itself.

Most people agree that one understands a declarative sentence like "Snow is white" only if one knows what it would be for the sentence to be true. A more controversial, but still widely held opinion, is that the converse obtains also: if one knows what it would be for a declarative sentence to be true, then one understands it. This suggests an approach to meaning which had a large impact in the twentieth century: meaning is truth conditions, because knowledge of meaning is knowledge of truth conditions. Tradition has it that this view is to be traced back to Gottlob Frege in the late nineteenth century. It's most salient advocate, in the second half of the twentieth, is Donald Davidson. The view needs to be understood in a rather nuanced fashion or else it is obviously false. Consider two necessary truths, for example, "Every triangle has three sides" and "Nothing is red and green all over." Under what conditions are these true? Under all conditions; that is, on one understanding of "truth conditions," they have the same truth conditions. Yet they evidently differ in meaning. We'll see shortly how Davidson provides the nuance which enables him to avoid this instant refutation. First, let's see how we might arrive from a different direction at the view that meaning is truth conditions.

We can't hope to describe the meaning of every sentence in a language using a sentence-by-sentence approach. That's because of the "creative" character of language use, which in turn depends upon the "compositionality" of language itself. Any of us can put words together in an entirely new way, producing a sentence which has never been used before. (The sentence you have just read might be one such.) As speakers we have no difficulty constructing, and as hearers no difficulty understanding, such novel sentences. That's creativity. The explanation is that the meaning of a sentence is determined by the meanings of the parts of which it is composed. Once we have understood a relatively small vocabulary and a relatively small number of ways in which words can be meaningfully strung together, we are equipped to understand any of the huge number of sentences that can be made up from those parts. That's compositionality.

In describing meaning in a language, we need to say something about the meaning of its words, and something about ways in which words can be combined in to whole sentences; this should deliver information about the meaning of all the sentences which can be formed from these words and these modes of combination, that is, about all the sentences of the language. How to proceed?

In what way should specifying the meanings of words relate to specifying the meanings of whole sentences? One suggestion is that the specification of word meanings are adequate only if they can be used to *derive* the specifications of whole sentences, by inferential processes that can at least in principle be made fully explicit by a system of logical rules. On this view, what we need is a "theory," in a somewhat technical use of that word: a system of sentences in which some are axioms, and the remainder follow from the axioms by specified rules of logic. As philosophers put it, a theory, in this sense (and it's how I'll be using the word "theory" in the rest of this chapter), is a set of sentences *closed* under the logical rules: anything which follows by the rules from any sentences in the set is also in the set. (For example, if some proposition p is in the set, and so is q, then the proposition "p and q" is also in the set, since it follows from other things in the set.) This answers a structural question: meaning needs to be described by a theory. But how?

Let's start with very simple sentences of English, like "Fido barks." We assume that "Fido" refers to some one dog (and we'll forget that in fact "Fido" is used for many dogs, and no doubt for many other things as well). We want to be able to say something about "Fido" and "barks" which will enable us somehow to describe the meaning of the whole sentence "Fido barks." Let's try this: "Fido" means (or stands for) Fido; "barks" means (or stands for) barking, or being a barker; and (here's the part that addresses the way words are put together) when a proper name (like "Fido") precedes an intransitive verb (like "barks") the resulting sentence means that what the name means has the property the verb means.

A problem is that this is false. "Fido barks" means that Fido barks; it does not mean that what "Fido" means has the property "barks" means. It's not about words and their meanings, it's about a dog and his barking. Can we attain a truth by taking a further step? Suppose Fido *is* the meaning of "Fido," and that barking *is* the meaning of "barks." Then we should be able to replace "what 'Fido' means" by "Fido" and "what 'barks' means" by "barking." Then we'd get: "Fido barks" means that Fido has the property of barking.

This is a whole lot better, but still not quite right, since having the property of barking is one thing and barking is another, seemingly simpler, thing. The very young, for example, could use "Fido barks" with the meaning that Fido barks, but, lacking the concept of a property, arguably could not use it with the meaning that Fido has the property of barking. Here's one way round the difficulty. Instead of describing the meaning of "barks" by associating it with a property, let's instead associate it with the things of which the word is true: "barks" is true just of things that bark. The axiom for putting names and verbs together could be modified like this: a sentence that results from prefixing an intransitive verb by a proper name means that the meaning of the name is among the things of which the verb is true. Again the result is not what's wanted: "Fido barks" does not mean that Fido is among the things of which "barks" is true. We would like to be able to replace "being among the things of which 'barks' is true" by "barks"; but this replacement can't be justified in the context: it's not a replacement which preserves meaning, as is made apparent by the fact that before the replacement we have the wrong meaning, and after it the right one.

These difficulties can be resolved if, instead of using *meaning* as the central notion by which to describe linguistic meaning, we instead use *truth conditions*. Our target would then be to establish, on the basis of things said about "Fido" and "barks," that "Fido barks" is true if, and only if, Fido barks. We can do this if we say that "Fido" stands for Fido, that "barks" is true just of things that bark, and that a sentence consisting of a name plus intransitive verb is true if, and only if, the referent of the name is among the things of which the verb is true. So "Fido barks" is true if, and only if, the referent of "Fido" is among the things of which "barks" is true, and now we can go on to infer that this in turn is so if, and only if, Fido barks. In a theory of truth conditions, we don't have to preserve meaning in making inferences, only truth conditions, and the relevant inference (to *barking*, from being among the things of which "barks" is true) does this.

Somewhat technical considerations about how to devise a theory of meaning coincide with more philosophical considerations to suggest that truth conditions should play a central role in an account of meaning. We need to revisit an earlier worry: don't any two necessary truths have the same truth conditions? So wouldn't a truth conditions theory of meaning be committed to the absurdity that any two necessary truths have the same meaning? In response, Davidsonian theorists have to say that they're not identifying meaning and truth conditions, if truth conditions are thought of in such a coarse-grained way that every necessary truth has the same truth conditions. Rather, a *theory* of truth conditions, taken as a whole, can "serve as" a theory of meaning. A truth condition, from this perspective, is what follows the "if, and only if," in a specification of truth conditions. A specification for "Every triangle has three sides" will be that it's true if, and only if, every triangle has three sides. A specification for "Nothing is red and green all over" will be different: it's true if, and only if, nothing is red and green all over. Just as the sentences are differently composed, their truth conditions will be derived by different routes, and so will count as distinct; this is what will mark the difference in meaning of the sentences for which they give the truth conditions.

Here's a further qualm: does " 'Fido barks' is true if, and only if, Fido barks" really tell us anything about meaning? Or, indeed, anything at all that we want to know? Isn't it just trivial? We didn't have to derive this from axioms relating to words; we could just have given a rule: take any sentence, write it within quotation marks, append "is true if, and only if," and then write the sentence again. Truth conditions theorists, like Davidson, are at pains to repudiate this claim of triviality. They point out that a monolingual Frenchman doesn't know that "Fido barks" is true if, and only if, Fido barks, and that's because he doesn't know English. The specification of truth conditions links the sentence to a state of affairs, Fido's barking, and thus describes the crucial connection between language and world in which meaning consists.

This crucial connection cannot be held in place by magic: it must somehow be effected by what speakers of a language do. We saw that if we conceive this behavior in terms of movement of matter, skepticism looms, whether of the Quinean or the Kripkensteinian variety. Suppose, however, we allow ourselves to describe behavior in terms of the intentions of speakers. Can we then give a satisfying account of the connection between language and the world, based on the way in which intentions relate to the world? That question will be addressed in the next section.

Meaning and Intentions

Linguistic intentions are very like nonlinguistic intentions. (Grice 1957)

In apparent opposition to truth conditions theorists of meaning, other philosophers, the most famous being Paul Grice, have urged that we should account for meaning in terms of the intentions of those who speak the language. Grice took as the first notion to analyze that of someone's meaning that such-and-such by an action, where the action may or may not involve language. His ultimate ambitious plan was to move on to describe the meanings of words in terms of conventions governing what speakers should use them to mean. To this ambitious part of the plan, he and others have paid relatively little attention; but the early part, in which Grice offers an analysis of speaker-meaning, has been highly influential.

Herod showed Salome the severed head of St. John the Baptist, trying to make manifest to her that he had kept his promise and that John the Baptist was dead. Herod tried, and succeeded, in getting Salome to form various beliefs, but intuitively, in showing her the head, he did not *mean that* John was dead, or that he had kept his promise. He engaged in intentional behavior, and behavior designed to induce beliefs in others, but he did not mean anything. Why not?

Grice puts his finger on a crucial issue in discussing two superficially similar cases. In one of them, I show Mr. X a photograph of his wife displaying undue familiarity with Mr. Y. In the other, I do a sketch which is supposed to represent the very same thing. Grice suggests that in the case of the sketch we are inclined to say that I meant that Mrs. Y was being unfaithful; but we are not inclined to say this in the photograph case. Grice explains the contrast as follows: in the case of the photograph, I can count on Mr. X to form the belief that his wife was unfaithful quite independently of his having any opinion about what I was up to. (Project back to the days before Photoshop, in which it was assumed that the camera could not lie!) In the case of the sketch, however, I would know that Mr. X would only form the belief that his wife was being unfaithful if he recognized my intention to get him to form this belief. I would know that if he thought I was just doodling, or fantasizing with pencil in hand, seeing the sketch would not lead him to form that belief.

The example brings out the central element of Grice's theory: speaker-meaning involves what has come to be called the "Gricean mechanism": the speaker (in the broadest sense, to include one who holds out a photo or a sketch) must intend his audience to recognize his intention that she should form a certain belief, and this recognition should be intended to supply a reason for the audience to form that belief. In the case of the sketch, one could reconstruct how I intend Mr. X to reason along the following lines: "he has shown me a sketch apparently representing my wife displaying undue familiarity with Mr. Y. It would be in terrible taste to do this in my presence merely as a doodle or distinctly off-color fantasy, so he must have had some serious purpose. He must believe my wife is behaving in the way he has sketched. If he believes that then, since he is reliably informed, it is probably true. So, probably, my wife is being unfaithful." By contrast, in the case of the photograph, I can't expect Mr. X to reason in this way. Seeing the photograph is likely to produce the belief quite independently of any beliefs Mr. X may form about my intentions. That's why I mean something by showing the sketch but don't mean something by showing the photo. And that's why Herod didn't mean that John the Baptist was dead by showing Salome the severed head: he would have realized that Salome, seeing the head, would believe he was dead quite independently of any appreciation of Herod's intentions.

Grice's idea has been subject to all kinds of criticism, but there is a wide consensus that he has put his finger on something interesting and important about how communication works, in particular in those cases in which communication is effected by linguistic means. What is less widely accepted is that the Gricean mechanism can play the role Grice cast it for in an analysis of speaker-meaning; some even doubt the robustness of any such notion.

One battle Griceans have had to fight is against truth conditions theorists. It has sometimes seemed to both parties that their views are mutually opposed: if meaning is truth conditions, then how can it be based on the notion of speaker's intentions and the Gricean mechanism? Maybe this sense of conflict is largely illusory. Truth conditions theorists do specially good justice to the compositional character of language. Griceans do specially good justice to the evident truth that language in some way depends upon use, and use is a species of intentional behavior. But a complete theory must do justice to both aspects: not just to the connection with use, but also to compositionality. Since countless sentences which have never been used are meaningful, Griceans have found it necessary to engage in some detours to incorporate the compositional aspects of language into their story. Some truth conditions theorists forge the link with use when they describe the kind of evidence that would ground a correct truth-theoretic account of a language: the evidence is, of course, how the language is used, and for Davidson the specific aspect of use is a tally of which of the sentences they utter the speakers hold true.

Each party must borrow material from the other: Griceans will somehow need to exploit the theoretical apparatus of truth theorists, or something like it; truth-theorists cannot entirely neglect the use of language and the intentions which animate that use. But one should not exaggerate the degree of rapprochement: truth-theorists can take cognizance of speakers' intentions without necessarily placing any weight on the Gricean mechanism; and although Griceans need to harness a theory, if they are going to provide a description of the meaning of every sentence of a language, it might be that they will regard this as a dispensable ambition: perhaps they are not offering such a description, but are, rather, providing an insight into what lies at the heart of meaning in any possible language.

Meaning and Use: Semantics and Pragmatics

So far in this chapter, linguistic meaning has been at the center of our discussion. Admittedly, the Gricean mechanism relates to speaker-meaning and not to sentence-meaning; but we introduced it in the context of the ambition to describe sentence-meaning. Grice himself was vividly aware that the impact of our use of language often diverges markedly from the meanings of the sentences we use. A simple example is irony: we say the opposite of what we mean. Saying goes with sentence-meaning, and what we mean is, of course, speaker-meaning, and the two diverge in the most obvious way: one is the opposite of the other.

Here is a more interesting example: I ask you whether you want coffee, and you reply "It will keep me awake." Does this amount to yes, or no, or neither? That depends on the context. Suppose I know you need to stay awake in order to finish an essay. Then I'll take you to have meant Yes. Suppose I know you want to have an early night to prepare for the next day. Then I'll take you to have meant No. There is no connection, merely at the level of language, between either "Yes" or "No" and "It will keep me awake." Yet we could hardly give a full account of the role of language in communication unless we observed the way in which such a connection can be forged.

As Grice's work made clear, a great deal of what we gather from the speech of others is sensitive to context in this kind of way. If you say "I'm nearly out of gas" and I reply "There's a gas station around the corner," you will assume that the gas station is open, or at least that I do not know it is closed, though what I strictly said did not mention whether it was open or not. If you ask me for a reference for a student and I write "She has beautiful handwriting" and nothing else, you will take it that I have expressed a negative opinion of her, though I have strictly speaking said nothing negative. If we use "semantic" correlatively with "sentence-meaning" and "pragmatic" correlatively with "speaker-meaning," the phenomenon we have started to uncover is that communication often involves an extra-semantic, pragmatic component; and sometimes this is more important than the semantic component.

As we reflect on these cases, we may begin to wonder whether any linguistic exchange can fail to exploit pragmatic features. In the ancient philosophy seminar, you say "Aristotle's logic is quite sophisticated." How do I know you are talking about Aristotle the philosopher, rather than about Aristotle Onassis, the shipping magnate? The words on offer do not themselves not settle the issue. The issue is settled by the context: we are in the ancient philosophy seminar, and the ascription to Mr. Onassis of such a property would be surprising. In this case, features of context help guide the audience to the right Aristotle. One might think that there are two words "Aristotle" spelled and pronounced the same, and with different semantics (one refers to the philosopher, the other to the tycoon). On this view, the features of context do not fill in semantic properties, but only help determine which semantic properties are present.

In other cases, the contextual information does more. Consider this sentence:

The policeman shouted to the robber to stop. He was in full uniform.

Who was said to be in uniform? Most people's first response is that it was the policeman. On reflection, they realize that it could have been the robber, too, but that's a less likely interpretation in most (not all) contexts. (Think of a context in which we have already been told that the robber was an army colonel.) Here again context helps resolve a semantic issue.

In the case of coffee, irony, or beautiful handwriting, the pragmatic contribution goes beyond anything that could be thought of as semantic. For some cases, it's hard to decide whether that's the best description or whether, as with Aristotle and the policeman, contextual information is simply rendering the semantic properties more determinate. Compare the following distinct conversations between me, in Brownsville, and you, in Austin:

A: You: Is it raining?
    Me: Is it raining? You know it never stops here.

B: Me: It is raining?
    You: No, clear skies as usual.

In A, my question "Is it raining" asks whether it is raining in Brownsville. In B, my question, asked with the same words, and with the speakers in the same places, relates to whether it is raining in Austin. On one view, "It's raining" has a semantic slot, waiting to be determined contextually. On another view, nothing in the semantics of rain determines a place; that information is a purely pragmatic addition.

These kinds of case raise a more general skepticism about whether sentence-meaning, the purely semantic contribution, ever determines truth conditions. (If it does not, truth conditions theorists are in trouble.) Try to think of a sentence whose meaning is completely independent of context. Charles Travis suggested what seems like a good candidate: "The ball is round," as spoken of a particular ball at a particular moment. At any moment, a ball has just one shape, round or not, so it seems that the sentence must have a single pragmatically independent meaning. Travis, however, thought that even this sentence does not. He illustrated the point by describing a squash game. You know nothing about squash and although you're watching a game your eyesight isn't very good and you ask whether the ball is round, like a cricket ball, or ovoid, like an (American) football. I say "The ball is round," and what I say is (surely!) true. Another spectator is a manufacturer of squash balls who has fitted this particular ball with very small sensors to determine its response to deformation (in the interests of product improvement). When the ball is deformed, the sensors should trigger a reading on the spectator's measuring device. Checking his equipment, he asks the same question, and I reply as before, "The ball is round." But I'm not paying attention: at that moment the ball was flattened against the wall and so not round. The very same sentence is false, on the understanding appropriate to the second question, though true on the understanding appropriate to the first. So perhaps pragmatic phenomena always play a role in settling how we are to understand the sentences we hear or read. Perhaps every sentence can be understood in more than one way, and semantic meaning, understood as rich enough at least to determine truth conditions, is an illusion.

Conclusion

Semantic meaning, the meaning of words and sentences, is determined by what people do, understood not as the motion of matter through space but as intentional action. Our communicative actions have layers of meaning that are much more complex than the meanings of the words we use. Quite how to draw the line between the pragmatic and the semantic aspects of meaning is not clear. But it does seem clear that linguistic meaning cannot be sharply separated from a wider notion of meaning that's applicable to everything we do. Understanding what someone says cannot be sharply separated from understanding the speaker. In John McDowell's words: "We have not properly made sense of forms of words in a language if we have not, thereby, got some way towards making sense of its speakers. If there is a pun here, it is an illuminating one" (1977: 160).

Further Reading

For a highly entertaining approach to language, focusing on empirical questions, see: Steven Pinker (1994) *The Language Instinct: How the Mind Creates Language*. To explore the questions raised in this chapter, I'd recommend visiting the Stanford Encyclopaedia of Philosophy (plato.stanford.edu). You will find it rewarding to sample at least these search strings: "gavagai," "Kripke's sceptical Wittgenstein," "Davidson meaning and truth," "pragmatics." For a book intruding the main themes, as these are understood in the analytic tradition, I would suggest: William Lycan (1999) *Philosophy of Language: A Contemporary Introduction*.

Note

1   Gilbert Ryle, a famous Oxford philosopher in the years after the Second World War, is said to have given this reply to the question.

References

Burgess, A. (1975). *Language Made Plain*, revd. edn., London: Fontana/Collins.

Davidson, D. (1967). "Truth and Meaning," *Synthese*, 7, 304–23.

Grice, H. P. (1957). "Meaning," *Philosophical Review*, 66, 377–88.

Kripke, S. (1982). *Wittgenstein on Rules and Private Language*, Cambridge, MA: Harvard University Press.

Lycan, William (1999). *Philosophy of Language: A Contemporary Introduction*, London: Routledge.

McDowell, J. (1977). "On the Sense and Reference of a Proper Name," *Mind*, 86, 159–85.

Pinker, Steven (1994). *The Language Instinct: How the Mind Creates Language*, London: Penguin.

Quine, W. V. O. (1960). *Word and Object*, New York: Technology Press of MIT and John Wiley and Sons.

Wittgenstein, L. (1953). *Philosophical Investigations*, Oxford: Basil Blackwell.

13
Scientific Inquiry

Marc Lange

The "Scientific Method" and Hypothetico-Deductivism

The first chapter of most high-school science textbooks is routinely devoted to explaining "the scientific method": the way that scientific theories are tested against observations. Here is a typical description of the procedure – from page 13 of *Biology: The Unity and Diversity of Life* by Cecie Starr and Ralph Taggart (1992), which looks a great deal like the biology textbook I used in high school:

1. Identify a problem or ask a question about some aspect of the natural world.
2. Develop one or more *hypotheses*, or educated guesses, about what the solution or answer might be. This might involve sorting through what has been learned already about related phenomena.
3. Think about what predictably will occur or will be observed if the hypothesis is correct. This is sometimes called the "if-then" process. (*If* gravity pulls objects toward the earth, *then* it should be possible to observe apples falling down, not up, from a tree.)
4. Devise ways to *test* the accuracy of predictions drawn from the hypothesis. This typically involves making observations, developing models, and performing experiments.
5. If the tests do not turn out as expected, check to see what might have gone wrong. (Maybe a substance being tested was tainted, maybe a dial was set incorrectly or a relevant factor overlooked. Or maybe the hypothesis just isn't a good one.)
6. Repeat or devise new tests – the more the better. Hypotheses that have been supported by many different tests are more likely to be correct.

This account of the way scientific theories are tested is sometimes called "hypothetico-deductivism" since it involves *deducing* observable predictions from *hypotheses*. If those predictions come out true, then the hypothesis is "confirmed": the prediction counts as evidence in favor of the truth of the hypothesis. On the other hand, if the prediction turns out to be false, then the hypothesis is "disconfirmed": the evidence counts against its truth.

Hypothetico-deductivism plainly makes a great deal of sense – whether the hypothesis being tested concerns the cause of a patient's unusual symptoms, the motions of the planets, or the reason why my car is refusing to start. Certainly it would be bizarre for us to violate hypothetico-deductivism by raising our confidence in a hypothesis in response to its making an *inaccurate* prediction! Furthermore, hypothetico-deductivism correctly recognizes that we cannot generally be justified in concluding that some hypothesis is true merely on the basis of its making a single accurate prediction. (Even a broken clock is right twice a day.) The more predictions it makes that are borne out – and the more diverse those predictions are – the more confidence we are entitled to place in the hypothesis. For example, suppose our hypothesis is that anyone who takes a certain vaccine is immune from contracting AIDS. This hypothesis is better confirmed by 1000 successful clinical tests than by 100 – and it is better confirmed by 1000 successful tests on a diverse range of subjects (men and women, young and old) than by 1000 successful tests on men between the ages of 20 and 25.

Unfortunately, hypothetico-deductivism fails to specify anything about *how much* confidence we are entitled to repose in a hypothesis when we discover some of its predictions to be true – nor does hypothetico-deductivism identify which successful predictions qualify as *stronger* evidence for the hypothesis. At best, then, hypothetico-deductivism is an incomplete account of the logic behind testing scientific theories. We would like to find a logical principle that determines which evidence would confirm a given hypothesis "beyond a reasonable doubt," which evidence would leave room for reasonable doubt but would still count as a "preponderance of evidence" favoring the hypothesis, and which evidence would fail to meet even this lower standard. Hypothetico-deductivism implies that a hypothesis is supported (to some degree, at least) whenever it makes a successful prediction. Surprisingly, this is mistaken. Indeed, an accurate prediction sometimes even *disconfirms* a hypothesis.

For example, suppose that your hypothesis is that all human beings are less than 9 feet tall. This hypothesis obviously predicts that the next human being you meet will be less than 9 feet tall. Suppose that this prediction is borne out: she is 8 feet, 11 ¾ inches tall. However, this evidence should actually *diminish* your confidence in the hypothesis. After all, you know that human heights are distributed in roughly a bell-shaped curve; there is no sharp cut-off at the high end. That one of the relatively small number of human beings whom you have met is just under 9 feet tall suggests that the high end of the curve slopes downward less steeply than you had thought, confirming that someone somewhere is more than 9 feet tall.

Likewise, suppose your hypothesis is that there are no rats in North Carolina. Suppose you visit a rat museum and see an exhibit of stuffed rats labeled with the locations from where they were captured. Rats are represented from all corners of the globe. Suppose that although there are stuffed rats from many states of the union, none is from North Carolina. Although your hypothesis successfully predicted this result, the evidence consisting of rats captured from "all over" confirms that there are rats in North Carolina, disconfirming your hypothesis. Thus, not every successful prediction confirms the hypothesis making it, contrary to hypothetico-deductivism.

Of course, you could travel to North Carolina in order to discover whether any rats live there. But you do not have to make the trip; the observations you make at the rat museum count as strong evidence against the hypothesis. The point of testing a hypothesis is often to justify using it to make *predictions*; we are able to know, in advance of actually traveling to North Carolina, whether any rats live there, just as we can justly be confident, in advance of actually inoculating Jones with the AIDS vaccine and observing the consequences, that doing so would immunize Jones against AIDS.

Sometimes it is impossible to "make the trip" to check the prediction directly – as when the prediction concerns an event in the distant future. For instance, suppose our evidence is that every emerald that we have ever observed (and there have been many) was green at the moment we observed it. Here are two rival hypotheses:

Green: All emeralds at every moment are green.
Grue: All emeralds are green at every moment before the year 3000 but blue at every moment thereafter.[1]

Both Green and Grue accurately predict our current evidence. But surely our evidence confirms Green, not Grue – and we do not have to wait to observe emeralds after 3000 in order to know their color.

Grue not only supplies another example where a hypothesis fails to be confirmed by making successful predictions, but also dramatically illustrates that even if some evidence confirms a given hypothesis enough to justify believing it true, a rival hypothesis could *possibly* be true instead. The evidence does not *contradict* all rivals to the justified hypothesis, even though the evidence is strong enough to justify our believing those rivals false. In other words, the evidence "underdetermines" the theory (a term interchangeable with "hypothesis").

One lesson of the "underdetermination of theory by evidence" is that when evidence justifies our believing in the truth of some scientific theory, the evidence has not *proved* the theory true in the way that mathematical theorems get proved. A proof is a good *deductive* argument: it is impossible for its conclusion to be false if its "premises" (what the argument proceeds from) are all true. Here is an example of a proof:

Premises:
All emeralds are green.
The stone in my hand is an emerald.

Conclusion:
The stone in my hand is green.

The conclusion cannot be false if the premises are true. But the confirmation of theories does not proceed by deduction. It requires *inductive* reasoning, and the conclusion of a strong inductive argument can possibly be false even when its premises are all true. Thus, when a scientific theory has been confirmed (even beyond a reasonable doubt), it *could* still be false. There have been occasions in the history of science when a theory that had been extremely strongly confirmed by evidence was revealed to have in fact been false (although evidently very accurate to a wide range of phenomena). The overthrow of Newtonian physics by Albert Einstein's theory of relativity in the early twentieth century is a famous example.

Although our evidence fails to *prove* our best scientific theories, it presumably *justifies* our believing those theories or, at least, justifies our placing a considerable degree of confidence in the predictions they make. However, in 1739, the Scottish philosopher David Hume formulated a simple but powerful argument for the astonishing claim that we could never be justified in having any degree of confidence, no matter how slight, in the predictions of scientific theories. For example, according to Hume, we are not justified in having 90 percent confidence that the sun will rise tomorrow, or in having 70 percent confidence, or even in being more confident that it will rise than that it will not. Here is Hume's argument in a nutshell. Our belief that the sun will rise tomorrow rests on our belief that the sun's future behavior will almost certainly resemble its past behavior. Hume challenges us to explain how we could ever know that. It does not follow *deductively* from our past observations; no *contradiction* would be produced by the sun's failing to rise tomorrow despite its having risen regularly in the past. Of course, we have observed that *in the past*, the sun's later behavior resembled its earlier behavior. This fact seems to justify our expecting that *in the future*, the sun's behavior will resemble its earlier behavior. But, Hume cleverly remarks, this argument runs in a circle; it presupposes what it aims to show. If we try to use the fact that the sun maintained the same pattern of behavior in the past to confirm that it will do so in the future, we must take for granted that the sun will behave in the future as it has done in the past. This belief is precisely what Hume challenged us to justify in the first place.

Few philosophers have been persuaded by Hume that we are not justified in having any confidence in the predictions of our best scientific theories. But it is difficult to find a flaw in Hume's argument. A few philosophers have instead embraced Hume's conclusion but tried to characterize science so that it does not involve our being confident that various predictions will turn out to be true. For instance, Karl Popper has suggested that although science refutes general hypotheses by finding them to be logically inconsistent with our observations, science never confirms (even to the smallest degree) the predictive accuracy of a general hypothesis. Science has us make guesses regarding what we have not observed by using those general hypotheses that have survived the most potential refutations despite sticking their necks out furthest, and we make these guesses even though we have no good reason to place any confidence in their truth. The trouble with Popper's view, however, is that if we are not justified in having any confidence in a prediction's truth, then it is difficult to see how it could be reasonable for us to rely upon that prediction.

Thus, the "underdetermination of theory by evidence" leaves us with Hume's challenge: to justify induction – that is, to explain how we manage to be justified in believing a hypothesis to be true although our evidence fails to prove it. The underdetermination of theory by evidence also teaches us that we are sometimes justified in believing a hypothesis to be false even when every prediction that the hypothesis has made and that we have checked has turned out to be true. (Once again, the Grue hypothesis is a good example.) Hypothetico-deductivism cannot tell us when we are justified in rejecting a hypothesis *despite* the success of every prediction it makes that we have checked. For that, we need a more adequate logic of scientific inquiry.

Falsificationism and the Testability of Scientific Theories

Some philosophers (such as Karl Popper, once again) have suggested that their testability against observations sets *scientific* theories apart from hypothesis that fall outside of the scope of science. For example, it does not seem to be the business of science to ascertain the truth of moral hypothesis (such as that capital punishment is immoral), aesthetic hypothesis (that Beethoven's late string quartets are more masterful than his early ones), or "metaphysical" hypotheses such as that there are "parallel universes" that do not causally interact with our universe, or that every object, at the stroke of midnight, suddenly discontinuously shifts two inches to the left (*my* left). These hypothesis seem unable to make any observable predictions; no observations are more likely if they are true than if they are false. Therefore, they are not *scientific* hypotheses – if its testability against our observations is what makes a hypothesis qualify as "scientific."

However, even some of the most famous scientific hypotheses are incapable, when taken all by themselves, of making observable predictions. Consider Isaac Newton's law of inertia: that a body feeling no forces remains at rest or moves in a straight line at a constant speed. From this hypothesis, no observations can be deduced – until we couple this hypothesis with "auxiliary hypotheses" specifying observable circumstances where a body feels no forces. Likewise, consider Charles Darwin's principle of natural selection: that an organism possessing a trait that increases its fitness is more likely to leave more offspring, other things being equal, and that differences in fitness are thereby a principal cause of changes in the frequency of traits over time within a population. Once again, without some independent specification of which traits in a given environment make an individual fitter, the "survival of the fittest" makes no predictions about which organisms are more likely to reproduce and thereby pass along their adaptations to the next generation.

Thus, what makes a theory "scientific" cannot be that taken all by itself, it has observable consequences. Of course, Newton's and Darwin's hypotheses have plenty of observable consequences once those hypotheses have been combined with other hypotheses. But this feature cannot be used to distinguish scientific hypotheses from hypotheses that fall outside of science's scope – since observable predictions can be coaxed out of *any* hypothesis once it is combined with the requisite auxiliary hypotheses. For example, an observable prediction about my weight follows from the two-inches-to-the-left hypothesis once it is combined with the hypothesis that my weight in pounds is greater than 60 times the number of inches to the left by which every object shifts at midnight. Plainly, this cheap trick would work on any hypothesis. It is not obvious, then, how *scientific* hypotheses differ in testability from moral, aesthetic, and metaphysical theories.

That typically, in grown-up sciences, no observable predictions are made by the theory being tested, when taken all by itself, is sometimes known as the "Duhem-Quine thesis" after two philosophers (Pierre Duhem and W. V. O. Quine) who emphasized it. One lesson of the Duhem-Quine thesis is that the logic of theory testing is not well-captured by "falsificationism," the view that science works principally by ruling theories out upon discovering that they make incorrect predictions about our observations. Of course, a true theory cannot make a false prediction. But typically, to make an observable prediction requires appealing not just to the theory that we were aiming to test, but to auxiliary hypotheses as well, so that if the prediction is untrue, some auxiliary hypothesis may be to blame. (If we then try to subject some auxiliary hypothesis to independent test, then further auxiliaries will need to be employed . . .) Hypothetico-deductivism fails to specify the *degree* to which each of the hypotheses that was used in making the inaccurate prediction is disconfirmed by it.

Scientific research often involves taking a well-established, broad theoretical framework and trying to figure out how to extend it to cover (more accurately) some additional phenomenon or further range of cases. For example, over the course of more than two centuries following the publication of Newton's *Mathematical Principles of Natural Philosophy* (in 1687), physicists worked to find the auxiliary hypotheses enabling Newton's laws of motion to be applied to optics, heat, electricity, magnetism, and so forth. During that period, there were frequent occasions in which the observable consequences of Newton's laws (coupled with the auxiliaries so far developed) failed to match these various phenomena. (After all, if these "anomalies" had not existed, then there would have been nothing for physicists to work on, no puzzles for them to try to solve.) But the existence of these anomalies did not strongly disconfirm Newton's laws of motion. On the contrary, scientists justly put the blame for these failed predictions on the auxiliary hypotheses they had used. Ultimately, scientists formulated more successful auxiliaries.

Following Thomas Kuhn, philosophers sometimes characterize a theory like Newton's as functioning (in a given scientific field, for a certain period of time) as a "paradigm": a model of scientific success guiding all research in that field, during that period, as scientists tried to find other theories that succeeded in the same way. When a paradigm encounters a long-standing anomaly, the anomaly fails to require scientists to take alternatives to the paradigm seriously. Rather, scientists are justified in treating a stubborn anomaly as "business as usual," expecting the problem to be resolved eventually – just as so many other anomalies that once afflicted the paradigm have been – without the need for a "scientific revolution" (where one paradigm supplants another, as when Einstein's relativity theory replaced Newtonian physics). As Kuhn emphasized, science requires a distinctive blend of conservative thinking and open-mindedness.

Scientific Realism and Anti-realism

It may seem especially difficult for our observations to settle which of two rival theories is true when those theories not only predict all of the observations that we have made so far, but furthermore have all of the same observable implications – disagreeing solely about the *unobservable* processes responsible for those observable facts. For example, Nicolas Copernicus' model of the solar system (published in 1543) places the Sun at rest and the Earth and other planets in orbit around it. Tycho Brahe, a Danish astronomer, proposed a rival model (1588) according to which the Earth is at rest, the Moon and Sun orbit the Earth, and the other planets orbit the Sun. (You may find it helpful to picture Tycho's model by imagining a three-dimensional toy model of the Copernican solar system. Imagine releasing your grasp on the orb of the Sun and holding the toy by the Earth instead, with the Sun now free to turn around the Earth, taking the other planets with it. That's the Tychonic system.) The Copernican and Tychonic models agree on all of the *relative* positions and motions of the Sun, Earth, Moon, and planets, and hence on all possible observations of them.[2] They disagree solely on unobservable facts: on which of these bodies are really moving and which are really at rest. Since we can observe only relative motions, how could our observations ever justify our believing one of these theories true and the other false? It would seem that any observation capable of confirming one of these hypotheses would equally confirm the other.

This argument has a venerable pedigree. Ancient Greek astronomers recognized that many different models of the heavens agree on all relative planetary positions and motions, but disagree on the particular arrangement of unobservable wheels within wheels carrying the planets and thus responsible for their motion. Accordingly, many ancient astronomers and mathematicians argued that the goal of astronomy is not to ascertain the unobservable causes of the observable facts, but merely to "save the phenomena": to devise theories that fit all observable facts (that are, in other words, "empirically adequate"). In accepting a theory, scientists should not be understood as believing in the theory's truth, but merely in its empirical adequacy.

Today, this interpretation of science is called "scientific anti-realism." In contrast, "scientific realism" interprets science as aiming not merely to save the phenomena, but also to explain them: to describe accurately the unobservable facts responsible for what we observe. According to scientific realism, scientists who accept a given theory believe it to be (approximately) true, even in its description of unobservables. Scientists can sometimes be justified in accepting one rival theory over another as true, even when those theories agree on all possible observations (in other words, even when they are "empirically equivalent").

Realists have sometimes pointed out that we are justified in believing that a dog lives in a house even if we have not seen the dog, namely, if we have seen many signs of a dog's presence (dog hair on the furniture, water and food bowl, pawprints, chew toys, and so forth). By similar reasoning, we justify believing in the existence of various unobservable entities. Many different, independent lines of evidence confirm the existence of atoms, for example. Anti-realists sometimes respond that it would not be a "miracle" (an amazingly improbable coincidence) for all of those phenomena to be just as if atoms existed even though they do not, considering that so many theories are empirically equivalent to atomism (whether or not anyone has bothered to devise these theories). A genuine "miracle" would be for the theory that scientists accept, from among all of these empirically equivalent theories, to be the one that is true.

Anti-realists argue that observations can never justify our believing one of these hypotheses true and its empirically equivalent rivals false. But anti-realists do regard our observations as able to justify our believing in a theory's empirical adequacy, and thus in making bold predictions going well beyond what we have already observed. Realists argue that anti-realists are arbitrary in treating evidence as able to favor one hypothesis over another (even when both hypotheses agree with all of the observations that we have made so far), as long as the hypotheses disagree on some other possible observations, but as unable to favor one hypothesis over another if the two hypotheses are empirically equivalent. Whatever reasoning justifies our going beyond what we have already observed, to confirm predictions regarding observables as yet unobserved, also justifies our confirming predictions regarding unobservables.

Anti-realists reply that to achieve its goal, science does not need to confirm the truth of theories over and above their empirical adequacy. Belief in the truth of theories about unobservables is dispensable to science. But realists take the goal of science to be the discovery not merely of empirically adequate theories, but also of the unobservable facts that explain our observations.

How might a scientist have argued for the truth of Copernicus' theory over Tycho's? Although these two theories make all of the same observable predictions regarding the planets, Copernicus' model is easier than Tycho's to couple with auxiliary hypotheses concerning the physical explanation of planetary motion. Consider these two auxiliary hypotheses, for which there was considerable evidence by the early seventeenth century:

1   Larger heavenly bodies have greater influence than smaller ones.
2   A heavenly body's influence diminishes with greater distance form it.

(The evidence for (1) included Galileo's telescopic observation that Jupiter's moons are smaller than Jupiter and orbit Jupiter, not vice versa. The evidence for (2) included that the moons farther from Jupiter orbit more slowly, and likewise for the planets farther from the Sun.) The Tychonic system is difficult to reconcile with these hypotheses. For instance, according to Tycho, the Sun orbits the Earth, not vice versa, so by (1), the Earth must be larger. But then when Venus, Mars, and Jupiter come nearer to the Earth than to the Sun, the Earth's influence on them should be greater than the Sun's, by both (1) and (2). Yet they orbit the Sun, not the Earth.

Realists, then, argue that we can sometimes justify choosing among rival, empirically equivalent hypotheses partly on the basis of their having different relations to well-confirmed auxiliary hypotheses. On the other hand, anti-realists might argue that scientists could justify believing (1) and (2) to be empirically adequate, but could not justify believing them true. These auxiliaries could then justify belief in the empirical adequacy of Copernicus' theory, though not in its truth.

Degrees of Belief as Probabilities

A natural way to think about our degree of confidence in a hypothesis is as a *probability*. When evidence confirms a hypothesis, it raises the probability that we assign to the hypothesis. Evidence that disconfirms a hypothesis lowers its probability. For example, the discovery that a patient has chest pain might confirm a physician's hypothesis that the patient is having a heart attack by raising her confidence in this hypothesis from 20 percent (0.2) to 60 percent (0.6). Of course, the probability that *I* assign to some hypothesis may differ from the probability that *you* assign to it; these are our "personal probabilities." Moreover, the probability that I give to some hypothesis need not take a sharp value. It could be somewhat vague; for example, I could be merely *highly confident* in some hypothesis without there being any precise probability value (say, 64.359 percent) that captures my confidence. (However, to understand the logic of theory testing, it is useful to think of a scientist as having precise degrees of confidence. We can always relax this idealization later.)

A probability is a function onto numbers between 0 and 1 inclusive. More precisely, a probability function "pr( )" is standardly taken to be a function that satisfies these three conditions (for any hypotheses h and k):

1   $pr(h) \geq 0$
2   $pr(h) = 1$ if it would be a contradiction for h to be false
3   $pr(h \text{ or } k) = pr(h) + pr(k)$ if it would be a contradiction for both h and k to be true.

A simple way to picture probabilities is in terms of a "muddy Venn diagram." A Venn diagram consists of circles representing various hypotheses. The region inside the circle representing hypothesis h stands for h being true. The region where two circle overlap represents the two corresponding hypotheses both being true. Now imagine that some mud is poured over the diagram and distributed among its regions. The fraction of the diagram's total mud that is contained within h's circle represents the probability of h being true. Thus, condition (1) above says that no circle can contain less than zero mud. Condition (2) says that if h must be true (or else a contradiction would result), then all of the mud must be inside the h circle. Condition (3) says that if the h and k circles do not overlap (since it is impossible for both h and k to be true), then the fraction of the total mud that is either in the h circle or in the k circle is the fraction of mud that is in the h circle plus the fraction of mud that is in the k circle. Figure 13.1 is an example of a muddy Venn diagram.

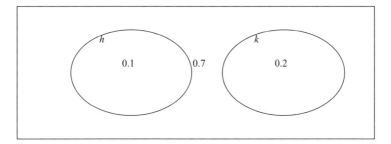

Figure 13.1 A muddy Venn diagram

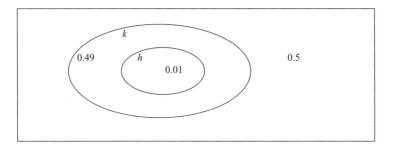

Figure 13.2 Our probabilities before we discover the evidence

In this example, 10 percent of the mud is in the h circle and 20 percent is in the k circle. So pr(h or k) = 0.1 + 0.2 = 0.3 (that is, 30 percent). (The total quantity of mud is 100 percent, so 70 percent of the mud must lie outside of both circles, in the "neither h nor k" region.)

Confirmation of h can be represented by the net movement of mud into h's circle in response to the discovery of some new evidence, increasing the amount of mud in h's circle. Even this simple picture captures some subtle features of confirmation. For example, suppose that k must be true if h is true. Then if some new evidence confirms h, it can nevertheless disconfirm k. For example, suppose we already are certain that Mary has one and only one pet: either a dog or a bird. Suppose we learn that Mary's pet has no hair. This evidence disconfirms the hypothesis (k) that Mary's pet is a dog but confirms the hypothesis (h) that it is an American hairless terrier (a rare breed of dog) – even though k must be true if h is true.[3] This situation is easily captured by the muddy Venn diagram (figure 13.2). Here are our probabilities before we discovered that Mary's pet has no hair; suppose we assigned equal likelihood to Mary's pet being a bird and to Mary's pet being a dog, but very little probability to its being an American hairless terrier.

pr(h) = 0.01
pr(k) = 0.5 (since the k circle includes both the outer "donut" containing 0.49 of the total mud and the inner "hole" containing 0.01 of the total mud).

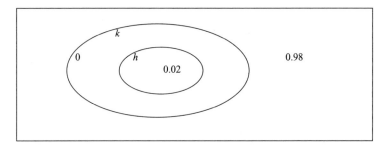

Figure 13.3 Our probabilities after we discover the evidence

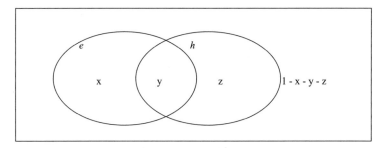

Figure 13.4 Our probabilities before we discover evidence *e*

Here, let's suppose, are our probabilities after we acquire the evidence (see figure 13.3).

pr'(*h*) = 0.02
pr'(*k*) = 0.02.

I have added a prime (') to "pr" to indicate that this is our *new* probability – that is, *after* taking our new evidence into account.

As a result of our new evidence, most of the mud that was in the outer "donut" of the *k* circle (standing for the hypothesis that Mary's pet is a dog but not an American hairless terrier) moved outside of the *k* circle (to the bird hypothesis), but some moved into the *h* circle. Consequently, the *k* circle lost mud and the *h* circle gained mud, even though any mud in the *h* circle is also in the *k* circle (since *k* is true if *h* is true).

To understand when evidence confirms *h* (and, if so, by how much), we must understand when a discovery results in the net motion of mud into the *h* circle. There is a natural way to think about mud movement. Suppose that before we discover evidence *e*, our opinions are represented by figure 13.4.

pr(*e*) = x + y (The lower this quantity, the less we expected to discover *e*.)
pr(*h*) = y + z
pr(*e* and *h*) = y

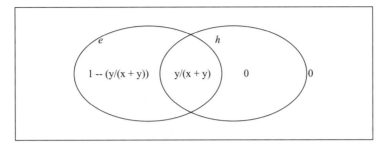

Figure 13.5 Our probabilities after we discover evidence *e*

When we discover *e*, all of the mud on the diagram that was not already inside the *e* circle moves into it, so pr′(*e*) = 1. How much of the new *e* mud should go into the region of the *e* circle that overlaps with the *h* circle? A natural thought is that the movement of the non-*e* mud into *e* should leave unchanged the *fraction* of *e*'s total mud that is also in *h*. For example, if y/x is 1 (so that prior to discovering *e*, half of *e*'s mud was in *h*), then the same ratio should hold after we discover *e*. That is, half of the mud initially outside of *e* should move into the *h* region of *e* (where the two circles overlap) and half should move into the region of *e* outside of *h*. We should push the non-*e* mud into *e* without fiddling with the distribution of *e*'s mud between the *h* and non-*h* regions of *e*'s circle (see figure 13.5).

Notice that in the previous diagram, the total amount of mud on *e* was x + y, and the total amount of mud on (*h* and *e*) was y, so the ratio of (*h* and *e*) mud to *e* mud was y/(x + y). In our new diagram (depicting our opinions after we discovered that *e* is true), 100 percent of our mud is in *e*, and the total amount of mud on (*h* and *e*) is y/(x + y), so the ratio of (*h* and *e*) mud to *e* mud is again y/(x + y), just as it was before. If we let "pr(*h*|*e*)" stand for the fraction of *e*'s total mud that is also in *h* before we discover *e* (that is, for pr(*h* and *e*) / pr(*e*), if pr(*e*) ≠ 0) and pr′(*h*|*e*) for the analogous ratio after we discover *e*, then our natural thought becomes that pr(*h*|*e*) = pr′(*h*|*e*).

Of course, pr′(*e*) = 1 since pr′ gives our degree of confidence *after* discovering that *e* is true. So:

pr′(*h*|*e*) = pr′(*h* and *e*)/pr′(*e*) = pr′(*h* and *e*)/1 = pr′(*h* and *e*)

Once again, since all of the mud is in the *e* circle after we discover *e*, any mud then remaining in the *h* circle is guaranteed also to be in the *e* circle, so pr′(*h* and *e*) = pr′(*h*). Thus, our natural thought that pr(*h*|*e*) = pr′(*h*|*e*) becomes that pr(*h*|*e*) = pr′(*h*). In other words, our degree of confidence in *h*, after we have discovered *e*, should equal what before this discovery had been the ratio between our degree of confidence in (*h* and *e*) and our degree of confidence in *e*.

The Bayesian Way

You will be relieved to hear that this idea about the relation between our old (pr) and new (pr′) degrees of belief is all we need to generate a proposal regarding the logic of scientific inquiry. That is because there is a powerful theorem, discovered by Thomas Bayes (and published posthumously in 1763), relating pr($h|e$) to pr(h). Let's now derive "Bayes's theorem." Suppose that pr(h) ≠ 0 and pr(e) ≠ 0. Then, as we know, "pr($e|h$)" is defined as the fraction of h's total mud that is also e mud:

pr($e|h$) = pr(e and h)/pr(h).

Multiplying both sides by pr(h), we find

pr(h) pr($e|h$) = pr(e and h).

We also know that by definition,

pr($h|e$) = pr(h and e)/pr(e).

Since obviously pr(h and e) = pr(e and h), we can use the second line above to substitute for pr(h and e) in the line immediately above, yielding

pr($h|e$) = pr(h) pr($e|h$)/pr(e)

That's Bayes's theorem. When we combine it with our result from the previous section, that pr′(h) = pr($h|e$), we arrive at the fundamental principle of "Bayesian confirmation theory":

$$\boxed{\text{pr}'(h) = \text{pr}(h)\ \text{pr}(e|h)/\text{pr}(e)}$$

This equation tells us that evidence e confirms hypothesis h – that is, pr′(h) > pr(h) – exactly when pr($e|h$) > pr(e).

  Let's apply Bayesian confirmation theory to a simple example. Suppose e is that the first emerald I observe today is green and h is that all emeralds are green. Since e must be true if h is true, pr(e and h) is just pr(h), and so pr($e|h$) = pr(e and h) / pr(h) = pr(h) / pr(h) = 1. Hence, by substituting pr($e|h$) = 1 into the fundamental principle of Bayesian confirmation theory (in the box above), we find that pr′(h) > pr(h) as long as pr(e) < 1. Therefore, as long as e is *new* evidence, it confirms h. We have found a kernel of truth in hypothetico-deductivism: if e constitutes our *total new* evidence and h deductively implies e, then e confirms h.

  But unlike hypothetico-deductivism, Bayesian confirmation theory is capable of specifying the *degree* to which e confirms h. The more surprising e's discovery (that is, the lower our pr(e)), the greater the amount by which e raises our confidence in h. For example, if pr(h) = 0.01, then

if pr(e) = 0.1   if pr(e) = 0.25
then pr′(h) = 0.01/0.1 = 0.1   then pr′(h) = 0.01/0.25 = 0.04.

The more we expected e before observing it to be true, the less e confirms h.

Bayesian confirmation theory also accounts for those cases we saw earlier where a hypothesis makes a successful observable prediction but is thereby *disconfirmed*. For example, suppose that h is that all human beings are less than 9 feet tall and e is that the next human being I meet is 8 feet, 11 ¾ inches tall. Unlike in the emerald case, h does not deductively imply e; rather, h entails only that the next human being I meet is less than 9 feet tall – not that she is just a tiny bit less. Hence, unlike in the emerald case, $pr(e|h) \neq 1$. This $pr(e|h)$ is the fraction of h's mud that is also e's mud. It is less than $pr(e)$, the fraction of the total mud that is e's mud, since if h is true, and so all human beings are less than 9 feet tall, then it is less likely that there is a human being who is just a tiny bit less than 9 feet tall. Since $pr(e|h) < pr(e)$, it follows from the fundamental principle of Bayesian confirmation theory that $pr'(h) < pr(h)$. Thus, e disconfirms h – the correct answer!

Bayesian confirmation theory is one of the liveliest current proposals regarding the logic of hypothesis testing in science. However, it must overcome some serious obstacles before it can serve as a complete theory of confirmation. For instance, by the fundamental principle of Bayesian confirmation theory, the hypothesis Green (from section 1 above) is confirmed by the fact that every emerald I have ever observed has been green at the moment I observed it, since $1 = pr(e|Green) > pr(e)$. But those same considerations would seem to apply equally well to the very bizarre hypothesis Grue that I also mentioned in section 1: $1 = pr(e|Grue) > pr(e)$. Yet we do not think that e confirms Grue nearly as strongly as it confirms Green. Bayesian confirmation theory might try to account for this result on the grounds that $pr(Green)$ is far higher than $pr(Grue)$. In that case, even if each of these probabilities is multiplied by the very same $1/pr(e)$ factor to yield $pr'(Green)$ and $pr'(Grue)$, respectively, the resulting $pr'(Green)$ will be far higher than $pr'(Grue)$. But why are we justified in assigning a far higher value to $pr(Green)$ than to $pr(Grue)$ prior to our having observed the relevant evidence? Bayesian confirmation theory seems able to account for the way in which we *update* our initial degrees of belief in the face of new evidence, but it cannot account for those initial degrees of belief themselves, and so seems insufficient to account for the degrees of belief that result from them after they have been updated in the Bayesian way in response to new evidence. Many philosophers today are hard at work on trying to resolve this "problem of the priors."

Let's look at one final application of Bayesian confirmation theory. Consider the competition between the Copernican model of the solar system (according to which the planets orbit the Sun) and the model it replaced, which had been developed by the ancient Greek astronomer Claudius Ptolemy, according to which the planets move on small circles ("epicycles") whose centers orbit the Earth (see upcoming figure). As evidence, consider the fact (known since ancient times) that a "superior planet" (that is, a planet that takes more than one earth-year to complete one circuit through the zodiac in Earth's night sky – for instance, Mars, Jupiter, and Saturn) is at "opposition" (opposite the Sun, as seen from Earth – rising in Earth's sky at sunset and setting at sunrise) exactly when it becomes brightest as seen from Earth (and so, presumably, when is at "perigee": its closest approach to Earth). The Ptolemaic model can explain this correlation, *but only by making each superior planet's epicycle turn at the same rate as the Sun orbits the Earth.*

A picture helps make this clear (see figure 13.6).

In contrast, the correlation between opposition and perigee falls immediately out of the geometry of the Copernican model; it would hold no matter what the orbital velocities were (see figure 13.7).

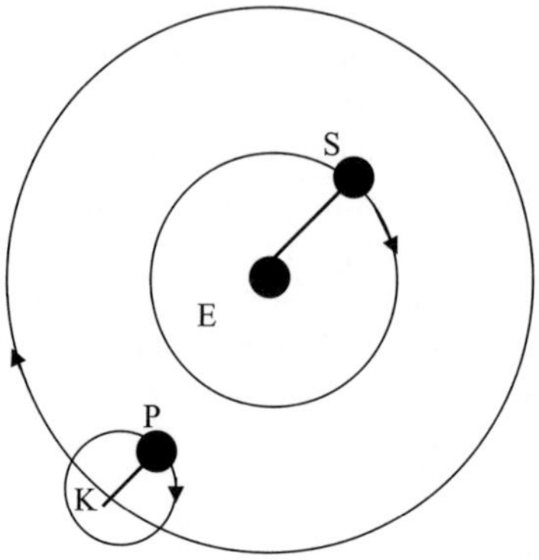

Figure 13.6 A superior planet (P) at opposition to the Sun (S) on the Ptolemaic model. The Sun orbits Earth (E) while the planet orbits on an epicycle, the center (K) of which orbits Earth on a larger circle. As long as the orbital velocities are fine-tuned so that line KP remains parallel to line ES, the planet will reach perigee exactly at opposition

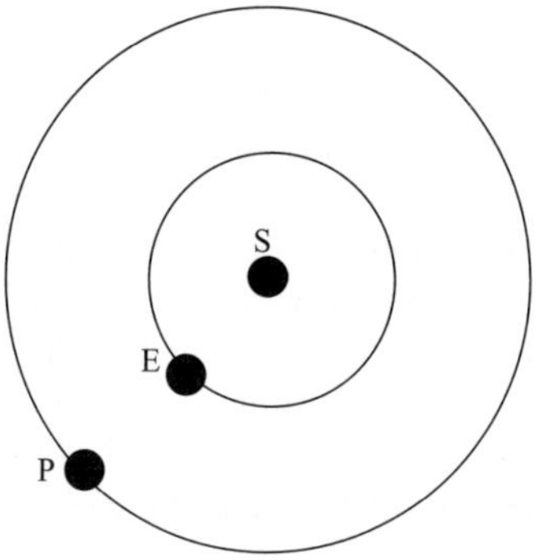

Figure 13.7 Perigee on the Copernican model occurs automatically at opposition

This difference between the Copernican (Cop) and Ptolemaic (Ptol) models was thought to count as evidence for Copernicus' theory. A Bayesian analysis bears this out. If the two models have the same initial probability, then (by the fundamental principle of Bayesian confirmation theory) $pr'(Cop)/pr'(Ptol) = pr(e|Cop)/pr(e|Ptol)$. Since e (the correlation between opposition and perigee) is guaranteed by Cop, but occurs in Ptol only for certain special values of the orbital velocities, $1 = pr(e|Cop) \gg pr(e|Ptol)$, and so $pr'(Cop) \gg pr'(Ptol)$.

Of course, there is a particular version of the Ptolemaic theory having the Sun's orbital velocity equal to the rate at which each of the superior planets' epicycles turns. Call that theory "t." Now since t deductively implies e, $pr(e|t) = 1$, and so e confirms t. But (as we saw in the previous section) from the fact that Ptol must be true if t is true (since t is a version of Ptol), it does not follow that evidence confirming t must confirm Ptol.

Thus, Bayesian confirmation theory nicely captures this famous episode of scientific reasoning. In the years ahead, accounts like this one will make confirmation theory an exciting subject in philosophy.

Further Reading

The famous Grue example comes from Nelson Goodman, *Fact, Fiction, and Forecast* (1983). He called it "the new riddle of induction." The "old riddle of induction" was the problem of justifying induction and thereby responding to Hume's challenge. Hume's 1739 argument can be found in book 1, part iii, section 6 ("Of the Inference from the Impression to the Idea") of his *A Treatise of Human Nature*. In 1748, Hume gave a pithier formulation of the argument in section iv ("Skeptical Doubts concerning the Operations of the Understanding") of *An Enquiry Concerning Human Understanding*. A brief, readable introduction to Popper's ideas is his paper "Science: Conjectures and Refutations" in his collection *Conjectures and Refutations: The Growth of Scientific Knowledge* (1963). A fuller account of Popper's falsificationism appears in his *The Logic of Scientific Discovery* (1959). A nice discussion of underdetermination and falsificationism can be found in Larry Laudan, *Beyond Positivism and Relativism* (1996). Duhem's discussion of the "Duhem–Quine thesis" appears in his *The Aim and Structure of Physical Theory* (1954). Today's leading version of scientific anti-realism is developed in Bas van Fraassen, *The Scientific Image* (1980). A comprehensive introduction to the debate over scientific realism appears in Stathis Psillos, *Scientific Realism: How Science Tracks Truth* (1999). Thomas Kuhn's influential views appear in his *The Structure of Scientific Revolutions* (1962) and *The Essential Tension* (1977). My discussion of Tycho was borrowed from Philip Kitcher, *The Advancement of Science* (1993), which in breadth and depth is a worthy successor to Kuhn. Bayesian confirmation theory is nicely elaborated by Paul Horwich, *Probability and Evidence* (1982). A more sophisticated, marvelously engaging introduction is Richard Jeffrey, *Subjective Probability: The Real Thing* (2004). Arthur Koestler's *The Sleepwalkers* (1968) presents a vivid account of Copernicus, Kepler, and Galileo.

Notes

1   If an "emerald" is *defined* as a certain type of green stone, then I would shift to a different property characteristic of emeralds, such as their chemical composition or their reactivity with acids.
2   They disagree on stellar parallax (Copernicus' theory predicting some, Tycho's predicting none), but stellar parallax was not observed until 1838, long after the Copernican model had been accepted. (Here we have a long-standing anomaly for Copernicus' theory that produced no second thoughts – at least, not after the seventeenth century.) Let's try to understand how astronomers were justified in rejecting Tycho's model even before stellar parallax had been detected.
3   I owe this cute example to Matthew Kotzen.

References

Duhem, Pierre (1954). *The Aim and Structure of Physical Theory*, Princeton, NJ: Princeton University Press.

Fraassen, Bas van (1980). *The Scientific Image*, Oxford: Clarendon.

Goodman, Nelson (1983). *Fact, Fiction, and Forecast*, 4th edn., Cambridge, MA: Harvard University Press.

Horwich, Paul (1982). *Probability and Evidence*, Cambridge: Cambridge University Press.

Hume, David (1739). "Of the Inference from the Impression to the Idea," in *A Treatise of Human Nature*.

Hume, David (1748). "Skeptical Doubts concerning the Operation of the Understanding," in *An Enquiry concerning Human Understanding*.

Jeffrey, Richard (2004). *Subjective Probability: The Real Thing*, Cambridge: Cambridge University Press.

Kitcher, Philip (1993). *The Advancement of Science*, New York: Oxford University Press.

Koestler, Arthur (1968). *The Sleepwalkers*, New York: Macmillan.

Kuhn, Thomas (1962). *The Structure of Scientific Revolutions*, Chicago: University of Chicago Press.

Kuhn, Thomas (1977). *The Essential Tension*, Chicago: University of Chicago Press.

Laudan, Larry (1996). *Beyond Positivism and Relativism*, Boulder, CO: Westview.

Popper, Karl (1959). *The Logic of Scientific Discovery*, New York: Basic Books.

Popper, Karl (1963). "Science, Conjecture and Refutations," in *Conjectures and Refutations: The Growth of Scientific Knowledge*, London: Routledge.

Psillos, Stathis (1999). *Scientific Realism: How Science Tracks Truth*, London: Routledge.

Starr, Cecie and Taggart, Ralph (1992). *Biology: The Unity and Diversity of Life*, Belmont, CA: Wadsworth Publishing).

14

Causation and Laws of Nature

Barry Dainton

A Crucial but Disputed Concept

It is widely agreed that average temperatures in many parts of the world have been rising in recent years. What's the cause? Some claim that it is due to the increasing quantities of human-made carbon dioxide being pumped into the atmosphere. If so, taking steps to reduce these emissions would be prudent, even if it would also be painful (an end to cheap flights, affordable petrol, and so on). But there are alternative explanations for global warming. To mention just one, some scientists believe it is caused by variations in the quantities of cosmic rays hitting the Earth: these rays affect the density of cloud cover, which in turn affects the amount of the sun's energy which gets absorbed and trapped in the atmosphere. If the latter account is correct, there is no point in taking painful measures to reduce carbon emissions – it is the next (cyclical) downturn in cosmic ray activity which will put an end to global warming.

Evidently, tracking down causes is an important business, and in several respects. It is important for understanding: we explain events by uncovering their causes, and when we know the cause of an event we know *why* it happened. It also matters pragmatically: it is only be discovering the real cause (or causes) of global warming that we can know what and whether there is anything we ought to be doing to prevent it. And since causes are responsible for their effects, tracking them down can also have moral significance: to murder someone is deliberately to cause their death.

If the concept of causation plays a key role in our everyday ways of making sense of the world, it plays an equally central role in contemporary philosophy. There are causal theories of knowledge, meaning, mind, perception and personal identity. Given the variety of ways philosophers *use* causation, developing an adequate philosophical account *of* causation is obviously a pressing matter.

The main philosophical problem of causation is easy to state: if an event C causes an event E, how must C and E be related? To put it another way, what differentiates events that are causally related from events that are not? Answers to this question fall into two main camps: *reductionist* and *non-reductionist*. Reductionists believe that it is possible to analyze causation in terms of one or more *other* (non-causal) relationships. According to their non-reductionist opponents no such analysis is possible: causation is not analyzable in other terms. There is a third option: denying the existence of causation. This *eliminativist* stance was advocated by Russell: "The law of causality, I believe, like much that passes muster among philosophers, is a relic of a bygone age, surviving, like the monarchy, only because it is erroneously supposed to do no harm" (1918: 180).

Although some philosophers have followed Russell's lead – we will be seeing why in due course – abandoning a concept that plays such an important role in our ordinary (and philosophical) thinking is not a step to be taken lightly. In recent years new accounts and analyses of causation have proliferated as never before. But before looking at these we need to take a step back.

Causes According to Hume

Hume's writings on causation are the most important and influential in the literature. Although his overall argument is quite complex, to understand Hume's impact on subsequent developments it will suffice to outline its main ingredients.

It is natural to think that for C to be a cause of E, C must immediately precede E, but what else is required? Mere temporal precedence is not enough, for many events are so related without being causally related. A plausible-seeming answer runs thus: "Causes *make* their effects happen, they *produce* their effects – events that occur in immediate succession without being related in this sort of way are not causally related." Or as we might put it, causes *naturally necessitate* their effects. That this is how we typically think of causation Hume does not question. What he does question is the extent to which this way of thinking is legitimate.

By way of a "perfect instance" of cause and effect he asks us to consider precisely what happens when a moving billiard ball strikes a stationary ball. We all know what we expect to see in such cases: after being struck, the stationary ball will itself move off, with a speed and direction that depends on the angle and speed at which it is struck. Here the cause clearly *precedes* the effect, and since the balls make contact, the cause and its effect are *contiguous* – i.e., they are right next to one another. But is the causal relationship itself visible? Hume argues not. All we can actually observe is one ball moving towards another, until finally contact is made, after which the other ball starts to move. There is no trace to be found of the *producing* that we naturally assume is essential to causation. Of course we know that this particular sequence of events is not a one-off: we have observed many other collisions between billiard balls, and know that they always behave in much the same way. In Hume's terms, there is a *constant conjunction* between cause and effect: they are events of a kind that are always found together. But again, constant conjunction is one thing (a pattern involving many event-sequences), causal necessitation is quite another (an intrinsic making-relationship which holds between a particular cause and a particular effect). Since all this applies to all other instances of causation – the billiard balls are perfectly typical in this regard, or so Hume maintains – he is led to the conclusion that *nothing in our experience* justifies the assumption that causes necessitate their effects.

This conclusion is surprising, but it also poses a potentially serious problem for Hume in particular. For as (what is commonly called) a *concept empiricist* he believes that all our basic concepts derive, in a direct fashion, from the contents of our immediate experience. If we never observe natural necessitation at work in the causal interactions we encounter, where does the concept originate? Hume's answer: a *feeling* in our own minds. When a pair of constantly conjoined event-types are repeatedly observed we come to *expect* the second to occur on seeing the first: "this customary transition of the imagination from one object to its usual attendant, is the sentiment or impression from which we form the idea of power or necessary connexion" (*Enquiry*: 75).

With this final piece of the jigsaw in place, Hume's account of causation is complete. A significant consequence of this account is a sharp division between our *concept* of causation, and causation as *relationship between objects and events in the world.* Causation as we conceive it involves natural necessitation; causation as a relationship that can coherently be supposed to exist in the real world involves nothing more than regular succession.

Humeans may be united in their rejection of natural necessities, but they disagree about how precisely the causal relationship should be construed.[1] Some are committed to the *regularity* theory, others to the *counterfactual* theory, others to the *process* theory. After taking a brief look at each of these in turn we will see what the Non-Humeans (or Realists) have to offer by way of an alternative.

The Regularity Theory

In its bare unqualified, form the regularity theory is easy to state:

The Regularity Theory (RT): A causes B if and only if all A-type events are followed by B-type events.

RT has three main merits: it has an agreeable simplicity, it offers a completely objective account of causation, and it has a good deal of *prima facie* plausibility: many causal interactions do involve event-types that are regularly found together – think of what (almost) invariably happens when eggs are dropped onto hard floors, or bricks are thrown through windows.

One cluster of problems can be grouped under the heading "singular causation." It is natural to think that if C causes E, what makes this so is the relationship between these two events: happenings elsewhere in the universe have nothing to do with it. In short, it is natural to think that causation is an *intrinsic* relationship between particular events. But according to RT this is wrong. Whether or not C is a cause of E depends *entirely* on what happens elsewhere: it is only if C-type events are followed by E-type events throughout the rest of the cosmos – from the distant past to the far future, in every galaxy from the nearest to the most remote – that C causes E.

Although this is a peculiar result we cannot conclude that RT is false – after all, our ordinary ways of thinking sometimes turn out to be mistaken – but RT is clearly a *stranger* (and more revisionary) doctrine than it initially seems. But there is a further aspect to this problem: what of *unique* sequences of events? Suppose E is a type of event that happens just once; event F occurs just after E, but is not caused by it. Since every instance of a E-type event (there's just the one) is followed by an F-type event, applying RT to this case delivers the result that E did cause F. To avoid this result the regularity theorist could stipulate that unique sequences of this kind are never causal. But this stipulation sometimes gets things spectacularly wrong. Take the Big Bang. It's not the sort of event that can happen twice, but wasn't it the cause of what came next?

Do the required *regularities* actually exist? It might seem obvious that they do – eggs dropped onto concrete floors tend to behave in a similar fashion, similarly for bricks thrown at windows – but matters are by no means so clear-cut. Suppose our effect is the breaking of particular window, and our cause a particular brick. Viewed from the perspective opened up by contemporary science, each of these events is *massively* complex, consisting as they do of shifting configurations of trillions and trillions of subatomic particles. This precise sequence of (micro-) events will almost certainly never be replicated (down to the last detail) anywhere, ever. Since the same will apply for all pairings of macro-level events, it seems regular, repeating event-sequences are extremely thin on the ground. The RT theorist may well say that causal regularities require only *approximately* similar event-sequences. But just how approximate will do? Taking this step leaves the existence of causal relationships dangerously dependent upon subjective judgments of similarity.

So-called "accidental regularities" are also a problem for RT, and historically speaking, probably the most significant. It seems quite conceivable that there could be types of event which invariably occur in succession, but which are not causally related, contrary to what RT entails. As Thomas Reid noted, night always follows day, but anyone who concludes from this that night *causes* day to follow would be mistaken. One option for regularity theorists is simply to accept that all such sequences are causal. This keeps the appealing simplicity of the theory, but brings with it a dramatic loss of plausibility. A second option is to introduce complications and qualifications in an attempt to distinguish genuinely causal from merely accidental regularities. This is not the place for an exploration of the measures which have been proposed – see Mackie (1974: ch. 3) and Psillos (2002: ch. 2) for further detail – but marking the required distinction without bringing in elements foreign to RT (such as counterfactual relationships) has proven difficult. Yet another option is to hold that causal regularities are underwritten by *laws of nature*, whereas accidental ones are not. This may sound promising, but the proponent of RT has to tread carefully here. While there are *non*-Humean accounts of natural law – accounts which invoke necessary connections – these are not an option for Hume-inspired regularity theorists. Unfortunately, by far the most obvious way to develop a properly *Humean* account of natural laws is in terms of universe-wide *regularities*, and many Humeans – e.g. the logical empiricists – have taken precisely this step. But this is not a step that should be taken by the proponent of RT who is hoping to distinguish between accidental and causal regularities by appealing to the laws of nature. This would be to move in an extremely small circle. Is there a viable Humean alternative to the regularity theory of laws? There is certainly *an* alternative – but as we shall see in due course, it is not without difficulties of its own.

The Counterfactual Approach

In the Enquiry (76), almost as a throwaway remark, Hume characterizes causation in counterfactual terms: "if the first object had not been, the second never had existed." He presents this as merely another way of characterizing his earlier definition in terms of regular succession, which is puzzling: the latter is a matter of patterns among events which actually occur, the new definition is about what *would have happened* if things had gone differently. In any event, we now have a new avenue to explore:

> *The Counterfactual Theory (CT)*: A is a cause of B if, and only if, had A not occurred, B would not have occurred either.

This new avenue has promise. The vase broke because I knocked it over; CT predicts that if I hadn't knocked it over, it wouldn't have broken – and this seems true. The autopsy concludes that the president's death was caused by the assassin's bullet; CT predicts that if the assassin's bullet hadn't been fired, the president wouldn't have died (at that particular time and place) – and this also seems true. CT gets a lot right: in many normal instances of causation, if the cause hadn't occurred, the effect wouldn't have occurred either. It seems natural to suppose causes *produce* or *necessitate* their effects, and the counterfactual theory captures something of what we mean by this. Effects *depend on* their causes because they wouldn't have occurred if their causes hadn't – and for the same reason causes *make a difference* to their effects. There are yet further advantages. According to RT, if A causes B this is because in virtue of patterns which obtain elsewhere (and elsewhen) in the universe; according to CT if A causes B this is because of the way *these particular events* are related. If singular causation isn't a problem for CT, nor are unique causal sequences: the Big Bang did indeed cause what came later – if it hadn't happened there wouldn't have *been* a "later."

These significant merits notwithstanding, the counterfactual approach only began to be seriously explored in comparatively recent times. Lyon (1967) was an early advocate, as was Mackie (1974: ch. 2). However, it was only with the appearance of David Lewis's "Causation" (1973) that the approach took off in a big way. For CT to be viable, we need a way of determining when counterfactual claims are true and false. Since the sequences of events they describe do not actually occur, we cannot appeal – at least in any direct or obvious way – to matters of actual fact. Mackie took the view that counterfactual statements can be more or less reasonable, but not objectively true or false. This lack of objectivity will obviously transfer to causal claims when the latter are analyzed in counterfactual terms.

Enter Lewis, who proposed a systematic and (purportedly) objective way of assessing the truth of counterfactuals. The details of this are interesting, but they needn't detain us here. There is, however, an important point that is worth noting. In outline, Lewis's proposal runs thus. A possible world is a way a whole universe might be; possible worlds are infinite in number, and some of these worlds are more similar (or "closer") to the actual world than others. In assessing counterfactuals of the form "if A hadn't occurred, nor would B" Lewis suggests that we consider possible worlds which are fairly similar to our own but where A doesn't occur. In some of these worlds B doesn't occur either, in others it does. If the worlds where B doesn't occur are closer to the actual world than the worlds where it does, then the counterfactual is *true*, if it's the other way around it is false. How are we to go about assessing which worlds are closest to our own? Lewis proposes a number of interlocking criteria for doing precisely this; the two most important criteria are these: a pair of worlds are similar to the extent that they (1) agree on particular facts (concerning what happens, where, and to whom) and (2) have similar laws of nature. The latter is significant. As a committed Humean, Lewis holds that laws of nature are (at bottom) nothing more than *regularities*, albeit of a distinctive sort. So if the CT-theorists are right in their contention that causal claims can be analyzed in counterfactual terms, if regularities play a key role in determining whether the relevant counterfactuals are true or false, it would seem that the regularity approach is alive and kicking within the CT-framework – even if it has been transposed to a different key.

For all its apparent advantages, the counterfactual approach also faces serious difficulties. How well does it capture the notion that causes produce their effects? Arguably, not well at all. It's one thing to be told that if A hadn't happened, nor would B. It's another to be told that A *made* B happen. The difference in meaning is as plain as could be. Consequently, there are grounds for doubting whether CT accurately captures what we ordinarily *mean* by "cause." This doubt connects with a worry: perhaps CT is getting things back to front. All sides can agree that there are systematic relationships between causal claims and counter-factuals, but what explains what? The CT-theorist would have us believe that "A caused B" is true in virtue of the fact that if A hadn't occurred, nor would B. But there is another explanation: perhaps the reason why B wouldn't have occurred if A hadn't occurred is that A *was the cause of* B – so inevitably, in A's absence, B didn't occur. This explanation looks all the more plausible when considered against the backdrop of Lewis's account of the relevant counterfactuals: is not relationships in *this* world which make such counterfactuals true, but rather happenings in *other possible worlds*. As with the regularity theory, it looks as though causation as viewed through the lens of CT is an extrinsic rather than an intrinsic relation.

Humean counterfactual theorists may well concede that their analysis doesn't fully capture what we mean by "cause," but go on to insist that the missing residue is simply that mysterious necessitation relationship which Hume rightly rejected. However, the conceptual gap separating CT from our ordinary concept is sufficiently large that damaging counterexamples are easy to devise. Consider the death of the president via the bullet of an assassin. Call the actual assassin "Killer-1." As it happened, there was a backup: if Killer-1 hadn't shot the president when he did, Killer-2 would have. For the CT-theorist, the claim that "Killer-1 caused the death-by-shooting of the president" is true in virtue of the truth of this claim: "If Killer-1 hadn't shot the president, the president wouldn't have died." But in the circumstances we are currently envisaging, the president would have died-by-shooting even if Killer-1 *hadn't* pulled the trigger, for Killer-2 would then have done the deed. So by the lights of CT, the person who actually shot the president cannot be regarded as having caused his death. CT's defenders have attempted to deal with such cases by introducing complex modifications into their account, but there is no agreement on what the best remedy is.

When introducing his version of CT Lewis wrote of the many difficulties facing the regularity theory, and wondered whether they could be overcome without "piling on the epicycles, and without departing from the fundamental idea that causation is instantiation of regularities" (1973: 557). In the eyes of many – though not all – an analogous epitaph should be carved on the tomb of CT.

Process Approaches

Regularity theories deny the plausible doctrine that causation is an intrinsic relationship between events, as does (arguably) the counterfactual account in its most influential

(Lewisian) guise. Is there a way of preserving the intrinsic character of causation without falling back on necessary connections of the sort Hume stigmatized? Perhaps connections of a different sort will do the trick: perfectly ordinary physical or material or mechanical connections. Shooter-1 caused the president's death because his pulling of the trigger was followed an explosion in the firing chamber of his rifle, this explosion accelerated a bullet, which then passed through space and into the body of the president. The (alas) fatal bodily damage is thus connected to the assassin's pulling of the trigger by a spatio-temporally continuous series of material objects and events.

The "process theories" developed by Salmon and Dowe are attempts to build a general account of causation around connecting mechanisms of this sort. The basic idea is that two ordinary events are causally related only if "a continuous line of casual processes and interactions obtains between them" (Dowe 2000: 147). Can we specify, in a quite general way, what *makes* a process or interaction a causal one, without relying on the notions of causality or necessary connections? Process theorists agree that we can, but disagree on precisely how. For Salmon it is the ability to transmit *structures* that is important. For Dowe it is a matter of the continuous possession of *conserved quantities* of the sort recognized by physics (momentum, charge, and so forth). For further details and variants see Psillos (2002: I.4) and Schaffer (2000).

Process theories preserve the intrinsic character of causation. They are also deliberately tailored to mesh with the world view of contemporary physics. While this is an advantage in one respect, it is also a significant limitation: the process theorists aim provide an account of causation *as it is in this world*. They make no claim to be providing a general conceptual analysis of "cause," an analysis which is applicable to other possible worlds. This is as well, for otherwise their account would immediately succumb to counterexamples: it is easy to envisage instances of causation which operate *at-a-distance*, without any spatially intervening material processes. The witch waves her wand, utters a spell, and turns her adversary into a pumpkin. We can easily make sense of this story, and if we are told that there is no physical connection or process linking the witch with her enemy – her spell simply *resulted in* the latter's turning into a pumpkin – our conviction that the witch caused the transformation is not weakened in the slightest.

Since the process theorists aren't claiming to be offering a fully general analysis, counterexamples of this sort are not fatal. Of course, the fact that they can't handle this sort of case means that we are still looking for a more general account that can. And there is a further point to consider. Causation-at-a-distance is not confined to fairy tales: Newton's theory of gravity operates in this manner. While it is true that Einstein's theory of gravity superseded Newton's and does not require causation-at-a-distance, can we be sure that future physical theories will follow suit? (Indeed, on some interpretations, causation-at-a-distance is already to be found in quantum theory.)

Process accounts are vulnerable to counterexamples of an altogether different sort. Your neighbor said he'd water you plants while you were away, but he didn't; by simply doing *nothing* your neighbor has killed your plants. Two planes are on collision course; you put a gun to the traffic controller's head, and stop him informing the planes, which collide a few minutes later, killing everyone on board – your actions were the cause of these deaths. These are examples of causation by *omission* and causation by *prevention*. If these are cases of genuine causation – and there are strong grounds for supposing they are, see Schaffer (2004) – they pose a severe problem process theories. You cause the planes to collide, but there is no physically continuous mechanism (of a causally efficacious kind) connecting you to the accident.

Causal Realism

Despite their differences, the regularity, process and counterfactual approaches have a lot in common: each is *reductive* (each explicates causation in terms of something else), and each is *Humean* (in the sense of rejecting necessary connections). Given the serious difficulties afflicting each of these approaches, there is room for an alternative. Let us use the term **causation** to denote the productive or necessitating relationship which Hume rejected. We now have a fourth main position to consider:

Causal Realism (CR): A causes B if and only if A **causes** B.

That CR provides a better approximation of what we ordinarily mean by "cause" is uncontroversial – Hume would have agreed that it does. What is more controversial, given Hume's arguments, is why we should suppose there is anything in the *world* which corresponds to this concept. After all, reality is under no obligation to conform to our ordinary ways of thinking.

One Realist response is to argue, contra Hume, that **causation** *is* directly discernible, at least on some occasions. Suppose I see you hammering in a nail. Doesn't *hammering in* involve **causation**? As you bring the hammer down, can't you *feel* it driving the nail in? For more along these lines see Anscombe (1971) and Fales (1990).

Another, and probably more influential, line is to argue that we would be justified in positing **causation** even if it can't in fact be observed. Most of us believe that the entities posited by fundamental physics – electrons, neutrinos, quarks, etc. – exist even though they are far too small for us to perceive, even using the most powerful of microscopes. Why do we believe in these things we cannot see? Because they are part and parcel of powerful theories which *can* explain much of what we want explaining. This mode of reasoning is *inference to the best explanation*: if one's best explanation for something which can be observed posits an unobservable X, it is reasonable to believe X exists. For advocates of CR, what needs explaining are all the observable regularities we find in the world. Colliding billiard balls conform to the dynamical laws discovered by Newton. Every billiard ball that has ever existed has conformed to the same laws, and so behaved in precisely the same sorts of ways in the same sorts of circumstance. What goes for billiard balls goes for objects of other sorts, throughout the universe, aeon after aeon. There are different rules for different kinds of object (electrons *don't* behave like billiard balls), but objects of the same kind conform to the same patterns of behavior wherever and whenever they are to be found. Can this be down to chance or coincidence? This seems unlikely. We could posit an all-powerful God who enforces this astonishing uniformity, but a more modest explanation is available. It is simply this: that objects of different kinds have different *natures*, and these natures *compel* the objects to behave in certain ways under certain conditions. Things behave in regular, predictable ways because they *have to*, given their natures. Natural or causal necessities, thus construed, explain in an economical fashion something which needs explaining. Given this, we are justified in believing that such necessities exist – and hence that **causation** is a real feature of the universe. This line of reasoning has been elaborated by Armstrong (1983), Foster (1982), and Strawson (1987, 1989).

While this reasoning may seem very compelling, Humeans are unmoved – e.g., Beebee (2006). That objects of the same kind behave in similar ways in similar circumstances is undeniable, but we needn't posit **causation** to explain this: a still more economical explanation is simply that *our universe is regular in certain ways*. The hypothesis concerning the patterns which characterize our universe has exactly the same predictive power as anything on offer from the causal realist, so why make the additional commitment to an unobservable entity?

We are entering deep metaphysical waters here. Why is the universe the particular way it is? If we leave God out of the picture, two responses to this question are available:

R1: As a matter of brute fact certain kinds of object exist; these objects have natures which compel them to behave in certain ways, and the observable regularities are a consequence of this.

R2: As a matter of brute fact the universe consists of a mosaic of unconnected objects and events, and this mosaic happens to be patterned in a certain way.

Realists find R1 more plausible than R2; their Humean opponents find the opposite. Both camps agree that explanations come to an end, they disagree only as to *where* explanations come to an end. For Humeans, the explanation found in R1 might be acceptable if we had a contentful understanding of how Realist necessitation works. For Realists we know enough: we have good reason to believe there is *something* which governs the behavior of objects, even if we cannot say anything informative about its character. They can also point out that this is by no means the only instance where our knowledge of the real nature of something we believe to exist is limited. We believe material objects exist, but do we have a positive understanding of the world described by quantum theory? We know what the theory says a photon can *do*, but does anyone have an understanding of what a photon *is*?

Laws of Nature

There are close connections between causation and the laws of nature. The laws of nature are often called "causal laws," and not without good reason: all sides agree that causality is associated with regularities, and it is natural to think that these regularities depend on the laws of nature – had the laws been different, different regularities would obtain. But just how should we conceive of these laws? Debates on this issue also tend to divide along Humean and Non-Humean lines.

Humeans may reject nomological necessities (i.e., necessitation deriving from natural laws), but most don't reject the existence of laws themselves. Rather, they take facts about the laws to be fully determined by *non-nomic* facts, i.e., facts about how the basic objects and properties are arranged, where the latter are construed as entirely lacking in powers of causal necessitation. What does "determined" mean here? Simply this: any two possible worlds indistinguishable at the base-level of non-nomic facts will also be indistinguishable at the level of nomological facts. Lewis called this doctrine "Humean supervenience."

So much for the programme, how can it be implemented? The most obvious non-nomic facts are facts concerning regularities. However, we cannot simply identify laws with widespread regularities, for as we saw earlier, there are *accidental* regularities (e.g., the night following day) which it is not plausible to regard as laws. As we also saw earlier, the option of appealing to causation to distinguish properly nomic from merely accidental sequences of events is unavailable to anyone who wants to analyze causation in terms of regularities, which most Humeans do, directly or indirectly. But there is at least one further option. When it comes to identifying the laws which actually hold in our universe we look to our best sciences; if we are looking for fundamental laws, we turn to physics. So why not say that the basic nomic regularities are those which correspond with the laws to be found in physics? To get around the fact that our current physics is incomplete and fragmented – where as the laws of nature, presumably, are not – we can identify the laws with the universal generalizations which would appear in the *ideal* physical theory of our universe – the theory a supremely intelligent being would come up with, were they apprised of all the relevant facts. This approach is sometimes known as the "best system theory" (BST), or the "Mill–Ramsey–Lewis" account – on the grounds that each of the latter has defended a version of it.

Most contemporary Humeans endorse BST. Although it has significant advantages over the alternatives, it is not without difficulties. One of the main worries concerns the extent to which it can offer a truly objective account of lawhood. Is there necessarily one *best* way to devise an empirically adequate physical theory? For Lewis the best system will have a "properly balanced" combination of *simplicity* (it won't have many axioms) and *strength* (it will be able to predict many particular events). However, in the eyes of some, it is unlikely that disputes about what constitutes the "proper balance" will be resolvable without appealing to subjective preferences.

The Humeans do not have the field to themselves. Contemporary Non-Humeans reject Humean supervenience. Since they believe there is more to the world than patterns amongst causally inert objects, qualities and events, they deny that such patterns determine the whole truth about the world. On their view, the world is more than just a passive patterning of occurrences, some events *make* others happen, and they do so because of the *laws* governing their behavior. Carroll (1994) takes laws to be basic and irreducible. Armstrong (1983), Dretske (1977), and Tooley (1977) offer something more informative: they take laws to be relationships of necessitation among properties construed as universals – Armstrong has developed this approach in most detail. Others regard laws as grounded in the causal powers of objects (e.g. Mumford 2004).

When it comes to arguments in support of their position, Nomological Realists often turn to the inference to the best explanation we met earlier: regularities require explanation, and laws which constrain and control how things behave provide such an explanation.

They also deploy thought experiments with a view to demonstrating the inadequacy of BST. Here is an example of the sort of case Carroll and Tooley propose. Suppose there is a world W_1 which contains five different types of particle. Particles of types T_1, T_2, and T_3 frequently collide, and the resulting interactions are governed by a small number of distinct fundamental laws L_1, L_2, L_3 for (T_1/T_2), (T_1/T_3), (T_2/T_3) interactions respectively. However, it so happens (by pure chance) that all the T_4 and T_5 particles are located at opposite ends of the universe, and so no T_4-particle ever bumps into any T_5-particle. Since there are no T_4/T_5 interactions, the simplest system of laws capable of covering everything which occurs in this universe will make no mention of a law governing this sort of case, and so according to BST there *is* no such law. But can't we easily make sense of there *being* a law governing these interactions, even though – by pure chance – they never occur? Can't we make perfect sense of this world conforming to law – call it L_4 – which ensures that T_4/T_5 interactions result in both particles being annihilated with a burst of energy? As it happens, no such interactions took place, but the world is such that if they had, then the particles involved would have behaved in just this way. Since this scenario seems perfectly intelligible, it seems that there are nomic facts BST fails to capture.[2]

Humeans will concede that such cases have some superficial plausibility, but insist that they resolve nothing. As they are described, the cases *presuppose* a conception of laws as governing or controlling what occurs. Since on the Humean conception laws merely *describe* what occurs, the cases beg the question – see Beebee (2000). Realists will concede that there is some truth in this, but insist that the cumulative force of their case is such that their conception of laws is more reasonable by far than the austere Humean alternative.

Pluralism

A tacit assumption was in play throughout our earlier discussion of causation, namely that there is just *one* kind of causal relationship. Perhaps this is wrong. Perhaps there are different forms of causation, different conceptions of causation. A number of recent writers have drawn precisely this conclusion: they have advocated *causal pluralism*.

Why opt for pluralism? Simply because it is difficult to see how any one relationship could do the jobs we commonly assign to causation. Recall the problem the counterfactual approach had in dealing with Killer-1 and Killer-2. Killer-1 is responsible for the president's death *not* because the latter wouldn't have died if he hadn't pulled the trigger (given the readiness of Killer-2 he would have), but because of the sort of process which connects Killer-1 to the bullet entering the president's body. This sort of case suggests that *productive process* rather than counterfactual dependence is what matters. But now recall some of our other cases. Your neighbor kills your plants by failing to water them; you are responsible for the deaths of hundreds of people because you prevent the warning being issued to the planes on collision course. When it comes to causation by omission and prevention it is not productive processes that matter – these play no significant role in these cases – rather it is counterfactual dependence: if you hadn't prevented the warning being issued, the planes wouldn't have crashed, if your neighbor had done the watering, your plants wouldn't have died.

Considerations such as these lead Hall (2004) to conclude that we are operating with two distinct conceptions of causation. There is causation as *dependence*, which Hall construes in straightforward counterfactual terms. There is also causation as *production*, a local and intrinsic making-relationship. It is often the case that these are found together, but (as just illustrated) they can also come apart. Hall offers a tentative account of causation-as-production in terms of nomological sufficiency, but Causal Realists could construe it in their own distinctive way.

Hall's "two concept" diagnosis is in many ways a plausible one – for variants and discussion see Godfrey-Smith (forthcoming), Hitchcock (2003) – but there is an alternative. Realists might well be inclined to argue that only causation-as-production is *really* causation. Process theorists might be similarly inclined – likewise regularity theorists who privilege regularities picked out by physical laws. Whatever the details of their position, these causal monists will need to undermine the case for thinking that instances of dependence which are not also instances of causation-as-production (or **causation**) are truly instances of causation. Dowe takes this line (2000: ch. 6), and Beebee (2004) argues that omissions can feature in causal *explanations*, but they cannot actually cause anything.

The Bigger Picture

The causal efficacy of omissions may be questionable, but there is a further issue: can anything *really* cause anything? We saw earlier that Russell opted for an eliminativist stance: he regarded causation as a pre-scientific concept, one that finds no application in the real world, in the manner of the ether or phlogiston. We encountered one of his reasons for adopting this stance, earlier when discussing RT: Russell realized that strict regularities are hard to find, perhaps non-existent, at the macroscopic level. He was also influenced what he found when he looked at actual scientific practice (e.g. in astronomy): he found little or no talk of *cause*, but much talk (and deployment) of *functional relations*, i.e. patterns of co-variation in properties precisely summarized by mathematical equations. A good many contemporary philosophers in possession of a good understanding of contemporary science agree with Russell that causation has no place in fundamental physics. If this is right, and we take physics as our guide to the ultimate nature of physical reality, it follows that the relationships which really govern the world are non-causal.

Of course this position is controversial – there remain plenty of philosophers who believe it is a mistake to base our metaphysics on physics – but even if it were to turn out to be correct, it would not mean we had no option but to abandon causation. There are many concepts – e.g., *liquid*, *animal*, *snowstorm*, *supernova* – which do not apply to systems comprising a small number of elementary particles, but which nonetheless have a useful and legitimate application at the macro-scale, and perhaps causation is another. It may well be that the concept is all but indispensable when it comes to dealing with larger systems – e.g. billiard tables, laboratories – whose constituents behave in ways sufficient regular to be exploited by us in our interactions with them. For some recent work along these lines see the essays in Price and Corry (2007).

Some very general metaphysical issues intersect with the topic of causation. One such is the nature of time. There are a number of very different conceptions of time, but for present purposes it will suffice to mention just two. Proponents of the *Growing Universe* model hold that whereas the past is real but future unreal; they also hold that as the present advances, moment by moment, new slices of reality come into being, via the process of "absolute becoming." This may not be quite how we ordinarily think of time, but it is closer to it by far than the alternative *Block view*, which many favor because of its consilience with relativistic physics. Proponents of this model hold that the universe exists as an eternal four-dimensional ensemble; the future is as real as the past, the present has no ontological significance, and there is no absolute becoming: the contents of the universe are fixed. Now, we naturally think of the causal relationship as *asymmetrical*: effects depend on their causes, in a way that causes don't depend on their effects. In a growing universe this asymmetry finds a place: when a cause comes into being, its (future) effect is as yet unreal. But is there room for this asymmetry if the block view of time is correct, where effects are just as real as their causes? Not obviously, a fact which had led some philosophers (e.g., Tooley) to conclude that the block view cannot be true. Others react differently, by holding that causation (if it exists at all) isn't asymmetrical in the way we commonly assume.[3]

The nature of time also impacts on the Realism issue. As we saw earlier, the debate between Humeans and their Realist opponents on the existence of causal necessitation largely hinges on whether law-like regularities require explanation. Perhaps surprisingly, there may be grounds for thinking the regularities are a good deal *more* puzzling for Growing Universe theorists. Just consider what the process of absolute becoming involves on the cosmic scale: trillion upon trillion of distinct creation-events, one for each momentary phase of each and every elementary particle, aeon after aeon. The Realist can thus argue: "How is it that these myriad creation-events give rise to our orderly world? In the absence of *any* constraints governing how things behave and evolve, wouldn't it take a miracle (many, many miracles) to keep the creation process coordinated?" Since this multiplicity of creation-event has no place in the block conception of time – such universes do not come into being slice-by-slice – this coordination problem does not arise with anything like the same vigor.

There is another grand metaphysical option which neutralizes the problem of why the regularities exist, and does so without any hint of natural necessitation. David Lewis subscribes to "modal realism," the doctrine that other possible worlds are just as real as this world. If all possible worlds are equally real, then there will be many worlds where regularities obtain, and many worlds where they don't (an infinite number in each case). If all these worlds exist, the existence of *this* particular world, regularities included, is not in the least surprising, or in need of explanation. Modal realism has its advantages, but it is also an ontologically extravagant doctrine – almost certainly, there is no doctrine which is *more* extravagant. Contemporary Humeans who for this reason are disinclined to follow Lewis in embracing modal realism are in a far less advantageous position when it comes to dealing with the troublesome regularities. And as for those who are also disinclined to follow him in embracing the four-dimensional view of time, their position may be even more precarious.

Further Reading

Psillos (2002) provides a detailed, accessible and up to date guide to all the main accounts of causation and laws. As a corrective to Psillos' (slight) bias in favour of the Humean line, and for more on Hume himself, see Strawson (1989).

Notes

1 Although accounts which reject natural necessitation are generally labelled "Humean" – and I will be adopting this usage in what follows – the appropriateness of this terminology has been called into question. According to the recent revisionists (or "New Realists") such as Strawson (1989) it was never Hume's intention to deny that causes necessitate their effects. Rather, his aim was a far more limited one: to persuade us that we can never hope to attain any positive understanding of the real nature of causal necessitation. See Reed and Richman (2000) for further discussion.

2 Humean supervenience is in trouble too. Consider W_2, which exactly resembles W_1 in all respects save one. In W_1 interactions of the T_4/T_5 variety are governed by L_4; in W_2, these interactions are governed by L_4^*, which ensures that when the relevant particles collide they *fuse* to form T_1 particles. It so happens that there are no T_4/T_5 interactions in W_2 – don't forget it is very similar to W_1 – but if there had been, they would have resulted in fusions, not explosions. Humean supervenience

entails that worlds that are indistinguishable in matters of particular fact are indistinguishable in every other way. W_1 and W_2 are indiscernible so far as matters of particular fact are concerned, but the nomic facts are very different. So Humean supervenience fails.

3   See Dainton (2001: chs. 4–6) for more on different conceptions of time, and their relationships with causation.

References

Anscombe, G. E. M. (1971). "Causality and Determination," in Sosa and Tooley.

Armstrong, D. M. (1983). *What Is a Law of Nature?*, Cambridge: Cambridge University Press.

Beebee, H. (2000). "The Non-governing Conception of Laws of Nature," *Philosophy and Phenomenological Research*, 61 (3), 571–94.

Beebee, H. (2004). "Causing and Nothingness," in Collins et al.

Beebee, H. (2006). "Does Anything Hold the Universe Together?" *Synthese*, 149, 509–33.

Beebee, H., Hitchcock, C., and Menzies, P. (forthcoming). *Oxford Handbook of Causation*, Oxford: Oxford University Press.

Carroll, J. W. (1990). "The Humean Tradition," *Philosophical Review*, 99, 185–219.

Carroll, J. W. (1994). *Laws of Nature*, Cambridge: Cambridge University Press.

Carroll, J. W. (forthcoming). "Anti-reductionism," in Beebee et al.

Collins, J., Hall, N., and Paul, L. (eds.) (2004). *Causation and Counterfactuals*, Cambridge MA: MIT Press.

Dainton, B. (2001). *Time and Space*, Chesham: Acumen.

Dowe, P. (2000). *Physical Causation*, New York: Cambridge University Press.

Dretske, F. (1977). "Laws of Nature," *Philosophy of Science*, 44, 248–68.

Fales, E. (1990). *Causation and Universals*, London: Routledge.

Foster, J. (1982). "Induction, Explanation, and Natural Necessity," *Proceedings of the Aristotelian Society*, 83, 87–101.

Godfrey-Smith, P. (forthcoming). "Causal Pluralism," in Beebee et al.

Hall, N. (2004). "Two Concepts of Causation," in Collins et al.

Hitchcock, C. (2003). "Of Humean Bondage," *British Journal for the Philosophy of Science*, 54, 1–25.

Hume, David (1888) [1739]. *A Treatise of Human Nature*, ed. L. A. Selby-Bigge, Oxford: Clarendon.

Hume, David (1902) [1748]. *An Enquiry Concerning Human Understanding*, ed. L. A. Selby-Bigge, Oxford: Clarendon.

Lewis, D. (1973). "Causation," *Journal of Philosophy*, 70: 556–67; repr. in Sosa and Tooley.

Lewis, D. (1986). *Philosophical Papers*, vol. 2, Oxford: Oxford University Press.

Lyon, A. (1967). "Causation," *British Journal for the Philosophy of Science*, 18, 1–20.

Mackie, J. L. (1974). *The Cement of the Universe*, Oxford: Oxford University Press.

Republic Revisited, Oxford: Oxford University Press.

Mumford, S. (2004). *Laws in Nature*, London: Routledge.

Price, H. and Corry, R. (2007). *Causation, Physics, and the Constitution of Reality: Russell's*.

Psillos, S. (2002). *Causation and Explanation*, Chesham: Acumen; Montreal: McGill-Queens University Press.

Reed, R. and Richman, K. (2000). *The New Hume Debate*, London, Routledge.

Russell, B. (1918). "On the Notion of Cause," in *Mysticism and Logic*, London: Allen & Unwin.

Salmon, W. C. (1993). "Causality: Production and Propagation," in Sosa and Tooley.

Schaffer, J. (2000). "Causation by Disconnection," *Philosophy of Science*, 67, 285–300.

Schaffer, J. (2004). "Causes Need Not Be Physically Connected to Their Effects: The Case for Negative Causation," in C. Hitchcosck (ed.), *Contemporary Debates in Philosophy of Science*, Oxford: Basil Blackwell, 197–216.

Sosa, E. and Tooley, M. (1993). *Causation*, Oxford: Oxford University Press.

Strawson, G. (1987). "Realism and Causation," *Philosophical Quarterly*, 37, 253–77.

Strawson, G. (1989). *The Secret Connexion: Causation, Realism, and David Hume*, Oxford: Clarendon.

Tooley, M. (1977). "The Nature of Laws," *Canadian Journal of Philosophy*, 7, 667–98.

Tooley, M. (1987). *Causation: A Realist Approach*, Oxford: Clarendon.

15

Ethical Value

Mark LeBar

Philosophical reflection on ethical value may be motivated in a number of ways. One common origin can occur when we observe that we often do not agree with people around us in their ethical commitments, and begin to puzzle how to make sense of that fact. Most of us have some strong beliefs as to ways our world can be a morally better or worse place: we agree for instance that the world is a better place for having less slavery in it than it used to. That is to say, we think slavery is a bad – a *morally* bad – thing. Similarly, most of us agree that the world is better off for our being in time to grab a small child out of the path of a speeding automobile than it would be if we came a moment too late. Saving a child from death or grave harm is a good – *morally* good – thing. The idea that the world includes ethical values like the goodness and badness of such things seems unproblematic when we focus on issues on which most of us agree. Yet our confidence that the world contains such values wobbles when we turn our attention to more controversial issues.

Consider the ethical values we express through voting for political candidates. Often we support such candidates because we believe they best represent morally good things and oppose morally bad things. Yet we hesitate to think that the world would be better off for *compelling* others to vote in the same way. We hesitate in part because we recognize that others in good faith can disagree with us; we think we ought to tolerate not only each other but (to some degree, anyway) our differing values and practices. But if our respect for these ethical values is a response to such values as part of an objective, shared, public world, how is it that others do not or cannot apprehend and respond to them as we do? That anvils are heavier than feathers is a fact of the objective, shared, public world, and it is no accident that nobody can mistake that fact without manifesting some serious mental defect. If ethical values are really elements of that objective world, how is it that there can be so much disagreement about them?

The fact that people disagree about ethical values thus can be one motivation for reflection on them. A second motivation may come from our understanding of the natural world in which we live. Advances in physics, chemistry, biology, and other sciences in the past two or three centuries have enriched not only our understanding of, but our ability to shape, the natural world. Yet these sciences accord no place to ethical values in their picture of the cosmos. At one point there seemed no alternative to understanding complex organisms like ourselves as the product of design – God's design – and thus as having some purpose. Many have thought that achieving that purpose might be among the highest of ethical values. But evolutionary theory explains not only the fact that we are here at all, but also our complexity, without any appeal to purpose or design, God's or otherwise. It instructs us that everything about us is just the upshot of the causal give-and-take of natural selection. Natural selection has no purpose and so neither do we. But without such purpose, this anchor for understanding ethical value too has been lost to us. We seem to live in a world which, so far as the best of our science can tell, doesn't include ethical values. What does that say about the nature of those values? Are we fundamentally mistaken in thinking there are such things? Skeptics or nihilists about ethical value urge an affirmative answer to that question, but their view is not the only one remaining available to us.

Realism

Realists about ethical value insist that, appearances to the contrary, ethical values are constituents of the world every bit as much as atoms or the gravitational force. Ethical values are, in a word, real. There are several varieties of realism.

One variety takes ethical value to be as much present in the world as the physical phenomena we interact with, without themselves *being* physical or "natural" phenomena. *Nonnaturalists* claim that ethical values are properties of natural things in the world, but are themselves not natural properties. The idea of a property being "non-natural" can sound a bit mysterious, but the air of mystery persists only if we insist on thinking about properties as having to be physical properties, like size, shape, and so on. If we think about the ways we ordinarily attribute value properties to things – *bad* to slavery and *good* to feeding the hungry, for example – it is plain that such properties are in one sense very ordinary and not mysterious at all. G. E. Moore, who made this sort of approach famous in the early twentieth century, argued that we should take the property *good* to be a *simple* property of things (that is, a property that cannot be analyzed into further component properties, as for instance the natural property *yellow* is simple) that is not natural, in the sense that it is not accessible by the natural sciences. Any attempt to understand the property *good* as merely some natural feature of the world, he claimed, was doomed to failure.

Moore's version of realism is a bit different from perhaps realism's earliest and most radical form. In his dialogue *Republic*, Plato lays out a view which may be construed as a robust form of non-naturalist realism. Plato maintained that there are really *two* worlds, and we are denizens of both of them. One is the world of material substance, which we detect with our senses. Things in this world are always coming into and going out of existence; their transience entails that we can really have no knowledge of them. The only reality that is stable and not in flux is the world of Ideas (or Forms), which we know by the use of reason. In this world the Idea of Good has pride of place. It is, Plato claims, only because of this Idea of Good that anything else even has being or existence. Things in the world around us which we call "good" are so (if we are right) only because they somehow "participate" in this Idea. On Plato's view, then, ethical value is not only real, it is more real than anything that science can contemplate.

But discomfort that the world might contain anything so bizarre as "non-natural" properties – let alone a world of Ideas – motivates skepticism that that is the right way to conceive of ethical values. After all, how could we know about such things on that picture? We have a ready model for knowledge from the sciences: there is nothing plainer than our knowledge, and our knowledge that we know, of shoes and ships and sealing-wax, and that pigs do not have wings. But by hypothesis ethical value would stand outside those ways of knowing.

Ethical naturalists are realists who see this problem as providing its own solution. Whereas non-naturalists claim that there are ethical values as part of the world, even though they are not themselves natural phenomena, ethical naturalists insist that ethical values *are* natural phenomena – they are constituted by facts or properties in the familiar, sensible world; there is nothing "non-natural" about them. But there are different varieties of ethical naturalism as well. One type takes as its point of departure the way natural features of the world and values intersect in unproblematic, non-moral cases. Suppose you have a lawn-mower. If its blade is sharp and it cuts grass well, you would think it is a good lawnmower; with a dull blade or some other defect in performance, it would be not such a good lawn-mower. In saying that the mower is good or not so good, you are attributing a value property to it. But what is that value property, other than something constituted by its capacity to do what it is intended to do (namely, cut grass)? There's nothing to that value beyond the familiar, physical, properties of the lawnmower; we don't need any spooky "world of ideas" or "non-natural" properties to make sense of the way a lawnmower can be good. Our first sort of ethical naturalist would extend this model quite generally into the ethical realm. Just as a lawnmower that cuts grass poorly is a bad lawnmower or a plant that can't absorb water is a bad plant, a human being that can't coexist peacefully with other people (say) is a bad person. Ethical value, on this picture, arises in the ordinary ways that natural things can have values. Since we are natural things, we can have these value properties as well.

Another sort of ethical naturalist draws our attention instead to close *parallels* between the way we think of ethical value and the way science contributes to our knowledge. Science proceeds, in large part, by providing theories that *explain* elements of our experience. We know that unobservable entities such as subatomic particles exist because they feature in the best explanations of phenomena we *can* observe. But ethical values feature in explanations in just the same way. It is the *badness* of slavery which explains people's opposition to it. We should think this badness is real, this sort of naturalist will insist, because the kind of property necessary to do this explanatory work will be something we can see to be *independent* of our attitudes about it (that is, slavery is bad whether we think it is or not; it was bad throughout the many generations of human society in which people thought it was unobjectionable: they were simply wrong), and which is something which can shape our thought and conduct (for example, societies that accept slavery simply will not thrive as do societies that reject it, not just because people resist it, but because its badness itself has implications for the working of human relationships and cooperation). Because ethical values can feature as parts of the best explanations of our experience of the world, we should regard them as real in just the same way we take other things that explain our experience (subatomic particles, the Big Bang) to be real.

All realists – naturalist or non-naturalist – will have responses to the two problems which launched our inquiry. Consider first the problem of moral disagreement. Realists will insist that the fact of such disagreement shows us precisely nothing about the existence of ethical values; such values are really part of our world, and people can be wrong about these features of the world just as they can be wrong about any others. By way of argument by analogy, they might point out that for centuries people were in deep disagreement over how the earth fits into the world: do the sun and other heavenly bodies orbit around it, or is the earth itself in orbit? Today, of course, there is little disagreement about this, but that is a relatively recent development. However controversial the question might have been at one time, however, there's no doubting there is a real matter of fact about the physical relations between the earth and the sun. Some people were right about it, and some people were wrong about it. At most, the disagreement reflects something about the difficulty of arriving at evidence that can be universally persuasive, rather than reflecting anything about the reality that that evidence points to. Similarly, what our moral disagreements point to is at most how difficult it may be to arrive at evidence about ethical value that is universally persuasive; they need show us nothing about the reality of that value. Indeed, realists will suggest that we consider our convictions that *toleration* of others holding views with which we disagree as an excellent example of a value that really is part of the world.

Realists may divide a bit more in response to our second concern. What exactly they have to say about the relation between the natural world and ethical values depends on the form of realism in question. Naturalists will insist that ethical values pose no problem for our understanding of the natural order because ethical values are *part* of the natural order and indeed are necessary to explain how we experience it as we do. Suppose, for example, that we think (as some utilitarians do) that it is right to maximize happiness. Then, if we can point to a situation in which happiness is, as a matter of natural fact, being maximized, we will have pointed to the presence of an ethical value. There is no problem for ethical values arising from our best science because these are just two different ways of thinking about the same thing, namely the order of natural facts.

Non-naturalist realists will take a different tack. Here they will insist that, though science does indeed inform us about the natural world, there is no reason to think that what science describes is all there is. Just because science does not afford us the tools to get a grip on goodness, rightness, or other ethical values, does not mean there is nothing there to know or understand. The mistake, from the non-natural realist's perspective, is thinking that if there is something there to know, science is the only credible way of getting at it. There is, this realist will argue, simply no reason to think this is so (and indeed that is a claim that cannot itself be substantiated by science!).

This strategy does blunt the force of that second concern, but it leaves another in its place for the non-natural realist. Suppose we grant that science is not the right tool for understanding ethical value. Nonetheless, we do aspire to ethical knowledge; we seek tools for sorting true from false ethical claims, and the like. If science is not to be our method for arriving at such knowledge, what is? What sort of account can the non-naturalist realist give us for how we can test claims of knowledge about ethical value, if science is not part of it?

The difficulty in mounting a persuasive response to this question may suggest that, if we are going to be realists, we at least ought to go for some form of naturalism, since at least we would not face this sort of epistemological hurdle. But the non-naturalist realist will argue that there are worse problems to be had by trying to make sense of ethical values as natural facts. Some of these are technical problems in understanding how the meanings of the terms we use in thinking about or describing ethical values come to have the meanings they do. But the deeper problem, the non-naturalist will insist, is that ethical values and non-natural (or *normative*) facts seem pretty clearly to be not the same things as *natural* facts. It is one thing to say *this act maximizes happiness*, and quite another to say *this act is right*. The former (if true) points out some natural facts about the world, but by itself imposes no demands for action upon us; by itself it gives us no reason to act. The latter, however, purports to do just that: saying that an act is right just is saying something about what we have reason to do, namely, that we have reason to perform that act – we *ought* to do it, we *should* do it, and so on. The non-naturalist realist denies that the latter can ever be fully captured in language that adverts only to natural facts about the world.

These difficulties with realism motivate some thinkers to give up thinking that ethical values are part of the world at all. Obviously we think and speak of them, but we aren't (on these other views) referring to parts of the world at all – natural, non-natural, or otherwise – in the way that we are when we speak of ships and kings and sealing wax. Instead, we are doing something else. Let us now turn to *irrealist* conceptions of ethical value.

Irrealism

Given the trouble in understanding how ethical values might fit into the natural world, or how we might know of them if they are somehow part of the world non-naturally, one plausible line of thought is that we should abandon the attempt to think they exist at all. What are we to think instead? Something like this: ethical values are reflections of our attitudes *toward* the world. Things that happen affect us in different ways: some we like, others we hate; some charm us, some repel us. What we do, on this way of thinking, is to *project* these attitudes out onto the world and the things that provoke them. When something repels us, we start thinking of it as having a value of (say) being *repulsive*, when in fact that "value" is just a matter of our own attitudes toward it. Saying of something else that it is "evil" is, likewise, a matter of projecting onto the "evil" thing the attitude or response we have to it. What is *not* happening is what the realist claims: that we are responding to some feature or property of the world. Things in the world don't *have* ethical value or properties; they simply are the objects of attitudes we project.

As in the realist case, there are variants of this approach. What these variants have in common, however, is a sort of "quietism" about the problems we began with. They will not try to solve those problems; they will accept that they *are* problems, but insist that these problems should not trouble us.

This is most clear in thinking about the concerns that faces us because science can make no place for ethical values in the natural world. The irrealist responds: of course not! There's nothing *there* to be made a place for. In fact, we misunderstand what ethical values are if we look around in the world (natural or otherwise) to find them. The only place such things exist is in us, and rather than looking outwards for them, we must look inwards.

Likewise, the problem of conflicting values doesn't go away but loses its urgency on this way of thinking. The fact is that people have varying attitudes toward things, including things we find abhorrent (child abuse, say, or slavery, or . . .). This ought not to surprise us, and it ought not to induce us to wonder how such people could be going wrong in detecting genuine ethical values, since there *are* no such values. At bottom people simply have different attitudes, and the different ethical values they take there to be are simply reflections of these differing attitudes. The mystery is dissolved.

Does that mean we must condone those who have such attitudes or accept abhorrent practices? Not at all. *Our* attitudes toward such practices are that they should be condemned. When we say that such attitudes or practices are abhorrent or ought not be to accepted, we are simply giving our attitudes voice, but that doesn't mean there are not genuine ethical values at work, since such attitudes are precisely what such values consist in. The irrealist is as comfortable as the realist in making the judgment that we should condemn slavery or injustice. Are we tempted to say more? Are we tempted, for instance, to think, "Yes, but we *should* condemn these things, and those who accept them *should not!*" The irrealist can say that too. In fact, it is very difficult to find something the realist wants to assert about the *morality* of practices, or the practical significance of values, that the irrealist cannot likewise assert. The two camps differ as to the *explanations* of what makes those claims true, when they are true (and even what it means to say of them that they are true). The realist claims that such judgments are true in virtue of lining up somehow with genuine ethical values, and the irrealist denies that there are any such things in the world to line up with. But that fact, the irrealist insists, cannot bar us from making all the moral judgments we are used to making, and on insisting on their truth in some different sense.

A different irrealist approach takes us much the same way. *Existentialists* maintain that it is turning things around to suppose there are ethical values "out there" which it is up to us to detect and respond to properly. To think this is to suppose there is some "blueprint" for what we are like, or ought to be like, which it is our function to fulfil or realize. And this is false. What we ought to become, or what values we ought to realize, it is up to us to *determine*, to bring into existence. The existentialist slogan for this position is that "existence precedes essence," which means that our essence – what we are or should aim to become – *follows from* what we make of ourselves. Our bare existence is the starting-point, not some planned-out picture of what we are or ought to be like. This is a more radical picture of our place in the world, and of the task of creation of ethical values, than the "projective" view character-ized above. On the existentialist picture, ethical values are more a matter of *will* for us than they may be on the projectivist picture. The projectivist may think we actually have very little control over, or play very little voluntary role in, the establishment of the attitudes that are the basis for projection. So there are different views as to exactly how values which don't strictly speaking exist in the world come to play the roles in our lives and practice that they do. The central point of agreement between these two forms of irrealism, however, is just on this crucial claim that ethical values are not to be found as part of the world outside us at all.

Some of the technical problems in understanding how our moral language comes to have the meaning it does afflict irrealists as well; in fact, the difficulties cited earlier for naturalist realists reflect deep disagreements on these issues between those realists and irrealists. But a different, and perhaps deeper, concern for irrealism arises directly from its conception of us, of the world we live in, and of what to make of ethical values in consequence. The realist will insist that, if the irrealist is right, we live in a very different world than the one we imagine we do, if (as seems plausible) when we make claims about what is good or bad, right or wrong, we take ourselves to asserting something about what the world is like, not just what *we* are like.

The irrealist must accept that this is true, but then will reply that this fact need make no great difference. After all, it does not matter to our senses of humor if we realize that, when we find something funny, we are not in doing so tracking a feature of the world, "funniness" (or "humorous value"), which we are accurately detecting and responding to. Even if we recognize that we are just projecting onto the world our reactions to some things as being funny, that need make no difference to us in practice. Things that are funny amuse us even so. Likewise, the irrealist claims, we can recognize that when we make ethical judgments, we are not in so doing tracking some feature of the world which we are accurately reflecting and responding to, without any great loss to our ethical practice. Evil things will merit our condemnation even so.

The realist will resist this analogy. Not a lot rests on what we find funny. But much *does* rest on our judgments about what is good or bad, right or wrong, and it cannot help but influence our attitudes about these things, and the ethical values we think they bear, to see our attitudes as disengaged from the real facts about the world around us, as they must be if the irrealist is right. At the very least there is a sort of instability in simultaneously seeking an accurate grasp of what is good and what is bad as though it were important in the ways we think it is, while thinking all the time that in doing so we are but tracing the contours of our own sensibilities. So, at least, the realist will argue.

It would be nice to find a way to reconcile the realist's reassurance that ethical values are really a part of the world we live in with the irrealist's ready solutions to questions about how we can know of them. A third approach, *constructivism*, claims to do just this.

Constructivism

Constructivism is, at first blush, less easy to make sense of then either the forms of realism or the forms of irrealism we have considered. The idea, however, is this. The constructivist agrees with the realist that ethical values really are part of the world. The constructivist does not agree with the irrealist, that is, that the world really has in it no ethical values of the sort to which we suppose our ethical judgments to be corresponding. However, the constructivist disagrees with the realist as to the nature of these values, and how they come to be, and agrees with the irrealist that an important part of that story is played by our dispositions and responses to the world in which we find ourselves. Whereas the realist wants to insist that ethical values are part of a timeless ideal world, or part of nature, the constructivist denies that there are or would be any ethical values were it not for *us* – some essential task we play in constituting or "constructing" such values. What exactly this role is, and the details of the picture, vary between versions of constructivism.

On some readings of Kant's account of ethical value, he is an exemplar of constructivism (but his view is in any event complex, and this is a contentious point). First, some background. Like Plato, Kant distinguishes between two worlds, the world of sense and the world of understanding. Unlike Plato, however, Kant does not claim that the latter is somehow more real or knowable than the former (in fact, just the opposite). Instead, the contrast between these two worlds that matters is this: the natural world (the "world of sense") we know to be governed by natural laws. Gravity, for instance, dictates how two masses will be attracted to each other any place, any time, without exception. The natural laws of cause and effect govern without exception in the world of sense.

But, Kant argues, we cannot help but see ourselves as *not* governed by natural law in the same way. We know that we can *choose* the principles or laws we act upon: when our desires pull against what we know we ought to do, we know we can choose between these courses of action and be governed by our knowledge of moral principles. This is because we are capable of being governed (or, better, governing ourselves) by *rational* laws – rules we impose on ourselves in virtue of our rationality. Kant thinks there is no ethical value in being governed by exceptionless natural laws, but there *is* value in choosing to be governed by moral principles. The "world of understanding" is the world governed by these principles, so ethical value is properly understood as having its home there, rather than in the world of sense. However, we belong to *both* worlds, so there is another sense in which ethical value is in the natural world in virtue of the choices we make in it.

Kant's constructivism consists in his claim that ethical value isn't something that by its very nature attaches to things in the world, or possible actions, or anything of that sort. Instead, ethical value comes to be in the world through the acts of willing we engage in when acting – through the ways we exercise our capacity for rational choice. When our wills are determined simply by the material incentives we have as part of the natural world (our desires, passions, and the like), there is no ethical value. After all, that is just the playing-out of natural laws. Just as there is no ethical value in (say) a mother bird feeding her chicks (that is just what mother birds naturally do), there is no ethical value in "doing what comes naturally" to us either. But, as noted above, we can instead choose to have our wills governed by rational principles, and when we do that, ethical value *is* constituted. Thus, there really is ethical value in the world, but it comes to be because of our choices as rational agents.

Constructivism is best-known through work, not in ethical value per se, but in the closely-related field of political theory. John Rawls, following Kant in thinking constructivistically about justice, held that just principles for political societies really are part of the world, but not in virtue of some timeless fact or feature of nature or some non-natural reality. Instead, he held, principles of justice are instituted in virtue of a certain sort of choice we can exercise in thinking rationally together about the fundamental principles of society. If we do this in a certain specified way, in which we impose a sort of "veil" of thought upon ourselves, so that we are ignorant of what we are like as individuals and what particular spot in society we occupy, we will settle on two principles of justice in particular. What these are doesn't matter for our purposes here; what matters is Rawls's view that these principles *really do exist* in the world just in virtue of being the objects of our willing and choice (provided we choose under the proper circumstances). There are no principles of justice as constituents of the world prior to and independent of our working these principles out through deliberating about them as moral agents.

What can constructivists say about the two problems for ethical value with which we began? For the most part, their responses will look similar to those of the realist. At least the sort of constructivists who focus on our *rationality* as the basis for "constructing" ethical values will insist that the values so constructed hold for all human beings, insofar as we are rational. That is to say, there will be facts about ethical values, and some people will get those facts right, and others wrong. Just as the realist insists, the fact that there is disagreement doesn't begin to show that there aren't facts of the matter. It's just that the constructivists' story about how those facts *are* facts will differ from the stories offered by realists, in that they will include a crucial role for human rationality.

The way those stories differ matters for the second question, how we can make sense of things like ethical values even though science leaves them out of its picture of the world. If constructivism is right, these values are in the world in part because of the operation of our rational capacities, and the study of those capacities, *as* rational, is not the subject of the empirical sciences. Instead, the empirical sciences *depend* in part on those very capacities, as scientists weigh evidence, compare the comparative satisfaction of different explanations for events and processes, adjudicate between competing theories, and so on. Here scientists, like other people, are using their rational capacities to make inferences and draw conclusions. This is one sort of operation of our rational capacities that isn't itself an object of empirical study (though related things like, say, what our brain is doing when we conduct these operations might be). So the constructivist would insist that it is not the case that all there is in the world is what scientists study.

Constructivism has attracted much attention in recent years, but really it is only a particular version of a way of thinking about ethical value as a kind of property things in the world can have, but only in virtue of our being in the world. The way that some have proposed we think about value as part of the world is on the model of the way we can think of colors as being part of the world. That is, we know that the yellow of a banana (say) is not *simply* a property of the banana. Creatures without the sort of color vision we possess will not see the banana as yellow, nor will we except under normal lighting conditions. The banana's yellowness is what John Locke called a *secondary quality*, in that this property it has doesn't depend on just features of the banana itself but also on our sensibilities. The project of construing ethical values on a similar model seems to "split the difference" between realist and irrealist camps. On the one hand, on the "response-dependence" model (as this approach is called, since on it the properties in question depend for their existence and nature on our responses to the world) insists with the realist that ethical values really are part of the world. The badness of slavery is really a feature of the world, just as is the yellowness of the banana. But on the other hand the response-dependence theorist agrees with the irrealist that these values are not somehow *already* out in the world, waiting for us to encounter them. If that is what we take ethical values to be, our attempts to find them will fail. The response-dependent theorist will claim that this approach thus benefits from the virtues of each approach, while the critic may complain that it is vulnerable to the problems which beset both! But, as constructivism illustrates, it is another promising path to explore in understanding how ethical value could be part of our world, and what it might be like.

Further Reading

The earliest, and perhaps still the strongest and starkest, version of realism about ethical values may be found in Plato's *Republic* (available in many translations, collections, and online). G. E. Moore's modern version of non-naturalist realism may be found in his *Principia Ethica* (1903); a later exponent of a similar view is in W. D. Ross, *The Right and the Good* (1930). Ethical naturalism is defended, more recently, by Philippa Foot in her *Natural Goodness* (2001); a similar approach may be found in Rosalind Hursthouse's *On Virtue Ethics* (1999). A succinct formulation of the second variety of ethical naturalism may be found in a paper by Peter Railton, "Moral Realism" (1986); a more extensive defense in David Brink, *Moral Realism and the Foundations of Ethics* (1989).

Irrealism's greatest historical spokesman is David Hume, who, in *A Treatise of Human Nature* (1888), set out the case for seeing values as projections of our sentiments in a way that philosophers have been adopting and refining since. Exemplary contemporary versions of this approach may be found in Allan Gibbard, *Wise Choices, Apt Feelings* (1990), and in a collection of essays in which Simon Blackburn has developed his own version of projectivism, *Essays in Quasi-realism* (1993).

The best-known expressions of existentialism are found in the philosophy and plays of Jean-Paul Sartre, such as *Being and Nothingness* (1992), *Existentialism and Humanism* (1948), and "No Exit" in *No Exit, and Three Other Plays* (1955), and Albert Camus, such as *The Stranger* (1988). These are twentieth-century expressions of ideas found in Soren Kierkegaard, *Fear and Trembling, and the Sickness Unto Death* (1954), and Friedrich Nietzsche, *On the Genealogy of Morals* (1967).

Kant's best-known work on ethical value, and the one in which many of the ideas discussed here are prominent, is his *Groundwork for the Metaphysics of Morals* (many editions). Also, his *Critique of Practical Reason* (1956), develops many of these ideas further, and sometimes in ways differing from the *Groundwork*. An excellent development of Kant's ideas along the lines suggested here may be found in Christine Korsgaard's *Sources of Normativity* (1996). Korsgaard has a lucid exposition of constructivism about ethical value in her paper, "Realism and Constructivism in 20th Century Moral Philosophy" (2003).

Rawls' constructivism is developed in *A Theory of Justice* (1971; 1999), and in a series of follow-up papers, among which the best on this point may be "Kantian Constructivism in Moral Theory" and "Themes in Kant's Moral Philosophy," both in *John Rawls: Collected Papers* (1999). The point that normative entities like ethical values are found not only in morality but also in science itself is made by Jean Hampton, in *The Authority of Reason* (1998).

Although they did not use the term "response-dependence" for their approaches (that terminology developed later), the best-known proponents of this approach are John McDowell, in "Values and Secondary Qualities" (1985), and David Wiggins, in "Truth, Invention, and the Meaning of Life," and "A Sensible Subjectivism," in his *Needs, Values, and Truth* (1987).

References

Blackburn, Simon (1993). *Essays in Quasi-realism*, Oxford: Oxford University Press.

Brink, David (1989). *Moral Realism and the Foundation of Ethics*, Cambridge: Cambridge University Press.

Camus, Albert (1988). *The Stranger*, tr. M. Ward, New York: Knopf.

Foot, Philippa (2001). *Natural Goodness*, Oxford: Clarendon Press.

Gibbard, Allan (1990). *Wise Choices, Apt Feelings*, Cambridge, MA: Harvard University Press.

Hampton, Jean (1998). The Authority of Reason, Cambridge: Cambridge University Press.

Hume, David (1888). *A Treatise of Human Nature*, Oxford: Clarendon.

Hursthouse, Rosalind (1999). *On Virtue Ethics*, Oxford: Oxford University Press.

Kant, Immanuel (1956). *Critique of Practical Reason*, tr. L. W. Beck, New York: Macmillan.

Kierkegaard, Soren (1954). *Fear and Trembling and the Sickness Unto Death*, tr. R. J. Lowrie, Garden City, NY: Doubleday.

Korsgaard, Christine (1996). *Sources of Normativity*, Cambridge: Cambridge University Press.

Korsgaard, Christine (2003). "Realism and Constructivism in 20th Century Moral Philosophy, *Journal of Philosophical Research, APA Centenary Supplement*, Charlottesville: Philosophy Documentation Center.

McDowell, John (1985). "Values and Secondary Qualities," in Ted Honderich (ed.), *Mrality and Objectivity*, London: Routledge and Kegan Paul.

Moore, G. E. (1903). *Principia Ethica*, Cambridge: Cambridge University Press.

Nietzsche, Frederick (1967). On the Genealogy of Morals, tr. W. Kaufmann, New York: Vintage.

Railton, Peter (1986). "Moral Realism," *Philosophical Review*, 95, 163–207.

Rawls, John (1971; 1999). *A Theory of Justice*, Cambridge, MA: Harvard University Press.

Rawls, John (1999). *John Rawls: Collected Papers*, ed. S. Freeman, Cambridge, MA: Harvard University Press.

Ross, W. D. (1930). *The Right and the Good*, Oxford: Clarendon.

Sartre, Jean-Paul (1948). *Existentialism and Humanism*, tr. P. Mairet, London: Methuen.

Sartre, Jean-Paul (1955). "No Exit," in *No Exit, and Three Other Plays*, New York: Vintage.

Sartre, Jean-Paul (1993). *Being and Nothingness*, tr. Hazel E. Barnes, New York: Washington Square Press.

Wiggins, David (1987). *Needs, Values and Truth*, Oxford: Clarendon.

16

Ethical Choice

Philip Stratton-Lake

What the Issue of Ethical Choice Is

In his monumental work the *Critique of Pure Reason* Kant claimed that all the interests of reason, speculative as well as practical, combine in the following three questions:

1. What can I know?
2. What ought I to do?
3. What may I hope? (B 832–3)

The second of these is the issue of choice. The issue of *ethical* choice is slightly more restricted. With this we are concerned not with what we ought to do in general, but with what we *morally* ought to do. But how are we to distinguish moral from non-moral oughts? Kant thought of oughts as imperatives, or commands, and distinguished moral from non-moral imperatives with reference to whether they are conditional on our goals or aims (ends). Non-moral oughts are what he called hypothetical imperatives. Hypothetical imperatives apply to you only if you happen to have a certain end of goal. They do not say that you must do this or that, but rather that you must do this or that *if* you have a certain end. So, for example, "you ought to brush" your teeth regularly is a hypothetical imperative. It only applies to you if you have the goal of having healthy teeth. If you do not have this goal, if that is, you do not care about having healthy teeth, it is not true that you ought to brush them regularly.

Moral oughts, Kant claimed, are not like this. They do not depend upon certain goals some of us just happen to have, but apply to everyone independently of any desires or ends they have. In Kant's jargon, moral oughts are *categorical* imperatives. There may be a non-moral reason to be honest, as Kant's honest grocer example illustrates. Being honest with all of your customers may be good for business, and being dishonest might be bad for business. But in addition to the thought that it is in the grocer's interest to be honest there is a quite distinct thought that the grocer ought *morally* to be honest to his customers. This moral requirement seems to be true even when it is not in the grocer's interest to be honest. So moral oughts seem to apply irrespective of whether the action furthers the agent's self-interest. It is for this reason that it is quite coherent to think that someone ought morally to do some act even where doing it would involve considerable sacrifice to the agent: it may even involve one sacrificing one's life.

I have said that the issue of moral choice asks the question: "what ought we morally to do?" But there is more to it than that. We are not concerned only with *what* we ought to do, but also with *why* we ought to do these acts. We might, for example, agree that we ought to keep our promises, but disagree about why we ought to keep them. So even if different theories agree about what we should do they will disagree about why we ought to do these acts.

In asking why we ought to do what morality requires us to do we are asking for a reason to do moral acts. Often acting morally will benefit us, but the reason why we ought morally to do certain acts cannot be that it will benefit us. For we have seen that we can be morally required to do certain acts even when doing those acts will not benefit us. So not just any reason to do what we morally ought to do will be of the right sort. The right sort of reasons must be as categorical as the oughts they explain – that is, they must be *moral* reasons.

Kant often seemed to think that there is only one moral reason, and that it is the fact that it is your duty to do that act. But if we are asking *why* we ought to do what we ought to do (why we ought to do our duty), we cannot answer in this way. We do not explain why some act is our duty by saying that it is our duty. So although we must answer the question of why we ought to do certain acts with reference to moral reasons, we cannot answer this question with this moral reason. Duty may be able to give us a reason to act, but cannot explain why some act is our duty.

Consequentialism

Consequentialists maintain that what we ought morally to do is determined solely by the amount of good our action will produce. So the first question for a consequentialist is to specify which things are intrinsically good, that is, which things are good in themselves and hence worth pursuing for their own sake. Once we know what the good is, we can say that the right act is the one that produces as much of that good as possible. So if, for instance, the only intrinsically good thing is pleasure, as utilitarians maintain, then the right act is always the one that will produce the most pleasure. Consequentialists need not, however, claim there is only one good thing.

Consequentialism has a lot going for it. It is a relatively simple theory. It says that we ought always to do those acts that will produce the best state of affairs, and we ought to do those acts just because they will produce the best state of affairs. It is able to show what the different act types that morality requires us to do have in common, and so is able to systematize and unify our thinking about morality. It is also very plausible, at least on first sight. If something is intrinsically good, then surely we should produce as much of it as possible. How could it be right to do anything less than the best action?

But despite its many virtues it is vulnerable to quite serious objections. First, it is insensitive to how the good is to be distributed. All that matters from a consequentialist point of view is that as much good as possible is produced. How this good is to be distributed is not relevant. But this generates quite counterintuitive conclusions. Suppose that human happiness is the only thing that is good in itself and human misery is the only thing that is bad in itself. Suppose further that we have to choose between two acts, A and B. Each act will produce equal amounts of happiness and misery for others, but different people will be made happy or miserable depending on which act we do. If I do act A the virtuous will be happy and the vicious miserable. If I do act B, however, the virtuous will be miserable and the vicious happy. Consequentialism would have to say that it does not matter whether we do A or B, since both acts have equally good consequences. But this seems quite wrong. It seems clear that we ought to do act A and that act B would be wrong.

Also other, apparent, moral considerations are given no independent weight according to consequentialism. So if, for example, keeping my promise will produce as much good as breaking it, then I am permitted to do either act. But once again this seems mistaken. It seems that when I could produce the same amount of good by keeping or breaking my promise, I ought to keep it. This could not be the case unless the moral relevance of promises was independent of good outcomes. Similar points can be made in relation to gratitude and reparation, which in turn suggests that these considerations have independent moral weight.

Another common criticism of consequentialism is that it cannot make sense of the idea that sometimes at least the end does not justify the means. Some acts seem quite wrong even though we know that they will have better outcomes. For instance it seems wrong to punish an innocent person even where we know that doing so would produce a better outcome, perhaps because we need to punish someone to deter others from committing some crime. Or suppose the only way to promote harmony within a community would be by ethnic cleansing. Many people would think that this would be wrong even if it produced the best outcome, as here as in many other cases, the end does not justify the means.

One way to try to deal with these difficulties is to modify consequentialism. What I have described so far is *act* consequentialism. For act consequentialism each particular act is made right by its particular good consequences. But some consequentialists maintain that what we ought to do is not determined by the good consequences of each particular act. Rather, what we ought to do is determined by the right set of principles, and the right set of principles is the one which, if generally followed, would produce the best outcome. Some of these rules might be absolute in the sense that they forbid certain types of act under any circumstances. Suppose the set of rules which would have the best consequences if generally accepted would include a rule that says that the innocent must never be punished. It would follow that it is always wrong to punish the innocent, even in those cases where punishing an innocent person would produce the best outcome. Of course an act consequentialist would deny this, and maintain that in those cases you ought to punish the innocent person, and you should do that because it would produce the best outcome. But a rule consequentialist would say that such acts are wrong, and are wrong because they are forbidden by the set of rules which would produce the best outcome if generally accepted.

The other problems with act consequentialism mentioned above could be dealt with in a similar way. The set of principles that would produce the best outcome if generally accepted might include principles requiring us to respect promises on their own account, and not merely because of the good consequences of doing so. If we acted in accordance to this rule, then we would be required to keep our promise in a situation where breaking it would produce as much good. Other principles within the right set might require us to treat considerations of gratitude and reparation as having independent moral weight.

Rule consequentialism has the further advantage over act consequentialism that it is easier to follow. If one is an act consequentialist, then for every act one considers doing one must work out what consequences it will have, and compare these to the consequences of other acts one could do in those circumstances. This would be extremely time consuming and difficult. A likely consequence of this is that we would spend more time deliberating about what will be for the best than we would doing the best acts. Consequently we would do less good than we would if we had some simpler way of deciding what to do. It seems probable then that we would do more good if we didn't aim to do most good in each of our acts. Rule consequentialism provides a way of getting round this problem, for it says that we do not need to decide in each case which act would produce the best outcome. All we need to do is decide, in our more reflective moments, which set of rules would produce the best outcome (if generally accepted). Once we have arrived at this set of rules, particular cases can be decided with reference to those rules.

But although rule consquentialism may get the right answer about what we ought to do, it remains to be seen whether it offers a satisfactory account of why we ought to do these acts. At first sight at least things don't look promising for the consequentialist on this score. For in relation to many duties it seems as though it is facts about the past, rather than about the future (actual or hypothetical) that explain why we ought to do certain acts. It seems as though duties of fidelity are explained by our past acts, namely acts of promising. Duties of gratitude seem to be grounded in past acts of others towards us. We ought to benefit them when we can because they benefited us. And duties of reparation seem to be grounded in past wrongful acts. We ought, for instance to compensate someone we have culpably harmed just because we have harmed them.

Consequentialists might respond that in criticizing them in this way we are simply begging the question at issue. They maintain that we ought to do certain acts because they will have good effects (in the future), or are required by principles the general acceptance of which would have good consequences. One cannot argue against this view just by asserting that what makes these acts right is facts about the past, since that is just what the consequential-ists deny.

But in objecting to consequentialism in the way I suggested above we can do more than simply deny what they assert. Certain facts about the past can capture better the fact that in failing to act in certain ways we *wrong* certain individuals. If I break my promise to you, then I wrong you. If I fail to benefit someone who benefited me in the past, then I wrong my benefactor. The view that it is certain facts about the past that explain why I ought to keep my promises and show gratitude easily accommodates the idea that in failing to do these acts I wrong certain individuals. It is because I promised *you* that I would do a certain act that both explains why I ought to do that act and why it I wrong you if I fail to do it. Similarly, if I ought to benefit you because you benefited me in the past, then this consideration will also explain why it is you I wrong when I fail to benefit you.

But if we ought to keep our promises because doing so will promote the good it is hard to see why it is that the promisee is wronged when we break our promises. If anyone is wronged it looks like it is those who would be denied the good consequences in the future. But although they may be wronged by such failures it is hard to accept that the promisee is not. Similar points can be made in relation to benefactors in relation to duties of gratitude and to those we have harmed in the past in relation to duties of reparation.

Deontology

Deontology is harder to characterize than consequentialism, as there are many differing accounts of what it is. Some philosophers define it as stating that right acts are determined by some set of rules, like the Ten Commandments, some as a view according to which certain types of acts are absolutely forbidden (forbidden in all circumstances), others define it as prioritizing the right over the good, and yet others as maintaining that there is an irreducible plurality of basic moral principles. Since "deontology" is a term of art, it doesn't really matter much which definition we work with, so long as we are clear about which definition we are working with and this definition allows us to hold onto the standard examples of deontology. Unfortunately, any single definition seems to rule out key figures. So what I will do in this chapter is focus on an exemplar from two very different versions of deontology: a monist absolutism and an pluralist non-absolutism.

Monistic absolutism is characterized by two theses. The first is that there is a single, non-consequentialist, fundamental principle of right action, or duty, and that all duties can be derived from this single principle. The second is that this principle implies that certain types of action are wrong in all circumstances. The classic monistic absolutist deontologist is Immanuel Kant. Kant maintained that all duties are ultimately grounded in a single principle, which he called the Categorical Imperative. He offers a number of different formulations of this principle, but the two most important ones are the formula of universal law, and the formula of humanity.

According to the formula of universal law, wrong acts are those that are based on maxims that cannot be universalized. A maxim is a subjective principle of action – that is, a principle on which the subject actually acts – and is contrasted to objective principles, or laws, which are principles on which the subject ought to act. Kant says that our maxims can be non-universalisable in two different ways. Some cannot even be conceived as a universal law, whereas others can be conceived as a universal law but cannot be willed as such without contradiction. Actions that fall under maxims that cannot be conceived as a universal law are absolutely wrong. Those that can be conceived, but not willed as universal law, allow of exceptions.

Kant thinks that lying promises and suicide cannot even be conceived of as universal laws, and are thus always wrong. To see how this is supposed to work, consider the following maxim: "When necessary, I will borrow money and promise to pay it back even when I know I will not be able repay it". This maxim basically involves a policy of using the institution of promise-keeping as a means of achieving one's end, which in this case is self-interest. So we must imagine a world in which everyone has such a policy, and has had it from the beginning of time. We must then imagine ourselves trying to act on that policy in that world. But this is impossible, for the institution of promise-keeping cannot survive such universal abuse. In such a world there would be no such institution. Consequently we would be trying to conceive of a world in which a certain institution is used for our own ends, but in which (because it is universally abused) this institution cannot be used for that end because it no longer exists. Since the maxim of lying promises cannot be conceived as a universal law, such acts are absolutely wrong.

Some maxims, such as a maxim of indifference to others' needs, can be conceived as a universal law, but cannot be willed as such. Suppose my maxim is "to be indifferent to other people's interests in order to further my own interests". We could easily imagine a world in which everyone acts on this maxim. But, Kant would say, we cannot will that they do so without contradiction. This is because we are not self-sufficient, and thus our interests depend upon others' help. If I will that everyone act from this selfish maxim, I will a world in which my interests are harmed. I thus will to further my own self interest and will a world in which my interests are harmed. This is, Kant says, a contradiction, and thus indifference to others' needs is wrong. But it is not absolutely wrong. It is not always wrong not to help others when one can. When you are enjoying reading a book, or a pleasant walk you are not helping others, but you are not thereby acting wrongly.

Many philosophers find it hard to accept Kant's absolute prohibitions. Lying is very often wrong, but it seems to give this consideration too much weight to insist *a priori* that it always outweighs all other moral considerations. Kant himself seems to show the absurdity of such a view when he argues that you should not lie to a murderer even when doing so would prevent him from murdering your friend. This view seems to give honesty far too much weight.

Also some maxims that fail Kant's universalisability test are plainly not wrong, let alone absolutely wrong. For instance, I may have a policy of always letting others through the door before myself. We clearly cannot all act on this maxim, but there is nothing wrong with such actions. Similarly, I might have a policy of giving more than the average to charity.[1] This maxim clearly cannot be acted on by everyone, but is not wrong.

Furthermore, Kant's principle seems ill equipped to explain what is so wrong about certain acts, such as murder or rape. It may be true that the maxims of such acts cannot be conceived or willed as universal laws, but this seems completely to fail to capture what is so terribly wrong about such acts.

Kant's formula of humanity fairs better with some of these problems. According to this formulation of the Categorical Imperative, we should treat humanity in ourselves and in others always as an end in itself, and never *merely* as a means. By "humanity" Kant means our rational nature. So the idea is that as rational beings we deserve to be treated as ends. But what does it mean to treat someone as an end? Put negatively, it means *not* treating them as a mere means – that is, as a mere instrument to be used as we wish in pursuit of our own goals.

This does not imply that we cannot use people for our own ends. We do this all the time when, for instance, we employ someone, or ask for help. The point is that we should not use them as *mere* means, so when we use them we must do so in a way which respects their rational nature. Which actions respect our own and others' rational nature? One very Kantian answer would be: those acts whose maxims can be universalized. But as we have seen, this answer runs into serious problems.

Some Kantians understand treating others as ends as acting in ways to which they could rationally consent. Someone could not consent to being raped or deceived, let alone rationally consent to being treating in these ways. So these acts would be ruled out on this criterion. But in other cases it is unclear. Is it rational for an innocent person to consent to being killed in order save many other innocent people's lives? They certainly have good reason to consent to being killed. This reason is provided by the fact that many other innocent people would be saved. Suppose the numbers saved were such that it would make it rational to consent to being killed. Would that make it permissible to kill the innocent person? If it would, then Kant's principle does not generate an absolute prohibition on killing the innocent.

But perhaps we should not focus on rational consent. Perhaps we treat others as ends when we treat them in ways to which they actually consent, whether or not that consent is rational. This seems to fit better with the idea of respecting *them* as ends in themselves. But in many cases treating people in ways to which they actually consent will not respect their *rational* nature. For instance, someone might consent to be treated in ways to which it is irrational to consent. Someone might, for instance, consent to having their arm amputated for no good reason. Since it is not rational to consent to have one's arm amputated for no reason, I cannot be said to respect their rational nature by cutting their arm off.

Kant's formula of humanity thus seems to generate a dilemma. In so far as we understand treating someone as an end in terms of what it would be rational to consent to, the agent's actual consent may be ignored, and in those cases it is hard to accept we are respecting actual individuals. Actual consent gets round this problem, but it is hard to see how treating people only in ways that they actually agree to is essentially respecting them as rational beings, for they may actually consent to things it is irrational to consent to, or fail to consent to things to which it is rational to consent.

The second version of deontology I will consider is non-absolutist and pluralist. Such deontologists maintain (1) that there is an irreducible plurality of basic moral principles, and (2) that any one of these principles can be overridden by any other. W. D. Ross is generally regarded as offering the best account of pluralist deontology with his theory of prima facie duties. Earlier pluralists regarded basic moral principles as stating what it is that we ought to do. Typically these principles would state that we ought to keep our promises, help others when we can, return a benefit with a benefit, make amends for past wrongs, etc. These principles can conflict in specific situations. In some situations it may be the case that we can only help someone by breaking a promise, and we can only keep the promise by failing to help someone. This means that whatever we do, we will fail to do what we ought to do, for we ought to keep our promise *and* ought to help. In this sort of case pluralists state that what we should do is determined by the most pressing, or weighty, obligation. But given that in conflict cases either act involves failing to do what we ought to do, this view has the paradoxical implication that in such circumstances we are obligated to do acts that are wrong – that somehow morality comes out in favor of doing wrong acts.

Ross tries to avoid this paradoxical implication by distinguishing between prima facie duty and duty proper. Our duty proper is what we morally ought to do all things considered. It is the *conclusion* of moral deliberation about how to act after we have taken into account all morally relevant considerations. If we act contrary to duty proper then we have acted wrongly.

Principles of prima facie duty do not tell us what we ought to do in this sense, but rather pick out features that tend to make acts obligatory. In effect these principles tell us that certain considerations, such as the fact that I have made a promise, or that I owe gratitude to someone, morally favor doing a certain act, e.g., whatever I have promised, or benefiting my benefactor. These different considerations count in favor of certain acts with different weights, and moral deliberation consists in trying to decide what our duty proper is by assessing which of the opposing considerations has the greatest weight, or significance. If the fact that I have promised to meet you morally favors meeting you more than the fact that I could help someone in need counts in favor of helping them, then my duty proper is to keep my appointment. The fact that by doing this I would be failing to help the other person does not mean that I would be failing to do what I ought, for the relevant moral principle does not state that it is my duty proper to help others when I can. It says simply that helping others is a *prima facie* duty, and failing to act in accordance with a prima facie duty is not necessarily failing to do what we ought morally to do.

Ross maintains that the only moral principles that are strictly universal (exceptionless) are principles of prima facie duty. This means that the fact that I have made a promise always counts in favor of doing what I have promised, and the fact that I can benefit someone always counts in favor of helping them. But for Ross there are no (strictly universal) principles of duty proper: there is no act that is always wrong, as absolutists maintain. This makes it very hard for consequentialists to criticize Ross's deontology. For Ross can allow that sometimes we ought to break our promises, or lie, when doing so would prevent a great harm to one or many others. Consequentialists will argue that this shows that fidelity to promises has no independent moral weight. Ross, on the other hand, can argue that these cases show nothing of the sort. He can maintain that promises have independent moral weight, but that in conflict cases this is sometimes outweighed by the good consequences of breaking one's promise. He can, therefore, have some of the advantages of consequentialism, but without being subject to the sort of objections raised earlier.

Initially Ross lists seven basic prima facie duties. These are duties of fidelity, reparation, gratitude, justice, beneficence, non-maleficence, and self-improvement. But, he argues, three of these (beneficence, justice, and self-improvement) can all be subsumed under the prima facie duty to promote the good. Ross thus ends up with a list of five principles of basic prima facie duties, and maintains that all the duties we have can be explained with reference to these five principles. We cannot, however, systematize the morality of right and wrong any more than this, as for instance, Kantians and consequentialists attempt to do. To do this would be to oversimplify morality and lead to distortions.

Ross's deontological ethics doesn't tell us what we ought to do, so does not answer the first question pertaining to the issue of ethical choice. It does, however, answer the second question of ethical choice, as it tells us what sort of consideration makes certain actions obligatory, and so can tell us why we ought, say, to keep our promises (when we ought to keep them). Furthermore, it answers this question in a very intuitive way. But just because it sticks so close to commonsense intuitions many philosophers feel that it doesn't really tell us anything we do not already know. Commonsense already accepts that we ought to do what we have promised just because we have promised, and that we ought to benefit our benefactors just because they have benefited us in the past, and so on. But what is wanted from philosophy is to ground these commonsense moral convictions in more fundamental principles in such a way as to systemize our moral thinking. All that Ross does, it is often objected, is provide us with an unconnected heap of duties. He does not show what unifies these various duties, or provide us with a way of deciding what we should do when they conflict.

We may have hoped for more from philosophy than Ross provides, but the claim that Ross merely lists our commonsense intuitions is unfounded. It is clear that he, and other deontologists, aim to systematize our moral thought as much as is possible. Ross manages to ground the diverse range of duties we have in five basic principles. But a theory that has five basic principles, though less unified than a theory that has one, is not unsystematic. Euclidian geometry has five fundamental principles, but could hardly be said to be unsystematic.

Some philosophers object to Ross's theory on the ground that it entails that no action is absolutely wrong, i.e. wrong under all circumstances. Kant, for instance, thought that lying is absolutely wrong, so if you could save a friend only by lying then you could not save your friend. Kant's view is hard to accept, but there are far more plausible absolute prohibitions. For instance one might think it always wrong to torture or kill the innocent no matter how much good you would produce by doing so.

Ross can go some way towards meeting this objection, for he believes that the wrong of inflicting harm is a greater wrong than benefiting others is right. So if we could confer a benefit on someone only be taking away a similar benefit from someone else, our act would still be wrong. This is so even if the benefit we take from another person is much less than the benefit we confer on someone else. But this response is very limited in response to the absolutist worry. For although it may mean that it is wrong to kill one innocent person in order to save two or three, there would be a number above which the benefits to others would outweigh the cost to the innocent victim, such that killing him would be morally required. To many people this still concedes too much to consequentialism, and some would regard the mere fact that a person would even contemplate weighing up the pros and cons of killing the innocent as a sure sign of a corrupt mind.

Virtue

Virtue ethics grew out of a dissatisfaction with modern moral philosophy's focus on the notion of duty and obligation. Virtue ethicists standardly reject the idea that we can decide what we ought to do by means of a set of principles, and *a fortiori* by means of a single principle. So they are skeptical about the ability of philosophy to deal with the issue of ethical choice. They think a more fruitful question to ask is what sort of life to lead. Aristotle maintained that all action is done for the sake of a good life for the individual, and so for him the most important issue is to articulate what constitutes a good life. Aristotle held that a good life for us would necessarily include virtue, so a focus on the good life would not be egoistic, or selfish. Contemporary virtue ethicists tend to follow Aristotle's lead on this.

The fact that virtue ethicists are skeptical about the possibility of coming up with one or more universal principles that would enable us to decide what to do in every situation does not mean that they have nothing to say about the issue of ethical choice. Typically they claim that the virtues make the good person sensitive and responsive to relevant moral considerations in whatever situations they find themselves. So, they claim, there is an answer to the question of what we ought to do and why. All they deny is that there is a *general* answer – that is, an answer that can accurately be captured by some manageable set of rules. So if you want to know what you ought to do, what you have to do is aim to acquire the virtues, and these will facilitate moral knowledge.

What virtue ethicists say about the moral virtues is plausible enough, but one might take issue with their claim that a good life must include these virtues. One does not have to be a hedonist to think that one can have a good life without having the moral virtues. One might think that a good life is constituted by success in ones rational aims. A rational aim is a goal we have reason to adopt and pursue. The reason we have to pursue some goal may be moral, but it need not be. Our goal might be the pursuit of artistic or scientific excellence. These goals are rational in the above sense, but are not moral goals, and they are significant enough that success in one of these goals would be sufficient for a good life. If this is right then virtue is not a necessary constituent of a good life.

But even if it were, virtue ethics does not seem to be something that deontologists like Ross need deny. Ross might agree that a good life must include the virtues, but maintain that this leaves his own moral theory untouched. He could claim his account explains what the right-making features are to which the virtues are responsive. He would have to deny their skepticism about the ability to codify morally salient features. But this skepticism is far more plausible against monistic theories like Kantianism or consequentialism than it is against a pluralist like Ross. If, as Ross claims, there are no principles of duty proper then judgment is still needed in deciding what we should do, and it is very plausible to suppose that to judge well one must have certain virtues, as virtue ethicists claim. But this is compatible with the view that the morally salient considerations they are sensitive to can be codified in the way Ross claims.

Conclusion

The issue of moral choice consists of two questions: "What ought we morally to do?" and "Why ought we to do these acts?" Not all of the moral theories we have considered answer both of these questions. Rossian deontologists and virtue ethicists do not tell us what we ought to do. For them moral theory cannot tell us what we ought to do in specific situations. To know this we need sensitivity to the morally salient considerations and good judgment in weighing up these considerations. It is not even clear that virtue ethicists can tell us why we ought to do certain acts, for they are skeptical of the ability of moral theory to capture these considerations in a manageable list of principles. Ross, however, is less skeptical about this, and provides us with a list of five basic moral considerations which can, he claims, explain all the obligations we have.

Consequentialism can answer both of the questions that constitute the issue of ethical choice, so in this respect consequentialism fairs better than Ross and virtue ethicists. Consequentialists claim that we ought to do those acts that produce the best outcome, and we ought to do them *because* they produce the best outcome. Kant's view does not tell us what we ought to do, but what we ought not to do. We ought not to act on maxims that cannot be universalized, or treat others merely as means. His theory thus tells us which actions are permissible (these are the ones that are not wrong), but it does not tell us which of the permissible acts we ought to do. Nonetheless, Kant can offer an account of why these acts are wrong. He can maintain that we ought not to do these acts just because their maxim cannot be universalized, or because we would be treating others as mere means by doing them. So he is able to answer a negative version of the two questions of ethical choice.

Ross and virtue ethicists would claim that the theoretical advantage that consequentialism and Kantianism have is illusory, for it is achieved by oversimplifying the moral realm. This objection has, I think, a great deal of force. Contrary to the claims of consequentialists, it is very hard to accept that good consequences are the only consideration that has moral weight on its own account. It is a stubborn fact of moral consciousness that considerations of gratitude, and fidelity also have moral weight on their own account.

Kant's view seems vulnerable to the same objection. Furthermore, despite the elegance of Kant's theory, universalisability by itself does not seem to capture what is so wrong with certain acts, such as murder and rape. His formula of humanity does better in this respect, but this advantage is undermined, to some extent at least, by the vagueness of the idea of treating others as ends in themselves.

Pluralist theories like the Rossian and virtue ethicists' accounts may not give us all we expect for from a moral theory, but they do seem to fair better in doing justice to the complexity of the moral realm. But perhaps the fault lies not with these theories for failing to live up to our expectations, but with our expecting more from a moral theory than it could reasonably be expected to deliver.

Further Reading

Perhaps the best place to start thinking further about these issues is with M. Baron, M., Pettit, P., and Slote, M. (1997), *Three Methods of Ethics: A Debate*. In this very useful book the central concepts and arguments of Kantianism, consequentialism, and virtue ethics are defended by Baron, Pettit, and Slote respectively. In later chapters, each author then responds to the criticisms of the other two. Another good general discussion of most of the positions covered in this chapter can be found in Rachels, J. (2002), *The Elements of Moral Philosophy*. Chapters 6 to 9, and 11 and 12 cover the subjects of this chapter, although Ross's pluralistic deontology is not covered.

Consequentialism

Bentham, J. (1961), *An Introduction to the Principles of Morals and Legislation*. Along with Mill's *Utilitarianism*, this is the classic consequentialist text. Here Bentham argues for the view that the right act is the one that produces the greatest human happiness, and argues that happiness is determined solely by pleasure and the absence of pain.

Hooker, B. (2000), *Ideal Code, Real World*. Hooker is a leading contemporary rule consequentialist. Here he outlines and defends his version of rule consequentialism.

Mill, J. S. (1998), *Utilitarianism*. Along with Bentham's work, Mill's *Utilitarianism* is the classic text of consequentialism. Like Bentham he argued that the only right acts are those that maximize happiness. Unlike Bentham, however, Mill distinguishes between higher and lower pleasures, and argues that the higher pleasures are to be preferred to the lower. Although he is generally regarded as an act consequentialist, one can, arguably, find the seeds of rule consequentialism in Mill.

Moore, G. E. (1993), *Principia Ethica*. Moore agrees with utilitarians that we ought always to produce the best outcome, but unlike utilitarians he argued that there is a plurality of different intrinsically good things, and that pleasure is not a very significant good. Moore thus defends here a pluralist consequentialism, which is often (rather misleadingly) called ideal utilitarianism.

Deontology

Kant, Immanuel (1998), *Groundwork of the Metaphysics of Morals*. This is the classic text of monistic, absolutist, deontology. In the first book he argues that wrong acts are those that fall under maxims that cannot be universalized. In the second book he elaborates this argument, and introduces the formula of humanity.

Paton, H. J. (1947), *The Categorical Imperative: A Study in Kant's Moral Philosophy*. Paton's book on Kant's moral philosophy still offers one of the best accounts of Kant's highly complex views.

Ross, David (2002), *The Right and the Good*. Here Ross outlines a classic statement of pluralist deontology with his doctrine of prima facie duties. The most important chapter for our purposes is chapter 2, where he argues for his five basic duties, and defends the view that morality cannot be further systematized.

Virtue ethics

Aristotle (2000), *Nicomachean Ethics*. This is the classic text for virtue ethicists. Here Aristotle argues that everything we do we do for the sake of our own *eudaimonia* (well-being, or happiness), and that eudaimonia is partly constituted by the virtues.

Crisp, Roger and Slote, Michael (eds.) (1997), *Virtue Ethics*. This is a very useful anthology collecting together seminal virtue ethicist writings.

Foot, Philippa (1978), *Virtues and Vices*. Philippa Foot was one of the first modern virtue ethicists. In this collection of essays she advocates an ethics of virtue, and addresses issues such as euthanasia, and abortion from this perspective.

MacIntyre, Alasdair (1985), *After Virtue*. MacIntyre is a leading modern exponent of virtue ethics. Here he argues that modern morality is fragmented and senseless. He proposes that the only way to recover a coherent idea of morality is to return to a virtue-based account of ethics of the sort we find in Aristotle.

Note

1   I owe this example to Derek Parfit.

References

Aristotle (2000). *Nicomachean Ethics*, Cambridge: Cambridge University Press.
Baron, M., Pettit, P., and Slote, M. (1997). *Three Methods of Ethics: A Debate*, Oxford: Blackwell.
Bentham, J. (1961). *An Introduction to the Principles of Morals and Legislation*, Garden City, NY: Doubleday.
Crisp, Roger and Slote, Michael (eds.) (1997). *Virtue Ethics*, Oxford: Oxford University Press.
Foot, Philippa (1978). *Virtues and Vices*, Oxford: Blackwell.
Hooker, B. (2000). *Ideal Code, Real World*, Oxford: Clarendon Press.
Kant, Immanuel (1998). *Groundwork of the Metaphysics of Morals*, ed. Mary Gregor, Cambridge: Cambridge University Press.
MacIntyre, Alasdair (1985). *After Virtue*, 2nd edn., London: Duckworth.
Mill, J. S. (1998). *Utilitarianism*, ed. and intro. Roger Crisp, New York: Oxford University Press.
Moore, G. E. (1993). *Principia Ethica*, ed. Thomas Baldwin, Cambridge: Cambridge University Press.
Paton, H. J. (1947). *The Categorical Imperative: A Study in Kant's Moral Philosophy*, London: Hutchinson's University Library.
Rachels, J. (2002). *The Elements of Moral Philosophy*, McGraw-Hill Humanities.
Ross, David (2002). *The Right and the Good*, ed. Philip Stratton-Lake, Oxford: Clarendon.

17

Artistic Value

Peter Lamarque

The rapid succession of artistic "movements" that swept through twentieth-century Europe and America – fauvism, cubism, Dadaism, surrealism, abstract expressionism, pop art, conceptual art, post-modernism – left in its wake not only a bewildered viewing public, wearily skeptical of "modern art," but also a community of critics and philosophers of art forced to return to basics in reconsidering what art is and why it matters. Philosophical questions about artistic value became both more pressing and more vexed.

In earlier ages, when change was less persistent, there were debates about taste and novelty in art but what counted as art, and for the most part what counted as good art, was not deemed unduly controversial. When eighteenth-century philosophers examined "judgments of taste" they were less concerned with judgments about art than with judgments about beauty more widely located. The twentieth century seemed especially sensitive to the question of value. Why? Apart from the relentless revolutions within art, as mentioned, there were also other factors: the arrival of new media like film, television, video, and latterly the internet; the massive proliferation of popular art, notably in music, fiction, and film; the internationalisation of art, which served to transcend and to some extent weaken particular artistic or cultural traditions; the democratisation of taste which meant that fashions were driven not by a self-selected elite but by mass markets, even if these were in turn manipulated by commercial interests; and in theoretical discourse the marked tendency towards relativism about value judgments, a refusal to admit either universal or objective standards in artistic value (other than that underpinned by the mass market).

But the philosophical perspective is less on historical or cultural developments, more on the underlying issues at stake. These turn out to be surprisingly complex, not because making judgments about art can be difficult (it can, but it is not the philosopher's role to say what is good or bad in art) but because there are so many different considerations that come into play. Above all, it is far from clear what a philosophical account of artistic value is expected to yield. What questions need to be addressed? What limits are imposed by "art" and "value"? It is helpful to divide the discussion into two broad concerns: first, about artistic value itself, how this value relates to other kinds of values and what, if anything, is distinctive about it; second, what the basis is for value judgments about individual works, what criteria are involved, or justifying reasons, what kind of objectivity, if any, is attainable.

Artistic Value among Other Kinds of Value

Preliminary obstacles

On the face of it, it might seem a hopeless task to try to give a uniform account of artistic value in the face of the extraordinary diversity of art forms, indeed of art works. Is it realistic to expect some common standard of value among, say, musical works, sculptures, paintings, films, plays, short lyric poems, novels, dance, opera, photographs, architecture, or the many multi-media forms of the post-modern age? Even within any one art form, such as painting, the range of styles, genres, and aims is so great – think merely of Giotto, Matisse and Jackson Pollock – that comparative value judgments seem pointless or impossible. Furthermore, looking across the arts, the kinds of reasons offered for valuing particular works can seem incommensurable. Lovers of film noir praise Fritz Lang's *Clash by Night* for its suspense and melodrama, Paulo Uccello's painting *The Battle of San Romano* is admired for its use of perspective in depicting the chaos of war, and Mahler's *Sixth Symphony* is exemplary in its emotional intensity. Music, surely, is valued, at least partially, for the quality of sound, painting for the quality of visual experience, the novel for narrative content, and so forth. Can there be a common measure of value across these modalities? Or should we drop any talk of a generic "artistic value" and limit ourselves to the discrete values of music, painting, literature, sculpture, film, and other forms?

As if the diversity of art forms were not problem enough for a theory of artistic value, there is cultural diversity to be accommodated as well. There might be a story to be told that links Giotto, Matisse, and Jackson Pollock, in our earlier example, within a "western" tradition of painting, a story that finds common underlying aims and aspirations. But traditions from different cultures are not amenable to any unifying narrative supplied by developments in western art. To understand Japanese Noh theatre or Chinese scroll painting or Indonesian gamelan music it is important to locate them in their own cultural narratives and to apply canons of value relevant to those distinct traditions.

These obstacles in the path of an account of artistic value might seem insuperable and promote radical kinds of relativism. Perhaps "artistic value" *per se* is a will-o'-the-wisp and we must be content with examining values in more narrowly defined spheres: culturally defined, or defined by art form, or subdivided further still. The trouble is this proposal threatens to undermine the idea of value altogether in the arts. Suppose we relativize value to particular art forms, let us say literature. Why should we assume there is some single standard applied to all literature? Should we not at least break it down further, even within a single cultural tradition, to poetry, drama, the novel, the short story? But why end there? Poetry itself is already a vast multifarious category: it includes the lyric, the epic, the ballad, the sonnet, free verse, rhyming verse, verse in iambic pentameters, as well as classical, romantic, metaphysical, modernist, surrealist genres. Do not each of these, and a hundred other such categories, admit of their own specific norms and value criteria? The answer is they do and it would be perfectly reasonable to narrow value criteria in this way. But this is not incompatible with taking another approach to value in the arts which involves broadening out rather than narrowing down. Those interested in, for example, the sonnet and its development can quite properly seek to identify sonnet-specific values which mark relative success or failure among sonneteers. Significantly, though, some, perhaps many, of the criteria for judging sonnets are certain to apply more widely to other kinds of poetry and even beyond that to literature and art generally. Even if there are entirely sonnet-specific values, this is compatible with sonnets exemplifying literary values more broadly conceived and even "artistic values." Narrowing the focus does not rule out seeking broad commonalities.

Other factors too encourage the thought that value in the arts need not inevitably atomize into narrowly defined sub-spheres. After all, we do have the single word "art" which purports to embrace all the forms we have mentioned and even to span cultures. And the term "art" is not entirely value-free. There can be bad art, of course, but to be a candidate for art an artifact must evidence some minimal aspiration to reward interest or appreciation, perhaps of a distinctive kind. "Art" hasn't entirely lost its honorific status. A culture's acknowledged art works indicate something important about the culture; and its artistic heritage – the items it preserves and reveres – can reveal what it values most deeply. The pursuit of artistic value in itself is the pursuit of some common value that helps to explain, for any culture, what makes an artistic heritage worth preserving.

Nevertheless, it remains to be seen if anything substantial can be said about artistic value over and above the genre-specific or culture-specific values associated with particular, more narrowly defined, classes of artifacts. One thing that is clear is that the value sought is value *as art*. There are other values that the relevant artifacts can have, most obviously values as commodities in the commercial market place. The market value of paintings or sculptures can be enormous, a recognition perhaps of their value as art but not equivalent to it.

Other kinds of value also seem distinct from *artistic* value. Take historical value. A work might be valuable to social historians as a source of information about a period, customs, dress, or beliefs, without being a work of much stature. A work might even have art historical value without implying high artistic merit. It might be the first, experimental work in a particular style, it might be a work that had a formative influence on an artist who went on to create a new art movement, it might be the last work of a well-known artist. None of these, though, would be reasons for valuing the work *as art*. Other non-artistic values might include personal or sentimental values; a work might be of high value for an individual because of personal associations without implications for artistic value as such. In general there are a range of *instrumental* values not reducible to artistic value. Instrumental values are those pertaining to the effects of art. Music is played in hospitals, lifts, and supermarkets to induce therapeutic, soothing, or mindless states and not any music is effective in this role; but therapeutically valuable music is not for that reason artistically valuable.

However, it seems wrong to rule out any effects that art has – thus all instrumental values – as part of artistic value and this is a topic to which we shall return. If art had no effect whatsoever on art appreciators then it is hard to see how it could have any value at all. Artistic value must be a *response-dependent* value. The question is *what* responses are integral to artistic value, not whether any responses are. It should be added also that the relevant responses are confined to human beings. Artistic value is a uniquely and distinctly human value, just as works of art are necessarily products of human activity. Whatever effects works of art – such as music – might have on non-human animals, these will have no bearing on the works' value as art. In that sense artistic value is not like the life-sustaining value of sunlight or oxygen, which is not species-specific.

Artistic value and aesthetic value

Some of the parameters for identifying artistic value have been laid out and at least some worries, that the task is futile, confronted. But there are further questions about the kind of value we are seeking. For example, there is an important distinction between artistic value and aesthetic value. Many things exhibit aesthetic qualities that are not works of art. Snowy peaks, the rising moon, shimmering water on a lake, all reward aesthetic appreciation and are enjoyed "for their own sake," affording pleasant experiences. In contrast, rubbish tips, dirty streets, and polluted rivers exemplify negative aesthetic value; we call them "ugly," "unsightly," "repellent." Aesthetic value is not always positive. But none of these is art. Even human artifacts designed to be beautiful, like furniture, wallpaper, clothes, or hairstyles, can have aesthetic value without being art, although the line between art and craft is not always clearcut.

There can be aesthetic value, then, that is not artistic value. Can there be artistic value that is not, or does not involve, aesthetic value? That question is more difficult. Much depends, of course, on how widely the notion of "aesthetic value" is drawn. In the twentieth century there was a strong reaction, both among artists and theorists, against giving a central place to *beauty* in art. If beauty is associated with sensuous and pleasurable experience, it is easy enough to find examples of art that is neither beautiful nor aims at beauty: much conceptual art, including Marcel Duchamp's "readymades," has no aspiration towards beauty, and does not even give much weight to "appearance," far less pleasure. But beauty is an elastic notion and even in the eighteenth century it was recognized that works of art with a horrific or "painful" content, such as crucifixions, battle scenes, or tragedies, might exhibit beauty. David Hume's seminal essay "Of Tragedy" is an attempt to explain how tragic drama can be pleasurable, even beautiful. In any case, aesthetic value should not to be limited to beauty. There are many other aesthetic qualities, as ably demonstrated by Frank Sibley, who offered this (non-exhaustive) set of examples: *unified, balanced, integrated, lifeless, serene, somber, dynamic, powerful, vivid, delicate, moving, trite, sentimental, tragic.* The broader question, then, is whether artistic value is essentially bound up with qualities of this kind. It should not simply be assumed that this is so, even if it might be hard to find works in which none of these is in evidence.

In this context an important distinction must be drawn between a work that is *anti-aesthetic*, in the sense that it aspires to being ugly, shocking, or repulsive, having negative aesthetic qualities, and a work that is genuinely *non-aesthetic* in the sense that it exhibits no aesthetic qualities whatsoever, positive or negative. No doubt some artists strive for the latter, hoping to rid their work of any aesthetic interest. But it is legitimate to ask: can they succeed? And if so, can they produce a work of any artistic value? On a broad enough interpretation of the aesthetic it does not seem likely that a work could be absolutely void of aesthetic interest, if it is an artifact of any kind. After all, the aesthetic need not be essentially linked to *appearance* as is shown in the literary case. Literary works, like poems or novels, can exhibit aesthetic qualities, for example of form or structure, without offering any essentially visual or auditory experience (they might simply be *thought*). Whenever we talk about the *way* something is achieved (an effect, a response) we are potentially in the realm of the aesthetic. As for the anti-aesthetic works, it is not entirely paradoxical to speak of the successful, even the aesthetically successful, use of ugly, repellent or shocking elements in bringing about some artistic end. Aesthetic value is here associated with the consonance of means to end.

Artistic value and conceptions of art

The reason why artistic value is sometimes thought to coincide with aesthetic value is that there is a common, if contested, conception of art whereby one of art's essential properties is beauty. Thus a work exhibiting beauty in any of its many forms is readily thought to be valuable as art. Of course, as we have seen, beauty is not a sufficient condition for art because non-art objects can be beautiful. It might be argued, though, that if a work can be independently established as art and shown to be beautiful then the positive evaluation necessarily follows. But even that doesn't seem right. Sometimes too much beauty in a work can be a flaw; "beautifying" or "prettifying" a subject might weaken its impact.

However, it does not seem unreasonable, in general, to seek a connection between artistic value and some essential or defining feature of art, even if that is not directly "aesthetic." The difficulty is only in finding any such feature, one that commands universal assent or is not open to counterexample. Traditionally, three principal candidates for an "essence" of art have been proposed: "mimesis," expression, and form. The classical mimetic theory, deriving from the ancient Greeks and revived in eighteenth-century neo-classicism, maintains that art is "imitation," that works of art hold a "mirror to nature." The romantic expression theory, emerging at the beginning of the nineteenth century, identifies art with the expression (and transmission) of emotion. Thirdly, formalism, associated with the twentieth century, finds the essence of art in formal properties, including "significant form."

Each of the three theories captures features of art – representation, expression, and form – that are widely recognized as important, and a potential basis for a general conception of artistic value. Each theory is also associated most comfortably with particular art forms. Mimetic theory applies best, obviously, to representational works, notably painting, photography, sculpture and drama, as well as certain other narrative art forms (film, epic poetry, some kinds of dance); expression theory fits music and lyric poetry best, but also other forms, such as dance and some painting where expressiveness is paramount; formalism finds encouragement in non-representational art forms, characteristic of the twentieth century, including abstract painting or sculpture and some purely "formal" modes of music or dance.

The view of art as "imitation" is probably the most ancient and revered of all theories of art. It also fits a simple paradigm of art: that art offers a picture of the world, it tells us or shows us how things are and we can learn from it. Some art does indeed aspire to "copy" things in the world: for example, naturalistic portraits, landscape painting, or realistic sculpture. In these cases accuracy of depiction might seem to be the straightforward criterion of value. The trouble is representational "accuracy" is not a simple concept in art nor always a mark of value; a portrait might offer a photographic likeness of its sitter (the sitter is immediately recognizable) but still be "lifeless," drab, without character. A better portrait might be one that slightly exaggerates some features (at the expense of "accuracy") to capture the underlying personality. Sometimes portraits or sculptures seek to "imitate" not how someone actually is but how they would like to be, an idealized version. Ingres's portraits of Napoleon or Van Dyck's of Charles I are of this kind, where not accuracy but aggrandizement is the mark of success. To make matters more complicated, mimetic theories of art are also applicable to fictional works. Novels, as well as some paintings and sculptures, can hold a "mirror" up to reality through portraying entirely made-up characters and events: characters who might be "like" real people but who are not real. Even Aristotle's account of mimesis in Greek tragedy rests on the idea of depicting not actual individuals but "kinds" of people and the actions they would "probably or necessarily" perform in certain kinds of situations. The values of Greek tragedy, for Aristotle, are not reducible to any simple criterion of "accurate" representation, but encompass formal features like plot structure and unity, emotional power, and the probability of the action. There are, then, different ways in which art can "imitate" reality and, seemingly, different values associated with this.

However, the main problem for mimetic theories as a source of artistic value is that they seem not to apply to all kinds of art. If we are looking for value *as art* it cannot be a value that excludes certain forms of art. Surely not all art aspires to be representational? What about the abstract color fields on canvases by Mark Rothko or Barnett Newman or Ad Reinhardt? In fact nearly all the prominent movements in the visual arts in the twentieth century seemed to reject classical imitation theories. And what about other arts: like music, for example, at least pure instrumental music? Does music imitate or represent? In some cases it might imitate the sounds of nature but that hardly accounts for what is most valued in music.

Perhaps, though, we should not be too quick to reject representation as a universal feature of art. There is a weaker notion of representation where it means simply "aboutness." A work might be said to represent, in this weak sense, whatever it is *about*; and, so the argument goes, all art must be about something to count as art. When Rothko described his color field paintings as "expressing basic human emotions – tragedy, ecstasy, doom, and so on," we might infer that that is what they are about. When the British Turner Prize winning conceptual artist Martin Creed exhibited *Work # 227*: "The lights going on and off" at Tate Modern – a work that consisted of the gallery lights being turned on and off at intervals of five seconds – the art gallery explained that "Creed plays with the viewer's sense of space and time . . . [W]e become more aware of our own visual sensitivity, the actuality of the space and our own actions within it. We are invited to re-evaluate our relationship to our immediate surroundings." Any work for which an interpretation could be offered or a meaning given, even in terms of what it expresses or the mood it conveys – thus including much music – might be said, on this account, to be *about* something, thus very broadly representational. Is not a sad piece of music in some sense an *imitation* of sadness? But even if this broadening gives new life to the mimetic theory in the face of abstract art, it does not seem to contribute much to the characterization of artistic value. The fact that a work is *about* something is not in itself a reason for valuing it. What seems to matter is how *well* a subject matter is represented, what novel thoughts an artist offers about that subject. But these seem to point to factors other than mere representation or "imitation."

The expression theory looks to the emotional sources of art. The power of art to express, explore and communicate emotion has long been thought to be one of its most valuable assets. Expressing feelings can seem a more closely human achievement of art, connecting art to the soul, than merely its ability to represent things in the world. The immense expressive power of music or poetry has sometimes been offered as a reason for the high regard of those art forms. And expression often seems to step in where representation fails. Rothko, we saw, spoke of his abstract paintings expressing emotion and the whole school of "abstract expressionism" had similar aims. Of course representational painting can also be expressive – think of Goya's series *The Disasters of War* – as can naturalistic sculpture – think of Michelangelo's *Pieta*. It seems gratuitous to ask, in many cases, whether the representational or the expressive properties are more important.

However, it just isn't convincing that expression is an essential property of all art. Take poetry, for example. It is customary to see a fairly sharp divide between the romantic poetry of William Wordsworth at the start of the nineteenth century, poetry that set out with the aim of expressing the "spontaneous overflow of powerful feelings," and the classical "mimetic" poetry of the eighteenth century illustrated by the likes of Alexander Pope and Samuel Johnson. The idea that Pope's "mock epic" poem *Rape of the Lock* (1714), satirizing eighteenth-century manners and frivolity, is an expression of personal emotion does it no justice. No doubt Pope had emotions towards the subjects he pillories, but wit and biting satire are the marks of the poem's value, not emotional expressiveness. Similarly, many novels, especially those based on action and adventure (Robert Louis Stevenson or John Buchan) are not valued for emotional expression, even though particular characters might express emotion. Finally, conceptual art, from Duchamp to Creed, is characteristically devoid of emotion; ideas, not feelings, are what make it significant. So, in summary, however important emotion has been in art, and continues to be, it is hard to find in it a basis for an artistic value that encompasses all art forms.

Then, lastly, there is form. Twentieth century formalism was a reaction partly to mimetic theories of art, partly to new developments within art such as Impressionism and Post-Impressionism. One of its most influential proponents, Clive Bell, wrote in his book *Art* (1914): "to appreciate a work of art we need bring with us nothing from life, no knowledge of its ideas and affairs, no familiarity with its emotions." Although apparently in one stroke thereby cutting off art from both the world and emotion, in fact Bell revived the idea of emotion, although less in the artist more in the art appreciator, as "aesthetic emotion," a distinctive experience aroused by what he called "significant form." In 1890 the Post-Impressionist painter and art critic, Maurice Denis, had written: "Remember, that a picture, before it is a picture of a battle horse, a nude woman, or some story, is essentially a flat surface covered in colors arranged in a certain order." One appeal of formalism is that it returns in this sense to basics. All art, it seems, exhibits form, conceived as an arrangement of elements, a means by which a work delivers its principal effect, be it mimesis or expression or something else. Form is inescapable in art and is readily associated with the skill or craft elements in the making of art, the manipulation of a medium. It is easy to see how form could come to seem the most important element in art. Bell did not deny that paintings could represent or that poems could express feelings but he reckoned that form (notably "significant form") was more important than anything else – and ultimately the source of art's value. Not all art is representational or expressive but all art exhibits form.

Is formalism, then, the route to artistic value? Possibly it is, although Bell's idea of "significant form" is generally accepted to be far too vague to be of much help. The trouble is, the price of accepting at least strong versions of formalism seems too high. Must we really give more weight to formal properties – properties of organization, structure, or unity – than to any other properties of works? That can seem unacceptable. Much art, across all cultures, is closely bound up with practical application, perhaps religious, political, or ritualistic. Paintings depict saints, statues glorify war heroes, music celebrates victories, films attack prejudice, novels expose social injustice. The thought that what makes these valuable as works of art rests ultimately on how they hold together, how they are structured or how the medium is manipulated, seems far too extreme, to ignore all that gives the works their power.

Perhaps the formalist might respond that whatever the *content* or the overriding *intention*, what makes something *art* must rest on facts about its form. Political art is art first, politics second. Where didacticism takes priority, art is disvalued. That, of course, takes us to the very issue we are exploring. Another objection to formalism is that in some conceptual works of art form has no role. Robert Rauschenberg's conceptual work *Erased de Kooning Drawing*

(1953) consists of a blank-looking page on which a drawing by Willem de Kooning has been erased (by Rauschenberg). It is now considered an iconic work in the conceptual art canon. It is not obvious that it exhibits significant formal properties. Nor for that matter do monochrome paintings by the likes of Ad Reinhardt. Also, if we drop "significant form" in favor of "form" alone then not only is there a danger of vacuity but the existence of many things with aesthetically interesting form, practical artifacts, for example, or even products of nature, will weaken the distinction between art and non-art.

For many people reflecting on artistic value, the properties we have considered – representation, expression and form – will seem indispensable. It is not fortuitous that the accompanying theories have had such a central role in attempts to identify art. What we have found in each case, though, is that these properties are not universally present across the full spectrum of art forms. As definitions of art, mimetic, expression, and formalist theories all strictly fail. Many but not all works represent things in the world, express emotions, or exhibit formal characteristics. Nor is it satisfactory to identify artistic value disjunctively as that which manifests any one or more of these properties to a high degree. Many quite worthless objects – artless drawings, sentimental tunes, or kitch – display our properties to a significant degree without any claim to art status. What they share with Rembrandt's portraits, Beethoven's string quartets, or *Citizen Kane* is not enough to explain the chasm of difference in artistic quality. The truth is that representation, the expression of emotion, and the presence of formal properties, while all importantly connected to the value of art, are not *in themselves* valuable. We need to look deeper at how art can make them valuable.

The failure of the traditional conceptions of art to provide secure defining properties has led philosophers to propound versions of "institutional" theories. Such theories forsake substantive qualities for mere relational ones: a work is art if it stands in the right relations to the "artworld" or to the history of art. It might be that only such accounts will be able to accommodate the diversity of art, not least problematic cases like post-modern art, which deliberately sets out to defy traditional conceptions. But institutional definitions can yield little insight into artistic value. They are silent altogether on issues of value because they offer no account of the kinds of reasons why the artworld selects the works it does; in fact they make a virtue of this on the grounds that the reasons are likely to be historically and culturally variable.

Instrumental and intrinsic values

We noted earlier that artistic value must be *response-dependent*. If humans were indifferent to art or showed no interest in it there would be no artistic value. Perhaps the kind of interest that art elicits is at the heart of what makes it valuable. Once again, though, it might be objected that any such interest will be far too diverse across art forms to underpin a substantial theory of value. Yet one prominent and long-standing thought is that to value a work *as art* is in some way to value it *for its own sake*. An extreme version was late nineteenth-century *aestheticism*, or the "art for art's sake" movement, epitomized by Oscar Wilde's aphorism that "all art is quite useless." In less extreme versions the value of art is associated with the intrinsic value of the experience that art offers. The contrast is with more utilitarian or instrumental values of art – the beneficial effects that art can bring about (like the therapeutic value of music mentioned earlier). One trouble with instrumental values of this kind is that they are variable and context-dependent; but also they seem not to focus on art *as art*. If art is valuable only for certain effects then arguably anything that produces similar effects is equally valuable. If a drug could produce the effect of listening to the "Moonlight Sonata" then the drug has the same value. Yet the drug has no *artistic* value. Also works of art seem to be unique and irreplaceable in what they can offer; experiencing a sonata in a musically informed manner seems to have an intimate connection with the distinctive features of the music which could not be reproduced in a non-musical way.

Identifying artistic value with the intrinsic value of an experience clearly needs much filling out. There is no implication, for example, that there is some one experience associated with all art. Each work offers its own unique experience. The kind of experience that is relevant to the value of art is informed experience, also normative, in the sense that it is derived from demands that the work itself makes. What makes the experience intrinsically valuable might vary considerably from case to case and here the very idea of what counts as an "experience" can become stretched. Experiencing Dostoyevsky's novel *Brothers Karamazov* and experiencing Martin Creed's *Work # 227* are as different as could be. But if these works are valuable as art, so the account goes, then each experience must itself have intrinsic value; it must be an experience that is valued in itself not merely for some further beneficial gains. All that the theory attempts to do is to find the right location for the peculiar kind of value that art exhibits.

It is not always clear where the line between instrumental and intrinsic values should be drawn. After all, experiencing a work is already a kind of effect, so perhaps all artistic values are instrumental to some degree. Especially controversial in this context are "cognitive" values, those associated with knowledge, insight or truth. Cognitivists will insist that the power of art to enrich understanding and deepen our sense of what it is to be human is at the heart of artistic value. Do we not value *Brothers Karamazov* for its profound examination of human psychology? While this might be readily conceded, other art forms seem less amenable to cognitive appraisal of this kind, in particular the non-mimetic arts. But even arts to which the expression theory or formalism seems more apt could be said to "explore" emotion or even to advance our understanding of art itself.

However, the issue about cognitivism concerns not just its general applicability across the arts but the status of knowledge as an artistic value. It is helpful to distinguish the possibility of acquiring new knowledge through exposure to art and the place of knowledge among intrinsic values associated with the experience of art. There is no doubt that art *can* be a source of knowledge, yielding facts about period or place right up to complex psychological or moral truths. To the extent that any learning is valuable then this too is valuable. But learning in itself does not look like a distinctive *artistic* achievement; maybe the same truths could be learnt in other ways; maybe some of what is learnt is incidental to the work itself (resting on personal circumstances). Learning from art seems to be an instrumental value of a kind that is set apart from true artistic value. Yet there is a kind of cognition that falls within the sphere of intrinsic values in the appropriate experience of art. A viewer or reader or listener, who carefully engages with a work, sensitive to its specific demands, reflecting on its meanings and themes, can undergo an experience partially constituted by a new clarity of mind or heightened awareness which looks unmistakably "cognitive" but is also uniquely attached to the work itself. If this is right then a species of cognition could be part of artistic value *per se*.

Somewhat similar considerations apply to emotional responses to art. Aristotle proposed that the value of tragic drama lies partly in its eliciting fear and pity in audiences and affecting a "catharsis" or purging of those emotions. On the face of it the arousing and purging of emotions look like instrumental values (a matter of cause and effect), if values at all, therefore, arguably, not pure artistic values. But it might be that something akin to the "tragic emotions" could find a place among the intrinsic values of an experience of tragedy. There is no necessity, for example, that the experience of art should be intrinsically *pleasurable*, only that it be intrinsically valuable, in the sense of being worthwhile for its own sake. Again, an intense involvement with the content of the drama, its themes, characters, and structure, could incorporate an emotional element; but the emotion would not be separable from, or characterisable independently of, an appreciation of the details of the play itself.

Artistic Value in Individual Works

Trying to establish some general kind of value that all art possesses *as art* is not the same as trying to identify criteria for making evaluative judgments about individual works of art, even if they cannot be completely unconnected. One task of the art critic – reviewing an exhibition, a concert performance, a theatrical production, a new novel or collection of poems, a film, a ballet or avant-garde dance, a piece of modern architecture, a photographic display – is to evaluate the works and in effect to advise potential audiences whether it is worthwhile attending, reading, or listening to them. Of course such critics are not always exclusively interested in *artistic value*. But when they are it is striking, in conformity with the more general outlook on artistic value, how far they will aim to characterize the *experience* the work affords, what a viewer or listener or reader might hope to get out of it. Any such judgment will only be of use to the extent that it is *specific*, that it offers reasons for a positive or negative appraisal that are closely tied to details about the work itself. Much art criticism is descriptive, saying what the work is like, what features of it are salient, what its aims are, and how far it succeeds in realizing them.

Here is a passage from a newspaper review of a horror film, Michael Haneke's *Funny Games* (2008). Following a detailed description of the film's plot, the reviewer writes:

> [Michael] Haneke has made interesting films about the way violence can suddenly burst through the thin crust of middle-class politesse – see *The Piano Teacher*, *Code Unknown* and the much-debated *Hidden* – and the neutral movements of his camera add up to a very distinctive directorial signature. In *Funny Games*, however, he has misjudged that sense of detachment. Ten years ago the [original German-language] film felt like an exercise in self-consciousness, a way of investigating our responses to atrocity. Now it feels more like an exercise in self-righteousness, luring us into its sinister scenario, subjecting the characters to harrowing abuse and then berating us for complicity in watching. Haneke is determined to boobytrap the whole movie, making it unapproachable as an entertainment and insufferable as a moral homily. (Anthony Quinn, *The Independent*, April 4, 2008)

The passage, not untypically, mentions a genre ("violence ... middle-class politesse"), identifies some "distinctive" formal techniques ("neutral movements of his camera") and some hypothesized directorial aims ("exercise in self-consciousness," "berating us for complicity"), and then offers a summary judgment ("unapproachable," "insufferable"). Other critics, it should be noted, have taken a more positive attitude, commending the movie as "thrilling," as "cruel and brilliant," and so forth, but that opens debate rather than poses a contradiction.

The example illustrates some general truths about critical evaluation. Merely offering bald value judgments – "good," "bad," "beautiful," "ugly" – is of little interest. What matters are the *reasons* in support of the judgments. A good critic will always argue a case, attempting to persuade through description, comparison, or interpretation. Substantive evaluations will be open to disagreement or qualification. Artistic value judgments are also intimately connected with interpretative judgments. The value of a work is its value-under-an-interpretation. At the most general level this involves placing the work in its correct "category" (to use Kendall Walton's term). If we fail to recognize that Pablo Picasso's *Les Demoiselles d'Avignon* is an early experiment in Cubism, that it deliberately sets out to challenge conventions of pictorial representation, then our experience of it will be misplaced. No doubt *Funny Games* should not be judged as "family entertainment."

Objective and subjective

The often heard concern about value judgments in the arts is that they are ultimately "subjective," resting on the preferences, opinions, likes and dislikes of critics, rather than on anything approaching true objectivity. But the terms "subjective" and "objective" are much abused in philosophy. On one simple interpretation, "subjective" can mean "pertaining to the subject" (i.e. the person making the judgment) and "objective" "pertaining to the object." Thus when critic C says "Work X is good," this is subjective to the extent that it identifies a fact about C, objective if it identifies a fact about X. But "pertaining to the subject" can mean different things: resting on personal preference alone or resting on some experiential state or "sentiment" (as Hume put it). We have seen that there is a strong case for saying that artistic value must rest ultimately on human experience, so on the latter meaning it must be "subjective" or at least "sentiment-based." But it does not follow that it is subjective in the former sense of being based only on the personal preferences of individual art critics. "Objective" too can mean not only "in the object" but "impartial." On the latter meaning an objective judgment is one that reflects the circumstances of its making as much as inherent qualities of the object judged. There is no reason to suppose that evaluative judgments are simply an expression of the preferences of a critic. It is not contradictory to say, as a critic, "I don't like it much but I recognize it is of high quality"; the impartial judgment is set against the personal one.

Matters of personal taste in the arts can, and should, never be eliminated altogether. The fact that individuals like or dislike certain kinds of art, or certain works, for whatever reason, is a legitimate aspect of evaluation. But if the only reason in support of a value judgment is "Because I like it" then both aspects of objectivity are missing: there is no reference to features of the object itself and no attempt to judge impartially. The critic striving for objectivity will advance reasons beyond personal preference. These reasons can take different forms, depending on the arts concerned. It is common, for example, to cite all of the elements discussed earlier, what a work represents, what emotions it expresses, and what form it exhibits. But, significantly, merely describing these aspects is never in itself enough to secure an objective evaluation: that a work is about the Battle of San Romano or develops the theme of rivalry in love or expresses a longing for peace or is in sonata form is never a reason in itself for a positive evaluation. It is only what a work does with its content or expression or form, in effect what experience it offers in that regard, that can be the basis for a judgment of value. It has long been a premise of value theory in all spheres that no value judgment can be derived logically from a mere statement of fact.

It is more common for the reasons supporting a value judgment to be a mixture of the descriptive and the evaluative. Aesthetic vocabulary is particularly amenable to this mixture, as evidenced in the list of aesthetic qualities given earlier from Sibley. So-called "thick" evaluative terms, like *unified, balanced, integrated, lifeless, serene,* in contrast to "thin" terms like *good* or *beautiful,* point to objective features of an object and also assign value to them. The handling of a theme might be "powerful," the emotional expression "lifeless," the form "balanced"; these can count as reasons for judgments. The peculiarity of aesthetic qualities, again as noticed by Sibley, is that they emerge from non-aesthetic features, such as colors, tones, movements, sounds, or metaphors, only in context. Similar non-aesthetic features in different contexts might ground different aesthetic characterisations. Patches of bright colors on a canvas might in one painting contribute to its vibrancy and dynamism, while in another might make the work seem merely strident or overpowering. Aesthetic value is a matter of an overall *gestalt,* an experience that arises out of a complex juxtaposition of features.

There is no guarantee that critics will agree on what aesthetic qualities are displayed in a particular work, or more generally what counts as a good reason for an artistic evaluation. Sometimes appeal is made to "ideal judges," those with especially strong qualifications, like experience, impartiality, sensitivity, and lack of prejudice. But in the end judgments of artistic value are based on experiences that humans find rewarding. Often there is agreement, but in culturally diverse cases or cases remote in time and place the assurance of commonality can weaken substantially. But that is to be expected. Artistic value might be rooted in matters that humans feel most deeply about but ultimately it also rests on how humans respond to human artifacts, on experiences, feelings, attitudes, and expectations. It is surprising how closely these can converge across cultures and across time but it is equally unsurprising how on occasion they diverge in irreconcilable ways.

Further Reading

Beardsley, Monroe C., *Aesthetics: Problems in the Philosophy of Criticism* (1958). A classic modern defence of the grounding of artistic value in aesthetic experience.

Budd, Malcolm, *Values of Art: Pictures, Poetry and Music* (1995). An important, though demanding, philosophical study of artistic value, emphasizing the intrinsic value of the experience that works of art afford.

Carroll, Noël, *Beyond Aesthetics* (2001). A selection of influential papers by Carroll, defending a pluralistic view of artistic value and attacking narrowly aesthetic views.

Davies, Stephen, ed., *Art and Its Messages* (1997). A useful collection of essays by contemporary philosophers on the different roles for cognition in art.

Dickie, George, *Evaluating Art* (1989). A helpful survey of competing theories, historical and modern, with incisive critical discussion.

Dickie, George, *Art and Value* (2001). A careful analytical account of where the values of art fit into the author's influential institutional definition of art.

Goldman, Alan, *Aesthetic Value* (1995). An analytical study of the grounds of aesthetic judgment applied to works of art, defending the irreducibly subjective element in such judgments.

Hume, David, *Of the Standard of Taste and Other Essays*, ed. J. Lenz (1965). Hume's essay "Of the Standard of Taste" (first published in 1757) is a classic defence of the view that while artistic value is rooted in "sentiment," there are nevertheless "standards" of judgment which are not merely subjective and are founded on the considered views of "true judges."

Nussbaum, Martha C., *Love's Knowledge: Essays on Philosophy and Literature* (1992). A passionate defence of the view that literature can educate the emotions and enhance moral sensibility.

Savile, Anthony, *The Test of Time: an Essay in Philosophical Aesthetics* (1982). An analytical exploration and defence of the "test of time" as a mark of artistic value.

Schaper, Eva, *Pleasure, Preference and Value: Studies in Philosophical Aesthetics* (1983). A collection of papers on aspects of aesthetic value by prominent contemporary philosophers, including Malcolm Budd, John McDowell, Philip Pettit, and Anthony Savile.

Sibley, Frank, *Approach to Aesthetics: Collected Papers* (2001). Sibley's papers in aesthetics, notably on the status and distinctness of aesthetic concepts, have been of considerable influence in analytic aesthetics.

References

Beardsley, Monroe C. (1958). *Aesthetics: Problems in the Philosophy of Criticism*, New York: Harcourt, Brace & World.

Budd, Malcolm (1995). *Values of Art: Pictures, Poetry and Music*, Harmondsworth: Penguin.

Carroll, Noël (2001). *Beyond Aesthetics*, Cambridge: Cambridge University Press.

Davies, Stephen (ed.) (1997). *Art and Its Messages*, University Park, PA: Pennsylvania State University.

Dickie, George (1989). *Evaluating Art*, Philadelphia, PA: Temple University Press.

Dickie, George (2001). *Art and Value*, Oxford: Blackwell.

Goldman, Alan (1995). *Aesthetic Value*, Boulder, CO: Westview Press.

Hume, David (1965) [1757]. *Of the Standard of Taste and Other Essays*, ed. J. Lenz, New York: Bobbs-Merrill.

Nussbaum, Martha C. (1992). *Love's Knowledge: Essays on Philosophy and Literature*, New York: Oxford University Press.

Savile, Anthony (1982). *The Test of Time: an Essay in Philosophical Aesthetics*, Oxford: Clarendon Press.

Schaper, Eva (1983). *Pleasure, Preference and Value: Studies in Philosophical Aesthetics*, Cambridge: Cambridge University Press.

Sibley, Frank (2001). *Approach to Aesthetics: Collected Papers*, ed. J. Benson, B. Redfern, and J. Roxbee Cox, Oxford: Clarendon Press.

18

Existence of God

Paul O'Grady

Introduction

Discussions of the existence of God, a topic historically addressed by most of the great philosophers, are carried on in contemporary philosophy within philosophy of religion. This branch of philosophy has seen a number of significant changes since the 1970s and I wish to examine some of these before broaching the topic proper.

In the mid-twentieth century, much of the work in philosophy of religion was devoted to questions about the intelligibility, or otherwise, of religious language. Given the dominance of logical empiricism, falsificationism, and ordinary language philosophy at that time, it was rare enough to see substantive work on the metaphysics or epistemology of theism, since the very intelligiblity of such endeavors was queried. Philosophers of language who accepted the empiricist account of meaning and yet wanted to keep a role for religion, (such as R. B. Braithwaite) attempted to show that religious language could still find a place, by expressing an attitude to reality, or as a framework for adherence to an ethical position. Religious Wittgensteinians rejected the empiricist account of meaning and defended a view that religious language was self-contained discourse with its own rules. An influential group of Welsh philosophers including Rush Rhees and D. Z. Phillips defended what came to be known as Wittgensteinian Fideism – that it was inapppropriate to use standards of scientific rationality to criticize religious discourse. Opponents accused them of defending an invidious form of relativism about rationality. As philosophy in general moved away from such a preoccupation with language as the obligatory starting place of inquiry, philosophers of religion turned again to tackle more substantive issues in the metaphysics and epistemology of theism.

By mentioning the term "metaphysics" (an inquiry into the ultimate nature of existence and existents), an area scorned by mid-twentieth-century empiricists, one can note a significant change that had an impact on philosophy of religion. A broad tradition deriving from Hume and Kant and finding twentieth-century expression in Carnap, Ayer and Wittgenstein, rejected any attempt to speak of metaphysical structures. Yet much has been recently written on properties, essences, causation, modality, universals, constitution, and so on by leading thinkers, such that there is no longer a blanket skepticism about the possibility of metaphysical knowledge. Recent philosophers of religion have used such developments as part of their discussion of both the existence and the nature of God. The works of great medieval and renaissance thinkers such as Aquinas, Scotus, Ockham, Molina, and Suarez have been re-examined in the light of contemporary metaphysics and their arguments feed into the contemporary debate. Yet some of the metaphysics conducted nowadays is found within an explicitly naturalistic programme. Naturalism, broadly construed, holds that science can ultimately explain everything. As a metaphysical position it involves the rejection of anything outside the realm of nature, hence entailing some kind of materialism or physicalism. As such it is usually explicitly atheistic. As an epistemological or methodological view it involves the rejection of substantive *a priori* knowledge (the view that we get real knowledge of the world in a way which doesn't rely on sense experience). Naturalism holds that all knowledge is connected to some kind of empirical input. This will rule out certain kinds of traditional arguments for the existence of God (for example the wholly *a priori* ontological argument), but is compatible with other approaches (for example the argument from the fine-tuning of the universe for there to be life).

Indeed developments in scientific knowledge have had quite a considerable impact on recent debates in philosophy of religion. If there were conclusive scientific evidence that the universe had a temporal beginning, it would block off an argumentative avenue favored by Bertrand Russell, who argued that the universe might always have existed as a brute fact. Whether the beginning of the universe has anything to say about the existence of God is debated in the cosmological argument for the existence of God. Relevant scientific data from physical cosmology is utilized by both defenders and opponents of this argument. The success of Darwinian accounts of evolution and the use of evolutionary theory to explain language, mind, even society, has influenced discussions of design. Few philosophers of religion reject the fact that evolution has occurred in a broadly Darwinian fashion, but much lively debate exists on the significance of this. Some defend the compatibility of appeals to design with an acceptance of the broad evolutionary account. Others focus on gaps in the evolutionary story, which they claim are not merely contingent gaps, but gaps in principle. A specific area of interest for philosophers of religion is the scientific account of mind. Many traditional religious philosophers were dualists about mind and body, holding that the mind is a non-physical soul-like entity. Few contemporary philosophers of mind are dualists. While not strictly connected to the discussion of the existence of God, there is an important question about whether theists can offer an account of the human person which could support post-mortem existence, an important concomitant of theistic belief. The significance of scientific method can be seen in the work of Richard Swinburne, one of the most important philosophers of religion of the last few decades. He has proposed the existence of God as a general hypothesis to be evaluated using the same canons of rationality as would be used in physical science. He also defends the thought that such a hypothesis can be defended on the basis of cumulative case arguments (that different arguments put together cumulatively can build up a stronger case than each on its own), while developing new and interesting versions of individual, traditional, theistic arguments.

A different strategy can be seen in a significant group of philosophers who belong to the Reformed church traditions and which has resulted in what is known as Reformed Epistemology. These challenge the epistemological framework of traditional debates abut theism. Specifically they reject evidentialism, the view that one must have appropriate evidence in order to be epistemically blameless in holding a belief. In so doing some of these philosophers have made significant contributions to contemporary epistemology (Plantinga, Alston, Wolterstorff).

A final issue worth noting is the phenomenon of religious pluralism. While much traditional philosophy of religion was carried out with Christian theism as the main religious tradition in question, a certain amount of Jewish and Islamic thought was also countenanced, generally involving what was common with Christianity. However, there is greater awareness nowadays of other, different traditions, including Hinduism, Sikhism, Daoism and Buddhism. Some of these are explicitly non-theistic, others could be seen as pantheistic. How are philosophers of religion to think of these? John Hick has defended an approach to religious diversity, which holds to a Kantian agnosticism about the deep nature of reality and treats each tradition as a kind of filter which sheds some light on that mysterious reality, showing personal and impersonal facts of the Godhead. Hick's view is regarded as being antirealist and has generated much debate. Others defend more realist forms of pluralism, while others again defend exclusivism. The point is that a greater awareness of cultural diversity and a sensitivity to claims of cultural chauvinism has colored recent debate about God's existence.

Given the wealth of material prevalent I shall limit this discussion to three main topics. First, I shall examine recent versions of traditional metaphysical arguments for and against the existence of God. Second, I shall discuss questions about the rationality or lack of rationality of belief in God. Third, I shall survey the burgeoning field of philosophical work on the coherence of theism, examining the divine attributes, their interrelations and the different conceptions of God which motivate current debates in the field.

Natural Theology

The role of arguments

It is rare to have general agreement in any branch of philosophy. Positions are defended, arguments analyzed, distinctions made. In philosophy of religion, different conceptions of divinity are presented, defended and attacked. Clusters of arguments have been discussed for millennia, for example the many different versions of the ontological argument. It is not unusual to find theists rejecting arguments for their position which they think unsound, e.g. Aquinas's rejection of the ontological argument, or Kant's dismissal of the cosmological argument. But what exactly are arguments for the existence of God supposed to *do*? It is rare for anyone to hold to belief in God's existence on the basis of an explicitly articluated philosophical argument. Atheists can suggest that this is a sign of credulity on the part of believers; that they are irrational. Theists generally split into two groups in response to this. Those who think that religious belief is something personal and subjective which is not subject to rational analysis (e.g. Kierkegaard, Phillips); and those who think that rational considerations do play a part in holding to religious belief, but there is more besides (e.g. Aquinas, Swinburne). These latter will propose arguments as a way of showing the rationality of theistic belief, but accept that the causes of belief may well be cultural or subjective. And furthermore they will argue that this is the case for atheism too, rejecting the notion that atheists operate solely in the cold light of reason, but maintain that subjective factors play a role in their beliefs too. Some atheists hold that atheism is a default starting position in that it is ontologically less extravagant than theism and so the onus is on theists to provide positive arguments for their position. Theists reply that atheism involves a distinct ontological claim and is therefore not a neutral default position, rejecting analogies between the existence of God and, for example, the existence of Santa Claus or The Tooth Fairy by virtue of the unique explanatory role of God.

So why still examine arguments for the existence of God? Theists use them to defend the rationality of their beliefs and atheists want to reject them. Nowadays arguments are often taken in clusters and rejected in clusters, seen as mutually supportive or mutually undermining, so simple knock-out arguments targetted individually tend to cut little ice on their own either way. Yet perhaps one of the main reasons for continuing interest in theistic arguments is the amount of illumination they offer on important philosophical issues. As an example, Plantinga notes of the ontological argument (rejected by the majority of *theist* philosophers) that "many of the most knotty and difficult problems in philosophy meet in this argument: is existence a property? Are existential statements ever necessarily true? Are existential statements about what they seem to be about? How do we understand negative existentials? Are there, in any respectable sense of 'are', some objects that do not exist? If so do they have any properties? Can they be compared with things that do exist?" (Plantinga 1974: 196).

Cosmological arguments

Cosmological arguments take some facet of the physical universe and argue from it to a creator God who is not physical and serves as an explanation of the universe. Aquinas's versions of these arguments rested on Aristotelian physics, Leibniz and Clarke had Newton in the background and recent discussions draw on developments in modern cosmology. William Lane Craig advances philosophical and scientific arguments for the beginning of the universe. His philosophical arguments use notions from Cantor on infinity and contend that an actual infinite is impossible in reality. Quentin Smith has challenged the philosophical arguments, but accepts the scientific case for the beginning of the universe. However, Smith blocks the inference from there being a beginning of the universe to the existence of God. He notes that in the quantum states present at the Big Bang, normal notions of causation do not hold. Hence, contra Craig, there is no irrationality in positing an uncaused universe. Steven Hawking has also advanced an account of the origin of the universe in which the universe is seen as expanding but finite and in which the notion of a boundary or edge makes no sense. Thus a temporal edge, a beginning, doesn't fit into this model.

Defenders of the cosmological argument argue that the fundamental issues addressed by the argument hold whether there a temporal beginning or not. Even if the universe had always existed, it would still have explanatory gaps, which can be exploited to make an argument for God. For example, Smith's use of quantum states to explain a causeless beginning relies on the existence of quantum fields, mathematical laws, and so forth – which themselves can be proper objects of further inquiry. Whether all versions of the cosmological argument rest on the Principle of Sufficient Reason is also a disputed point. Such a principle holds that every event, entity or true proposition has a reason which explains it. How such a principle might be formulated, defended, rejected and connected to God has received much attention.

Design arguments

While very popular in the aftermath of Newton's physics, design arguments fell foul of Darwinian evolutionary theory. Design arguments take some example of order in the universe and argue that this is evidence for design, arguing against chance as an explanation of such order. Darwin damaged this approach precisely by showing that random mutation, a sufficient population, huge stretches of time, and contributary environmental factors could lead to the very phenomena which were supposedly designed. So random mutation and environmental adaptation explained e.g. the eyes of eagles and beaks of finches, which hitherto were held to require the creator's hand. Modern defenders of design shift the focus to more general features of scientific explanation. Biological evolutionary theory requires the operation of more basic laws in order to work, chemical and physical laws, not to mention the mathematics involved. How are these factors to be explained?

Richard Swinburne has advanced a detailed cumulative case argument for theism which deals with this issue specifically. He sets up the evaluative criteria for very general scientific hypotheses, including simplicity, fit with background knowledge and explanatory power. Using Bayes' theorem, he shows how one can determine the relative probabilities of competing hypotheses. The two competing theories he pits against each other are theism versus a general physicalism. Theism contends that there is an immaterial agent with maximal power and intelligence who causes the world by intention. Physicalism holds that explanation terminates with very general physical laws and a set of elementary particles. Swinburne argues that on the basis of the evaluative criteria set out, theism is more probable than physicalism. The evidence for theism includes a concatenation of traditional natural theological arguments, reworked by Swinburne. Swinburne's opponents challenge his ability to give a numerical value to the relative probabilities involved, thus denying that the Bayesian framework he uses can get off the ground. Furthermore, they challenge the persuasiveness of the simplicity of theism (which Swinburne sees as being greater than the complexity of physicalism) against the implausibility of the kind of agent defended by theism (which they say goes against the background knowledge of the kinds of agent with which we are familiar).

Ontological arguments

Ontological arguments are wholly *a priori* arguments attempting to demonstrate God's existence on the basic of certain logical and linguistic truisms. Anselm produced the first of these arguments in the eleventh century, Descartes a less sophisticated version in the seventeenth, and many think that Kant produced the definitive refutation in the eighteenth century. Anselm's argument is probably best interpreted as a kind of *reductio ad absurdum*. If one takes as premise that God only exists in the mind, one can be led to the contradiction that "that-than-which-no-greater-can-be-thought" has something which can be thought greater than it – namely that very concept with existence added. To generate this contradiction, it is required that existence is a "great-making" property, making one concept greater than another. Kant showed it is no such thing – that there is no difference between the *concept* of 100 thalers in the mind and the *concept* of 100 thalers with existence added. Existence doesn't alter the concept and so Anselm's contradiction isn't generated.

Despite this criticism, various versions of the ontological argument have been formulated in the twentieth century seeking to avoid this criticism. Norman Malcolm, Charles Hartshorne and Alvin Plantinga have developed significantly different versions. Plantinga's usues the machinery of possible-worlds semantics and carefully refines a series of arguments which he believes avoids Kant-type objections.

The problem of evil

This is a key issue in philosophy of religion. There seems to be a *prima facie* contradiction between holding that there is a God who is all-good and all-powerful and also that evil exists. Evil can be glossed in this context as "all of life's minuses – whether small or big" (Adams and Adams 1990: 1). If God is good, then he would be motivated to not have people suffer and if God is all-powerful then he would be capable of ensuring this. Yet since people patently suffer, this seems a powerful point against the existence of God. If stated in a strong way – that the existence of God is logically incompatible with evil, then the argument is hard to sustain. The theist just needs to suggest some logically possible scenario where God would allow evil to exist and the contradiction is resolved. Hence atheists tend to advance the argument in terms of evidence and probability rather than strict logical incompatibility. That is, while it may be logically possible that God and evil co-exist, the prevalence of evil renders it highly improbable that God exists. Theists argue that evil is required as a necessary condition for God granting humans free choice and free choice is required for the existence of moral beings – hence there is a reason why God allows evil. Atheists, such as John Mackie, challenge this position.

Talking in this fashion about the probability of the existence of God carries us to the issue of the rationality of religious belief, which will be discussed in the next section. Theists typically nowadays tend to hold that the rationality of religious belief rests on a wide set of factors which cumulatively build up to show that belief in God is reasonable. Hence they want to view the evidential problem of evil as one element within a larger picture. Theists want to hold that it is of the nature of God not to be fully explicable. God is the terminus of all intelligibility and explanation and goes beyond our cognitive capacities. Hence there is no full answer to the problem of evil, one has to acknowledge that it goes beyond our comprehension. Indeed to affirm the existence of God is to acknowledge limits to our understanding. Against this, atheists argue that it is inconsistent to advance the existence of God, on the one hand, as a purported explanation of the existence of the universe and on the other hand to turn agnostic at hard issues about evil, claiming that it is beyond our comprehension. Theists retort that there is no inconsistency whatsoever in affirming the existence of things, aspects of which may be beyond our comprehension; mathematicians and physicists do it all the time. Some theists want to claim that the problem of evil as advanced by atheists is a different problem to the one dealt with by religious believers. D. Z. Phillips argues that the quasi-scientific weighing up of opposing probabilities is a quite different activity to a prayerful consideration of evil and suffering and shouldn't be confused with it. Theist opponents of this find such a separation of the sacred and the secular unsustainable, on both philosophical and religious grounds.

The Rationality of Religious Belief

Most of the protagonists in the debates over natural theology share a specific assumption. This is, that in order to be reasonable, the issue of the existence of God must be settled on the basis of evidence. They disagree on the kinds, relative weighting, and success of that evidence, but nevertheless share the emphasis on the role of evidence. Some philosophers seek to defend religious experience as a distinctive kind of evidence for belief in God.

However, other philosophers challenge the evidentialist assumption and seek to argue that belief in God may properly have grounds other than epistemic ones, arguing for a pragmatic grounding for religious belief. Others still suggest that belief in God may be held legitimately without evidence, yet not relying on a pragmatic justification either (the Reformed Epistemology position). I shall discuss these three approaches to the rationality of religious belief in the order just mentioned.

Defense of religious experience

Richard Swinburne and William Alston have recently defended claims that religious experience provides good evidence for belief in God. The key idea behind such approaches is to argue for a parallel with discussions of perceptual experience. Unless one accepts a *prima facie* case for the truth of the deliverances of the senses, it is difficult not to fall into skepticism. That is, one assumes that what one percieves is true unless there are various conditions present which would lead one to think that it is not true. These conditions are "defeaters", for example sensory impairment, use of drugs, misleading environmental conditions, the presence of deceiving apparatus and so on. Defenders of religious experience argue that there is parity between religious experience and perceptual experience in this respect. Religious experience is *prima facie* justified in the absence of defeating conditions, of a similar kind – drugs, evident deception, inconsistency of result etc.

Opponents deny the analogy between religious experience and perception, pointing out the many differences between the two. Everyone employs perception whereas religious experience is the preserve of a sub-set of perceivers. Much information comes from perception, little from religious experience. Perception is capable of intersubjective justification, religious expeience is not. Different accounts of religious experience yield different and conflicting sets of beliefs (for example differences in Hindu and Christian religious experience). Defenders respond to such objections, arguing that they do not discredit the parallel. Even if religious experience is had by a smaller group of people and less knowledge is gained thereby, that mere fact of limited scope does not discredit the information gained. The intersubjective verification of perception is gained on the basis of other perceptual experiences – it is what is called "norm-circular" – using a method to justify itself. So, in parity, religious experiences can be used to confirm each other. That different results arise from religious experience may be accommodated by religious pluralism and defenders of religious experience point out that it still serves as an argument against generalized naturalism, a position incompatible with all main religious traditions. Responding to such challenges, defenders of religious experience argue that double standards are being used – if the same kinds of objection were to be levelled at perceptual beliefs, the result would be a general skepticism.

However, further issues arise about the actual nature of such purported religious experience. While it is not perceptual, it is still analogous to perception and worries exist whether it could count as an entirely separate epistemic practice, whether it is a genuinely separate source of knowledge. Appeals are made to religious literature (for example William James's *Varieties of Religious Experience*, or the writings of the mystics, such as St. John of the Cross) to illuminate such experience. Critics wonder how the object of such purported experience can be identified as God – what sort of criteria are to be used? Indeed could the experience be explained on purely naturalistic causal grounds (a range of options from hallucination, to wish-fulfilment, to expectation might produce such experiences, rather than a veridical experience of God). Once again defenders of the epistemic usefulness of such experience argue that it must be seen as part of a cumulative case, as William Alston says "Thus I take the "cumulative case" and "mutual support" perspective on the grounds of Christian belief to be clearly superior to any story according to which the whole thing rests on some particular basis, a basis that will inevitably be subject to serious doubts that it cannot satisfactorily resolve with its own resources alone" (Alston 1991: 307).

Pragmatic accounts of religious belief

There have been accounts of religious belief which seek to argue that they do not rest on reason, but perhaps on some other aspect of human subjectivity. That is, there may be prudential as well as epistemic reasons for belief. Pascal's famous wager argument and Kierkegaard's account of faith fall into this category and have been hotly contested on account of their perceived vulnerability to charges of irrationality. Pragmatic accounts of religious belief are significant in that they challenge the alleged dichotomy between reason and irrationality used against prudential arguments and they are associated primarily with William James and his legacy.

One of the features of contemporary pragmatism is its rejection of certain kinds of dualism, particularly that of mind and body and of fact and value. The challenge to this latter dualism (which holds that facts and values are quite distinct orders of things) argues that the very notion of a fact is tied to human interests, and hence to values. Thus this kind of pragmatism advocates a kind of constructivism about the world – that it makes no sense to speak of the world independent of perspective. While those who developed James's initial insights had little sensitivity to religious issues (e.g. Clarence Iriving Lewis, Carnap, Quine, Davidson, Rorty), James himself thought that pragmatism was a way of bringing together two conflicting temperaments, the tough and tender minded. Tough-minded philosophers tend to empiricism and skepticism, tender to rationalism and religion. James combined both in himself; he was a medical doctor and empirical psychologist but also deeply interested in religious experience.

James disagreed with the views advanced, for example, by W. K. Clifford, namely that "it is wrong, always, everywhere and for everyone to believe anything on insufficient evidence". Yet such a view seems eminently sensible, so why did James reject it? He, in fact, accepts the view for a large range of cases, but argues that it doesn't work in a specific context, namely when one is faced with a choice that is *living, momentuous* and *forced*. A choice between two views is living if both seem genuine options for that person. It is momentous in that something important is to be gained or lost by the choice and it is forced in that there is no neutral stance, suspending judgment is to fall on one side of the options. In such a situation, where there are no rational grounds left to judge between the options, something important is at stake and there is no option but to choose, James claims that Clifford's maxim doesn't work. One's "passional nature" may make the choice: that is, one's inclinations and desires can legitimately motivate one in making the choice, even without rationally compelling evidence. Clifford's maxim is one which "would absolutely prevent me from acknowledging certain kinds of truth if those kinds of truth were really there" and as such is irrational in such contexts.

Against the charge that this is a license to believe anything, James can point to the constraints that it has to be about something living, momentuous and forced. However, opponents challenge the view that the religious versus the irreligious options are so finely balanced. There is no widely agreed-upon general argument that this is so (otherwise philosophy of religion wouldn't exist!) and it seems odd to think that by comparing all the specific arguments one might find them exactly matched. So they challenge the thought that rational considerations don't push one way or the other, which is required for the condition of "openness". A further challenge is that James's characterisation of the religious hypothesis, (namely that (1) the best things are the more eternal things and (2) we are better off even now if we believe the proposition (1) to be true), is anaemic, lacks content and fails to capture essential features of religious traditions.

Reformed epistemology

Alvin Plantinga has outlined, defended and refined a position, in a series of papers and books since the 1970s, which is known as "Reformed Epistemology" (the name deriving from the Reformed church). Recent epistemology has been preoccupied with debates about foundationalism, coherentism, internalism, and externalism. Most traditional philosophy has been internalist and foundationalist. By internalist is meant that anyone who holds a justified belief must be in a position to give a reason for holding it as justified. A foundationalist is one who thinks that justified beliefs divide into two main kinds. Basic beliefs are those which do not rest on any other beliefs for their justification. They are in some sense self-justifying. Typical candidates for such beliefs are self-evident truths of logic or mathematics and beliefs about one's own perceptual states: "2+2-4," "either p or not-p," and "I am having the visual experience of a red patch" are examples of these. The other kind of belief is a derived belief, one which is inferred from these basic beliefs, for example beliefs about physical objects or other persons. Descartes and Locke are generally held to have made foundationalism central to the method of modern philosophy, although it can be found in Aristotle. What is distinctive about recent epistemology is that both foundationalism and internalism have been challenged in a variety of ways.

Plantinga's challenge to foundationalism is that, first, it cannot justify many normal beliefs we think of as paradigmatically reasonable to hold, and, second, it is self-refuting. An example of such a normal belief is one's memory of having had toast for breakfast. I believe I had toast for breakfast, but it is very difficult for me to show how this rests on whatever supposed basic beliefs I might have had and their inferential connections to my current belief (critics of foundationalism always point to its schematic and programmatic nature). In relation to self-refutation he points out that the principle of rational belief expressed in classical foundationalism (i.e. that a rational belief is either a basic belief or appropriately derived from one) is not supportable by classical foundationalism – it isn't a basic belief itself or in any clear way derivable from one. However, rather than moving to coherentism, Plantinga suggests an alternative to classical foundationalism.

With his account he broadens the range of what counts as properly basic. That is, there are beliefs we can hold without having other beliefs to support them, and without being self-evident. The controversial example he uses is the belief that God exists. One is rationally entitled to hold that God exists without providing evidence for that belief and without seeing it as self-evident. Opponents charge that this is a license to hold all sorts of crazy beliefs. However, Plantinga defends himself against what he calls the "great pumpkin objection" (the belief that a great pumpkin will appear every halloween). While belief in God may not have evidence for it (that is, other beliefs standing in evidential relation to it), it does have grounds. Grounds are states which are not doxastic (not belief-like), but which generate associated beliefs. Certain perceptual grounds have associated beliefs (for example, that I am now seeing red is grounds for believing that I am now seeing red). Plantinga holds that belief in God has grounds, that is circumstances or conditions, which confer justification on the belief. Such conditions include "guilt, gratitude, danger, a sense of God's presence, a sense that he speaks, perception of various parts of the universe" (Plantinga 1983: 81) (strictly, these serve to justify beliefs such as "God is present, forgiving, speaking to me etc," which trivially entail the belief that God exists). Plantinga doesn't think there are necessary and sufficient conditions for specifying what counts as a properly basic belief, but holds that we can argue inductively from those which clearly seem basic. Furthermore, there is an onus on holders of properly basic beliefs to defend them against further evidence which might count against them, against potential defeaters, as the terminology has it. So if Freudian or Marxist critics of religious belief hold that they are the result of wish-fulfilment or of economic interest, it behoves the reformed epistemologist to reply to these (typically along the lines that these critiques are question-begging or assuming the truth of atheism in order to demonstrate it).

Critics of Plantinga can note that his position is still too close to classical foundationalism (it just widens the range of basic beliefs) and is therefore still open to challenges to foundationalism. They might, however, accept that theism could be defended on coherentist grounds (see Helm 1997). However, even if one accepts the general foundationalist approach, one might challenge the use of theistic beliefs as candidates for properly basic beliefs. That is, one might accept that perceptual experience of red is a ground for a belief in seeing red because there is a strong connection between the content of the experience and the content of the belief, but deny this in the theistic case. The purported grounds advanced by Plantinga (guilt, gratitude etc) are too far distant from the belief that God exists to be credible grounds. As Nicholas Everitt remarks, "if the experience of reading the Bible grounds any belief as properly basic, it would be the belief 'I am reading the Bible' " (Everitt 2004: 27).

The Coherence of Theism

One of the main challenges proposed against theism is that it is an incoherent position. This claim can include the thought that some individual divine attributes seem problematical in themselves (for example the claim that God is a simple being, without parts), that some of the attributes conflict with each other (God's omnipotence means he can do anything, while his goodness means he won't perpetrate evil) or that his attributes conflict with other phenomena theists want to hold to (that God's omniscience conflicts with human free will). Much work has emerged recently on all these issues by both proponents and opponents of theism.

One important divide in recent discussions of the nature of God is between those who think that God exists outside of time and those who think that God must be within time. Classical theism (a tradition including Augustine, Boethius, Anselm, and Aquinas) defends the view that God is eternal, outside of time. Such a view has implications for many of the other divine attributes. For example, God's knowledge of future contingent events is not regarded as "future," but rather that God knows them as happening in an eternal present.

That God is outside of time is closely connected to the view that God doesn't change (construing time as a measure of change). Apart from querying what sense can be given to a changeless, timeless reality, theistic critics of the classical view suggest that it is religiously inadequate. How might a timeless, changeless being communicate with and relate to temporal beings, as standard theism claims? Therefore, such critics seek to defend a temporal view of God, which entails the view that God does change and argue that this fits better with religious data, such as the view of God presented in scripture.

Defenders of the classical view argue that it is not incompatible with God responding to beings in time. An important objection to the classical view is that it leads to paradoxical views about time. If God is held to communicate with temporal beings from his eternal vantage point, then it must follow that he is simultaneous with such beings as he communicates with them – for example communicating with Moses and with the Apostles. However, simultaneity is transitive – if A is simultaneous with B and A is simultaneous with C, then B must also be simultaneous with C. This means that Moses and the Apostles must be simultaneous with each other (and indeed any other person God putatively communicates with). Responding to this, classical theists have argued that "simultaneity" has different meanings in different contexts. Relativity theory in physics has made acceptable the thought that what counts as simultaneous depends on the vantage point of the observer. Thus there is a difference between "simultaneous-with-eternity" and "simultaneous-in-time". While God may be "simltaneous-with-eternity" with Moses and the Apostles, it doesn't follow that these are "simultaneous-in-time" with each other.

Such a position also allows a response to the charge that God's knowledge is incompatible with human free will. The argument standardly goes that if God necessarily foreknows something, then it has to happen. Theism claims that God does foreknow all facts, therefore all things have to happen and as a result, free will is impossible. The view that God is eternal counters this with the claim that God doesn't foreknow facts. Rather, God's knowledge from an eternal now is simultaneous with events as they happen. Hence there is no incompatibility between God knowing such facts and them freely happening.

Conclusion

Contemporary philosophy of religion is a flourishing field. It uses resources from metaphysics, epistemology, philosophy of language, philosophy of mind and philosophy of science, applying insights from these to questions about the nature of ultimate reality. While certain tendencies in modern thought had forecast the demise of religious belief, its global resurgence in the early twenty-first century makes all the more important the philosophical analysis of religious claims.

Further Reading

Two excellent introductions to philosophy of religion are Davies (2003) and Everitt (2004), the former defending a theistic position, the latter atheistic. Haldane and Smart (1996) present a good debate between these positions in a single volume. Specific topics in contemporary philosophy of religion have been debated in Peterson and VanArragon (2004). Good anthologies of classic texts include Davies (2000), Craig (2002), and Taliaferro and Griffiths (2003). Quinn and Taliaferro (1997) is a good overview of topics in the field, while Swinburne (1979) and Mackie (1982) remain two modern classics.

References

Adams, M. and Adams, R. (eds.) (1990). *The Problem of Evil*, Oxford: Oxford Unversity Press.
Alston, W. (1991). *Perceiving God: The Epistemology of Religious Experience*, Ithaca, NY: Cornell University Press.
Barrett, C. (1991). *Wittgenstein on Ethics and Religious Belief*, Oxford: Blackwell.
Craig, W. L. (1980). *The Cosmological Argument from Plato to Leibniz*, London: Macmillan.
Craig, W. L. (ed.) (2002). *Philosophy of Religion: A Reader and Guide*, Edinburgh: Edinburgh University Press.
Craig, W. L. and Smith, Q. (1983). *Theism, Atheism and Big Bang Cosmology*, Oxford: Oxford University Press.
Cupitt, Don (1984). *The Sea of Faith*, London: BBC.
Davies, B. (1992). *The Thought of Thomas Aquinas*, Oxford: Oxford University Press.
Davies, B. (ed.) (1998). *Philosophy of Religion: A Guide to the Subject*, London: Cassell.
Davies, B. (ed.) (2000). *Philosophy of Religion: A Guide and Anthology*, Oxford: Oxford University Press.
Davies, B. (2003). *Introduction to the Philosophy of Religion*, 3rd edn., Oxford: Oxford University Press.
Davies, P. (1992). *The Mind of God*, London: Penguin.
Davis, S. T. (1997). *God, Reason and the Theistic Proofs*, Edinburgh: Edinburgh University Press.
Evans, C. S. (1998). *Faith Beyond Reason*, Edinburgh: Edinburgh University Press.
Everitt, N. (2004). *The Non-existence of God*, London: Routledge.
Fischer, J. M. (ed.) (1989). *God, Foreknowledge and Freedom*, Stanford, CA: Stanford University Press.
Flew, A. (1966). *God and Philosophy*, London: Hutchinson.
Flew, A. and MacIntyre, A. (eds.) (1963). *New Essays in Philosophical Theology*, London: SCM Press.
Gale, R. M. (1991). *On the Nature and Existence of God*, Cambridge: Cambridge University Press.
Gaskin. J. C. A. (1978). *Hume's Philosophy of Religion*, London: Macmillan.
Gaskin, J. C. A. (1984). *The Quest for Eternity*, Harmondsworth: Penguin.
Geivett, N. and Sweetman, B. (eds.) (1992). *Contemporary Perspective on Religious Epistemology*, Oxford: Oxford University Press.
Haldane, J. and Smart, J. (1996). *Atheism and Theism*, Oxford: Blackwell.
Hasker, W. (1998). *God, Time and Foreknowledge*, Ithaca, NY: Cornell University Press.
Helm, P. (1988). *Eternal God*, Oxford: Oxford University Press.
Helm, P. (1997). *Faith with Reason*, Oxford: Oxford University Press.
Helm, P. (ed.) (1999). *Faith and Reason*, Oxford: Oxford University Press.
Hick, John (1963). *The Philosophy of Religion*, Englewood Cliffs, NJ: Prentice-Hall.
Hick, John (1989). *An Interpretation of Religion*, London: Macmillan.
Hick, John (ed.) (1964). *The Existence of God*, London: Macmillan.
Hoffman, J. and Rosenkrantz, G. (2002). *The Divine Attributes*, Oxford: Blackwell.
Hughes, G. J. (1995). *The Nature of God*, London: Routledge.

Hume, D. (1993). *Dialogues and Natural History of Religion*, Oxford: Oxford University Press.

James, W. (1956). *The Will to Believe*, New York: Dover.

Kenny, A. J. P. (1969). *The Five Ways*, Notre Dame: Notre Dame University Press.

Kenny, A. J. P. (1979). *The God of the Philosophers*, Oxford: Oxford University Press.

Kenny, A. J. P. (1992). *What is Faith?*, Oxford: Oxford University Press.

Kenny, A. J. P. (2005). *The Unknown God*, London: Continuum.

Kretzmann, N. (1997). *The Metaphysics of Theism*, Oxford: Oxford University Press.

Kung, H. (1980). *Does God Exist?*, London: Collins.

Leftow, B. (1991). *Time and Eternity*, Ithaca, NY: Cornell University Press.

Le Poidevin, Robin (1997). *Arguing for Atheism*, London: Routledge.

Mackie, J. (1982). *The Miracle of Theism*, Oxford: Oxford University Press.

Masterson, P., (1971). *Atheism and Alienation*, Harmondsworth: Penguin.

Mitchell, B., (ed.) (1971). *The Philosophy of Religion*, Oxford: Oxford University Press.

Morris, T. V. (1987). *The Concept of God*, Oxford: Oxford University Press.

Nielson.K. (1982). *An Introduction to the Philosophy of Religion*, London: Macmillan.

Peterson, M. and VanArragon, R. (2004). *Contemporary Debates in Philosophy of Religion*, Oxford: Blackwell.

Phillips, D. Z. (1970). *Faith and Philosophical Enquiry*, London: Routledge.

Plantinga, A. (1974). *The Nature of Necessity*, Oxford: Oxford University Press.

Plantinga, A. (1983). *Faith and Rationality*, Notre Dame: University of Notre Dame Press.

Plantinga, A. (2000). *Warranted Christian Belief*, Oxford: Oxford University Press.

Plantinga, A. (ed.) (1968). *The Ontological Argument*, London: Macmillan.

Quinn, P. and Taliaferro, C. (eds.) (1997). *A Companion to Philosophy of Religion*, Oxford: Blackwell.

Rice, H. (2000). *God and Goodness*, Oxford: Oxford University Press.

Robinson, T. (ed.) (1996). *Readings in Philosophy: God*, Indianapolis: Hackett.

Ross, J. (1969). *Philosophical Theology*, Indianapolis, IN: Bobbs-Merrill.

Rowe, W. (2004). *Can God Be Free?*, Oxford: Oxford University Press.

Stone, M. (1998). "The Philosophy of Religion," in A. C. Grayling (ed.), *Philosophy*, vol. 2, Oxford: Oxford University Press, 267–350.

Stump, E. (2003). *Aquinas*, London: Routledge.

Stump, E. and Kretzmann, N. (2000) "Eternity," in Davies.

Swinburne, R. (1977). *The Coherence of Theism*, Oxford: Oxford University Press.

Swinburne, R. (1979). *The Existence of God*, Oxford: Oxford University Press.

Swinburne, R. (1981). *Faith and Reason*, Oxford: Oxford University Press.

Talieferro, C. (1998). *Contemporary Philosophy of Religion*, Oxford: Blackwell.

Talieferro, C. and Griffiths, P. (ed.) (2003). *Philosophy of Religion: An Anthology*, Oxford: Blackwell.

Van Inwagen, Peter (1995). *God, Knowledge and Mystery*, Ithaca, NY: Cornell University Press.

Ward, K. (1996). *God, Chance and Necessity*, Oxford: Oneworld.

Ward, K. (2003). *God: A Guide for the Perplexed*, Oxford: Oneworld.

Wolterstorff, N. (1983). *Faith and Rationality*, Notre Dame: University of Notre Dame Press.

Wolterstorff, N. (1995). *Divine Discourse*, Cambridge: Cambridge University Press.

Yandell, K. (1999). *Philosophy of Religion*, London: Routledge.

Zagzebski, L. (1991). *The Dilemma of Freedom and Foreknowledge*, Oxford: Oxford University Press.

19

The State

Michael Huemer

The Problem of Political Authority

The state is an organization that issues commands ("laws") to the rest of society and enforces those commands with a threat of punishment against those who would disobey. These punishments, in turn, are imposed, directly or indirectly, by the exercise of physical force or threats of physical force. The state finances its activities through compulsory payments from the population ("taxes"). States may do other things as well. These, however, seem to be the state's most salient and essential activities. The famous sociologist Max Weber provided the best-known definition of government: "The state is a human community that (success-fully) claims the *monopoly of the legitimate use of physical force* within a given territory."[1]

This naturally raises two philosophical questions:

1 What gives the state the right to rule – to make and enforce laws, collect taxes, and so on? Any non-governmental person or group that tried to engage in similar activities would be thought to be acting wrongly, so what is special about the state? The presumed right to rule possessed by (some) governments is often called *political legitimacy*.
2 Why ought citizens to obey the state? Again, one would typically not be obligated to obey a non-governmental person or group who issued commands backed up by force, so what makes the state special? The presumed obligation on the part of citizens to obey their government is often called *political obligation*.

Together, these questions constitute the *problem of political authority*. Political authority is the characteristic governments are often thought to have, in virtue of which they have the right to rule and their subjects have the obligation to obey.

Those who believe in political obligation do not generally think that one must obey *all* laws all the time. There may be some restrictions on the content of legitimate laws and on how they are arrived at, imposed by a government's constitution and by general moral con-siderations. For instance, a law requiring one to assist in committing murder would generally be agreed to be wrong – the state would have no right to make such a law – and one would not be obligated to obey. However, provided that a law is made in the right way and that there are no strong reasons against doing what the law requires, it is usually thought that one has an obligation to do what the law requires, because the law requires it.

Both aspects of political authority – political legitimacy and political obligation – are difficult to account for. Most discussion in the field has focused on political obligation, so most of the following will deal with that aspect of the problem. We will discuss three well-known accounts of political obligation, followed by the skeptical theory that denies the existence of political authority.

The Utilitarian Account

The basic idea

The idea behind the utilitarian account of political authority is simple: the state is entitled to rule because its doing so is necessary to provide great benefits, or to avoid great harms, to society. In the absence of government, the argument goes, theft and violence would be rampant and society would degenerate into chaos. It is, therefore, right for the government to continue its activities. For the government to provide these vital services, the citizens must pay taxes and obey the laws. Therefore, we should pay our taxes and obey the laws.[2]

Objections

Not everyone finds the utilitarian argument convincing. Some have suggested that the goods provided by government could be provided by alternative means. We discuss this idea below in the section on practical anarchism.

The more common objection is that the utilitarian argument fails to account for why the individual citizen must obey the law, because the disobedience of an individual citizen is unlikely to have any real impact on the state. We may accept Plato's observation that a government would collapse if its commands were *generally* disregarded. But it would not collapse if *I* disobeyed a law. In any sizeable modern society, many violations of the law occur every day. One additional violation, or even a series of violations by one individual, is not likely to bring down the government, nor to produce any detectable effect on social order generally.

In some cases, there are good reasons for doing what the law requires (or avoiding what the law forbids). For instance, one ought not to steal from one's neighbor, because (perhaps among other reasons) to do so would harm him. Such behavior also happens to be against the law, so one ought to comply with the law in that regard. But the issue is whether one should do what the law requires *because* the law requires it. One test for this is to ask whether one has reason to follow the law in those cases in which one judges that what the law requires is not independently good. The utilitarian account provides no convincing reason for obedience in such cases, given the unlikelihood of one's transgression precipitating a general collapse of social order.

The Rule-utilitarian Theory

In response to this, defenders of a utilitarian approach may argue that, although a single person's transgressions are unlikely to bring down the government, we should choose our actions on the basis of what would happen if everyone behaved as we did.[3] If everyone broke the law whenever they felt like it, social order would collapse. Since this result would be disastrous, we should not break the law.

This kind of reasoning is open to a simple objection. Consider the following principle:

The "What if everyone did that?" principle: If it would be disastrous if everyone did A, then it is wrong to do A.

This seems to underlie the present argument for the obligation to obey the law – since it would be disastrous if everyone broke the law, it is wrong to break the law. Now consider another situation. You are deciding on a career. Let's say you are considering whether to become a computer programmer. You think to yourself: "What if everyone became a computer programmer? What a disaster that would be! There'd be no farmers, so we'd all starve!" It is true that it would be disastrous if everyone became a computer programmer. But that does not show that it is wrong to become a computer programmer. So the "What if everyone did that?" principle appears false.[4]

In response, one may argue that the principle has been misinterpreted. Perhaps the proper principle is that, if it would be disastrous if everyone followed the general *rule* one would be following in doing A, then it is wrong to do A. And perhaps the rule one would be following in becoming a computer programmer is not simply, "Be a computer programmer," but rather some more nuanced rule, such as, "Join a profession you are well suited to, provided that there are enough people in other professions that no very bad consequences will result." If everyone acted on *that* rule, no disastrous consequences would ensue. So it is not wrong to become a computer programmer.

However, if this response succeeds, then a similar response could be made on behalf of one who chooses to selectively violate laws. The law-violator may say: "The rule I am acting on in violating the law is not simply, 'Violate the law,' but rather a more nuanced rule, such as, 'Violate bad laws, provided that there are enough other people obeying the law that no very bad consequences will result.' If everyone acted on *that* rule, no disastrous consequences would ensue. Hence, it is not wrong for me to violate these laws."

It is difficult, then, to find a way of understanding the "What if everyone did that?" principle so that (1) the principle is not absurd, and yet (2) the principle supports a general obligation to obey the law.

The Fair Play Account

The basic idea

Another theory of political authority, more specifically of political obligation, appeals to the notion of fair play.[5] The government provides vital services. These services come at a cost, which most of your compatriots have undertaken. They have accepted both monetary costs and restrictions on their liberty, because their doing so is necessary for government to function to provide benefits that everyone, including you, enjoys. Given this, it would be unfair to your fellow citizens if you did not also do your part. You would be acting as a free rider on the efforts of others.

To illustrate the idea of fair play, consider this scenario. Suppose your neighbors have paid to have a well dug in the center of town, to provide fresh drinking water. If you periodically take water from the well, then it seems that your neighbors could justly demand that you pay a fair share of what it cost to dig the well.[6] Perhaps, similarly, the government can justly demand that individuals who receive governmental benefits – which, arguably, includes all those occupying the territory claimed by the state – undertake a fair share of the burdens necessary for provision of those benefits. These burdens would include obedience to the laws and payment of taxes.

The nature of fairness obligations

To better understand the obligations imposed by this notion of fairness, we may ask two things. First, when does fairness demand that we cooperate with beneficial schemes? Second, what sort of things must we do to discharge this obligation?

Fairness does not require us to cooperate with all beneficial schemes, even when we receive some of the benefit. To be obligated to cooperate, normally we must have agreed to the scheme or voluntarily accepted the benefits of the scheme in a situation in which we did not have to. To illustrate, suppose that your neighbors have gotten together and instituted a public address system for the neighborhood.[7] Each day, one of your neighbors provides a daylong entertainment program over the PA, playing music, telling stories, and so on. You are occasionally entertained by the music or amused by your neighbors' funny stories. After 138 days of this, your turn, as determined by your neighbors, arrives: they now expect you to provide the entertainment for the day. Are you obligated to do so?

Whether you are so obligated depends upon further conditions. For instance, if you promised to participate, then you are obligated to do so. But suppose you did not. The entertainment scheme was implemented entirely by other people, without consulting you. You benefited from the entertainment system, since you were home when some entertaining programs were broadcast; nevertheless, you never solicited the entertainment, nor did you ever voluntarily communicate to any of your neighbors that you were willing to participate in providing it. In this case, it seems that you are not obligated to contribute. While your neighbors may complain of the unfairness of your not contributing, it would seem at least equally unfair that your neighbors should be able to impose obligations on you unilaterally, by deciding on their own to give you benefits. Before adopting a plan requiring sacrifices of you, your neighbors must first verify your willingness to fulfill the part they have in mind for you. Their failure to do so leaves them with no claim upon you. This case suggests that consent or voluntary acceptance of benefits is essential to fair play obligations.[8]

Next, what does the obligation of fairness obligate one to do? In cases in which there is an obligation of fairness to contribute to a cooperative scheme, this will generally be an obligation either to support the scheme, in the sense of doing things that contribute materially to the provision of the benefits, or an obligation to help defray the costs, for example by providing monetary compensation to others who have made sacrifices to provide the benefits.

All these points are illustrated in the case of the town water well. In that case, you voluntarily seek out the benefits provided by the well. This puts the other town members in a position to ask you for some monetary compensation in return, which would help defray the costs that they have already undertaken. It of course does not give rise to a free-floating entitlement on their part to make unrelated demands, such as to demand that you pull weeds from their gardens or that you change your diet to a healthier one.

Objections

Does fairness require that we obey our government? Given what we have said above, this depends on whether we have agreed to obey the government or voluntarily accepted benefits from the government that we did not have to accept.

Your government was probably set up by other people, without consulting you. So initially the government seems analogous to the above example of the entertainment scheme devised without your participation. However, some would argue that you have in fact *agreed* (perhaps implicitly) to the presence of the government. This is the central contention of the social contract theory, to be discussed below. For now, we should take note that, *if* the claim of agreement is correct, then the fair play account is superfluous: if we have agreed to obey the government, then we are obligated to obey the government under that agreement. No separate appeal to *fairness* would be required. We may therefore set aside the agreement claim until we discuss the social contract theory.

Even if you haven't agreed to support the government, you might be obligated to support it if you voluntarily accepted benefits from the state that you needn't have accepted. Have you done so?

There are two sorts of benefits to consider. First, the government provides certain *non-excludable* goods (often called "public goods"): these are goods that must be provided either to all or to none of the members of some pre-existing group. For instance, the military provides the good of defense against foreign invasion. They must provide this good either for everyone or for no one living in a given region; they cannot feasibly protect your next-door neighbor against foreign invasion but not protect you. Similarly, the deterrence against crime provided by the police benefits everyone in a given neighborhood. The police cannot feasibly deter crimes against your neighbor without also deterring crimes against you.[9] In that sense, national defense and deterrence against crime are non-excludable. When we consider whether citizens have voluntarily accepted the benefits of government, we should set aside these non-excludable goods, because these are goods that we do not seek out, and that we have no choice but to receive. (More precisely, one would have to bear large costs to avoid receiving them.)

The more relevant sort of good is the *excludable* goods provided by the state. These are goods that could feasibly be provided to other members of your community without being provided to you. This includes such goods as public roads, schools, and the postal service. You could be excluded from using these services; more to the present point, you could exclude yourself from them. To receive the benefits of roads, postal service, or schools, you must undertake positive actions. So it is these sorts of goods that make a more plausible case for your having incurred an obligation to do your fair share in supporting the state.

There are, however, at least two difficulties for this case. One is that the state, while providing you with certain excludable goods, also to some extent interferes with your obtaining those goods from other sources. Sometimes this is done by prohibiting competition (for instance, private companies may not deliver first class mail to your mailbox), and sometimes it is done merely by placing competitors at a great disadvantage in the marketplace (for instance, by requiring citizens in effect to pay for the government-provided service whether they use it or not). Another difficulty is that the state typically does not represent payment of taxes or obedience to the law as a condition on one's receipt of government services. For instance, the public schools will not expel your children if they discover that you have not paid your taxes; by the same token, you will not get a tax break if your children do not attend the public schools. This makes it less obvious that use of the public schools obligates one to support the state, since the state itself does not even claim any connection between the use of the schools and the alleged obligation.

Nevertheless, suppose that individuals are under an obligation, based on fairness, to support the state. How should we go about discharging this obligation? Advocates of the fair play account hold that we can discharge it only through general obedience to the law. It is, however, unclear why this would be so. Given what we said above, the notion of fair play would seem to give rise only to an obligation to contribute materially to the provision of governmental benefits. In the example of the town water well, you had an obligation to contribute money to help pay for the well; you did not have a free-floating obligation to obey commands issued by your neighbors. Similarly, we can see why one's use of public roads might be thought to obligate one to provide a reasonable payment for the building and maintenance of roads. But it is unclear why it would create an obligation, say, to refrain from consuming illegal drugs. It is easy to see how our payment of taxes makes it possible for the state to build roads. But it is unclear how citizens' compliance with the drug laws helps make it possible for the government to build roads.[10] It is, therefore, hard to see how compliance with that law would constitute support for the government in its provision of that benefit, as required by fair play. Similar points apply to many other benefits and laws. So it is not clear that the fair play account explains the sort of general political obligation that most political theorists have sought to justify.

The Social Contract Account

The basic idea

Since the 1600s, the social contract theory has been the most influential account of political authority.[11] This theory postulates a contract between citizens and their government, which calls for the government to protect the citizens, chiefly against thieves, murderers, and other criminals. In return, the citizens agree to make monetary payments to the government and to obey its laws. Traditionally, the theory is arrived at through roughly the following line of thought.

First, imagine a situation in which human beings are without government or laws. This situation is called *the state of nature*. The state of nature would have various problems. With no authority to provide laws, some individuals would attack, rob, or kill others. If such theft and violence were widespread, a further problem would result: no one would bother working to produce large amounts of goods, or goods of great value, since to do so would only invite others to attack one to steal the goods. As a result, everyone would be reduced to poverty.[12]

There would be problems even for interactions between basically moral people. Disputes would sometimes occur, over such things as who is entitled to a particular piece of land, what a particular clause in a contract should be taken to mean, and so on. Without a neutral third party to arbitrate these disputes and to specify detailed principles for the interpretation of contracts, property rights, and so on, such disputes would be likely to devolve into violence or other socially harmful consequences.[13]

For these reasons, the state of nature would be found unsatisfactory. The individuals living in such a state would be wise to gather together and agree to establish some sort of authority with the power to resolve disputes, to define precise rules for interpreting individuals' rights, and to enforce people's rights by punishing those who rob or harm others – in short, a government. The person or group who took on this role would naturally want certain things in return: they would want some monetary payment, and they would want the agreement of the rest of the community to follow their decisions.

Once this *social contract* had been made, the government would have the right to rule because the citizens had granted it that right, and the citizens would be obligated to obey because they had agreed to do so.

The idea of implicit consent

The story so far is hypothetical. If a scenario such as I have just described unfolded, then it seems that the government of that society *would* have legitimate authority. The question is, why do at least some *actual* governments *actually* have legitimate authority?

The most common response to this is that we have actually agreed to some form of social contract, even though we have not stated our agreement in words. Instead, we have agreed *implicitly*.[14] An implicit agreement is an agreement that one accepts through one's conduct, without explicitly stating one's acceptance. To illustrate, consider two examples.

The board meeting: You are at a board meeting, where the chairman says, "Next week's meeting will be moved to Tuesday at 8:00. Any objections?" He pauses. No one says anything, and the new meeting time is thus accepted.[15]

The restaurant: You enter a restaurant and are seated. When the waitress arrives to take your order, you say, "Please bring me the shrimp scampi." She brings the food and you eat it. Then she brings you the check, to which you react indignantly: "What's this? I never said I was going to *pay* for any of this! I just asked you to bring me some food. If you wanted *payment*, you should have said so at the start. I'm sorry, but I have no obligation to pay you."

In the first example, it seems that you have accepted the chairman's scheduling change, even though you have not said anything. Your failure to object when given the opportunity is reasonably taken as indicating consent. In the second example, despite your protestations to the contrary, you implicitly accepted the obligation to pay by ordering the food. It was not necessary for the waitress to state that payment would be expected, because this is generally understood in our society. Given the way restaurants work, and are generally known to work, anyone who orders food in a restaurant is understood as agreeing to pay for it, unless he says otherwise.

Perhaps, similarly, citizens of a state can be understood as implicitly agreeing to be governed, despite their lack of explicit statement to that effect. What might we have done that would indicate such agreement? One popular suggestion is that we implicitly endorse the social contract merely by living in the geographical territory controlled by the state. If an individual does not wish to accept the contract, he must emigrate once he reaches the age of consent.[16] Another suggestion is that individuals implicitly embrace the social contract when they voluntarily accept goods or services provided by the state.[17]

Conditions for valid agreements

Agreements typically generate obligations to do what one has agreed to do. But in some cases, an alleged agreement may be "invalid" in the sense that it does *not* generate an obligation to follow through. (In these conditions, it may not be considered a real agreement at all.[18]) This is so in the case of agreements made under duress, for example. We note three principles about valid agreements.

First, valid consent, whether implicit or explicit, requires the availability of a reasonable way of opting out. If an individual is offered no way of refusing to enter into a particular contract, or if the only ways offered him of avoiding entering the contract impose unreasonable burdens on him, then his acceptance of the contract is not genuinely voluntary, and the contract is not valid. To illustrate, consider a variation on our earlier board meeting example:

> *The coercive chairman*: You are at a board meeting, where the chairman says, "Next week's meeting will be rescheduled for 8:00 Tuesday. Anyone who objects, kindly signal this by lopping off your right arm."[19] No one lops off his arm, and the chairman thus declares the new meeting time accepted.

In this case, you have not genuinely, voluntarily agreed to the chairman's schedule change, because you were offered no reasonable way of opting out. Cutting off your arm is not a reasonable way of opting out, because it requires you to give up something of great value that belongs to you, as the price of refusing the chairman's proposal. This is unjust since you have a right to your arm, and the chairman has no right to your arm. The demand is also gratuitous, since less costly but effective methods of communicating dissent are available. Under such conditions, the board members' failure to adopt the specified method of communicating dissent cannot be taken to evidence assent.

Second, in normal conditions, explicit statements should be accepted as means of conveying agreement or disagreement with a proposal, and when such an explicit statement is made, it trumps any alleged implicit agreements to the contrary. Thus, consider a modification of the restaurant example:

> *Restaurant with explicit dissent*: You enter a restaurant and are seated. You say to the waitress, distinctly and loudly, "I will not pay for any food that you bring me. Nevertheless, please bring me the shrimp scampi."

In this case, unlike in the previous restaurant case, you have not agreed to pay for the shrimp scampi. Although normally one who asks for food in a restaurant is understood as agreeing to pay for it, this obviously cannot be so if the person at the same time explicitly states his refusal to pay. In this case, if the waitress brings you the food anyway, you are not obligated to pay.

Third, an individual's performing some action, A, can be taken as expressing agreement to some terms only if the individual had reason to believe that if he did *not* do A, then he would not be held to those terms. Thus, return to the board meeting example. Suppose that the chairman, while inviting objections to his rescheduling of next week's board meeting, also announces that any such objections will be ignored. In this situation, if board members express no objections, this cannot be taken as signaling their agreement. Some board members might oppose the rescheduling but see no point in impotently voicing their objections when the schedule change is a *fait accompli*.

Consent through residence

Individuals who are dissatisfied with their government are in most cases free to emigrate from their country of origin, in which case they will no longer be subject to the laws of that country. They also know that as long as they remain in the country, they will be expected to obey the laws. Does one therefore, by remaining in the country, implicitly agree to obey the laws?

Given what we have said above, this depends on whether one has a reasonable way of opting out. Exiting the country is a way of escaping the dominion of one's original government. Individuals who wish to escape government altogether, however, have only the option of moving to Antarctica, the only known land mass not currently claimed by some government. Even if an individual considers the government of another country acceptable, he would still most likely have to undertake large costs in relocating. For most individuals, the greatest cost involved in moving would not be the economic one, but rather, the social cost of abandoning all of one's family and friends. For these reasons, it may be doubted that emigration constitutes a *reasonable* way of opting out of the social contract.[20]

Defenders of the social contract theory may argue that the costs of emigrating do not invalidate it as a way of opting out.[21] Suppose that, at a party at my house, I announce that everyone who remains at the party must agree to remove their shoes. You do not wish to remove your shoes, but you do not wish to leave the party either, since all your friends are there, it is very cold outside, and you are too drunk to drive home. Even so, it seems that I can legitimately demand that you either remove your shoes or leave, irrespective of the cost to you of leaving.

We should note, however, that this is not because, by remaining at the party, you *agree* to remove your shoes. You might be loudly and explicitly proclaiming that you do not agree to remove your shoes. In that case, I could not claim that you have agreed; yet I would still be entitled to demand that you remove your shoes or leave. The reason is that I *own* the house, and thus I have the right to exclude others from using it. Contrast the case in which I am attending a party at *your* house and I make the same demand: that you either remove your shoes or leave. In this case, my demand is illegitimate. By analogy, then, the state would have the right to demand that citizens either obey the laws or leave the country, *if* the state *owns* the territory that the citizens occupy. If the state does not own this territory, then it may not make this demand.

The agents of a government appear to regard the state as owning the territory over which it claims control. Is there a morally legitimate basis for this claim? How might the state have acquired such ownership? The state could have acquired ownership of the land, if the citizens of the country voluntarily granted ownership to the state, perhaps as part of the social contract.[22] This suggestion, however, is of no help here, since we are presently asking how the social contract might be established in the first place. If we must assume that the social contract has *already* been accepted in order to see why the state owns the land, then we cannot use that ownership to explain why the state has the right to demand that citizens accept the social contract. Alternately, perhaps if the state had legitimate authority for some other reason, then the state could pass a law saying that it owns all the territory. But this proposal is similarly unhelpful in the present context, since we are seeking an account of how the state acquires legitimate authority to begin with. In such an inquiry, we may not simply presuppose that the state has authority.

So far, then, we have not uncovered a way in which citizens generally have endorsed the social contract.

Consent through acceptance of benefits

Let us turn to the suggestion that citizens implicitly accept the social contract by accepting benefits provided by the state. We discussed a similar idea above, in our discussion of the fair play account of political obligation. There, we saw that benefits provided by the state can be divided into two categories: excludable goods and non-excludable goods. We automatically receive the *non*-excludable goods, just by being present. Excludable goods are thus the only goods for which it might be plausible to say that our acceptance of them implies agreement to the social contract. The excludable goods include schools, roads, the post office, and governmental currency, among other things.

Some of the same observations made above with respect to fair play apply here. Often, one implicitly accepts a contract by intentionally taking a good provided by another party, as in the case of ordering food in a restaurant. But this will typically not be the case – one will not have made a valid contract – if any of the following conditions holds:

1   The other party has used coercion to make it difficult for you to obtain the good from another provider. In this case, it may be that the other party is obligated to provide you with the good whether or not you agree to their terms.
2   The other party does not represent your acceptance of the contract as a condition on provision of the good. For instance, the provider makes no effort, even verbally, to deny you the good if you do not follow the terms of the contract.
3   You reasonably expect that the terms of the contract will be imposed on you whether or not you accept the good.

All of these conditions typically hold in the case of individuals' acceptance of excludable goods from the state. The state has exercised some degree of coercion to make it more difficult or costly for you to receive the goods from other providers; the state does not represent your obedience to the law as being connected to your entitlement to social services; and you may reasonably expect the state to impose laws on you whether or not you accept social services. Under these conditions, it does not seem that your acceptance of social services commits you to the social contract.

Implicit consent and explicit dissent

Recall the principle mentioned above that explicit statements trump alleged implicit consent. That is, one does not accept X by doing Y, if one at the same time explicitly declares that one does not accept X. If political obligation is founded on implicit consent, then, one can escape the obligation by explicitly stating that one does not consent to the social contract. One should, for example, be able to send a letter to one's political leaders explaining that one does not agree to the social contract, whereupon the terms of that contract would no longer apply to one. The state would then be free to deny one access to governmental services, of course. But in fact, this is not what will happen. If you send such a letter to the public officials, your letter will most likely be ignored. You will not be denied government services, nor will you be excused from tax obligations or any other laws.[23]

A defender of the social contract theory need not defend this aspect of actual government policy. The social contract theorist might agree that, if one explicitly renounces the social contract, one should not be considered bound by it.[24] Of course, this position, if adopted by the state, could create practical difficulties, as individuals with large tax liabilities might begin rejecting the social contract, leading to revenue problems for the state.

But to return to the central question, have all or most citizens actually consented to the social contract? It is well known that legal obligations will be imposed on one regardless of whether one clearly dissents from the social contract. Because of this, it could be argued that any apparent consent to the social contract is not entirely voluntary. Consent is voluntary only if the consenter is permitted to opt out. Normally, an explicit statement of dissent should be included among the ways of opting out of a contract. If this means of opting out is disallowed, as it appears to be in the present case, solely to prevent too many people from exercising the option, then the resulting alleged consent to the contract is not valid.

Anarchism

At least two distinct doctrines have gone under the name "anarchism" in political philosophy. First, what is usually called philosophical anarchism maintains that individuals do not have any general obligation to obey the law – we are not morally obligated to do things merely because they are legally required.[25] Second, a view we might call *practical anarchism* maintains that some sort of non-governmental social system would actually be preferable to any state-centered social system.[26]

Philosophical anarchism

Two points about "philosophical anarchism" must be clarified. First, philosophical anarchism does not entail that one should feel free to violate any and all laws – for instance, that one should feel free to murder, rape, and rob other people. One should not feel free to do those things, because there are *moral* obligations to treat others with respect, consider others' rights and interests, and so on. These moral obligations are independent of the state and its laws.

Second, philosophical anarchism does not entail practical anarchism: there are some theorists who believe that government is generally a good thing, but that even so, an individual is not obligated to obey the law as such.[27] Nor does the claim that we need not obey laws in general imply that we ought to dismantle the state. In situations in which violating the law does not conflict with any of one's natural moral obligations, one may feel free to do so. This does not entail that one ought to overthrow the government, nor that a stateless society would be desirable.

Nevertheless, some worry that the widespread acceptance of philosophical anarchism would threaten social order.[28] Philosophical anarchists deny this, arguing that citizens who accepted their doctrine would still follow general *moral* requirements in their dealings with other people. If the state confined its laws to ones that enforced such moral requirements – as in the case of laws against murder, theft, and the like – the state would have no need to worry about widespread disobedience.[29]

Some consider philosophical anarchism too far from our commonsense beliefs to be defensible.[30] In response, philosophical anarchists argue either that commonsense political beliefs are unreliable for various reasons, or that philosophical anarchism is not really so far from commonsense.[31] Many people routinely violate laws that they disagree with, without appearing to feel that they have done anything wrong. Examples of frequently flouted laws include the speed limits and laws against underage drinking, consumption of drugs, and sodomy.

Practical anarchism

On the practical side, some anarchists have argued that government-like services could be better provided by non-governmental institutions. The most developed proposal along these lines is *market anarchism*, a theory according to which competing businesses would provide such goods as security, dispute resolution, roads, and so on.[32]

The most controversial aspect of this theory is its proposed privatization of police and court functions. Individuals who wished to be protected would purchase services from private security companies. In the event that one was attacked or robbed, one's security company would attempt to apprehend the criminal and extract compensation. Security companies might also offer such further services as video surveillance for one's home or business, and regular patrols by security guards. Multiple companies could operate in a given geographical region; thus, if one was dissatisfied with one's security company, one could sign up with a different company instead.

In the market anarchist theory, resolution of disputes would be accomplished by means of private arbitration companies instead of government courts. These companies would seek to build their reputations by making the decisions that were the most satisfactory, or the least unsatisfactory, for the parties to the dispute, and that, moreover, were regarded as fair by outside observers. More precisely, they would seek to decide by procedures that most observers who might be potential customers would perceive as the way they, the observers, would want a dispute to be resolved if they were in one.

To illustrate, suppose I accuse you of stealing my television. You deny it. I call my security company to retrieve the television; you call your company to protect the television.[33] At this point, our respective security companies hire an arbitration company to resolve the dispute. They proceed in this manner because it is the least costly way of resolving the dispute, far less costly, for example, than resolving the dispute through violence. The arbitration company collects evidence and makes a decision. Suppose they conclude that you stole the television. Our respective companies, having agreed to accept arbitration, now both agree that you have to return the television.

Given the radical nature of this proposed social order, concerns naturally arise about how it would work. Some think the system would devolve into warfare among security companies.[34] Others question the ability of the system to provide suitably uniform legal rules.[35] Others doubt its ability to provide public (non-excludable) goods.[36] Others believe that once established, the system would or should naturally evolve into a state.[37] These issues cannot be addressed here. But it is worth briefly mentioning what advantages the system is thought to have over a traditional governmental system.

There are two key differences between market anarchism and traditional government. First, subscription to a security company would be voluntary. Security companies would avoid the problems raised above for the social contract theory by providing actual, explicit contracts, which their customers would literally sign. Second, security companies would be in competition with one another, with multiple companies in the same region. In contrast, traditional governments hold territorial monopolies. Market anarchists claim that the competitive market in security would produce benefits similar to those produced by the free market in other goods. Competition tends to keep prices down, improve quality, and enable individuals to choose products better tailored to their needs.

Summary

We began with a philosophical problem, and have ended with a practical proposal. The philosophical problem asks how we can account for the state's authority and our own obligation to obey the state. We considered three solutions to this problem. One seeks to derive political authority and obligation from the great benefits provided by the state and the disastrous consequences that would allegedly result from disobedience. This account can be questioned on the grounds that a single individual's disobedience is unlikely to noticeably affect the state's provision of social benefits. Though general, society-wide disobedience would threaten the government's survival, it is unclear how this shows any individual act of disobedience to be wrong.

The second account of political authority holds that it would be unfair for you to disobey the state or refuse to pay taxes, since other members of your society have accepted both monetary costs and restrictions on their liberty to make it possible for the state to provide benefits for everyone, which you have accepted. There were three reasons to doubt this theory. The first was that the state prevents citizens from receiving the mentioned benefits from another source. Second, the state does not itself represent obedience as a condition on receipt of the benefits. Third, even in cases where one is obligated to do one's fair share in supporting a cooperative scheme, fairness does not typically require general obedience to commands issued by persons providing the benefits.

The third theory that we discussed, and historically the most popular, holds that political authority and obligation stem from a contract accepted by the citizens, which calls for the citizens to pay the government and obey its commands, in exchange for the protection provided by the state. The most popular versions of this theory hold that we have accepted this contract implicitly, by remaining in the territory controlled by the state, or by accepting benefits provided by the state. We saw grounds for doubting that continued residence could be taken as a sign of consent, because emigration may impose great burdens on individuals, and the state would have no right to demand emigration unless it could be independently shown to legitimately own the land one occupies. The acceptance of benefits is also difficult to read as implying binding consent to the social contract, since (1) most governmental benefits are received non-voluntarily (the non-excludable benefits), (2) the government prevents one from receiving the benefits from other sources, (3) the government does not represent obedience as a condition on receipt of benefits, and (4) the government demands obedience even if one does not take or receive the benefits. Finally, the fact that the state does not recognize explicit statements of dissent from the social contract calls into question the voluntariness of that contract.

In sum, the major theories of political authority face serious difficulties. This has led several recent political theorists to reject the notion of political authority, arguing that we are not after all under a general obligation to obey the state, nor does the state have a general right to rule. Since most of us assume as a matter of course that government is necessary for any livable society to exist, the difficulty of justifying the government's authority may be disturbing. Additionally, we may worry about the practical consequences, should the secret get out that individuals are not generally obligated to obey the law.

In this context, some economists and philosophers have advanced a practical anarchist proposal. Practical anarchists would see governmental services assumed by competing private businesses. They claim that the general advantages of free-market provision of goods and services would apply as well to traditionally "governmental" goods and services. If correct, this theory would render the initial philosophical problem moot: we need not devise ingenious rationalizations for state authority, nor need we worry about disturbing practical consequences should the truth about the state become widely known.

Further Reading

The classic, historically important works on political authority and obligation – those by Plato, Hobbes, Locke, Rousseau, Hume, Kant, and Mill – are all available online (see www.epistemelinks.com/Main/MainText.aspx).[38] Plato's very readable dialogue, the *Crito*, provides a good starting point, as it contains the germs of several different accounts of political obligation, including the utilitarian account, the social contract theory, and the gratitude account (not discussed in the present chapter). The most important works on the social contract are Hobbes's *Leviathan* (especially chs. 13–15 and 17) and Locke's *Second Treatise of Government* (especially chs. 1–5 and 7–9). Hume's "Of the Original Contract" provides a classic criticism of the social contract theory, together with a defense of the utilitarian approach. Mill's famous *On Liberty* provides a classic account of the proper limits of government.

For readers interested in the contemporary debate, a good starting point is the debate between Wellman and Simmons in *Is There a Duty to Obey the Law?* Wellman there provides a defense of political obligation based on "Samaritan duties" (not discussed in this chapter for reasons of space). Other accounts omitted here for reasons of space include Rawls' (1999: 99–100) account based on the duty to promote just institutions, Walker's (1988) account based on gratitude, Christiano's (2004b) account based on the authority of democratic processes, and Horton's (2007) account based on associative obligations. For further discussion of the accounts of political obligation discussed in this chapter, see Hare (1976) on the utilitarian account and Klosko (1992) on the fair play account. Wolff (1998) and Simmons (1979) present influential defenses of philosophical anarchism, the latter trenchantly criticizing several contemporary accounts of political obligation. On practical anarchism, Miller (1984) provides a useful, critical overview, while Stringham (2007) collects essential writings from numerous authors. Caplan's very accessible FAQ answers many important questions and provides a fair, sympathetic introduction to anarchist thought.

Notes

1   Weber (1946: 78), emphasis in original.
2   See Plato (1992: 50b), Hume (1987: 480–2); Hare (1976).
3   This is the rough idea behind "rule utilitarianism" – that one should act on the basis of the general rules that would have the best consequences (Brandt 1992: ch. 7). *Rule* utilitarianism contrasts with *act* utilitarianism, which holds that one should always choose the individual act that, given the particular circumstances one is in, would produce the best consequences.
4   See Sartorius (1975: 15–18, 102) for further objections.
5   See Hart (1955: 185–6), Rawls (1964), Klosko (1992; 2005).
6   The example is from Simmons (1979: 126–7).
7   This example is from Nozick (1974: 93–5). See Klosko (1992: 39, 44–5) for criticisms of Nozick's analogy.
8   See Arneson (1982) for criticism of this argument.
9   This, at any rate, is what is usually argued, particularly in discussions of why these goods must be provided by government.
10 Klosko (1992: 101–7), however, claims that obedience to the law in general supports the maintenance of law and order in general.
11 The most famous social contract theories are those of Rousseau (1950), Hobbes (1996), Locke (1980), and Kant (1991). Plato (1992) advances an early version of the theory.
12 Hobbes (1996: 86–90).
13 Locke (1980: ch. IX).
14 Locke (1980: sections 119–20). However, some theorists treat the social contract as purely hypothetical (Kant 1991; Rawls 1999). Dworkin (1975: 17–22) criticizes their view.
15 The example is from Simmons (1979: 79–80).
16 Plato (1992: 51d–e), Locke (1980: sections 119–21).
17 Steinberger (2004: 219–20). In addition, some have argued that we consent by participating in the institutions of the state (Steinberger 2004: 218–19; Plamenatz 1968: 168–72).
18 Hereafter, I shall neglect the distinction between an invalid (non-binding) agreement and something that is not a real agreement at all. This distinction does not matter for our purposes.
19 This example is from Simmons (1979: 81).
20 See Hume (1987: 475); Simmons (1979: 99–100).
21 See Beran (1987: 105–6); Christiano (2004a: section 4.9).
22 Locke (1980: ch. VIII) takes this view, postulating an original, explicit social contract as an actual historical event. Hume (1987: 470–4) rightly disputes the historical claim.
23 The United States government has procedures for renouncing US citizenship. However, this step is not permitted for those living in the territory claimed by the US government, and even those

living in foreign countries who successfully renounce their citizenship may still be subject to American taxes (see http://travel.state.gov/law/citizenship/citizenship_776.html).

24 Compare Beran (1987: 49–50, 99–100).

25 Wolff (1998), Simmons (1979), Raz (1979), Green (1988), Smith (1973).

26 Practical anarchism is more commonly called "political anarchism," but the latter label is misleading, as it falsely suggests that a contrast between philosophical and political theories is intended.

27 Simmons (1979: 198–200). Wellman (2005: 26–9) questions whether this stance can be plausibly maintained.

28 Horton (2007: 15–16).

29 Simmons (1996: 31–2). But see Senor's (1987) argument that philosophical anarchism would undermine acceptance of the duty to pay taxes.

30 Klosko (1992: 16–26). David Hume (1987: 486–7), writing in the 1700s, used this sort of argument against the social contract theory.

31 Green (1996), Simmons (1996: 33).

32 Also known as "anarcho-capitalism," this theory's most prominent defenders are Friedman (1989) and Rothbard (1973); Stringham (2007) collects numerous writings on the subject. For reasons of space, I omit from this discussion the historically prominent tradition of socialist anarchism, represented by Bakunin (1953), Kropotkin (1975), and Proudhon (1994).

33 This example is from Friedman (1989: 115–16).

34 Rand 1964, pp. 112–13. Friedman (1989: 116) responds.

35 Wellman, in Wellman and Simmons (2005: 14–16). See Friedman (1996: 236–7) for discussion.

36 Miller (1984: 41–2); see Miller (1984: 12) for further objections. Friedman (1989: 135–43, 156–9) addresses the public goods problem.

37 Nozick (1974: 15–17, 101–19). See also the exchange between Cowen and his critics in Stringham (2007).

38 The relevant essay by Kant is listed as the "Introduction to the Metaphysic of Morals." The relevant Hume essay is included in "Essays: Moral, Political, and Literary" and in "Selected Essays."

References

Arneson, Richard (1982). "The Principle of Fair Play and Free-Rider Problems," *Ethics*, 92, 616–33.

Bakunin, Mikhail (1953). *The Political Philosophy of Bakunin*, New York: Free Press.

Beran, Harry (1987). *The Consent Theory of Political Obligation*, London: Croom Helm.

Brandt, Richard (1992). *Morality, Utilitarianism, and Rights*, Cambridge: Cambridge University Press.

Caplan, Bryan (n.d.). "Anarchist Theory FAQ," www.gmu.edu/departments/economics/bcaplan/anarfaq.htm, accessed February 13, 2008.

Christiano, Thomas (2004a). "Authority," in Edward N Zalta (ed.), *Stanford Encyclopedia of Philosophy*, http://plato.stanford.edu/archives/fall2004/entries/authority.

Christiano, Thomas (2004b). "The Authority of Democracy," *Journal of Political Philosophy*, 12, 245–70.

Dworkin, Ronald (1989). "The Original Position," in Norman Daniels (ed.), *Reading Rawls*, Stanford, CA: Stanford University Press, 16–53.

Friedman, David (1989). *The Machinery of Freedom*, LaSalle, IL: Open Court.

Friedman, David (1996). "Anarchy and Efficient Law," in Sanders and Narveson, 235–53.

Gilbert, Margaret (2006). *A Theory of Political Obligation*, Oxford: Clarendon.

Green, Leslie (1988). *The Authority of the State*, Oxford: Clarendon.

Green, Leslie (1996). "Who Believes in Political Obligation?" in Sanders and Narveson, 1–17.

Hampton, Jean (1997). *Political Philosophy*, Boulder, CO: Westview.

Hare, R. M. (1976). "Political Obligation," in Ted Honderich (ed.), *Social Ends and Political Means*, London: Routledge & Kegan Paul, 1–12.

Hart, H. L. A. (1955). "Are There Any Natural Rights?" *Philosophical Review*, 64, 175–91.

Hobbes, Thomas (1996) [1651]. *Leviathan*, revd. student edn., ed. Richard Tuck, Cambridge: Cambridge University Press.

Horton, John (2007). "In Defense of Associative Political Obligations," part 2, *Political Studies*, 55, 1–19.

Hume, David (1987) [1777]. "Of the Original Contract," in *Essays, Moral, Political, and Literary*, Indianapolis, IN: Liberty Fund, 465–87.

Kant, Immanuel (1991). *The Metaphysics of Morals* in *Kant's Political Writings*, ed. Hans Reiss, tr. H.B. Nisbet, Cambridge: Cambridge University Press, 131–75.

Klosko, George (1992). *The Principle of Fairness and Political Obligation*, Lanham, MD: Rowman & Littlefield.

Klosko, George (2005). *Political Obligations*, Oxford: Oxford University Press.

Kropotkin, Peter (1975). *The Essential Kropotkin*, ed. Emile Capouya and Keitha Tompkins, New York: Liveright.

Locke, John (1980) [1690]. *Second Treatise of Government*, ed. C. B. Macpherson, Indianapolis, IN: Hackett).

Mill, John Stuart (1978) [1859]. *On Liberty*, Indianapolis, IN: Hackett.

Miller, David (1984). *Anarchism*, London: J. M. Dent & Sons.

Morris, Christopher (1998). *An Essay on the Modern State*, Cambridge: Cambridge University Press.

Nozick, Robert (1974). *Anarchy, State, and Utopia*, New York: Basic Books.

Plamenatz, John (1968). *Consent, Freedom, and Political Obligation*, 2nd edn. Oxford: Oxford University Press.

Plato (1992) [ca. 360 BC]. *Crito* in *The Trial and Death of Socrates: Four Dialogues*, tr. Benjamin Jowett, New York: Dover.

Proudhon, Pierre-Joseph (1994). *What Is Property?*, ed. and tr. Donald R. Kelley and Bonnie G. Smith, Cambridge: Cambridge University Press.

Rand, Ayn (1964). "The Nature of Government," in *The Virtue of Selfishness*, New York: Signet, 107–15.

Rawls, John (1964). "Legal Obligation and the Duty of Fair Play," in Sydney Hook (ed.), *Law and Philosophy*, New York University Press, 3–18.

Rawls, John (1999). *A Theory of Justice*, revd. edn., Cambridge, MA: Harvard University Press.

Raz, Joseph (1979). *The Authority of Law*, Oxford: Clarendon.

Rothbard, Murray (1973). *For a New Liberty*, New York: Macmillan.

Rousseau, Jean-Jacques (1950) [1762]. *The Social Contract*, in *The Social Contract and Discourses*, tr. G. D. H. Cole, New York: E. P. Dutton & Co.).

Sanders, John T. and Narveson, Jan (eds.) (1996). *For and Against the State*, Lanham, MD: Rowman & Littlefield.

Sartorius, Rolf (1975). *Individual Conduct and Social Norms*, Belmont, CA: Dickenson.

Senor, Thomas (1987). "What If There Are No Political Obligations?" *Philosophy and Public Affairs*, 16, 260–8.

Simmons, A. John (1979). *Moral Principles and Political Obligations*, Princeton, NJ: Princeton University Press.

Simmons, A. John (1996). "Philosophical Anarchism," in Sanders and Narveson, 19–39.

Smith, M. B. E. (1973). "Is There a Prima Facie Obligation to Obey the Law?" *Yale Law Journal*, 82, 950–76.

Steinberger, Peter (2004). *The Idea of the State*, Cambridge: Cambridge University Press.

Stringham, Edward P. (ed.) (2007). *Anarchy and the Law: The Political Economy of Choice*, New Brunswick: Transaction Publishers.

Walker, A. D. M. (1988). "Political Obligation and the Argument from Gratitude," *Philosophy and Public Affairs*, 17, 191–211.

Weber, Max (1946). "Politics as a Vocation," in *From Max Weber: Essays in Sociology*, ed. H. H. Gerth and C. Wright Mills, New York: Oxford University Press, 77–128.

Wellman, Christopher Heath (2001). "Toward a Liberal Theory of Political Obligation," *Ethics*, 111, 735–59.

Wellman, Christopher Heath and A. John Simmons (2005). *Is There a Duty to Obey the Law?*, Cambridge: Cambridge University Press.

Wolff, Robert Paul (1998). *In Defense of Anarchism*, Berkeley, CA: University of California Press.

20

Liberty

Matt Zwolinski

Introduction

One of the striking facts about political debate is the extent to which people with sharply different political views agree about the value of liberty. Libertarians and democratic socialists, representatives of the political right and left, and individuals from a strikingly diverse set of cultural and political backgrounds are united in believing that the protection and promotion of liberty is one of the chief tasks of governments, and one of the most important ways in which they can contribute to the well-being of their citizens.

This agreement on the value of liberty, however, belies a wide array of disagreements regarding the meaning of liberty, its relative importance compared to that of other political values such as equality or prosperity, which actions or policies which can be said to interfere with liberty, and which are appropriate ways to promote it. This should not surprise us. Our disagreements over substantive questions of public policy, after all, are *real*. And those disagreements – such as whether to impose progressive income taxes on the rich for the purpose of providing social welfare programs for the poor – often reflect deep divisions in the way we conceptualize and value liberty. Does coercive taxation interfere with the liberty of those on whom it is imposed? Is poverty a condition which limits the liberty of those who live in it? If the answers to both these questions is "yes," can we meaningfully compare the *amount* of liberty lost by taxation to the amount gained through social welfare programs so as to say that the policy represents a *net* gain or loss in liberty? But even if poverty doesn't limit the liberty of those who live in it, it is certainly bad for them in *some* way. Can the loss of liberty (if such it is) brought about by increased taxation be justified by the way in which it addresses this other, distinct kind of moral value? Is the value of liberty absolute, or is it something we can trade off against other goods in order to achieve the most desirable overall balance of valuable things?

Negative and Positive Liberty

Imagine a man – call him Jim – too sick to get out of bed and leave the house. What should we say about Jim's freedom? Does he have the liberty to leave, or not? In one sense, he does.

After all, no one is stopping him from leaving. There are no laws, penalties, or externally imposed obstacles standing in the way of his leaving. Still, there is an obvious sense in which Jim is *not* free to leave. Even if no external obstacles stand in the way of his leaving, *something* does – his illness. And the illness is just as effective as any external force in preventing him from acting in accordance with his goals.

One way of analyzing Jim's situation is to say that although he has freedom in the *negative* sense to leave the house, he, nevertheless, lacks freedom in the *positive* sense. To have freedom in the negative sense (negative liberty or freedom) is to be free from externally imposed obstacles, especially those that are created by other human beings. This kind of freedom is negative insofar as all it requires is the *absence* of something – external obstacles. To have freedom in the positive sense (positive liberty or freedom), on the other hand, is to be able to act in a way that is in accordance with one's autonomous and/or truly rational desires. This freedom is called positive because it requires not just an absence of external obstacles, but the presence of something more – autonomy, power, or self-mastery.

Since Jim is not *able* to leave, which is what he truly and autonomously wishes to do, he lacks positive freedom. It does not matter that the source of his inability is a physical disease, rather than someone holding him to his bed with a gun. Nor would it matter if the source of his inability was a crippling agoraphobia, or a hypnotic suggestion. If what Jim *truly* wants is to get up and leave, then *anything* that prevents him from fulfilling this desire is an infringement upon his positive freedom.

In a way, the notion of positive freedom asks us to see Jim as two different persons. Consider the case where he suffers from agoraphobia. On the one hand, Jim desires to go outside and live a normal life. At the same time, Jim has another, stronger, desire to avoid the outdoors because of the psychological pain he fears it would cause him. Part of him wants to go out, and part of him does not. But most of us would not say that these two selves are on equal footing, when it comes to having a claim to govern Jim's life. Insofar as the part of him that wants to avoid the outdoors is being driven by a psychological disease, we will quite likely be tempted to say that it is the less authentic of the two desires. As a desire, it is less truly an expression of who Jim is – *Jim* is not responsible for this desire, his *disease* is. Positive freedom, then, is the ability not to act on just any old desire – but only on those desires of *one's true self*.

Speaking in this way about someone who suffers from a serious psychological impairment seems natural enough. But the extension of this line of thinking to broader questions of social and political morality was something that was deeply disturbing to Isaiah Berlin, who was the first to identify the concepts of positive and negative liberty by name in his famous 1958 essay. For while the distinction between Jim's true desires and those desires caused by his disease seems uncontroversial enough in the example above, who is to say that we do not have to dig still deeper in order to find Jim's *real* true self? Perhaps what Jim wants to do once he gets outside is go to a mall and shop. But if this desire is simply a product of the consumerist culture in which Jim was raised, is his positive freedom really advanced by his ability to satisfy it? Indeed, maybe Jim's desires as an individual agent are the wrong place to look altogether. After all, man is a social animal, and so perhaps the only way that Jim's *true* essence can be actualized is through acting in accordance with the collective will of the community – a greater whole of which his individual self is but one part. The problem with this line of reasoning, Berlin thought, is that it paves the path for tyranny in the name of liberty. For once I define freedom in this way, he wrote, "I am in a position to ignore the actual wishes of men or societies, to bully, oppress, torture them in the name, and on behalf, of their 'real' selves, secure in the knowledge that whatever is the true goal of man (happiness, performance of duty, wisdom, a just society, self-fulfillment) must be identical with his freedom – the free choice of his 'true', albeit often submerged and inarticulate, self."[1]

The distinction between negative and positive liberty is intuitively powerful, and can often prove helpful in analyzing the fundamental basis for various political disagreements. Classical liberal thinkers such as John Stuart Mill and Adam Smith, for instance, generally understood liberty in the negative sense. For these thinkers, the abridgment of any individual's negative liberty by government was something which required considerable justification. Contemporary libertarians, who can be seen as representing an extreme form of this doctrine, go even further by holding the value of negative liberty to be nearly absolute. Both these groups hold that the primary purpose of government is to promote liberty by protecting individuals against certain sorts of forcible interference with their actions. Theft, assault, and rape all constitute infringements with individuals' negative liberty, and hence the state may legitimately prohibit actions of these kinds. Those in the classical liberal or libertarian tradition do not, however, generally view poverty as an infringement of negative liberty. To lack resources is to lack a kind of power, they hold, but it is not to lack liberty. Instead, it is government programs that try to reduce poverty which constitute an infringement of liberty, whenever those programs involve redistributive taxation. For libertarians and classical liberals, taking a person's property without their consent generally *is* thought to be an infringement of negative liberty, regardless of whether it is done by a private person or by the taxing apparatus of the state.

For those who view liberty in the positive sense, on the other hand, redistributive taxation is generally seen as being morally unobjectionable, and maybe even morally required. For while it is true that those who are taxed are deprived of some positive liberty insofar as they lose the ability to use that wealth to pursue their ends, those who receive the benefits of that taxation thereby *gain* in positive liberty. The evaluation of redistributive taxation thus depends on a comparison of the respective amount or value of the positive liberty lost on the part of the taxpayers with the amount or value of positive liberty gained on the part of tax beneficiaries. In many cases, defenders of this view argue, the conclusion will be obvious. The positive liberty lost to taxation by a multi-millionaire is trivial compared to the positive liberty gained by those who benefit from that taxation by receiving tax-funded housing, education, and basic medicine. Understanding liberty in a positive sense thus makes it easier to accept a wider role for government in *promoting* liberty. While negative liberty can be protected with a minimal "night-watchman" state restricted to policing and adjudicating disputes, positive liberty can be promoted by a education, medicine, economic development initiatives, and a whole host of other endeavors. To say that the state's role should be limited to the promotion of liberty can thus mean very different things, depending on whether one means liberty in the negative or the positive sense.

Liberty for Whom, and from What?

Of course, even Berlin was not simply arguing "for" negative liberty and "against" positive liberty. Rather, his main concern was to avoid conceptual confusion and the distortion of moral and political reasoning that he believed could result from it. Berlin thought that we have a natural tendency to use the term "liberty" as a label for everything that we care about. And we can certainly find cases which seem to bear this point out. Franklin Delano Roosevelt, for instance, delivered a famous address to Congress in 1941 in which he proclaimed the necessity of recognizing and protecting "four freedoms" – freedom of speech and expression, freedom to worship God in one's own way, freedom from want, and freedom from fear. One of the reasons that this speech was so influential was that it led people to think about a concept they already prized – freedom – in a broader and more expansive way, and in so doing led many to recognize that their commitment to freedom in some areas also, in a way they hadn't yet recognized, committed them to other kinds of policies or values as well. As those who lived through the Great Depression had seen, being in a state of severe and continuous economic hardship could be just as detrimental to one's ability to live a self-directed life as could forcible interference by others. Berlin's point, however, was not that positive freedom was not as *valuable* as negative freedom, but simply that it was not the same *thing* as negative freedom, and that our policies and moral judgments would be on firmer ground if they recognized the inevitable trade-offs between different sort of values that are masked by a common name.

But even by the criterion of conceptual clarity, many have questioned whether Berlin's distinction between positive and negative liberty is helpful. Gerald MacCallum, for instance, has argued that Berlin's distinction rests on a confusion and has led theorists of freedom to spend their time on tiresome verbal disputes at the expense of substantive debate about the truly important questions of political philosophy.[2] Instead, MacCallum argues, we should recognize that both so-called negative and positive freedoms are really just unhelpful ways of speaking about a single broader and more accurate understanding of freedom. That more accurate understanding of freedom, according to MacCallum, is one where freedom consists of a "triadic relationship" between three variables. On this analysis, every instance of freedom is a case of freedom "*of* something (an agent or agents), *from* something, *to* do, not do, become, or not become something." All cases of freedom thus take the format "x is (is not) free from y to do (not do, become, not become) z," where "x ranges over agents, y ranges over such 'preventing conditions' as constraints, restrictions, interferences, and barriers, and z ranges over actions or conditions of character and circumstance."[3] This analysis can accommodate both paradigm cases of negative and positive liberty. Freedom from assault, for instance, could be understood as something like freedom *of* each individual *from* unwarranted assault *to* engage in lawful behaviors. And Roosevelt's "freedom from want" could be understood in terms of the freedom *of* each individual *from* economic inability *to* meet their basic needs. Once we understand that *both* of these are kinds of "freedom," we are able to move past mere semantic disputes and onto the important questions – which agents are the proper subjects of freedom, what kinds of "preventing conditions" are the most serious obstacles to freedom, and how should we weigh the respective values of different kinds of freedom?

Following MacCallum, the remainder of this chapter will look more closely at some of the substantive questions of liberty. The next section will explore the question of which agents are properly regarded as the subjects of liberty. Then, we will look at various candidates for "preventing conditions" such as force, poverty, and internal psychological barriers. Finally, we will turn to questions about the value of different kinds of liberty, and the role that the state ought to play in promoting or protecting them.

The Subject of Liberty

When we think of freedom as value, who or what are we thinking of as *possessing* that freedom? The US Declaration of Independence speaks of "all men" (which we now read to mean "all persons") being endowed with the right to liberty, and the UN Declaration of Human Rights says similarly that liberty is a right that "everyone" has. Both of these suggest an understanding of liberty on which it is *individuals* who are the primary subjects of freedom.

Contrast this with what Benjamin Constant has famously called "the liberty of the ancients."[4] This kind of liberty, according to Constant, consisted not in the freedom of individuals from external obstacles, or even in the ability of individuals to satisfy their own individual desires or projects. Rather, it consisted in the exercise of *the people as a whole* in their collective self-governance. Constant thought that this sort of liberty characterized the society of Ancient Greece, where freedom in the sense of collective self-determination was prized, even while freedom in the modern sense of individual freedom from external obstacles was rarely to be found.

But this understanding of freedom also has appeal for those wishing to provide a philosophical defense of contemporary democracy. Rousseau's characterization of the social compact, for instance, wherein each person "in giving himself to all, gives himself to nobody," expresses the idea that collective self-determination is the essence of social freedom.[5] A democratic society governed according to the "general will" is one that is ruled by itself. And each individual, as a member of that society, is free insofar as the only restrictions to which she is subject are those in which she imposes on herself through her collective deliberation with others.

The fact that collective freedom, in this sense, is compatible with a great lack of individual freedom has deeply troubled many modern liberals. After all, even Rousseau himself admitted that many individuals might be unwilling to comply with the dictates of the general will, and that they would have to be compelled by the force of law to submit. This fact did not trouble Rousseau, who thought it merely amounted to forcing individuals to be free. But one need not deny that there is a form of freedom to be found in collective self-governance to be troubled by Rousseau's dismissal of the significance of individual freedom as it is ordinarily understood. John Stuart Mill, for instance, writes in his treatise *On Liberty* that talk of "self-government" obscures the fact that "the 'people' who exercise the power, are not always the same people with those over whom it is exercised, and the 'self-government' spoken of, is not the government of each by himself, but of each by all the rest. The will of the people, moreover, practically means, the will of the most numerous or the most active part of the people; the majority, or those who succeed in making themselves accepted as the majority; the people, consequently, may desire to oppress a part of their number; and precautions are as much needed against this, as against any other abuse of power."[6] Mill should not be understood here as saying that there is no value to the notion of freedom in the collective sense, but, rather, as saying that we must be aware of the way in which it can come into conflict with freedom in the individual sense, and be on guard against the dangers of tyranny which come from eliminating the latter notion entirely by understanding freedom purely in terms of the former.

So far in this section we have spoken as though the only question were whether it is individuals or groups of individuals who are the proper subject of freedom. But even if we restrict our focus to individual freedom, it is not entirely clear just what exactly we are referring to in talking about individuals. Let us return to the case of agoraphobic Jim. Does Jim remain in his house freely? There is an obvious sense, of course, in which he does. No one, as they say, is holding a gun to his head and forcing him to stay there. If he remains in his home, it is because he *chooses* to do so. And what is freedom if not doing what one chooses to do?

But Jim need not be unequivocal about his choice to remain in his house. We can imagine that part of him very much wants to leave. Furthermore, we can imagine that he wishes he didn't have his strong aversions to going outdoors, and that he *identifies* more with his wish to go outside than with his strong fear of doing so. His wish to go outside seems authentic and truly *his*, whereas his fear seems like something *imposed* on him, something that he *gives in* to. This, too, seems a perfectly natural way of analyzing Jim's case, and would lead many of us to say that there is an important sense in which Jim's staying in his house is *not* something that he freely does. The choices that Jim makes are unimpeded – no one stops him from doing what he chooses, whether it be to stay in the house or to leave. But while his ability to *act* on his choices is free, his choices themselves, we might say, are not. They are not free because they are caused by something alien to him – his disease.

Many wish to resist the claim that there is any sense in which Jim is not free. But it is not clear why. The problem cannot be that the obstacle to Jim's leaving is an internal, rather than an external one. To see this, just imagine that Jim's reluctance to leave, instead of being caused by his agoraphobia, is caused by a hypnotic suggestion, or by brainwashing. In this case, like the one just described, nothing would stop Jim from leaving if he chose to do so. But because he has been manipulated by some outside force, he cannot choose to leave. Surely, all of us would admit that in a case like this Jim's remaining in his house is not truly free. But the only difference between the hypnosis/brainwashing case and the agoraphobia case is that the former is an internal obstacle caused by *some agent*, whereas the former is an internal obstacle caused by natural events. And it is not clear why the *cause* of the obstacle should make a difference to Jim's freedom.

The reason many of us wish to resist the claim that Jim is not free, I suspect, is that we share Berlin's fear of dividing the individual in to two parts, and claiming that what a person *says* they want does not necessarily tell us what their *true* self wants. Berlin thought that such a move paved the way for tyranny. After all, a troubling implication of those views which would hold Jim's staying in his house to be unfree is that they render us unable to say that Jim is free merely because he is doing what he wants to do. Such views might even imply that Jim might not *know* what would promote his freedom. If our real self is not simply the self we present to others in our everyday interactions, but instead something deeper and harder to detect such as our "autonomous" or "rational" self, then there is no reason to expect that we will always know what this self wants, and hence what would make us free. We might be so conditioned by our fears and inauthentic desires that we will have simply lost touch altogether with what we would truly and autonomously like to do or become. In this case, it is possible that *other* people – some cadre of expert psychologists employed by the government, for instance – might know better than us what would make us free. And this opens once more the frightening possibility of individuals being forced to be free, regardless of how much they might protest against it.

As a rhetorical and certainly as a historical matter, there are no doubt good reasons to share Berlin's worry. But as a matter of strict logic, there is simply no connection between the "split-self" positive view of freedom and tyranny. First, while it *might* be the case that some other individuals know better than you what would make you free, it also might not be, and nothing in the split-self view of freedom entails that this would be the case. Second, even if someone else did know better than you what would make you free, it does not follow that forcing you to act in that way would actually promote your freedom. Positive views of freedom are often based on the idea that freedom is a matter of *autonomy* and *self-realization*. For such views, there is a large difference between performing some action because one freely chose it, and performing that same action because someone else compelled you into doing so. Third, and possibly most seriously, even if we granted everything that we have just denied, there are a whole host of pragmatic reasons for why endorsing tyranny in the name of freedom would not be a good idea. Even if some people know what would make other people free, how do we identify them so that we can make sure we hand the keys to the coercive apparatus of the state to the right person? And once we hand them the keys, how do we know they will use it only in those ways designed to promote the freedom of others? After all, if the case for positive freedom is based on the idea that people are often irrational and lacking in autonomy, shouldn't we be concerned that those in power will be flawed in those same ways? And what incentive will those in have to refrain from using that power for their own benefit? Who, as Juvenal famously asked, will guard the guardians?

All of this is just to say, of course, that settling questions about the meaning of liberty does not settle *all* our moral and political questions. One can agree that there is an important sense of freedom captured by the split self-view without concluding that it is the *only* sense of freedom, and certainly without concluding that such freedom is the most important moral value and one that the state ought to promote at all costs.

Constraints on Liberty

To a large extent, one's views on the possible sources of constraints on liberty follow from one's views regarding the proper subject of liberty. Someone who thinks of the subject of liberty as an ordinary person with all their idiosyncratic and less-than-ideal psychological characteristics will tend not to view an irrationally strong desire as a *constraint* on a person's freedom. Rather, they will view such a desire as *part of who the person is*. Similarly, someone who views the subject of liberty as a collective body such as a nation will tend not to view the coercion of individual members of that collective as a loss of freedom, because such coercion is simply part of the way that the collective realizes its freedom. In general, the more narrowly defined the subject of freedom, the greater the range of conditions that will count as a constraint on the subject's freedom; and conversely, the more broadly the subject is defined, the narrower the range of conditions that will count as a constraint will be.

Still, one's view on the subject of liberty does not settle all questions about the range of possible constraints. Someone who conceives of the subject of liberty as ordinary persons, for instance, will typically view only those factors *external* to the person as constraints on her liberty. But *which* external factors? Is gravity a restriction on my freedom because it prevents me from flying? If I am poor, is society restricting my freedom even if no one ever acted in a way with the intention of making me poor (or preventing me from buying what I want)?

Does a constraint have to make it *impossible* for me to do what I want in order to count as a constraint on my liberty, or is it enough that it makes my doing it more difficult, costly, or unpleasant?

Let us take the question about gravity first. Gravity does, of course, restrict our ability to do things that we might like – maybe even *truly* like – to do. So why would anyone deny that it can be a restriction on our freedom? To see why, we must keep in mind the *context* in which our discussion of freedom is taking place. The reason we are thinking about freedom at all is that it is an important concept in *moral and political theory*. But both moral and political theory are *normative* enterprises. They are theories about how we *ought* to behave as individuals, or about how our political and social institutions *ought* to be designed or reformed. As moral and political theorists, then, we are interested in the concept of freedom only insofar as it has some relevance for *what we ought to do*. But gravity is not like this. If we invented special anti-gravity packs that allowed people to fly or float around as they wished, then it might be useful to talk about how our decision to allocate those packs in one way or another might affect an individual's freedom. This is because we would be faced with a *choice*, and we could therefore appeal to the value of freedom as a reason for making that choice in one way rather than another. But where there is no human choice involved, there is simply no point for us as moral or political philosophers in talking about the value of freedom. The only things that can count as constraints on freedom, on this view, are those things that are brought about or contingent in some way on human choices and the actions that follow from them.

What, then, should we say about poverty? In a capitalist society, it is typically not the case that some one person *makes* another person poor. There is no centralized mechanism for the distribution of wealth or other resources in such an economy.[7] Things are distributed according to the countless decisions of countless individuals. Your mother gives you some money because you are her daughter; consumers give Steve Jobs money (indirectly) because they want to own his company's software; I give Jack a job because he is my friend, and so on. The distribution which ultimately results from this nexus of transfers is something which no one could foresee, and which no one intended. A person might end up poor in such an economy because no one wanted to purchase the labor or goods she was selling, because she poorly invested what resources she had, or for countless other reasons. If we cannot trace her poverty to the act of any specific human agent, can we nevertheless say that her poverty constitutes an infringement of her freedom?

This question has proved to be extremely difficult to settle. Some, such as Hillel Steiner, David Miller, and G. A. Cohen, hold that poverty constitutes a limitation on freedom insofar as it stems from institutional structures for which other people are responsible in either a causal or a moral sense. The market system, such philosophers argue, is not an inevitable fact of nature. Even if it arose gradually and was not the product of deliberate human design, it is nevertheless something that we have the power to deliberately alter if we wish. Philosophers who take this position tend to argue that we should recognize that that the poor lack freedom in a capitalist economy, and often go on to claim that we should reform capitalist institutions in order to provide protection for the liberty of the poor, or at the extreme, perhaps do away with capitalist institutions altogether. Those on the other side of the debate tend to make one of two kinds of argument to support their position. Some, such as Friedrich Hayek, define freedom in a way such that only certain kinds of choice-limiting relationships between persons count as limitations on freedom. For Hayek, freedom is defined as the absence of coercion, and coercion in turn is defined as being subject to the arbitrary will of another. Since, according to Hayek, it is only in highly unusual cases that market relationships involve coercion in this sense (such as when one person holds a monopoly over a necessary resource), it is not generally the case that capitalism renders the poor unfree. So long as the rule of law is in place – so long, that is, as each citizen is subject only to the same sorts of general rules as everyone else – individuals are free, even if their choices are severely limited. The other strategy, employed largely by libertarian philosophers such as Robert Nozick, is to argue on the basis of a *moralized* concept of freedom. A moralized concept of freedom is one that defines freedom (and losses of freedom) in terms of some other moral concept. So, for instance, a theory might hold that the boundaries of one's (proper) freedom are specified by principles of justice, so that losing the ability to do what would be unjust for one to do is no real loss of freedom at all. Such a strategy has some appeal. We do not think that in proscribing rape we must "trade-off" the liberty thereby gained by potential rape victims against the liberties lost by potential rapists. The restriction of the rapist's actions results in no loss of *real* liberty at all. Applying this strategy to the case of poverty, though, is more difficult, as it requires making a prior moral argument to show that poverty is not itself a violation of justice, and/or that any attempt to rectify it by redistributive taxation would be. And this move thus seems merely to trade one difficult problem (showing that the poor are not unfree) for another (showing that the poor are not treated unjustly).

Finally, there is the question of the kind of limitation a constraint must place on our action in order to count as a restriction on our freedom. Some, such as Hillel Steiner, take a very narrow view of the nature of possible interferences, arguing that only those actions of others that make our performing some action literally *impossible* thereby render us unfree. The difficulty with this position is that many intuitively freedom-reducing obstacles do not make it *impossible* to do what we want, just difficult or costly. A gunman's threat to hand over our money or be shot, for instance, doesn't literally make it impossible for us to keep our money, just much more costly than most of us would care to accept! On the other hand, this position has a nice advantage in not having to deal with "degrees of freedom." If the gunman's threat to shoot us in the head unless we pay him makes us unfree, does his threat to shoot us in our left hand make us *less* unfree, since the options it forecloses are (somewhat) less valuable? On Steiner's position, we are either free to do something or we are not. Questions of how free we are and questions about the *value* of our different freedoms are entirely separate.

Liberty and Politics

How important are philosophical questions about the nature of liberty for settling the difficult questions of politics? Many of the questions we have looked at in this chapter are questions about the *meaning* of liberty. And while these are certainly of some importance, they are clearly not sufficient to decisively settle much of political significance. Whether or not someone in poverty can be correctly described as lacking in liberty seems a question of secondary importance. The fundamental question is whether there is something *wrong* with people being in poverty, or with a system that allows people to live in poverty. If this is a question about liberty at all, it is a question about the *value* of liberty, not its meaning. What we really want to know is whether the situation of the poor is justifiable in the sense that their lack of liberty (if such it is) is compensated for by gains in liberty or some other value elsewhere.

Even agreement on the nature and value of liberty, however, will still leave many important questions concerning its proper political implementation unsettled. For the answers to those questions will depend not just on our philosophical principles, but on our empirical beliefs about the way the world works. Take, for instance, the case of T. H. Green. Green was a nineteenth-century British political thinker who operated with a strongly positive conception of liberty. Liberty, for Green, was a matter of having the power to do those things which were truly worth doing, and doing them in common with others. And while, as we have seen, positive conceptions of liberty tend to be associated with those thinkers who favor a more activist role for the state, nothing in this definition entails, or even suggests, such a conclusion. Green's belief in the necessity for state activism sprung not merely from his understanding of the nature or importance of liberty, but also from his empirical belief that human beings are not to be trusted to do what is worth doing on their own. The law is designed, according to Green, for those "overworked women [and] ill-housed and untaught families" who, Green thought, were incapable of directing their own lives (Green, 2006, p. 27). This led Green to favor policies which many classical liberals would view as restrictions on liberty – regulations controlling trade in liquor, laws mandating compulsory state schooling, and various sorts of factory legislation.

But just as Green's political conclusions do not follow from his understanding of liberty, neither must classical liberals' opposition to those conclusions follow from theirs. Hayek, for instance, while he did in fact operate with a very different understanding of liberty than Green, also had radically different empirical beliefs which in and of themselves would suffice to yield quite different policy conclusions, even if he were to take Green's understanding of liberty on board. For Hayek, like many libertarians, was impressed with the idea of spontaneous order. This is the belief that so long as society establishes certain basic ground rules governing property rights and freedom of contract, individuals will often organize their actions in such a way as to achieve good social outcomes even though such outcomes are not intended by any of them. The development of language and money are two important examples of spontaneous order, but the example most cherished by libertarians is the free-market itself. For in the market, as Adam Smith noted, individuals who are motivated only by their own concern for profit are moved "as though by an invisible hand" to create an outcome which was no part of their intention – a betterment in the lives of their fellow men and an increase in the wealth of nations. Thus, legislators need not force individuals to do what they ought to do, for Hayek and for Smith, not because these two thinkers are operating with a conception of what it is that individuals ought to do which is radically different from Green's, but simply because they have more confidence in people acting on their own to do what they ought (and less confidence in the ability or interest of legislators to bring these desirable outcomes about directly by force of law).

While questions about the philosophical nature of liberty are important, then, they cannot be considered in a vacuum. Liberty is only one value among others, and questions of its importance must always be questions of its importance *relative* to other values. And the ultimate philosophical question of what we should *do* about liberty's value is one which will need to take into account not only other moral and political values, but contentious empirical claims about human nature, the respective functioning of government and markets, and the operation of various social forces. There is, in short, no shortage of questions to be asked!

Further Reading

An articulation of the nature of negative liberty and a defense of its value can be found in the writings of a variety of classical liberal and libertarian philosophers. The origins of the term itself can be found in Isaiah Berlin's essay, "Two Concepts of Liberty" (Berlin 1969), wherein the author both articulates the distinction between negative and positive liberty, and argues in favor of the former and against what Berlin sees as a tendency to confuse other, distinct values with it. A similar distinction is certainly implicit in earlier works, though such as John Stuart Mill's *On Liberty* (Mill 1978), wherein Mill defends the principle that individual negative liberty can only be restricted in order to protect others from harm. Friedrich Hayek (Hayek 1944; 1960) and Robert Nozick (Nozick 1974) provide useful over-views of the classical liberal and libertarian concepts of negative liberty, respectively, while Eric Mack and Gerald Gaus (Mack and Gaus 2004) provide an extremely useful overview of the classical liberal and libertarian tradition of political philosophy, and the role of liberty in that tradition.

The nature of and case for positive liberty, on the other hand, can be found both in classic works such as Rousseau's *Social Contract* (Rousseau 2002), and even Plato's *Republic* (Plato 2004), and in more modern and contemporary works such as T.H. Green's important speech on "Liberal Legislation and Freedom of Contract," (Green 2006), Charles Taylor's essay "What's Wrong with Negative Liberty?" (Taylor 2006), and G. A. Cohen's book-length critique of Nozickian libertarianism, *Self-Ownership, Freedom, and Equality* (Cohen 1995).

More recently, philosophical discussions of freedom have tried to move past the debate between negative and positive freedom. Much of this may be due to arguments like those of Gerald MacCallum (MacCallum 2006) that the negative/positive distinction fails to highlight anything important about our real political disagreements. Many philosophers, for instance, have become interested in reviving the classical tradition of freedom as self-government, a conception of freedom which does not map neatly onto either the nega-tive or positive understanding. This conception of freedom has come to be known as the "Republican" tradition of liberty, and has been most forcefully defended by Quentin Skinner (Skinner 2006) and Phillip Pettit (Pettit 2006). See Christopher MacMahon's essay (McMahon 2005) for a critique. Other philosophers have turned their attention to more narrowly focused questions about liberty, such as the extent to which liberty can be meaningfully measured and compared (Carter 2004), or the way in which freedom relates to other philosophical concerns such as coercion (Wertheimer 2006) or autonomy (O'Neill 2000).

Notes

1   Berlin (1969: 133).
2   See MacCallum (2006).
3   MacCallum (2006: 102).

4   See Constant (1988).
5   See Rousseau (2002).
6   Mill (1978: ch. 1).
7   See, on this point (Nozick (1974: ch. 7)).

References

Berlin, I. (1969). "Two Concepts of Liberty," in I. Berlin (ed.), *Four Essays on Liberty*, Oxford: Oxford University Press, 118–72.
Carter, I. (2004). *A Measure of Freedom*, Oxford: Oxford University Press.
Cohen, G. A. (1995). *Self-ownership, Freedom, and Equality*, Cambridge/New York, Cambridge University Press; Paris: Maison des sciences de l'homme.
Constant, B. (1988). "The Liberty of the Ancients Compared with That of the Moderns," in B. Fontana (ed.), *Constant: Political Writings*, New York: Cambridge University Press, 309–28.
Green, T. H. (2006). "Liberal Legislation and Freedom of Contract," in D. Miller (ed.), *The Liberty Reader*, Boulder, CO: Paradigm Publishers, 21–32.
Hayek, F. A. (1944). *The Road to Serfdom*, Chicago, IL: University of Chicago Press.
Hayek, F. A. (1960). *The Constitution of Liberty*, Chicago, IL: University of Chicago Press.
MacCallum, G. (2006). "Negative and Positive Freedom," in D. Miller (ed.), *The Liberty Reader*, Boulder, CO: Paradigm Publishers, 100–22.
Mack, E. and Gaus, G. (2004). "Classical Liberalism and Libertarianism: The Liberty Tradition," in G. Gaus and C. Kukathas (eds.), *Handbook of Political Theory*, London: Sage, 115–30.
McMahon, C. (2005). "The Indeterminacy of Republican Policy," *Philosophy and Public Affairs*, 33, 67–93.
Mill, J. S. (1978). *On Liberty*, Indianapolis, IN: Hackett.
Nozick, R. (1974). *Anarchy, State, and Utopia*, New York: Basic Books.
O'Neill, O. (2000). *Bounds of Justice*, Cambridge: Cambridge University Press.
Pettit, P. (2006). "The Republican Ideal of Freedom," in D. Miller (ed.), *The Liberty Reader*, Boulder, CO: Paradigm Publishers, 223–43.
Plato (2004). *The Republic*, tr. C. D. C. Reeve, Indianapolis, IN: Hackett.
Rousseau, J.-J. (2002). "The Social Contract," in S. Dunn (ed.), *The Social Contract and the First and Second Discourses*, New Haven, CT: Yale University Press.
Skinner, Q. (2006). "A Third Concept of Liberty," in D. Miller (ed.), *The Liberty Reader*, Boulder, CO: Paradigm Publishers, 243–54.
Taylor, C. (2006). "What's Wrong with Negative Liberty?" in D. Miller (ed.), *The Liberty Reader*, Boulder, CO: Paradigm Publishers, 141–62.
Wertheimer, A. (2006). *Coercion*, Princeton, NJ: Princeton University Press.

Index